History

The Inner Quarters

Marriage and the Lives of Chinese Women in the Sung Period

Patricia Buckley Ebrey

UNIVERSITY OF CALIFORNIA PRESS

Berkeley   Los Angeles   London

University of California Press
Berkeley and Los Angeles, California

University of California Press, Ltd.
London, England

© 1993 by
The Regents of the University of California

Library of Congress Cataloging-in-Publication Data

Ebrey, Patricia Buckley, 1947–
    The inner quarters: marriage and the lives of Chinese women in
the Sung period / Patricia Buckley Ebrey.
        p.   cm.
    Includes bibliographical references and index.
    ISBN 978-0-520-08158-1 (alk. paper).
    1. Marriage—China—History.   2. Women—China—Social
conditions.   3. China—Social conditions—960–1644.   I. Title.
HQ684.A25   1993
306.872'0951'09021—dc20

92-31376
CIP

Printed in the United States of America

08   07

9   8   7

The paper used in this publication meets the minimum requirements of
ANSI/NISO Z39.48-1992 (R 1997) (*Permanence of Paper*). ∞

To my sisters,
Mary Buckley Anderson and Barbara Buckley Boyles

CONTENTS

FOREWORD

By Bonnie Smith

"The Sung was above all a period of change," writes Patricia Buckley Ebrey, "a turning point in the long sweep of Chinese history." There was a time not too long ago when women were considered beyond the realm of change and thus outside of or irrelevant to history. Incapacitated by law or custom from appearing on the public stage of great events or absorbed by the supposedly unchanging roles of wife or mother or daughter, their lives were often credited with being important in perpetuating the species but not historically so. *The Inner Quarters* disputes this traditional historical wisdom, mapping atop the structural complexities of Sung legal and cultural life a millennium ago a realm of struggle, contest, and endeavor where women participated in shaping the society in which they lived and thus the course of history. Often working against the grain of legal strictures, these women's lives as Ebrey has painstakingly reconstituted them take part in modern history's *telos* of freedom and agency. For Ebrey, women played their assigned, even longstanding roles in the great drama of Sung history, but they were also extraordinary improvisers in a world that seemed structured to their disadvantage.

The assigned role of Sung women was that of wife, and in preparation for it they learned useful household skills, the ways of showing deference to elders, and personal—we might even say sexual—refinements that would make them appealing. Increasingly the display of charm came to include the painful practice of footbinding, borrowed for respectable women from actresses and courtesans with whom wives had to compete for their husbands' favors. Once married, a woman's role was dominated by service to her husband's family, for a wife moved not to a home of her own but became part of a patrilineal and patrilocal kinship system. Performing sacrifices in memory of her husband's family's dead ancestors or caring for the offspring of his concubines were as much a part of a wife's duty as bearing and raising children of her own. Laws, religious ethics, high culture and low—all molded the marital role of women and gave it a highly determined shape. The story of great men in history is often told in terms of face-to-face combat with competing men and their armies. Sung women, more anonymously, faced and struggled with a limiting set of circumstances, canonic prescriptions, duties, and social strictures; as a result of this confrontation, Ebrey sees these women becoming historic actors and thus gaining historic stature.

Sung women used the institution of the dowry, the laws of divorce, the right to remarry, and many other social practices to act on their own behalf or on that of their children. Additionally, those who behaved as exemplary wives and daughters-in-law gained credit and standing where others earned only shame or oblivion. Women who raised their children to succeed but also to be deferential and loyal were able to assure themselves a measure of comfort and even affection in old age. Women even pursued literary ends, not only by pushing their sons to follow the arduous road toward the state examinations that would ensure a prestigious future in the bureaucracy, but also by writing themselves or studying the religious and ethical classics. In special circumstances their learned husbands or sons brought them renown through commemorative biographies. Financial acuity, religious devotion, and perseverance in maintaining family solidarity gave others posthumous fame, even if they did not always guarantee a smooth life.

All of us fascinated by history recognize that change—its texture, meaning, and motor—is the past's most intriguing component, for it addresses the question of human efficacy. How did Napoleon change the course of history, or Mao, or Gorbachev? Finding these agents of change gives societies and individuals hope that human life has ultimate meaning. The long progress of individual heroes who have been shown to bring change makes us believe that there is a place for us all to be historical actors, not just the acted upon. Perhaps these insistent fantasies of historical actors executing great historical change draw us to the study of history in the first place. But when we see the changes wrought by Sung women, we are forced to ask whether Ebrey's study is a case of women's history imitating men's; we are, in short, encouraged to create a fantasy world of the inner quarters, one in which women readers of history can imagine a realm of female action, perhaps even female autonomy.

We might also ask ourselves whether the subject matter of Chinese women makes that imaginary realm still more exotic and thus enticing to us because of the ghosts, concubines, matchmakers, and other characters in Sung history that are so unfamiliar to us. Even before the days of full-blown imperialism, Westerners like the English traveler and writer Lady Mary Montagu were fascinated to discover life in places like the harem and to write about it. From her letters one sees how the sexuality, deportment, and social position of Ottoman women provided Montagu with a fascinating vision of a different sexual economy, which she then relayed to the court back in London. Descriptions in her letters formed the basis for subsequent portrayals of Turkish baths and the harem itself, until photographers of the late nineteenth century began gaining access, thereby feeding still different exotic depictions of non-Western women. Does Ebrey's work do that to Chinese women, doubling our fantasies by providing us with heroines in the struggle for freedom, agency, and change, made perhaps more interesting because they are all dressed up in Oriental garb?

My own opinion is that Ebrey's book (perhaps like other historical studies of women) defuses some of the most dangerous fantastical elements in history by making the entry into the world of Sung women an uneasy one, not impossible but also not direct. Instead of rollicking in, say, Hitler's cruel world of jackboots and conquest, a student must puzzle out the complex patrilineal, patriarchal, and patrilocal system of marriage with its restrictions on intermarrying. Difference is not a matter for fantasy, but for rigorous intellectual work. The author's own path was one through Chinese language, by means of difficult documents (few of them in a woman's own hand) representing three centuries, and past numerous impediments to the imagination. At the end there was no picture of larger-than-life heroines, but rather more personal depictions of the quotidian duties of splicing hemp or directing servants, both unimaginable and ordinary hardships, small pleasures and great luxury, whose full import we may be able to talk about satisfactorily, though perhaps with less energy than the heart-pounding stories of male conquerors inspire. Historical understanding reached painstakingly across the trajectory of gender and cultural difference—not just difference in time—tarnishes history's heroic fantasies, as Ebrey suggests when she expresses her concern not to let "my imagination run too free." Consequently, the historic stage for this drama has different scenery, a bigger cast, no leadng characters, and the voices reaching the audience are less distinct, speaking more fragmented lines, and demanding more attention to catch any message at all.

But here we approach a fantasy realm once again, where the belief reigns among many historians of women (both students and authors) that their enterprise "changes" the nature of history itself, that is, that women's history is in a sense a heroic genre, for it reconstructs a different past and exercises still another kind of agency by making the analytical practices of the historical profession less sexist and biased. Again, I would like to point to the muted register in which Ebrey as a historian has made most of her claims. She insistently casts the insights she has garnered as questions posed against mainstream Chinese history. It is always important to be able to imagine that our knowledge will reshape the world, but at the same time we must ensure that our methodological fantasies are expressed as questions, thus allowing space for other acts of interpretation and other historical narratives. *The Inner Quarters* opens itself to readers' questions and to other scholars' insights rather than aiming to have the last word.

This book does not provide a comforting (or terrifying) narrative with which one can easily identify, nor does it revel in the exotic difference of Sung women's lives. Instead it provides material that is sometimes difficult to grasp, and at other times more familiar to us and our own lives. Raising questions about women's lives, about gender, about why we read history and how we write it, Patricia Buckley Ebrey has made *The Inner Quarters* a place we need to enter.

PREFACE

For more than a dozen years I have been studying family, kinship, and marriage in Sung China (960–1279). For a long time I planned to write a book that centered on women, but found myself repeatedly diverted by the need to research related topics such as property law, family rituals, and Confucian ideology. I was also procrastinating, hoping to overcome the feeling that no approach to the subject could ever be satisfactory. I did not want to gloss over unpleasant facts like the traffic in women, footbinding, or female infanticide; neither did I want to depict gender differentiation in China in an ethnocentric way, implicitly judging China by a modern Western standard. As a historian I found generalized descriptions of "the position of women in traditional China" too simplistic, implying as they did that women were somehow outside of history, their lives unaffected by changes in culture, society, or the economy. Presenting women above all as victims always bothered me, as it seemed to demean them. Didn't most Chinese women have some room to maneuver, and didn't some—the fabled tyrannical mothers-in-law at least—exert considerable control over others? I knew that much of the primary historical evidence, written by the male writers of the time, was built on moral premises that we today do not necessarily share. Would I be able to find ways to look sympathetically at all sorts of women, not only dutiful daughters-in-law and self-sacrificing mothers, but wives who gave in to jealous hatreds, concubines who had lost all trust in others and spent their time scheming for favor, and widows who abandoned their children to remarry?

Despite these doubts, I gradually began assembling bits and pieces for this book. At first my goal was a scholarly monograph on marriage, and I wrote several essays that examined particular facets of marriage in depth. In 1990, when I finally had time to work full time on this book, I decided to give up writing for specialists and instead prepare a broad survey of the ways marriage shaped women's lives. Writing an overview has proved both challenging and exciting. Normally, when I address fellow historians, I can confine my efforts to well-documented issues like Confucian thought or property law. Now, though, to be comprehensive, I had to tackle elusive ones like sexuality, jealousy, and gender symbolism.

By trying to see the larger whole I gained new insights into the better-studied topics; there was a cost, though, the need to keep treatment of any one topic short. Fifty pages instead of five or ten on subjects such as divorce, widow remarriage, or marriages among relatives would certainly have allowed for more nuanced analyses. But this book would quickly have reached unmanageable proportions and thus have failed to serve its intended purpose. I will therefore have to be content with the hope that my brevity on important topics will provoke energetic scholars to investigate them more thoroughly.

As I struggled to get the larger whole into focus, I found partial solutions to the nagging doubts about approach with which I began. By putting my emphases on context and women's agency, I came to feel, I could give women their due without violating my sense of the complexity of history. The context of Sung women's lives encompassed both the structures of power and the ideas and symbols that helped them orient themselves within those structures. It was embedded in history, its features shaped by and shaping other social, political, economic, and cultural processes. Kinship and gender systems, after all, did not exist in isolation. Stressing women's agency means seeing women as actors. Women occupied positions of vastly different power, just as men did, and made choices that helped to recreate and subtly change the family and kinship system. Existing evidence can be read in ways that bring to the fore women responding to the opportunities open to them and accommodating or resisting those around them.

University professors today are inevitably indebted to others for allowing them the time and wherewithal to conduct research and write. Much of the research presented in this book was begun in 1983–84, a year I spent at Princeton with support from a grant from the Committee on Chinese Studies of the American Council of Learned Societies and the Social Science Research Council. The Research Board of the University of Illinois repeatedly provided funds for research assistants. Miss Bau-hwa Sheieh helped at the initial stage of this book, and Miss Ch'iu-yüeh Lai at the final stage. A grant from the Illinois-Tamkang Exchange program made possible research in Taiwan during the summer of 1990, and the Center for East Asian and Pacific Studies contributed toward the cost of the illustrations. A grant from the University of Illinois's Center for Advanced Study for 1990–91 gave me time to devote exclusively to writing. I was able to spend six months of that year at the Institute for Humanistic Research, Kyoto University, as perfect a place as any to check sources and reflect on larger themes.

My gratitude goes not only to these institutions, but also to colleagues who were generous with their time and counsel. Julia Murray offered advice on the illustrations, and Francesca Bray and Angela Sheng on the technology of women's textile work. Colleagues at the University of Illinois—Kai-wing Chow, Thomas Havens, Sonya Michel, and Ronald Toby—read revised chapters on short notice. I owe the most to the friends who read the entire manuscript: John Chaffee, Charlotte Furth, Peter Gregory, JaHyun Haboush, Dorothy Ko, Susan Mann, Brian McKnight, Ann Waltner, and Rubie Watson. They contributed to the clarity of my presentation by pointing out where I had to give more background, where I contradicted myself, and where I could develop my arguments more forcefully. I am also grateful to those who responded to talks or papers I presented on topics covered in this book. These include seminars at Stanford, Davis, Rutgers, Harvard, and the University of Washington; presentations at the premodern China study group in Kyoto, the group for research on women in Chinese history in Tokyo, and the social history group at the University of Illinois; and papers at conferences on lineage demography (Asilomar, 1987), on marriage and inequality in Chinese society (Asilomar, 1988), on the social and cultural history of early modern China (Taipei, 1990), and on family process and political process in late imperial China (Taipei, 1992). Finally, I would like to thank the students in my seminars on women in Chinese history, who have contributed by their enthusiasm for the topic and their willingness to discuss issues from almost any angle.

NOTES ON CONVENTIONS

1. Wherever possible, women are identified by name, rather than as a man's daughter, wife, or mother. The wife of Ssu-ma Kuang, for instance, is referred to as Miss Chang (1023–1082). Chang was the name of her natal family, a name she retained her whole life. If her given name was recorded, it is also given in Chinese style after the family name, as in Miss Shen Te-jou (1119–1179). In most cases, given names are not known. In ordinary social life, a married woman was called by her original family name with the polite term *shih* attached. *Shih* is translated here as Miss because it was attached to the woman's natal family name, not her husband's family name. By itself, it did not indicate marital status. Although *shih* could also be attached to a man's family name, men were much more commonly referred to by their family names and a personal name. In the uncommon case in which a woman is only known as the wife of a named man, she is referred to by his family name prefaced by Mrs. Referring to men by their family and given names alone (i.e., not as Mr. Ssu-ma Kuang) and women by names prefaced by Miss or Mrs. may violate contemporary American rules on the avoidance of sexist language, but it was adopted here as the least of several evils. It captures Chinese usage quite accurately; in the case of men, it is less cumbersome than using Mr. as well; yet it still alerts readers to the sex of everyone mentioned.

2. Other than the six authors discussed in the Introduction (Hung Mai, Ssu-ma Kuang, Yüan Ts'ai, Ch'eng I, Chu Hsi, and Miss Li Ch'ing-chao), all men and women have their dates indicated if known, even when their dates seem to have nothing to do with the points being made. This is intended to underline that they were specific people, not generic stereotypes, and also to keep separate the many women called Miss Chang or

Miss Wu. Providing dates also allows concerned readers to consider issues of historical change, such as the gradual increase in the influence of Neo-Confucianism.

3. Ages are given by Chinese reckoning in *sui*. A phrase such as "he died at forty" means he died at forty sui. On the average, sui ages will be a year older than Western ages. By sui reckoning, a person is one from the date of birth until the first New Year's Day, when he or she turns two. Thus, a girl who marries at eighteen sui could be anywhere from a day over sixteen by our reckoning (if she was born on the thirty-first day of the twelfth month of the year 1000 and married on the first of the first month of the year 1017) to a day under eighteen (if she was born on the first day of the first month of 1000 and married on the thirty-first of the twelfth month of 1017).

4. For convenience, places are identified according to modern province names rather than Sung circuits. See the following map for the borders of Northern and Southern Sung superimposed on the modern provinces of China proper.

5. All translations given here are my own. When a translation into English is available, it is cited after the primary source citation as a convenience to readers who would like to check the full passage.

6. The only abbreviation used in the body of this book is *c.s.* with a date. This refers to the year a man passed the *chin-shih* examination, and is given when the man's birth and death dates are not known.

The Borders of Sung China (960–1279)
(set against modern province boundaries)

INTRODUCTION

The Sung period began just over a thousand years ago, in 960, and lasted more than three centuries, to 1279. It has long been a favorite period among Western students of China, in no small measure because the art of the period appeals to modern tastes. Sung paintings, calligraphy, silk tapestries, and porcelain all convey a sense of restraint and mastery, subtlety and refinement. Gazing at a delicately colored porcelain dish, a meticulously rendered depiction of a busy city street, or a sketch of a lone figure before a lofty mountain, we feel it would have been pleasant to live among these objects and the people who made them or cherished them. What we know of the politics of the period corresponds to this image of civility. The Sung is remembered not for despotic or cruel emperors, corrupt eunuchs, or regional warlords, but for highly principled scholar-officials who entered the civil service by means of a competitive literary examination and were motivated by a strong desire to serve their rulers and aid the common people.

The image of the Sung period among Chinese is less positive. Many prefer the previous dynasty, the T'ang (618–907), a period they associate with virile emperors, military expansion, passionate poets, and cultural confidence. To them, the Sung seems an effete period, when China's leaders became too refined, sophisticated, and thoughtful for the country's good. High-mindedness was not enough at the beginning of the dynasty to oust the Khitan from borderlands previously held by the T'ang, in the middle of the dynasty to prevent the Jurchen from conquering the ancient northern heartland of China, or in the final half-century to resist the steady incursion of the rapidly expanding Mongols.

But the Sung should not be summed up in likes and dislikes. Current scholarly opinion among Chinese, Japanese, and Western historians is that the Sung was above all a period of change, a turning point in the long sweep

1

of Chinese history.[1] The changes that occurred between the mid-T'ang and the mid-Sung went beyond the rebellions, invasions, and dynastic wars that have marked all periods of Chinese history. They reached the most basic social, cultural, political, and economic structures of Chinese civilization, features that normally change very slowly over the long term. The late T'ang government gave up interfering in the distribution of land, which could thenceforth be freely bought and sold. It also overhauled its taxation policies, deriving less from land and more from commerce. Between 700 and 1100 the population doubled to about one hundred million. Migration on a huge scale shifted the population southward; those living in central and south China rose in number from about a quarter to over half of the total population.

People moved south to avoid war, but also to take advantage of economic opportunities. Convenient water transportation and a milder climate made possible rapid commercial and agricultural expansion. Steady improvements in wet-field rice productivity were allowing denser settlement in rice-growing regions. All over the country commerce burgeoned, from local trade in agricultural products to maritime trade in porcelains that extended throughout Southeast Asia. The government assisted by increasing the money supply, even issuing paper money. Ten to twenty times as much cash circulated at the end of the eleventh century as ever had during the T'ang. In 1107, in addition to copper cash and silver bullion, over twenty-six million units of paper money were outstanding, each worth a "string" of a thousand copper coins.

Commercial expansion fueled the growth of cities. Kaifeng, the capital of the Northern Sung (960–1126, the period when the Sung government held most of "China proper"), was conveniently located near the north end of the Grand Canal and not far from major deposits of coal and iron. It was about as populous as the T'ang capital, Ch'ang-an, had been at its height, but was a more commercial city, dominated as much by markets of all sorts as by palaces and government offices. Other cities also grew at an unprecedented pace, dozens reaching populations of fifty thousand or more, leading to urban-rural cultural differences more marked than in any earlier period. During the Southern Sung (1127–1279, when the government did not hold the northern third of the county), the capital, Hangchow, at the southern end of the Grand Canal, grew extremely rapidly, reaching an estimated two million people—the largest city in the world at that time.[2]

Of the many technological advances during these centuries, the invention of printing warrants special note, as it revolutionized the spread of ideas, old and new, and contributed to fundamental changes in social structure. No longer was it necessary to copy books laboriously by hand. From mid-T'ang to mid-Sung the price of books dropped to perhaps one-tenth of its previous level. The Confucian classics and the Buddhist and Taoist canons were all published in their entirety. But these were not the only books to circulate in large numbers: there also appeared a profusion of books on agriculture, medicine, and divination, collections of anecdotes and stories, individual authors' prose and poetry, religious tracts and treatises, and reference guides that served the needs of local magistrates, candidates for the examinations, and anyone who wished to compose elegant letters.[3]

Economic expansion and easier access to books facilitated growth in the educated class. This development was further stimulated by changes in the way men were selected to become government officials, long the most prestigious occupation. Already in the late T'ang, the old aristocratic families that had been politically dominant for centuries were losing their claim on the central government as their special preserve. After bringing an end to a century of warlord domination, the early Sung government took steps to expand the civil service examination system. By the middle of the dynasty about half of those holding government posts had entered the bureaucracy after passing these examinations (with most of the rest gaining entrance thanks to privileges extended to the close relatives of higher officials). Competition to gain office through the examinations increased steadily over the course of the dynasty. In the early eleventh century, fewer than 30,000 candidates took the prefectural examinations; this number rose to nearly 80,000 by the end of the century and perhaps 400,000 before the dynasty's end. By the mid-1000s, indeed, it is fair to say that social and political leadership had been taken over by the educated class (*shih-ta-fu*), landholders, by and large, who prepared their sons to take the civil service examinations and to occupy positions of leadership at local and national levels in politics and culture. And now, for the first time in Chinese history, a large proportion of this ruling class was from central and southern China, often from families that had settled there fairly recently, in the waning years of the T'ang or even later.[4]

The growth of the examination system and the steady increase in the size of the educated class contributed to the intellectual ferment of the Sung. Although basic Buddhist doctrine and practice had by Sung times been completely sinified and incorporated into general Chinese culture, Buddhist philosophy and metaphysics no longer dominated speculative thinking. The best minds, it seems, turned instead to perfecting the arts of the literati: poetry, painting, calligraphy, history, philosophy, and classical studies. Confucian teachings were revived in a form so new that they are generally termed in English Neo-Confucianism. Teachers attracted hundreds of students, many of whom, though intent on preparing for the examinations, were drawn into discussion of subjects such as the nature of sages and restoring government by sages. Leaders of the movement to revive Confucianism sought ways to reconcile the vision of an ideal order found in the classics with the rapidly changing social and political order of their day. They argued, often bitterly, about the examination system. They sought to revitalize ancestral rites, combat such Buddhist practices as cremation, and give ritual definition to educated men's responsibilities toward their kinsmen. Personal self-cultivation became a major concern of thinkers, especially among followers of Ch'eng I (1033–1107) and Chu Hsi (1130–1200). In the Southern Sung, Confucian scholars, frustrated with the failure of the government to regain the north, took increasing interest in building a more ideal society from the bottom up —reforming families and local communities, establishing academies, and spreading their message through publishing.[5]

Ordinary working people, generally illiterate, were affected by cultural changes as well. Urbanization, denser settlement, expanded interregional commerce, and the growth of the educated class altered patterns of cultural communication. As communities that had been largely isolated from one another came into greater contact, local cults spread across wide regions of the country. At the same time, new forms of localized kinship groups emerged, bringing educated men and their peasant cousins together for joint ancestral rites, joint protection of graves, and the pursuit of other common interests. For every man who attempted the civil service examinations, a dozen must have gone to school long enough to learn to read or write but not enough to master the classics. It thus became more likely that every county, if not yet every market town, had schools and learned men.[6]

THE SUNG AND CHINESE WOMEN'S HISTORY

Women's history, as it has developed in the West, has been closely tied to feminism and the goal of improving women's lives. As activists have shifted their rallying cries, historians have been stimulated to ask new questions of the past. In the last couple of decades, they have analyzed the ideological basis of women's subordination and the historical processes by which particular constructions of gender differences have come to be accepted as matters of fact. Through assiduous searching, they have discovered that women left a much larger literary record than previously supposed. Women's history can even be credited with enlarging and recasting the questions historians ask, thus, for instance, stimulating new interest in the personal and emotional in the lives of both men and women. Today, even for periods as early as the Middle Ages and the Renaissance, there is a large body of scholarship showing what women were doing and analyzing gender as integral to the basic structures of culture and society.[7]

The volume of historical studies on women in China is still much smaller than that for women in the West, but gradually we are gaining a more nuanced understanding of how women's experiences have been tied to the development of Chinese history. It is now possible, for instance, to provide a relatively sophisticated analysis of the role women played as the mothers, wives, and sisters of the emperors and of how imperial marriage politics functioned in the overall political structure.[8] The connections between gender differentiation and basic philosophical and religious ideas have been analyzed, and minute attention has been directed to the didactic works that instructed women in their roles.[9] Notions of women's spheres, we now see, had enormous influence on the sorts of public roles women were able to play in religion and the arts.[10] The entertainment quarters provided some women with opportunities to develop their literary, musical, and artistic talents, yet inhibited other women who did not wish to be associated with that milieu.[11] In the late Ming (1368–1644), however, women writers and artists began to appear in greater numbers, a development that led, by the eighteenth century, to debates among scholars on women's roles.[12] The cult of widow fidelity ironically reached its peak in the same period. The extraordinary honor and rewards given to young women who renounced remarriage or even committed suicide have been analyzed from many angles—ranging from the state's interest in promoting virtue, to popular attitudes about suicide, to regional economic circumstances, to family structure among the educated elite, to widows' rights to property.[13] Indeed, it is now clear both that widows were actively making choices and that the cultural framework that shaped those choices rewarded certain forms of self-sacrifice. Even more research has been done on Chinese women in the twentieth century, especially on efforts to improve women's situations through political means. The focus here has been on connections between the feminist movement and successive political reforms and revolutions, with most scholars emphasizing the difficulty of effecting fundamental change in gender relations or of removing all the institutionalized disadvantages that hinder women.[14]

Why pick the Sung as the period to study Chinese women? Historians of Chinese women have usually selected a particular period in order to make a point of contemporary relevance (a time-honored practice also among Chinese historians, who call it using the past to criticize the present). Thus the T'ang (618–907) has attracted scholars who wish to show that in such a prosperous and vibrant age elite women participated in society with considerable freedom.[15] They can point to some T'ang women as role models, but, more importantly, they can demonstrate that granting greater autonomy to women is not incompatible with Chinese culture. By contrast, those who would rather expose the cruelties imposed on women—such as footbinding, infanticide, prostitution, and pressure on widows not to remarry—have generally been drawn to the Ch'ing (1644–1911), when such practices are best documented.[16]

The Sung has attracted scholars because it was a time when women's situations apparently took a turn for the worse.[17] It is associated with the spread of footbinding and strong condemnation of remarriage by widows. Because male dominance in Chinese history has so often been explained as a matter of ideology, scholars have looked to the revival of Confucianism in the Sung to explain these changes. In his influential *History of the Life of Chinese Women* (1928), for example, Ch'en Tung-yüan argued that women's lives started to deteriorate after the philosophers Ch'eng I and Chu Hsi promoted "the idea that women must value chastity," making the Sung "the turning point in women's lives."[18] Some authors have gone so far as to credit particular Sung scholars with actively promoting footbinding, infanticide, and widow suicide.[19] Placing the blame on Neo-Confucianism has been a convenient way for modern writers to condemn patriarchy in China without condemning Chinese culture as a whole.

Another reason for focusing on the Sung would seem on the surface to be quite contradictory: the evidence that women had particularly strong property rights during that period.[20] From surviving legal decisions we know that Sung judges, when called on to supervise the division of an estate, would set aside shares for the daughters for their dowries that were half the size of the sons' shares. Moreover, all women who brought dowries into marriage retained considerable control over their use and disposal as long as they lived, even taking them with them into second marriages. Neither in earlier nor in later periods did as much property pass through women's hands as a matter of course.

The conjunction of these two rather different signs of change in women's situation was what motivated me to focus on the Sung period. The great historical changes of the T'ang-Sung period could hardly have escaped having some impact on women's situation. Because the family is a property-holding and tax-paying unit, strategies for family survival and advancement must have been affected by changes in land tenure and taxation policies. The intensive character of wet-field rice cultivation had to have influenced the division of labor in the household. Urbanization and commercialization must also have had some effect on women's opportunities to support themselves. Cultural conceptions about gender differentiation necessarily fit into larger mental maps of the nature of human existence, the bonds between individuals, the moral basis of authority. Cultural changes so sweeping as the sinification of Buddhism and the revival of Confucianism must have influenced how people thought about basic issues. Given that much of the rhetoric on family had a clear class character, new class structures and new modes of interaction across class lines would certainly have reshaped this rhetoric. The task, then, is to discover how the history of women during the Sung fits into our understanding of the broad historical changes associated with that period.[21] How do we make sense of the spread of footbinding, especially when it seems to have occurred at the same time that women's rights to property were particularly strong? How valid are the charges against Sung Neo-Confucianism? What were the effects of economic growth and a new sort of elite? Does knowledge of what was happening to women raise new questions about these historical transformations?

MARRIAGE AND WOMEN'S LIVES

In this book I focus on the intersection of women and marriage. The over-whelming majority of Sung women married and had no public career. Men effectively dominated the public sphere: they ran the government, operated the businesses, wrote the books, and built the temples. To understand the lives of the majority of women, we must look at them where they were— in the home. Their interactions in this sphere with one another and with men were central both to individual women's sense of identity and to men's conceptions of women as persons and as a category of persons.

Historians who see women's history as a means of breaking down stereo-types about women's place in society tend to neglect the married women who stayed home rearing children and tending to family affairs, preferring instead to uncover exceptional women who gained power or prominence in the largely male worlds of rulers, artists, writers, or rebels. Even though most women in premodern societies identified themselves with their roles in their families, the history of women and the history of the family have been treated as two distinct, at times even antagonistic, disciplines. Historians of women who look on the family as the central institution of women's oppres-sion have criticized historians of the family for writing about families in ways that obscure gender-based differences, whether in interests, resources, or goals. They have argued that men's and women's experiences of the family are quite different, and that the family most historians have studied is the family as defined by men.[22]

In the Chinese case, a reluctance to focus on women within families may reflect distaste for the profoundly male-centered ideology of the Chinese family. The descent line from father to son to grandson was taken to be the core of the family: obligations to ancestors, family property, and family names were all transmitted along the patriline. Texts that can be broadly labeled Confucian presented family and kinship as at bottom a set of con-nections among men; indeed, people could and did compile family histories that failed to mention any women. Legal texts presented an equally idealized model of authority relations in the family. Senior generations had authority over junior ones, and men had authority over women. At all social levels, land, tenancies, houses, furniture, and most other property was conceived as family property; when transmitted to the next generation, sons alone got shares. Because sons had to stay home to continue the descent line, wives were brought in for them. Marriage thus moved a girl from one family to another, from a position of subordination to her father to one of sub-ordination to her husband and his parents. Wives were not free to divorce or abandon their husbands at will; men, though, could divorce wives on a wide variety of grounds. They could also take concubines, for although monogamy restricted them to one wife at a time, it did not restrict them to one woman. According to the dominant ethical and legal model, in short, the Chinese family was thoroughly patrilineal, patriarchal, and patrilocal. Women were well aware of that model and their marginality in it. Still, most found it to their advantage to respond to the incentives and rewards that this family system offered women and to work within it.[23]

It is easy to criticize the traditional Chinese family system as being oppressive to women, as Chinese reformers of both sexes have been doing since the beginning of this century. But no one is trying to revive this system; so pointing to its disagreeable features is not as useful as examining how women came to fashion their lives in terms of it and work as hard as men at keeping it going. Emphasizing women's victimization, in other words, only tends to obscure what women were able to accomplish.

To admit the power of the dominant ideology and legal structure does not mean that they must be used as the organizing framework for inquiries into women's lives. In this book I have adopted two strategies to give a truer picture of women's experiences. First, I focus on marriage rather than the family. By making marriage the central issue, we can see family life more from women's perspective. Marriage was many things: it was a series of rituals; it was a legal framework determining authority over people and goods; it was a way of creating affinal ties to other families; it was a set of gender-specific roles, laden with expectations about how men and women acted toward each other; it was a sexual union; it was the foundation of parenthood and family membership. It came in a variety of recognized forms: standard patrilocal first marriages; second marriages for either men or women; uxorilocal marriages of daughters or widows; and the quasi-marriages of concubines. Men's experience of family was marked by continuity, women's by discontinuity. Most men remained tied to the family into which they were born. A woman, in the best of circumstances, moved once to be married. In less fortunate circumstances, she could be sold and resold as a maid or concubine; she could be divorced; she could be sent away when widowed.

My second strategy is to view marriage as a cultural framework encompassing a variety of partly contradictory and often ambiguous ideas and images. To grasp these ideas and images we must set aside our usual ways of thinking. To modern sensibilities (including modern Chinese sensibilities), the best foundation for personal happiness and social order consists in strong ties between husbands and wives based above all on love. We may realize that the individual pursuit of love is not always successful, but we tend to assume that the total sum of human happiness is best realized when people are given considerable freedom to find loving spouses. In premodern China, by contrast, it was the parent-child tie that was viewed as central to personal happiness and social order. Women were at a disadvantage in that their ties to their parents were weakened when they moved away to marry. Yet their sons would stay home, so they might end up living twice as long with their sons as they had with their husbands. Thus the emphasis on parent-child ties gave women ample opportunity to build satisfying lives as mothers.

The value placed on motherhood and on parent-child ties more generally did not, however, make Chinese women's lives any less conflicted than our own. Partially contradictory notions of gender, sexuality, and affinity were also part of the cultural framework in which they fashioned their lives. Sung sources are full of husbands and wives who considered themselves tied to each other by forces of destiny, widows who sued their relatives for property, and wives who talked their husbands into keeping their daughters at home and bringing in husbands for them, not to mention all the tales of passion and jealousy, so disruptive of domestic relations. The existence of these assorted ideas and practices was widely recognized and tacitly accepted even if not synthesized into a single, coherent model. Most people understood that no matter what the legal and Confucian models might imply, families were not units in which members shared assumptions, interests, and goals uniformly; rather, they were contexts within which young and old, men and women, wives and concubines, negotiated their relations with one another, often pursuing different interests and thus coming into conflict.

I am not suggesting that Sung society was any different from our own in these regards. We are aware that in our society actions rarely have unambiguous meanings: parents do not all convey the same meanings when they urge a child to eat more, nor do clothing styles convey sexual messages unambiguously. And people are certainly not always consistent: a wife may defer to her husband one minute and undercut him the next. Such inconsistency is not necessarily based on class, regional, or gender differences; after all, a single individual can adhere to contradictory ideas and feel conflicting emotions. The coexistence of multifaceted, ambiguous, and often opposed ideas makes life confusing, but it is not necessarily bad in itself, for it gives people room to maneuver and thus to alter, at least slightly, the circumstances in which they live. Sung women's lives become more interesting and believable when we begin with the assumption that they lived in a world as complex, fluid, and riddled with ambivalence as the world of today. Even if men made sense of their lives primarily in terms of the dominant ideologies, for women, I would argue, the contradictory ideas and ambiguous images that swirled around them were every bit as crucial.

NARRATIVES

Given the many things I set out to do in this book—explore the complexities of a changing society, perceive both individuals and structures, detect both the possibilities for negotiation and the weight of convention—I have drawn on all the sources I could find. To understand the legal system, I turned to the standard histories, government document collections, and the Sung code, the *Sung hsing-t'ung*. I gleaned details of wedding rituals and the market in maids and concubines from descriptions of local customs, and information about prevailing ideas on pregnancy and childbirth from medical treatises. To discover images or symbols that helped shape people's thinking, I turned to such sources as poems, marriage proposals and agreements, and the phrases used to decorate a house for a wedding. Paintings proved a good medium for learning about gender distinctions. For the vocabulary of family relations and family ethics, I made use of advice books, most notably Ssu-ma Kuang's (1019–1086) *Precepts for Family Life* (*Chia-fan*) and his "Miscellaneous Proprieties for Managing the Family" (*Chü-chia tsa-i*) and Yüan Ts'ai's (ca. 1140–ca. 1195) *Precepts for Social Life* (*Yüan-shih shih-fan*).[24] Because these two authors saw problems differently, they often complement each other, confirming the prevalence of certain practices or else indicating where educated men might disagree. Philosophical writings have also proved useful, particularly those of Ch'eng I (1033–1107) and Chu Hsi (1130–1200), influential thinkers who put greater emphasis on patrilineal principles than Ssu-ma Kuang or Yüan Ts'ai.[25]

The drawback of these prescriptive and discursive texts is that they were written largely by men whose intellectual framework tended to deny multiplicity and change. Those who set words to paper can record only a tiny fraction of what goes on around them; the act of writing, moreover, forces them to impose order on the object, issue, or event in question and thus to simplify and rationalize. In China, the order they imputed was generally one that denied change. Thus writers, in deciding what to say about family, marriage, gender, and related topics, focused on what they saw as most true, and what was most true was what matched eternal patterns: basic human relations such as the parent-child bond, they assumed, were uninfluenced by time. As a consequence, the legal, ritual, and philosophical texts that set out to explain the principles of family organization obscure not only the messier side of social life, but also change over time.

Because generalizing authors left out so much, in this book wherever possible I have drawn on narratives of specific people in specific circumstances. The advantages of narrative can be illustrated by a story that is cited twice more in this book, once each in the chapters on concubines and on divorce. It was recorded by Hung Mai (1123–1202), one of the most engaging writers of the Sung period.

> Wang Pa-lang was a rich man from Pi-yang in T'ang-chou [Honan]. Every
> year he went to the Chiang-huai area, where he was a large merchant. While
> there he fell in love with a prostitute. Each time he went home, he would treat
> his wife badly, trying to drive her out. His wife was intelligent. She had borne
> four daughters, three of whom were already married, but since the youngest

was only a few years old, she figured she could not leave. Consequently, she responded to her husband meekly, "I have been your wife for over twenty years. Our daughters are married and we have grandchildren. If you chase me out, where can I go?"

Wang left again, this time bringing the prostitute back with him and setting her up in an inn in a nearby street. The wife, at home, had little by little to pawn or sell everything she had stored in her cases, until there was not a thing left in the house. When Wang returned and saw this, he was even angrier. "You and I can never get together again. Let's settle things today." His wife, finally becoming agitated, said, "If that is how it is, we must go to court." She grabbed him by the sleeve and dragged him to the county court, where the magistrate granted the divorce and divided the property in two. Wang wanted to take the little girl, but his wife objected. "My husband is shameless. He abandoned his wife and took up with a prostitute. If this girl goes with him, she will certainly end up in degraded circumstances." The county magistrate agreed with her and so she got custody of the girl.

The woman went to live in another village. She bought such things as jars and jugs and lined them up by her door the way shopkeepers do. One day her ex-husband passed her door and spoke to her as though they were on the same familiar terms as before. "How much money can you make on these? Why not try something else?" She chased him away, railing at him, "Since we have broken our relationship, we are like strangers. How do you get to interfere in my family affairs?" Thereafter they never saw each other again.

When the daughter came of age, she was married into the T'ien family of Fang-ch'eng [a county within their home prefecture of T'ang-chou]. By then the woman's property had grown to one hundred thousand strings of copper cash, and the T'ien family got it all. Mr. Wang lived with the prostitute and died away from home in Huai-nan. Several years later his ex-wife also died. When she was ready to be buried, the daughter, troubled that her father's body had not been brought back, sent someone to get it, wanting to bury him with her mother. After the two bodies were washed and dressed, they were laid on the same table, and while those in charge were not paying attention, the two bodies turned their backs on each other. Thinking this a coincidence, the daughter cried and put them back in their original place. But before long it happened again, so she knew that this couple were as emotionally estranged in death as in life and still hated each other. Nevertheless, she buried them in the same grave.[26]

This story is just one of thousands of surviving narratives about women written in the Sung dynasty. It is full of potent images. It depicts a smitten man, alienated from his wife because of his attraction to a prostitute. It also depicts a resourceful woman who, though she could not do whatever she pleased, was still capable of resisting pressure and pursuing goals. We are given some context: we see that the woman had to fashion her life within legal and economic limitations on what a woman could do inside or outside of marriage. The letter of the law on divorce—for instance, the rule that a man could not divorce his wife without grounds, or even with grounds if she had nowhere to go—is shown to mean little if he could simply abandon her. Still, women could benefit from flexible application of the law—as in this case, where the magistrate set aside the husband's claims to custody of his child.

From this narrative we see that wives and daughters had possibilities not often mentioned. Wives could have property of their own that they were free to sell; a family with no sons might pass its property to a daughter and her husband; and that daughter would be expected to take on the ritual duties normally expected of sons, such as burial. This story also depicts conflict between a husband and wife—Wang's wife knew her interests were not the same as her husband's—but at the same time it underscores the strength of Confucian values that favor overcoming conflict by moral effort. Without such values the daughter would not have tried to bring her parents' bodies together and, indeed, forced them to cohabit despite their apparent objections. We thus are left with many disparate, unintegrated truths: male dominance and female resourcefulness, the power of sexual attraction and the power of a mother's devotion to her child's welfare, marital incompatibility and the value placed on the unity of parents.

A great many other narratives exist that are in some ways comparable to the story of Wang Pa-lang and his wife. Hung Mai collected stories from all sorts of people, including domestic servants, monks, strangers he encountered at taverns, and colleagues he got to know during his years as a provincial official.[27] Most of the 2,692 stories in the surviving edition of his *I-chien chih* concern uncanny phenomena like the postmortem hatred between Wang and his wife, but since strange events often occurred at home, the tales inadvertently reveal some of the dynamics of domestic life. His stories were not crafted to fit didactic models, and he did not suppress or resolve the contradictions that occurred in ordinary thinking. And even if we read his stories as highly inventive ghost stories, Hung Mai presented them as true accounts of actual events—events hard to explain perhaps, but events that did happen.

Dozens of other authors besides Hung Mai recorded short narratives of events in women's lives. Particularly plentiful are anecdotes based on gossip about famous men.[28] Gossip may not always be accurate in its details, but it is not without a certain historical significance. To evaluate depictions of virtuous people, after all, we also need to know what was considered unattractive, inept, foolish, or scandalous, something in which such anecdotes excel. And we need a sense of what was taken as a reasonable explanation for unattractive behavior—the circumstances authors mention to help their readers understand why men might trade concubines or wives leave their husbands.

A brief anecdote recorded by Chou Mi (1232–1308) can serve as an example of these sources. It impugns the paternity of the much-hated chief councillor, Han T'o-chou (d. 1207).

When Wang Hsüan-tzu was an erudite at the imperial academy, one of his maids got pregnant. Because his wife would not tolerate the situation, the maid was sent to a female broker [to be resold]. The father of Han P'ing-yüan [i.e., Han T'o-chou] was from the same prefecture as Wang and serving at court with him. When he heard that the Wang family's pregnant maid had been discharged, he took her, first telling Wang his intentions. Before long, she had a son, who was none other than P'ing-yüan.[29]

Those reading this story would understand that Han wanted a son and saw in the pregnant maid an opportunity to get a child who could be raised as though it were his natural child. We may well wonder about the factual basis for stories like these, but people of the time accepted them; indeed, they sometimes ended up recorded in the official biographies of leading political figures in the *Sung History*. The biography of Wang Yen (890–966), for instance, records the following incident:

When Yen was military commander, he was friends with Wang Hsing of P'ing-lu, and their wives treated each other like sisters. After Yen reached high rank, he slighted Hsing, who felt bitter about it. When Yen's wife got sick, Hsing told people he could cure her. Yen then hurried to visit Hsing. Hsing told him, "I am not a competent physician, but think [the illness may be related to the fact that] when you were in Shan, you had just your one wife but now you have lots of courtesan-concubines. Couldn't it be that having to put up with poor treatment has made the lady discontent and thus ill? If you could discharge your female attendants, her illness would probably be cured." Yen took this as a personal insult. He falsely accused Hsing of something else and saw that he and his wife were both executed.[30]

Gossipy anecdotes like these are particularly useful for the insight they provide into ideas about sexuality and sexual attraction, touching as they do on the whole gamut of upper-class men's connections to the market in women. We see men purchasing concubines, having them entertain their guests, and getting into trouble when they lose control over them. We see wives unable to contain their jealousy and sons suspected of incest with their fathers' concubines. We see fathers and mothers in the lower classes looking for ways to profit from the demand for attractive young girls. Telling these stories allowed men to work out some of their feelings about the fragility and dangers inherent in their relations with women.

Standard historical sources can also be mined for narratives of particular women. The *Judicial Decisions* (*Ming-kung shu-p'an ch'ing-ming chi*), for example, contains over two hundred rulings concerning family disputes that reached the government courts. The rulings were written by judges, who were educated men, but the litigants were ordinary people in all walks of life. Of most relevance to this book are the accounts of disputes concerning incest, the validity of marriages, the claims of daughters, wives, and widows to dowries and other property, and the rights of widows to adopt heirs or otherwise decide family affairs.[31]

The collected writings of Sung authors are a rich source for funerary biographies. As eulogies, these biographies follow rather fixed conventions and unfortunately survive only for members of the educated class.[32] Each biography gives a basic account of its subject: dates, ancestry, native place, spouse, children, character, accomplishments, and virtues. The subjects of these biographies were usually officials or their relatives, both male and female; many were the friends and relatives of prominent writers, since these are the people whose collected works have been best preserved.

The men, and occasionally women, who decided what to reveal about a deceased woman close to them—a mother, sister, wife, daughter, or daughter-in-law—were crafting an image of her that also reflected on them and their identity. When this information was further organized and edited by a skilled writer (almost invariably a man), the account naturally took on more and more the characteristics of a literary creation. But biographies are not all artifice. When authors knew their subjects, especially when they wrote about their own mothers, wives, and sisters, their feelings come through clearly. Actions women took upon being widowed, for instance, are recounted in apparently factual ways. And when read carefully, biographies contain a wealth of details useful for determining the criteria on which people selected spouses for their children.[33] Funerary biographies also provide the only significant information from the Sung on such vital data as age at marriage, numbers of children, length of marriage, and length of widowhood. To make use of these data I collected biographies of women whose husbands' biographies also survived. By going through the standard index of Sung biographical materials, I found 189 couples for whom biographies exist for both husband and wife; 166 of these biography pairs give birth dates for both spouses, making them more useful for quantitative purposes. Of these 166 pairs, 135 were for a man and his first wife, and 31 were for a man and his second, third, or fourth wife. All of the statistics given in this book are based on these biography pairs.[34]

Here is the first half of a fairly typical funerary biography, written by Han Yüan-chi (1118–1187) about Miss Shang-kuan (1094–1178), the mother of an acquaintance.

Tomb Notice and Inscription for Miss Shang-kuan, Lady of Jung-kuo

Miss Shang-kuan was of a prominent descent group of Shao-wu [Fukien]. Her father quickly attained the rank of senior grand master of the palace through his Confucian scholarship and held a series of prominent posts, the first to bring eminence to their family. Miss Shang-kuan was sedate from birth and never spoke or laughed foolishly. Her father was impressed with her and spent a very long time picking a mate for her. The late Mr. Chi, [who eventually rose to] vice minister of revenue, had a good reputation while in the imperial academy and had passed in the top class, so she was sent to marry him. His home was in Lung-ch'uan in Ch'u-chou [Chekiang]. He had been orphaned at a young age and was poor. Miss Shang-kuan thus did not get to serve her parents-in-law, but at each of the seasonal sacrifices she would make offerings to them in accord with the family's means, meticulously attending to purity. She and her husband both admired those who would not stop once they had started something. She once sighed and said, "I am a daughter-in-law of your family and should serve the dead in all ways as I serve the living."

After her husband was appointed an instructor at the preparatory school of the imperial academy, a bad person in the Chi clan surreptitiously sold the graves of their ancestors at Ch'ing-p'ing village to a Buddhist temple. Her husband took leave to come back to redeem [the land] but, since he had no savings, was going to take out a loan. Miss Shang-kuan, with tears in her eyes, said, "The reason my parents sent me with a dowry was so that I could help your family. How could I use it while your graves are not protected?" She then emptied out her dowry chests to redeem the hill, and with the remainder bought a lot more land and had a temple built to protect [the grave property], saying, "This way later generations will know that they got this from you and outsiders will not dare interfere." With this, everyone in the Chi clan, young and old, praised her as worthy and went along with her plan. Even today woodcutters do not dare look at the grave forest, saying, "This was donated by Miss Shang-kuan."

Her husband served as edict attendant at the Hui-yu Hall and then was assigned to Kuang prefecture. After three years he was granted a temple guardianship [a sinecure], but before he left Kuang he died. None of their sons had reached maturity, so Miss Shang-kuan took charge of the coffin, bringing it back several thousand li to be buried in the Ch'ing-p'ing graveyard, managing everything meticulously. When finished, she said sadly, "I will not turn my back on the Chi family, and will educate their sons so that they can take their place in the ranks of the literati. But there is no one to depend on in my husband's family. Why not depend on my own parents?" So she brought her children across the mountains to live with her father. At the time, all of [her father's] sons had already died; she was the only surviving child. Every day [Miss Shang-kuan] served her two parents, then personally taught her sons to read and recite, not going to bed until midnight. This was her normal schedule.

Both of her parents were over ninety when they died. After their deaths, [Miss Shang-kuan] left their home and built a house in the prefectural capital, where she lived in a complex household of a hundred members. Her sons proved capable, and one after the other served as prefects. She had over ten grandsons, some of whom have received office, some of whom have studied for the examinations. Her six or seven grandsons-in-law are known for their Confucian cultivation and local service.

Unfortunately, over the last decade or so, three of her sons died, leaving only the youngest, Kuei, to serve her. [Miss Shang-kuan] was over eighty, and other people would not have been able to bear the grief, but she had been familiar with Buddhist scriptures from her youth, so she remained composed, not giving in to grief. The evening before she died, feeling slightly ill, she still sat up straight with her eyes shut and recited the Hua-yen sutra, her words flowing like a torrent without a single error.[35]

After thus alluding to her death, Han Yüan-chi described how her surviving son came to request that he write this biography, his connection with their family, and his admiration for her virtues. He also details her ancestry, the names and offices of her four sons, and the names of sixteen grandsons and of the husbands of eight granddaughters.

Like other funerary biographies, this one depicts its subject in a highly positive light. Miss Shang-kuan is described as possessing such stereotypically feminine virtues as never speaking or laughing foolishly and knowing how to gain the affection and gratitude of her relatives, both in her natal family and in her family of marriage. A rich source for the values of its author, this biography shows that Han Yüan-chi was impressed by tales of overcoming adversity; that he put a positive construction on a woman's education, at least when she used it to educate her sons; that he thought a woman who could chant sutras in the face of death deserved to be admired for her composure and possibly for her religious attainments. By reading many such biographies, one gets a sense of what male authors considered most special in their experiences with women, what gave them warm feelings when they thought about family life.

Still, I think these works reveal more than just the values of their authors. This one, for instance, gives concrete details about particular events in Miss Shang-kuan's life. I have used it in this book not only in quantitative summaries (it was a case, for instance, of a marriage between people from different circuits, and of a woman widowed between forty and forty-five), but also as an example of an educated woman from a family of means, with an interest in Buddhism, who accompanied her husband when he took a provincial post. From this epitaph we can see some of the things that could happen when the wife came from a more prosperous family than her husband: she might use her dowry for such family purposes as buying grave land; she might bring her children home with her to her parents' household after being widowed.

Although it is difficult to build an analysis of marriage and the way it shaped women's lives from narratives, it is the only way to get at context and complex motives. Hung Mai, Chou Mi, and Han Yüan-chi could have written essays (as Ssu-ma Kuang and Yüan Ts'ai did) on divorce and the problems of widows. Their generalizations would be interesting evidence of their thinking but would not tell us nearly as much as their narratives of particular women do about what women would say and do in given circumstances. Having read many narratives, I find that some of the generalizations made by Sung authors ring true, but in many cases they seem to have missed an important part of what was going on. For instance, the construction of emotions—from class prejudices, to sexual desire, to feelings toward mothers—are given relatively little weight in generalizing texts but emerge clearly in narratives of particular individuals.

CLASS- AND GENDER-BASED BIASES IN THE SOURCES

The sources I have used complement one another but do not provide equally abundant evidence for all the questions I would have liked to pursue. Evidence is fullest for ways of representing women and marital arrangements. It is also quite good for detecting ways of thinking, feeling, and acting on the part of both men and women. Issues of context—what sorts of circumstances would lead to certain actions—are also fairly well covered. But judging the actual incidence of particular forms of behavior is nearly impossible. The sources often allow me to say that an action was common, a common variant, or uncommon but recognized, but not to say that it characterized 10, 20, or 30 percent of the people in a particular place.

A class bias in the sources must be recognized as well. Much of the evidence in this book concerns people outside the educated class: most of the litigants in legal cases and perhaps half those discussed by Hung Mai and similar storytellers were ordinary people, neither officials, nor their relatives, nor necessarily educated. Wang Pa-lang, for instance, was a merchant, and his wife may well have been totally illiterate. Details about uxorilocal marriages, adultery, incest, and divorce, widows' tribulations, and widows who took in second husbands, come largely from these sorts of sources. By contrast, funerary biographies, the best source for evidence concerning matchmaking and the virtues sought in women, are overwhelmingly for the educated class and their dependents (including concubines, wet nurses, and nannies). The result is a definite asymmetry: information about ideal women comes largely from narratives of the lives of upper-class women, whereas information about irregular marriages, despised behavior, and unfortunate circumstances comes mainly from narratives of the lives of ordinary men and women.

Because no one today would suppose that virtue exists so disproportionately among the elite or depravity so disproportionately among the poor, I have by and large avoided linking either set of traits to class. Rather, I have interpreted the asymmetry of the rhetoric as an *expression* of class. Claiming that its women were virtuous added to the legitimacy of the educated class. A topic like adultery or incest was easier for authors to discuss if they could distance themselves from it: such behavior was a vice of those not adequately indoctrinated in moral values. This is not to say that class differences in values or behavior did not exist. Among peasant women, reserve and physical modesty were probably less central to notions of what is attractive in women than they were among upper-class women. Divorcing a childless wife probably carried less stigma for those who could not afford to take concubines. Men with no source of income other than inherited land may more readily have tried to oust heirs appointed by a brother's or cousin's widow in the hopes of installing their own sons. But proof of these differences is not forthcoming from the sources, given their biases.

An even more serious limitation to the sources is that virtually all of them were written by men. (The only woman to leave much of a corpus of writings is Li Ch'ing-chao [1084–ca. 1160], and while she will be cited several times, what survives from her pen are mostly poetic songs conveying feelings of love, grief, and despair but providing little in the way of concrete detail about her life.) Male authors, of course, did not see things as women of their time would have. In no society do women in a mixed group of men and women act just as they would in groups composed solely of women, especially women they know well. Women may, in the presence of men, have seemed entirely deferential but in all-female groups been quick to make fun of men's pretensions or preoccupations. An anthropologist studying rural women in contemporary China found that women would admit to their own power only when men were not present to hear them.[36] In addition, topics related to women's bodies—menstruation, pregnancy, looking attractive, growing old—were surely discussed much more among women than between men and women. Women must, for instance, have talked about binding their own or their daughters' feet, but we find no reflection of their conversations in the observations recorded by men. And could women have failed to discuss the everyday joys and trials of child rearing? But alas, we have no access to what women said among themselves. Those women who did write stayed largely with topics made conventional by male writers, such as the sadness of separation. And whereas men who enjoyed women's company and were deeply attached to their mothers, wives, and daughters might sympathetically and candidly report what they observed, they might misconstrue some of what they learned from hearsay. The tendency for writers to bifurcate everything associated with women into the very good (gentle, loving, dependent, beautiful) and the frightful (jealous, gossipy, petty, demanding, seductive) probably derives from an inability to see a connection between what makes mothers so wonderful and other women so dangerous. I thus have continually had to ask myself how far to push my reading of narratives. The argument for making them say things their authors did not intend is that my questions are different from theirs. The argument against it is that Sung men knew all sorts of things about their world that the passage of centuries prevents me from knowing, so if I push too hard I may be letting my imagination run too free. All I can hope is that I have attained a reasonable balance. I am well aware that in this book I present evidence about marriage in a way that no Chinese man or woman in the Sung would have. But I try to stick fairly close to the sources, and indicate who said what about a certain woman or women generally.

DETECTING AND EXPLAINING CHANGE

Running throughout this book is the question of change: In what ways were women's situations changing? What accounts for changes that did or did not occur? Because sources for the T'ang are less abundant than and often not comparable to sources for the Sung, it is important not to overestimate the extent of change, to mistake more references for more activity. Even change over the course of the Sung can be hard to prove conclusively, since many sources do not exist in comparable form for all periods. Judicial decisions nearly all date from the thirteenth century. Laws and edicts, by contrast, survive better for earlier periods. Anecdotal narratives of the sort Hung Mai compiled are fullest for the late eleventh and twelfth centuries. Even funerary biographies, which do survive from all periods, must be approached with some caution, for differences among them are not necessarily tied to changes over time; they could instead reflect class or regional differences, accidental differences in circumstances (age when widowed, for instance), or differences in personality. If I had thousands of cases, I could exclude some possibilities by statistical analysis, something rarely feasible with only a couple hundred cases. Thus my first task in considering change was to make sure that the evidence for believing change occurred is strong enough to warrant further discussion.

Because I rely so heavily on narratives, the sources that suggest the occurrence of change do not explain it. To analyze why attitudes or practices shifted, I had to look for correspondences to other historical developments. In particular, I looked for connections to changes in the economy, including increased commercialization and urbanization and shifts in the ways landed property was transmitted; to changes in the geographical situation of the Sung, such as the occupation of areas in the north by non-Han ethnic groups and steady southward migration; to changes in the nature of the elite, particularly in the ways men could attain office and otherwise gain or preserve social standing; and to the revival of Confucianism and the gradual success of a particular strand of Confucian thought identified with Ch'eng I and Chu Hsi.

The connections I draw between these historical currents and changes in marriage practices and women's lives will, I hope, be persuasive, or at least plausible. I argue, for instance, that the examination system stimulated competition for desirable sons-in-law, which in turn pushed the value of dowries up. I also argue that urbanization, increased prosperity, and growth in the size of the educated class all stimulated demand for women from the lower classes to serve the upper class as maids, concubines, and courtesans, and that the growth of this market subtly altered ideas about female attractiveness and male-female relations. But my arguments about such historical links must remain hypotheses, since the sorts of evidence one would need to prove causal connections simply do not exist. Nonetheless, issues of change are important enough to warrant discussion, even when I have to be content with rather speculative hypotheses.

ONE

Separating the Sexes

The many paintings that survive from the Sung period give indications of what the Sung world looked like. The bustle of the streets in the capital of Kaifeng in the early twelfth century, for instance, is depicted in a long handscroll painted by Chang Tse-tuan (fl. 1100–1130). On a fine spring day more than six hundred people are out on these streets, working, shopping, chatting, or observing the commotion. Porters carry bundles on shoulder poles; literati and monks greet each other; wheelwrights, fortune-tellers, and innkeepers vie for customers. But this mixed lot of people had one thing in common: with remarkably few exceptions, they were all men. In the small scene shown in Figure 1, men of all sorts are visible, and, peeking out of a sedan chair, one woman. Men could be seen everywhere in the business districts of the capital; women were a rare sight.

Another long handscroll by an unknown Sung painter reveals where the women were. This painting narrates an incident that occurred in the Han dynasty (202 B.C.–A.D. 220): Miss Ts'ai Wen-chi's return to her home after being held captive for twelve years by nomadic tribesmen. In the final scene of the scroll (Fig. 2), the party bringing her back reaches her parents' home, which, like other upper-class homes, was built around a courtyard. Most of the men in the escort party remain outside the front gate. Behind this gate is a screening wall that keeps passersby from seeing into the inner quarters of the house. On the far side of the courtyard the women have gathered to welcome Wen-chi home, in their excitement spilling a bit beyond the gate to the inner quarters, but still keeping themselves out of the sight of strangers.[1]

Fig. 1. A street in Kaifeng
Detail from the handscroll *Spring Festival on the River* by Chang Tse-tuan
(fl. 1000–1130). The Palace Museum, Peking. From Ku-kung 1981:78.

Fig. 2. The separation of the inner and outer quarters
From an anonymous late Northern Sung handscroll depicting Lady Ts'ai Wen-chi's
return from captivity. Denman Waldo Ross Collection. Courtesy, Museum of Fine
Arts, Boston (28.62–65).

INNER AND OUTER

The physical separation of the sexes underlined by the contrast between
these two paintings was given high value in Confucian ritual and ethical
teachings. The classic *Book of Rites* called for punctilious attention to the
"separation of male and female" (*nan-nü chih pieh*). Men and women should
spend most of their time out of each other's company and, when they had to
be together, should observe a general avoidance of physical contact. In his
"Miscellaneous Proprieties for Managing the Family," Ssu-ma Kuang para-
phrased and elaborated on the rules for sexual segregation presented in the
"Domestic Regulations" chapter of the *Book of Rites*, presenting an ideal
only those with considerable wealth could attain:

> In housing there should be a strict demarcation between the inner and outer
> parts, with a door separating them. The two parts should share neither a well,
> a washroom, nor a privy. The men are in charge of all affairs on the outside;

the women manage the inside affairs. During the day, the men do not stay in
their private rooms nor the women go beyond the inner door without good
reason. A woman who has to leave the inner quarters must cover her face (for
example, with a veil). Men who walk around at night must hold a candle.
Menservants do not enter the inner quarters unless to make house repairs or
in cases of calamity (such as floods, fires, or robberies). If they must enter, the
women should avoid them. If they cannot help being seen (as in floods, fires,
and robberies), they must cover their faces with their sleeves. Maids should
never cross the inner gate without good reason (young slave-girls also); if they
must do so, they too should cover their faces. The doorman and old servants
serve to pass messages and objects between the inner and outer quarters of
the house, but must not be allowed to enter rooms or kitchens at will.[2]

Elsewhere, Ssu-ma Kuang summed up the situation bluntly: "A girl ten or
older does not go out, which means she remains permanently inside."[3] He
also said that a father should not enter his daughter's room after she has
become engaged, and a brother should not sit next to his married sister
on her return visits home.[4] Yüan Ts'ai praised Ssu-ma Kuang's teachings on
the segregation of the sexes, saying it contained "over half of what is needed
to manage a household."[5] The importance of women staying out of sight of
men was underlined in the *Analects for Girls,* a primer written in T'ang
times, in this way: "Inner and outer each have their place. Males and
females gather separately. Women do not peek through the walls, nor step
into the outer courtyard. If they go out, they must cover their faces. If they
look out, they conceal their forms."[6]

The concept of keeping men and women physically apart was extended
analogically to encompass separation of functions and differentiation of
behavior. Men and women should do different things, or the same things
differently. For instance, each degree of mourning garments had a male
and a female version; thus, a son and a daughter required to perform largely
similar mourning obligations would do so in visibly dissimilar ways.[7] This
dimension of the separation of the sexes tended to merge with the differentiation in duties and proprieties of husbands and wives within families.
In fact, it was in terms of husbands and wives that inner and outer were
conceived as complementary spheres, with men dominant in one and women
in the other. In his *Elementary Learning,* Chu Hsi quoted the *Book of Rites*:
"Men do not discuss inside affairs nor women discuss outside affairs." Men,
however, were rarely if ever told not to get involved with what their wives
were doing; rather, their attention was directed to taking precautions to
ensure that women did not intrude into the men's sphere. Chu Hsi cited an
early ritual text which stated that women should spend all day within the
women's quarters and "never initiate affairs or take action on their own."[8]
He also cited Yen Chih-t'ui on the dangers of letting women take part in
the governance of either states or families: "Do not allow the disaster of the

hen announcing the dawn."[9] Elsewhere, in his commentary on a poem in the *Book of Songs,* Chu Hsi wrote: "Men correctly establish themselves on the outside and are the rulers of states and families. Therefore, when they are wise they can establish states. . . . Beautiful and talented women, by contrast, are evil omens, for through talking too much they can get things started on the road to disaster."[10]

How widely accepted were Confucian ideas on sexual segregation? Certainly they were taken for granted by members of the educated class, who have left virtually all of the surviving records. Wives in upper-class households, if they had any interest in the men's activities, stayed behind screens and listened to conversations with guests but never joined them. Still, when Confucian authors underlined the importance of maintaining the separation of the sexes, they were in effect implying that some girls and women were not naturally compliant. And a few such women do appear in the histories. In 1212, a girl named Wu Chih-tuan tried to take the examination for precocious children, but the officials in charge objected. Those who had read the *Book of Rites,* they argued, would know that women's responsibilities were spinning, weaving, and sewing, and that when they leave the house they must cover their faces; this girl's claim to be well read was thus spurious, since she ran around with no sense of shame.[11] Other evidence of the resistance to strict segregation is the attitude of women's biographers: they considered it worthy of special note when women were truly content to stay at home. One woman who accompanied her husband and son to various posts was praised for not even wanting to look at famous places nearby, "such as nationally famous parks like West Lake in Ju-yin, Hundred Flowers Land in Nan-yang, and Little Gold Hill in Chin-ling," even though family members tried to get her to come. Miss Fan (1015–1067), her biographer reported, never once went to see any of the splendid court ceremonies, always choosing to remain at home. Miss Chang Chi-lan (1108–1137) epitomized the woman happy to stay home because she declined to go sightseeing with her husband, saying it was not something women did.[12]

Naturally, unrelated men and women were never kept totally apart. Poets occasionally described women outdoors doing such agricultural tasks as picking tea or mulberry leaves (see Chapter 7). In *Ts'ai Wen-chi's Return Home,* mentioned above, some women are out on the street (see Fig. 2). Figure 3 is one of several Sung paintings depicting working-class women with children at their side stopping to negotiate with a peddler.[13] In this one, the woman apparently considered it of no consequence that a couple of men were there on the same errand. Clearly, the artist recognized that strict segregation of the sexes was most marked among the well-to-do with large homes and servants to run errands. Thus gender distinctions were intimately connected to class distinctions; or, to put it another way, one way the upper class made its distinctiveness visible was by making its women invisible.

Fig. 3. A woman making a purchase from a tea-seller
An album leaf attributed to Liu Sung-nien (ca. 1150–after 1225). Collection of the
National Palace Museum, Taiwan, Republic of China (VA 127).

Still, it would be inaccurate to think that there were two separate and
unrelated sets of standards, with the upper class insisting on the separation
of the sexes and ordinary people ignoring it. For age, and thus implicitly
sexuality, were also involved. In all classes, women of an age to be sexually
attractive or vulnerable (say, from ten to thirty-five or forty) were more
obliged to keep out of men's sight than the old or very young. In a painting
depicting an emperor's visit to a rural village, the men and boys have come
out in large numbers. In the detail shown in Figure 4, the men bow, salute,
or prostrate themselves. Three old women are also out on the street, two
staying somewhat behind, but one bowing right in front of the emperor. Yet

Fig. 4. Villagers turning out to greet an emperor
From an anonymous Southern Sung hanging scroll. The Shanghai Museum.

two young mothers with children at their skirts stay behind a rustic fence, catching a glimpse of what was going on without fully exposing themselves to others' view.

YIN AND YANG

After *inner* and *outer,* the pair of terms most often used to sum up the differences between men and women were *yin* (dark, passive, female) and *yang* (bright, assertive, male), the complementary forces that account for movement and change in the cosmos.[14] Underlying the theory of yin and yang is the assumption that all things are interrelated and interdependent; no part has a life of its own, for each is shaped by and helps to shape other constituent parts in a continuum of interactions. All things contain some yin and some yang, although in most cases one predominates. The classic source for yin-yang theory is the divination manual the *Book of Changes,* together with the traditions of interpretation that grew up around it.

In this book, as well as in treatises on biology, medicine, weather, or other natural phenomena, yin and yang were generally regarded as equally essential and important. In medical literature, men being more yang and women more yin accounted for the differences in their life cycles. For women, seven was the key number: they have all their teeth by seven, are sexually mature by fourteen, at full powers by twenty-one, and lose their reproductive capacity by forty-nine. For men the key number was eight: they get their teeth by eight, are sexually mature by sixteen, have full powers by twenty-four, and lose their reproductive capacity by sixty-four. In this conceptual framework, men and women are not conceived as opposites; rather, women are simply on a different cycle from men. Not only are they smaller, but they mature and age at a faster pace than men, giving them a shorter youthful period. Illnesses that strike both men and women thus had to be treated somewhat differently in each case. Men's physiology was based on vital energies (*ch'i*), women's, on blood, for "in women, blood is the basis."[15]

In Confucian models of social relations, it is tacitly accepted that yang is superior to yin, that action and initiation are more valued than endurance and completion. Thus yin-yang cosmology was used to explain gender hierarchy, making male dominance a matter of nature. The *Classic of Filial Piety for Girls* states:

> The way of establishing heaven is called yin and yang; the way of establishing earth is called gentle and tough. Yin and yang, gentle and tough, are the beginnings of heaven and earth. Male and female, husband and wife, are the ·beginnings of human social relations.... The wife is earth and the husband is heaven; neither can be dispensed with. But the man can perform a hundred actions; the woman concentrates on a single goal.[16]

Ssu-ma Kuang expanded on these ideas when he wrote:

> The husband is heaven; the wife is earth. The husband is the sun; the wife is the moon. The husband is yang; the wife is yin. Heaven is honored and occupies the space above. Earth is lowly and occupies the space below. The sun does not vary in its fullness; the moon alternates between being round and being incomplete. Yang sings out and gives life to things; yin joins in and completes things. Therefore wives take as their virtues gentleness and compliance and do not excel through strength or intellectual discrimination.[17]

Chu Hsi echoed this type of language when he cited the explanation in the *Book of Rites* on why the groom goes to fetch the bride in wedding ceremonies: "The man taking precedence over the woman is based on the principle of one being tough and the other gentle. The principle is identical to that of heaven taking precedence over the earth and rulers taking precedence over their subjects."[18]

Ch'eng I brought gender distinctions into his commentary on the *Book of Changes*. One hexagram had appended to it the judgment that "the female's correct place is in the inside; the male's correct place is on the outside." Ch'eng I explained: "Yang occupies five and resides on the outside; yin occupies two and stays on the inside; thus male and female each attain their correct place. The way of honored and lowly, inner and outer, correctly corresponds to the great meaning of heaven and earth, yin and yang."[19] Elsewhere Ch'eng I wrote that four hexagrams conveyed the principles underlying the unions of men and women. Below each of them he made comments about male-female differentiation:

> A man's will is sincere and so he lowers himself to come into contact with her. The woman's heart is pleased, so she responds up to him; this shows the priority of the man's influence.
>
> Enduring in compliance and obedience are the way of the wife. For a woman they are good and thus auspicious. For a man to endure in compliance and obedience to others is to lack the proper toughness of yang and thus is inauspicious.
>
> Yang on the top and yin on the bottom is proper for honored and lowly; thus male and female are proper and attain their place.
>
> [This image] illustrates the distinction between male and female. Even the highest-ranking woman must not lack gentleness, mildness, or act with arrogant will.[20]

From our perspective it is easy to recognize that Ch'eng I was moving from the attributes associated with women in his time and place to what was natural or intrinsic to men and women. But that is beside the point. To him and his contemporaries the fact that women were yin and men were yang was an adequate explanation of why men acted on their wills, women on their feelings; why men initiated and women endured; why men were associated with the outside and women with the inside.

The view of women as innately more emotional than men was certainly not confined to a narrow circle of philosophers, nor did it have to be explained in terms of yin and yang. Poets regularly described women as overcome by their emotions, unable to act because of the intensity of their feelings. Yüan Ts'ai saw women as more inclined than men to indulge their children, to want to give money to a married daughter facing hardship, and to respond to servants with angry outbursts. Men had to guard against both the generous and the temperamental side of women's more emotional character.[21]

AESTHETIC IDEALS: LOVELY YOUNG WOMEN WAITING ON SCHOLARLY MEN

The Confucian literature, with its emphasis on separate spheres for men and women and the complementarity of their roles, can be seen as giving wives considerable dignity.[22] In visual art and poetry we encounter another conception of what is desirable in women: beautiful, deferential, attentive service to men. Men would seem to have enjoyed imagining having young, well-dressed, attentive, and compliant women about them to see to their needs. Sexual segregation did not mean men could not have women around them, only that the women around them would be assumed to be under their domination, social and sexual—a situation unfitting for women married to other men or girls who would one day so marry. In depictions of women attending to men, women may outnumber the men, but the men are the central figures, the women are the marginal ones, there to make the men's life more pleasant. Such women were commonly portrayed as palace ladies attending to emperors, maids and concubines attending to scholars, or courtesans attending to scholarly guests. The presence of female attendants, in other words, demonstrates that the man was powerful enough to command the services of many women.

Figure 5 shows a detail from a handscroll narrating the adventures of Duke Wen of Chin during his twenty-year exile before recovering his state in 636 B.C. The ruler of Ch'in, when Duke Wen visited, presented him with five women, and in this scene three of them help him wash his hands: one holds the basin, one pours the water, and one is ready with a towel.[23] Scholars, too, enjoyed the services of female attendants. In Figure 6, a scene from a handscroll depicting a group of sixth-century scholars collating texts, we see four men busily examining and copying texts, one servant boy removing a shoe, and five women, all in similar clothes and hairstyles, carrying armrests, towels, water, and other objects the scholars might need.

Women attending to men could be present for purposes of amusement or entertainment, as in a long handscroll said to depict a party the painter had attended at the home of Han Hsi-tsai. At this private gathering, twenty-five women are keeping nineteen men amused, one of whom is a monk. The women, we must assume, were courtesans hired to entertain the guests for the night, perhaps helped out by Han's own maids or concubines. Some of the women are playing musical instruments (see detail, Fig. 7), some are carrying trays of food, some are sitting with several men chatting, some are waiting for orders, some are in private conversations with a single man. In two scenes we see beds with their curtains open, revealing rumpled bedding. In another scene a man has his arm around one of the women and seems to be persuading her to go somewhere with him. This painting, in other words, does not conceal the erotic overtones of women entertaining men. The women here do not look especially young, though we know from other sources that youth was prized in courtesans. The poet Liu Yung (987–1053), for instance, described one courtesan as having glossy black hair, a tiny waist, and being just fifteen, and another as just past sixteen (fourteen or fifteen by our counting; see "Notes on Conventions").[24]

Although the image of woman as handmaiden was epitomized by the maid, concubine, or palace lady (that is, not by the wife), the notion that demure and attentive service makes a woman attractive certainly carried over into husband-wife relations. In biographies, wives were repeatedly praised for being *wan*—agreeable, accommodating, compliant, a term used

Fig. 5. Women attending to a ruler
From a handscroll narrating an incident in ancient history attributed to Li T'ang
(fl. 1120–24). The Metropolitan Museum of Art, Gift of the Dillon Fund 1973
(1973.120.2).

exclusively to describe women. Echoing ancient usage, authors often referred
to wives as attending their husbands "with towel and comb." The poet Ho
Chu (1063–1120) concluded a poem lamenting the death of his wife by
asking who now would trim the lamp for him or mend his clothes.[25]

Attending to another person was not something that women alone did,
or that they did only for men: male servants could attend men; maids and

Fig. 6. Women attending to a group of scholars
From a Sung copy of an earlier handscroll narrating how scholars in the
Northern Ch'i collated texts. Denman Waldo Ross Collection. Courtesy,
Museum of Fine Arts, Boston (31.123).

young boys could attend women; even occasionally one sees men attending
women, though this seems to be confined to scenes of palace life where the
men were probably eunuchs. Still, a remarkably large proportion of women
depicted in Sung paintings were shown attending to men's needs. This is, of
course, as much a construction of masculinity as of femininity: a successful
man has women to attend to him. Attending to men may well have been an
aesthetically appealing image for many women too. Rewarded for pleasing
men with their appearance and their service, such women probably found it
gratifying to know that important men enjoyed the sight of them and wanted
them around.

Other dimensions of the depiction of men also deserve to be noticed.
The men with women to attend them are generally represented as literati
types, men more likely to compose poems or collate texts than ride horses.
It has long been noted that the Sung period marked a general shift in ideals

of manhood toward the literatus. This cultural shift was manifested on many levels, from increased use of sedan chairs, to fads for collecting antiques and delicate porcelains, to a decline in the popularity of hunting. The model literatus could be elegant, bookish, contemplative, or artistic, but did not need to be strong, quick, or physically dominating. The popularity of the literatus ideal undoubtedly owed much to the spread of printing, the expansion of education, the triumph of the examination system for recruitment to office, and the revival of Confucianism. It also, I suspect, was influenced by the international situation. For Sung men in the ruling elite to cultivate the image of the refined literatus accentuated the contrast between the Chinese and their northern rivals, the Turks, Khitan, Jurchen, and Mongols, all much more martial types. Tacitly asserting the superiority of the literary way of life was thus a way of asserting the superiority of Chinese over non-Chinese culture.

BODY IMAGES

Artists, in their paintings, reflected gender distinctions much more than they created them: works of the sort illustrated here were not seen widely

Fig. 7. Women entertaining men at a party
From a Sung copy of a painting by Ku Hung-chung (ca. 950). The Palace Museum,
Peking. From Chung-kuo mei-shu 1984 hui-hua pien 2:131.

enough to shape people's thinking. But people in Sung times did receive
powerful visual images of gender distinctions on an everyday basis through
clothing, hairstyles, cosmetics, and jewelry. Symbols inscribed directly on
bodies are powerful ways of communicating ideas about the differences
between men and women.

As mentioned above, in Confucian ideology it was deemed important
for men and women to do things differently as a way of manifesting their
differences. To give some trivial examples from Confucian ritual writings,
in greeting his parents in the morning, a man would say, "At your service,"
whereas his wife would say, "Bless you." When participating in ceremonies
together, men would bow two times and women four times.[26] Several of the

Fig. 8. A husband and wife being served by their son and daughter-in-law
A painting on the wall of a tomb in Honan dated 1099. From Su 1957: pl. 22.

paintings already discussed show how this desire for differentiation carried over into how men and women presented their bodies, particularly *Han Hsi-ts'ai's Night Revels* and *Ts'ai Wen-chi's Return Home.* To these let me add two further illustrations, in the form of religious paintings that were in no sense meant to carry erotic overtones. Figure 8, a wall painting from a tomb dated 1099, portrays two couples, the deceased husband and wife seated at a table, and their son and his wife serving them (with female servants or other relatives behind them). Figure 9 comes from the bottom of a portrait of the bodhisattva Kuanyin, dated 968. The two people are a husband and wife, donors of the scroll.

Although these four paintings date from different periods of the Sung and were created for different purposes, they reveal quite a few similarities

Fig. 9. Pious donors, husband and wife
From the bottom of a painting of the bodhisattva Kuanyin, dated 968. Courtesy of
the Freer Gallery of Art, Smithsonian Institution, Washington, D.C. (30.36).

in how the differences between men and women were manifested in bodily
appearance. There seems little doubt that, in upper-class society at least,
androgynous styles were not in favor. Clothing, hairstyles, and makeup were
used to draw attention to and heighten the differences between the sexes.
Even the clothes of ordinary people (see Figs. 3 and 4) roughly follow these
patterns.

The coding of clothing is most striking. In all cases, the women are
dressed more brightly than the men. The men wear clothes that are pre-
dominately a single color, generally black or off-white, but the women wear
more vibrant clothes that combine more than one pattern or hue. The men
are generally in one-piece garments, whereas the women wear multipiece
ones, with a jacket or vest setting off a dress or skirt, or a scarf or ribbon
draped over their shoulders, or both.

Notice also the differences in the hair. The men have pulled their hair up
and covered their topknots and sometimes all their hair with small black
hats. Since ancient times, wearing a hat of this sort had been seen as a sign
of manhood; indeed, putting on such a hat for the first time was one of the

standard Confucian life-cycle rituals for boys.[27] By contrast, the women and girls in these paintings also have their hair tied up, but do not cover it with hats. Sometimes they decorate it with jewels or headdresses, but usually quite a bit of the hair can be seen. Their hairstyles vary, perhaps reflecting changes in taste, regional differences, or class differences. Lower-class women, as seen in Figure 4, were portrayed as wearing scarves over their heads when outside, perhaps as a form of modesty, for authors sometimes mention the importance of women wearing "head covers" outdoors.[28]

Applying cosmetics to their faces was another way women drew attention to their gender. It was common in paintings for men's flesh to be left without added color, but for women's to be whitened, probably reflecting different ideals of skin color as well as the related practice of women applying cosmetics to their faces. Men, who could go outside, did not need to be white. Women, who ought to stay inside, could demonstrate it by their pallor. Women also wore more jewelry than men and, though not clearly illustrated in any of these paintings, pierced their ears so that they could wear earrings.

Sung China was not entirely without androgynous images. One goal of Buddhism was to transcend the distinctions between male and female along with those of class and ethnicity. The enlightened beings called bodhisattvas were described in sutras as neither male nor female but rather combining traits of each; Chinese artists, accordingly, often portrayed them with ambiguous sexual identity. Yet even here a trend toward making the sexes more distinct is apparent: during the Sung the popular bodhisattva Kuanyin came to be portrayed more and more regularly in distinctly female form.[29]

FOOTBINDING

In these paintings the women tend to be a bit smaller than the men, and generally somewhat more slope-shouldered. Sung artists, in contrast to T'ang artists, portrayed women as slender, even fragile. This may well be a self-image women shared. Li Ch'ing-chao in one song described herself as more slender than a flower.[30]

A general desire to see women as delicate and diminutive probably had something to do with the gradual spread of footbinding during the Sung. To people of the twentieth century—Chinese and non-Chinese alike —footbinding has been among the most potent symbols of the evils of the past. To the Chinese it has symbolized not merely the subjection of women, but also the self-imposed subjection of China.[31] To radical Western feminists it has gained notoriety as the most extreme of the many ways women have felt compelled to endure pain, discomfort, and inconvenience to meet standards of beauty that do women little if any good, even when they embrace them wholeheartedly.[32] One test of our ability to understand the mentality of Sung China is to set aside these modern readings of the symbolism of footbinding and to try to see how, in Sung times, both men and women, at least in the upper classes, could have seen tiny bound feet as symbols of beauty rather than subjection.

Footbinding seems to have spread during the Sung from the palace and the entertainment quarters to the homes of the elite who frequented those quarters.[33] Chou Mi (1232–1308) attributed to an anonymous source the story that three centuries earlier a dancer in the palace of the ruler of the Later T'ang (923–935) had bound her feet to make them small and curved up like new moons.[34] The practice could plausibly have started among dancers in the tenth century who bound their feet to make them stronger and more elegant-looking. In the eleventh century, the rather staid scholar Hsü Chi (1028–1103) apparently knew something of the custom, for he praised a widow for "knowing about arranging the four limbs [for burial], but not about binding her two feet."[35] By the early twelfth century, the custom was widespread enough for one scholar, Chang Pang-chi, to inquire into its origins. Chang offered the opinion that true bound feet, bowed in shape and artificially rather than naturally small, were a recent phenomenon, as they were mentioned by no poets in the T'ang or earlier.[36]

From the late twelfth century on, casual references to footbinding become slightly more common.[37] By this period footbinding was no longer associated with dancing, and its practice was not confined to entertainers. There is even reference to a kitchen maid in a well-to-do household who had bound feet.[38] By the thirteenth century, archaeological evidence shows clearly that footbinding was practiced among the daughters and wives of officials (Fig. 10). The tomb of an official from Chekiang with strong scholarly interests whose first wife died in 1240 included a pair of silver shoes for bound feet inscribed with her name. They were 14 cm long and 4.5 cm wide at the widest point, tapering to a narrow point that was turned up.[39] These were probably not actual shoes that had been worn, but mementos to remind him of his first wife and her tiny feet. Actual bound-foot shoes were found in the Fukien tomb of Miss Huang Sheng (1227–1243), the daughter of a high-ranking official from Fu-chou (Fukien). In 1242, at sixteen sui, she married an imperial clansman very distantly related to the throne, whose father was dead but whose grandfather, still alive, was a successful official. Her coffin contained several sets of shoes for bound feet, each about 13.3 to 14 cm long, and her feet were in fact bound with a long strip of gauze cloth.[40] Further evidence was found in the Kiangsi tomb of Miss Chou (1240–1274), also the daughter and wife of officials. The seven pairs of bound-foot shoes discovered in her tomb were somewhat larger than the others (18 to 22 cm long, and 5 to 6 cm wide).[41]

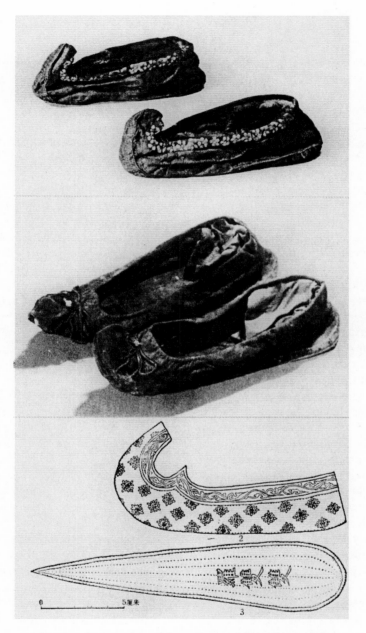

Fig. 10. Shoes for bound feet excavated from three tombs
From Fu-chou 1982: pl. 62; Ch'ü-chou 1983:1007; Chiang-hsi 1990: pl. 3.

Sung writers associated bound feet with exquisite beauty. Su Shih (1036–1101) composed a song describing a dancer who was eager to try this "palace" style but found it painful. In this song, tiny feet were depicted as objects of wonder, to be held in the palm of the hand. Other poets marveled at the slender arcs of bound feet or used phrases like "moons forever new."[42] Chang Tun (d. 1105) reportedly said that his age surpassed prior ages in three regards, one of which was women's feet. Ch'en Liang (1143–1194) once made fun of himself by saying he was like an ugly woman of thirty or forty who uselessly endures the pain of trying to bind her feet.[43] To him, footbinding was something women did voluntarily in their efforts to make themselves beautiful, but it worked only if started young.

Despite its associations with women's efforts at beautification, at least one Sung man questioned the propriety of footbinding. In the mid–thirteenth century, Ch'e Jo-shui, in what may be the first protest against footbinding, wrote: "Little children not yet four or five sui, who have done nothing wrong, nevertheless are made to suffer unlimited pain to bind [their feet] small. I do not know what use this is."[44] Other men may have discouraged footbinding for the very reason that it was associated with the pursuit of beauty. An early Yüan observer noted that among the sixth-generation descendants of the strict moralist Ch'eng I, the women neither bound their feet nor pierced their ears.[45]

By the end of the Sung, footbinding was firmly entrenched. T'ao Tsung-i (fl. 1300–1360), writing in the first century of the next dynasty, reviewed the evidence of the history of footbinding. He began with the same source Chou Mi had cited regarding the dancer at the court of one of the pre-Sung states, then repeated Chang Pang-chi's arguments for the relatively recent origins of the practice, and finally speculated that the practice, though still rare through the eleventh century, had become progressively more common owing to imitation. In his day, he reported, people were ashamed not to practice it.[46]

As a type of beautification, bound feet remained quite private. In the paintings of women checking their appearance or thinking about absent men—paintings clearly meant to have at least mildly erotic overtones—the women's feet were concealed under floor-length skirts. The only painting from this period depicting women with bound feet shows actresses, denizens of the entertainment quarters, who, like courtesans, probably were quick to adopt footbinding. Because one of the women is playing the part of a man, she has to show her tiny feet (Fig. 11).

Modern writers have often compared footbinding to high-heel shoes because it affected gait, or to tight corsets because it involved unhealthy constriction. These comparisons, however, do not bring out the degree to which women's bodies were permanently altered by footbinding. Footbinding did not merely accentuate or advertise the differences between the sexes:

Fig. 11. Actresses with bound feet
Late Sung or Yüan album leaf. The Palace Museum, Peking. Photograph by
Wan-go Weng.

it rendered men and women physically more different than nature had,
making it closer to cosmetic surgery. Yet even here the comparison is in-
sufficient; for even silicon implants and liposuction do not affect other parts
of the body to the degree footbinding did. Footbinding was an alteration of
the body that changed everything about a woman's physical being. She
would move about less, sitting rather than standing, staying home rather
than going out. With less exercise, she would be softer, more languid. From
poetry, we know of men's attraction to languid women, especially unhappy
beauties longing for absent men.[47] For women to be smaller, softer, more
stationary, and more languid would of course enhance the image of men as
larger, harder, more active. Because the ideal upper-class man was by Sung
times a relatively subdued and refined figure, he might seem effeminate
unless women could be made even more delicate, reticent, and stationary.

What better than tiny feet to accomplish this? In this way, new notions of masculinity stimulated the creation of revised standards of feminine beauty. Other associations may have been mixed in. That the feet were bound and not simply small, for example, probably had erotic appeal for some men.

But I do not think we can be satisfied with seeing why men might have been attracted to women with bound feet. We must also come to grips with women's apparently eager participation. After all, it was mothers, not suitors, who bound little girls' feet despite the great pain it caused. The violence of footbinding was a violence that they afflicted on their own. Did they do it with regret because they felt otherwise men would not consider their daughters attractive? Did they share the perception that tiny feet were beautiful? Did they take pride in creating a perfect foot?

We cannot understand how they would have felt about female attractiveness without keeping in mind the competition for favor between wives and concubines that was a basic reality in their lives. As will be discussed in later chapters, with the great increase in the money economy in the Sung and the growth of commercial cities throughout the country, concubinage flourished among the well-to-do. By mid–Northern Sung times, the sorts of men who in earlier dynasties might have been satisfied to visit the entertainment quarters and have affairs with the courtesans there had the means and desire to purchase women to bring home as concubines. Mothers who knew the strength of men's attraction to courtesans and courtesan-like concubines had to consider carefully how to groom their daughters for their later lives as wives. Could they make them as appealing as courtesans without diminishing their respectability? It was fine to teach them to select becoming clothes and arrange their hair attractively. But it was also essential that they appear modest, reserved, and reluctant to show off in any way so that they would not be confused with courtesans who brazenly showed their faces to unrelated men. Would what was playfully attractive in a courtesan seem like competition in a wife? Was it a good idea to teach daughters to compose poetry, or would that make them too much like courtesans? I suspect that mothers took to binding their daughters' feet because little feet were one of the tricks courtesans used to enhance their beauty, yet this attribute could not be classed in any way as too forward. Bound feet were private, not something that one showed off. Even if courtesans had bound feet, binding them was very "inner," involving no competition with men.

It took a couple of centuries for footbinding to become common among the wives and daughters of good families. During this time, bindings may have gradually gotten tighter as the ideal foot size diminished. Certainly no one could have danced with feet shaped to fit the tiny shoes found in thirteenth-century tombs. In the early stages of the spread of footbinding, mothers whose own feet had not been bound were making the decision to bind the feet of their daughters, perhaps having seen bound feet for the first time when a young concubine was brought into the house. They wanted for their daughters something they did not have themselves. As these girls grew up, there were naturally more mothers whose own feet had been bound. Those who had frequently been praised for the beauty of their feet may well have internalized this standard of beauty and been more than willing to help their daughters attain it as well.

In broad outline, Sung ideas about the differences between men and women are far from unusual in world history. The concepts of yin and yang may be distinctively Chinese, and compared to Western notions may stress relations more than essences; still, association of women with the responsive and fruitful earth and men with the active exploitation of it has similarities with the nature/culture dichotomy identified as basic to Western ideas about gender. Certainly a polarity of inner and outer is found many places, along with the view that the two spheres are complementary rather than opposed or antagonistic. Physical separation of the sexes has occurred to varying degrees in many locations, especially in Asia, with higher social status generally associated with greater seclusion of women. And in almost all societies, it would seem, people feel a need to wear their clothes and hair in sex-specific ways.[48]

It is important, however, to get beyond this very general level. Chinese ideas about gender were embedded in Chinese society and culture. They changed along with changes in the larger social and cultural environment: thus, as we have seen, during the Sung the cultivated literati gained dominance as the masculine ideal in the wealthier classes, and footbinding spread among both courtesans and upper-class wives and daughters. Power was involved in these processes. Conceptions of gender differentiation and gender hierarchy evolved in social environments in which men had much more legal, economic, and cultural power than women. Gender distinctions made these differences in power seem part of nature, part of the unchallengeable way life is.

Without denying the power of gender distinctions, we should still notice the tensions in them. In many formulations what is natural and what is desirable are elided, leaving unanswered the question of whether the differences between men and women come above all from their natures or are simply desirable because they contribute to the order of society. The polarities of yin and yang and inner and outer are each built on tensions; each presents the relations between the poles as simultaneously complementary and hierarchical. There are also tensions between these two formulations. Yin-and-yang thinking highlights the continuum and the movement from one to the other, while inner and outer evokes the need to keep the two apart; the one creates the possibility of boundaries blurring, the other tries to banish it. A woman may be relatively yang to her son, but she is not relatively outer. Equally important, both these relatively desexualized models of the differences between male and female existed alongside images that touched on the erotic, further complicating the messages conveyed. Were women there to please men with their appearance, or should they not be seen?

Here, again, Sung China was not unique; ideas about gender are often untidy. Recent scholars have noted that within a given culture there may be several competing gender ideologies, each of which can contain inconsistencies and contradictions. Individuals may gravitate toward those ideologies that benefit them the most, even shifting during different stages of their lives. Moreover, a given set of ideas may both empower and oppress women at the same time.[49] In Sung China, association of women with the inner both limited and empowered: it kept women out of the public sphere but legitimated their authority in the domestic sphere. The male authors cited here certainly did not envy women for their authority in that realm, but we should not assume that women evaluated their social and familial roles the same way.

What were the psychological consequences of the physical separation of the sexes? Since we live in a society in which men and women mix quite freely, we must guard against assuming that women in Sung times felt the sorts of frustrations we might if constrained by their rules. In modern societies where the demands for female modesty and seclusion are high, women are not passive or dispirited, or even necessarily less self-confident than their husbands.[50] Sung women may well have been just as capable as modern Indian women, for example, of finding self-worth in spatially and socially constricted worlds. To get some sense of what Sung women thought of themselves, we will have to look at them engaged in their domestic roles.

This chapter has far from exhausted the subject of gender distinctions in Sung culture—indeed, nearly every chapter that follows will add to the list of common ways of thinking about the differences between men and women. This chapter has dealt only with very basic attitudes, ones that underlie many others. Yet it is already necessary to offer a major qualification, for in Sung China, thinking of people in terms of roles frequently overpowered thinking of them in terms of gender. To put this another way, ideas about the differences between men and women were usually merged in one way or another with ideas about social roles, which for women were particularly the roles assigned by the family and marriage system: daughter, wife, daughter-in-law, mother, mother-in-law, grandmother, mother's sister, father's sister, and so on. In the next chapter I examine how understandings of marriage shaped conceptions of these roles, especially the role of wife.

TWO

Meanings of Marriage

"The Meaning of Marriage," a chapter in the ancient classic the *Book of Rites,* begins by explaining, "Marriages are for the good of the two surnames that are joined. Looking toward the past, they provide for service to the ancestral temple; looking toward the future, they provide for the continuation of descendants."[1] Sung writers often cited this saying—just one of the many indications that their concepts of marriage were by no means identical to ours.

In this chapter I examine Sung understandings of what it meant to get married, relating these ideas to larger social and cultural contexts. My goal is to reveal the prevailing assumptions about marriage in Sung society, especially when they differ from ours, and at the same time point to sources of disagreement or tension among them. I begin with basic assumptions, then examine systematic and rationalized models of marriage as a dimension of the family, then turn to the less organized but no less powerful ideas conveyed through literary images. Although I analyze these concepts, ideas, and images on the basis of Sung usage, much of what I describe in this chapter was true in earlier and later periods as well.

MEANINGS EMBEDDED IN LANGUAGE

The words people used to talk about marriage implied a lot about what the institution meant. The term *hun-yin,* for instance, implied that marriage was a relationship between families. According to an ancient lexicon, *hun* and *yin* were the terms the parents of the bride and groom used to refer to each other.[2] Marriage could also be alluded to as *hun-li,* literally, the marriage ritual. This term stressed that marriage, like other rituals, was based on rules handed down from the past; like other rituals, too, it served to create social distinctions, ones rooted in the cosmological order and thus unquestionable.

Marriage could also be conceived of as an act, the joining of two parties. In English we can say, "he married her," "she married him," or "they were married by the justice of the peace." In China, different verbs were used to refer to the actions of different parties. The man's family took (*ch'ü*) a daughter-in-law, and the man himself could be said to take a wife. From the bride's side, her parents could be said to give (*yü*) her to someone, to get her a home (*chia*), or to confer her as a bride on someone (*ch'i*). Generally, a woman's parents or guardians were portrayed as the active agents with regard to her marriage. One could, however, say that she had "gone" (*shih*) or "returned home" (*kuei*) to her family of marriage to describe her entry into it.

Marriage in the narrow meaning of the union of a husband and wife was best expressed in Chinese by *fu-fu* or *fu-ch'i*, terms for couple made up of the words for husband and wife. *Fu*, or husband, meant little more than man. The other *fu*, for wife, meant daughter-in-law as much as wife, thus stressing the woman's place in the man's patriline. A woman could be called the *fu* of a family, of the family head, of her father-in-law, or of her husband. Chinese philologists derived the meaning for this word from homophones for "support" or "submit."[3] A wife, in short, was someone who submitted to her husband and assisted him. *Ch'i* was the common legal term for wife. As a *ch'i* she was not a concubine (*ch'ieh*); indeed, she was the mate of a particular man and shared in his social status. Philologists said *ch'i* meant "identification"; a husband and his *ch'i* became one unit, one entity, sharing the same status and honor.[4] In other words, a woman lost her separate identity by marrying; her identity was absorbed in her husband's.

In polite conversation other men's wives were also commonly called "rooms" (*shih*) or "persons of the room" (*shih-jen*), and acquiring a wife was termed "getting a room." Calling a wife a room alluded both to the fact that a young man would get a room for himself and his wife when he married and to the idea that his wife would have a special connection to this room. It implied that although the man was identified with the entire family, the wife had a much stronger tie to a particular room, the bedroom for her and her husband and later their young children. Yet whereas a man referred to other men's wives as "rooms," he referred to his own wife, in casual conversation, as *nei* or *nei-tzu*, "inner one." This choice of terms drew on the inner/outer distinction discussed in the last chapter. It was a belittling term that diminished the significance of the wife because she was closely identified with the speaker, but it did so in a very specific way: it made her part of an inner, private world.

These ways of talking about marriage and married couples, like the legal and ritual codes to be discussed below, assumed and reinforced patrilineal,

patriarchal, and patrilocal principles. It was from the perspective of the patriline from father to son to grandson that the same term could be used to
mean both daughter-in-law and wife. It was from the perspective of a family
system with fathers in control that one could speak of giving brides. And the
idea of brides as rooms, and of the wedding as a "going home" for the bride,
made sense only if one assumed patrilocal marriage, with women moving
into the homes of their husbands.

LEGAL FRAMEWORK

In Sung times one did not have to go to a government office to get permission to marry or to register a marriage, but marriage was nonetheless a
legal institution, for laws promulgated by the state recognized only certain
sorts of unions as valid.[5] Monogamy was a key requirement. The Sung code
stated, "Anyone who has a wife and then takes another wife is subject to one
year penal servitude. The woman's side is subject to a penalty one degree
lower. In cases of deception, those taking the wife are subject to a year and
a half of penal servitude, but the woman's family is not implicated."[6] Both
men and women could remarry if the first marriage ended by death or
divorce, but not before.

Monogamy, in this model, did not limit a man to one woman at a time,
but it did limit him to one wife. Wives and concubines were not interchange-
able: "Anyone who makes his wife into his concubine or his maidservant
into his wife is subject to two years penal servitude. Anyone who makes
his concubine or female retainer into his wife or his maidservant into his
concubine is subject to a year and half penal servitude. Each woman should
be returned to her proper status." In other words, raising a woman's status
two levels or dropping it one brought two years of punishment; raising it
one level brought a year and a half. The code did provide for some leeway at
the lower levels: "A maidservant who has borne a child or been freed is
permitted to be made a concubine."[7] One definitely could not make her a
wife, however. The commentary explained: "A wife transmits the family
affairs and carries on the ancestral sacrifices. She is married with the full
six ceremonies, then the two rites. How could a maidservant, even if freed,
be qualified to perform the important responsibilities of a legal wife?"[8]

The Sung code treated engagements as binding on the girl's family.
"Anyone who has already replied to a marriage letter promising to marry
out his daughter or who has made a private agreement and then suddenly
changes his mind is subject to a sixty-stroke beating. The same is true if
there is no document agreeing to the marriage but betrothal gifts have been
received." If the girl's family betrothed her to someone else, the punishment was increased to one hundred strokes; if the wedding had already
taken place, to one year of penal servitude. The commentary noted that the

groom's family was permitted to change its mind, but in such a case could
not expect the betrothal gifts to be returned.[9] These laws assume a betrothal
system in which the groom's family makes a deposit for a bride; they thus
had every right to expect her to be delivered at the agreed-upon time. If
they did not ask for her within three years, however, the bride's family could
assume they were no longer interested and marry her to someone else.[10]

Laws on exogamy show that the legal model of marriage was tied to
notions of patrilineality. From very early times, it was agreed that people
should not marry even remote patrilineal relatives; by Sung times, that
restriction had been extended to include all those of the same surname.
The Sung code stated: "Those who marry someone of the same surname are
subject to two years penal servitude." Penalties were even greater when the
parties had a common patrilineal ancestor within the past four generations,
and the closer their kinship, the more serious the offense.[11] Concubines,
like wives, could not be taken from a family of the same surname. The commentary to the code repeated the ancient rule that those who purchased a
concubine of unknown family name should perform a divination to make
sure her name was not the same as theirs.[12] Rules also governed marriage
with maternal or affinal kin, but in those cases only generation mattered:
men could marry cousins of other surnames, but not aunts or nieces.[13] When
a woman remarried, her ex-husband's relatives were then also included
among the prohibited spouses. In one legal case, a judge ordered the divorce
of a woman who three years earlier had married a second cousin of her
former husband. He cited a rule that divorce in such cases was compulsory
unless the marriage had already been in existence twenty or more years.[14]

The laws on marriage supported the authority of family heads. Fathers
and family heads controlled the marriages of their children and thus were
responsible if the law was broken. If a grown son while away from home
entered into an agreement to marry only to discover later that his parents
had betrothed him to someone else, only the betrothal his parents had
arranged would be valid.[15] Paternal authority was also reinforced by the laws
on divorce. The husband's parents could send back a wife who displeased
them or bore no children. The woman, by contrast, could not unilaterally
leave her husband and his family, nor could her parents take her back
against their will. Indeed, running away was a punishable offense. The code
specified that a wife or concubine who left of her own accord was subject to
three years penal servitude. The commentary explained that "wives follow
their husbands and lack the authority to make decisions themselves."[16]

Getting married, in the legal model, did little to alter a man's identity.
His status as a married man had no legal consequences for his relations to
outsiders: after he married it was no more serious for him to have sexual
relations with a married or unmarried woman than it had been before his

marriage, just as it was no more—or less—serious for him to injure or kill his father or brother. In other words, his primary identity remained that of the son of his father. His status as husband of his wife governed his relationship with her and her parents, but not much else.

For a woman, in contrast, marriage brought a fundamental change in identity. From the moment she married, she was above all daughter-in-law of a certain family and wife of a certain man. Anyone outside that family (other than her natal family) regarded her before all else as a married woman. After her marriage into a new household she came under the authority of the head of that household. She was not, however, merely a subordinate member of that household; she had a specific place in it, meticulously defined in the statutes on criminal offenses. A woman who killed her father-in-law by accident was subject to a punishment of three years penal servitude, a penalty one degree lower than her husband would suffer in the same situation, but much higher than what her brother or sister would get, since as outsiders they could get off by paying restitution.[17]

Penalties for offenses classed as illicit sexual behavior carried heavier penalties when the woman involved was married. Rape of a married woman had a penalty of two and a half years penal servitude; of a woman without a husband, two years. Adultery (consensual sexual relations between a married woman and a man other than her husband) carried a penalty of two years penal servitude, whereas fornication (consensual sexual relations between a man and a woman without a husband) brought only a year and a half.[18] In the cases of both adultery and fornication, the penalties were the same for the man and the woman.

Sung laws paid relatively little attention to gender but treated kinship roles as being of fundamental importance. It was, in short, not men and women who had markedly different standing, but husbands and wives. Men were not all alike: some were family heads, some were sons or younger brothers of family heads, and these differences mattered. Nor were women a uniform category: daughters and daughters-in-law, wives and concubines —all were treated quite distinctly. In the law, what mattered was a person's position in a given relationship much more than his or her gender.

The laws on marriage were of considerable consequence in Chinese society, but they were laws, not a description of how people behaved or even how they were punished. Sung laws against behaviors hard to police—laws against adultery, bigamy, promoting concubines to wives, marrying widows of cousins—should probably be looked on as comparable to laws against robbery. They indicate not that the offenses were rare, for they were not, but that those in authority wished to label them as being very wrong. Even judges found it difficult to think in terms of the simple principles of the laws. Judges presented with evidence of offenses seem to have been almost as willing as other people to consider nonlegal issues. They rarely enforced the provisions of the code when they conflicted too greatly with their sense of what was right.

CONFUCIAN ETHICAL AND RITUAL MODELS

Much of people's sense of what was right was based on Confucian family ethics, which placed marriage in the context of the universal obligations to parents and to patrilineal ancestors. Confucian didactic writing from Han times on regularly stressed the need for sons to obey and honor their parents and wives to serve their husbands' families.[19] In the Sung, Confucian family ethics were summarized in handy form by Chu Hsi in his *Elementary Learning.* Chu selected passages from the classics and earlier writers to stress the seriousness of marriage, a wife's obligation to remain loyal to her husband, and the principles of sexual segregation. He quoted the statement attributed to Confucius in an early ritual text: "A wife is someone who submits to another. Therefore she has no independent authority, and there is the rule of the three obediences: while at home she obeys her father, after marriage she obeys her husband, after he dies she obeys her son." Chu Hsi also quoted Ssu-ma Kuang on what to look for in wives, Ch'eng I on the impropriety of widows remarrying, and Liu K'ai on wives' tendencies toward partiality and contention.[20]

Confucian teachings on the virtues of wives were often conveyed by recounting exemplary models. In his *Precepts for Family Life,* Ssu-ma Kuang cited the following case as exemplifying the woman devoted to her husband's family:

> Han Chi's wife was Miss Yü. (Her father, Shih, was a grand deputy for the [Northern] Chou.) At fourteen she married Chi. Although she was born and grew up in a wealthy house of great eminence, she observed ritual decorum and was personally frugal and restrained. The entire clan respected her. When she was eighteen [her husband] Chi died in battle. She became so emaciated through grief that even passersby were moved. Every morning and evening, she offered the funerary oblations with her own hands. At the end of the mourning period, her parents wished to marry her to someone else, as she was still young and had no children. She swore she would not consent, then made Shih-lung, her husband's son by a concubine, the heir and raised him herself, loving him as much as if she had actually borne him. She trained him methodically, and in the end he succeeded in establishing himself.
>
> From the time she began to live as a widow, she never went anywhere other than on occasional visits home or to relatives. When senior relatives called on her, she never went out of her house to greet or bid farewell to them. To the end of her life she ate only vegetarian food, dressed in plain cloth, and did not listen to music.[21]

Miss Yü illustrated the wifely virtues central to the Confucian model. Her husband's family became the focus of her identity and attention. She forgot the wealth and comfort of her parents' family, displayed restraint and frugality, and thought of heirs from a patrilineal point of view—as heirs to her husband—indifferent to whether they were her own children. She in no way acted like a courtesan: frugality and duty were her concerns, not beauty and entertainment. Her husband's death in no way weakened her commitment to his patriline.

Conceiving personal identity in terms of roles and relationships within the family was given further ethical foundation in Confucian writings on ritual, beginning with the *Book of Rites* and the *Etiquette and Ritual*. This tradition of scholarship had a broad impact on what was accepted as normal, natural, and right in family relations.[22] In ritual writing, the nature and intensity of various kinship bonds were conceived schematically in terms of five grades of mourning obligations. A man was duty bound to mourn most of those descended from his great-great-grandfather. The three heaviest grades were entirely for his patrilineal relatives and their wives. He owed his father the first grade, which involved austerities lasting twenty-seven months (a nominal three years). He owed his paternal grandfather (father's father) grade two mourning, for one year; his paternal uncle grade three, for nine months; his father's first cousin grade four, for five months; and his father's second cousin grade five, for three months. He also mourned quite a few relatives of other surnames, but at lower grades. He owed his mother's parents and siblings and his sister's children grade four mourning. His cousins through his father's sister and his mother's brothers and sisters he owed fifth-degree mourning, as he did his wife's parents.[23]

Getting married, in this model, changed how both the bride and the groom stood in relation to others, but to different degrees. For the new husband, the only change was the addition of obligations to mourn his wife and her parents. A husband would mourn his wife at grade two (one year), whereas she was to mourn him at grade one (three years). His obligations to her parents, however, were reciprocal and equal: they mourned each other at grade five. If his wife died, a husband was still obligated to mourn her parents. After her marriage, a woman did not end participation in mourning rituals of her natal home, but her obligations were reduced one degree. Thus, a married daughter did not owe her parents three years of mourning, but only one year; and her mourning for her brothers likewise was reduced from one year to nine months. These changes were reciprocal: her natal relatives also reduced their mourning for her by one degree. As commentators regularly noted, reducing but not eliminating mutual mourning expressed the incompleteness of the women's change of status. In her new family, a wife took on many mourning obligations. The Sung appears to have been a period of change in this regard. The classical rule was that wives mourned their husbands' relatives one degree lower than he was obliged to; thus, for instance, she would mourn her father-in-law's brother at grade three instead of grade two. Ritual guides generally retained this rule, but in practice wives often performed the same mourning as their husbands.[24]

These mourning rules conveyed as incontrovertible the principle that a woman's identity undergoes a much greater transformation at marriage than does a man's. The ties between a man and his wife's family were reciprocal: they dealt with each other as equals and also as outsiders. The obligations between a wife and her husband, his father, and his grand-father, however, were all unequal, revealing both the inequality between the husband and wife and her incorporation into the family as a lineal subordinate. A man mourned his father and grandfather at higher degrees than they did him; his wife followed a similar pattern.

Whereas mourning obligations stressed the woman's dual nature as both outsider and insider, rituals of ancestor worship attached her quite firmly to her husband's patriline. An unmarried daughter participated in ancestral rites in her parents' home in a minor capacity—standing in line with other young women of her generation, behind the more senior women, watching the presiding man and his wife, the presiding woman, place offerings of food and wine in front of the ancestral tablets. Once the girl was married, she had a similar role in her new home, standing in line with the wives of her husband's brothers, gradually moving up in seniority so that one day, if her husband was the oldest son, she would serve as the presiding woman in charge of the preparation and presentation of food at the rites.[25]

Full ritual status as a wife (as opposed to a concubine) was supposed to guarantee a woman that she would not be neglected after death. Even a wife who died young and whose husband remarried would have a tablet set up for her, eventually to be cared for by her husband's descendants, whoever their mother might be. Generally, though, her tablet was not put with the other ancestral tablets until her husband died. In other words, her status as an ancestress was primarily that of the wife of a father, rather than that of a mother. In the meantime, her children could place offerings before her tablet in a private room. (In an analogous way, it was common to store a woman's coffin until her husband had died and joint burial could be arranged.) After both husband and wife had died, their tablets would be paired in all subsequent ancestral rites. This ritual complementarity of husbands and wives is captured visually in the tomb painting illustrated in Chapter 1 (Fig. 8), in which the husband and wife are seated next to each other while junior family members serve them.

There are many congruences between the Confucian ritual model of kinship and the laws on marriage. Both stress roles and relationships over age and gender, obligations over rights. But there are also subtle differences. The Confucian model gave more dignity to wives than the legal model did.

Men as actors in the ancestral cult were not complete without wives to assist them. Not only were wives needed so that men might have heirs, but the wives themselves had to participate in ancestral rites. Other women, such as concubines, could bear a man heirs, but only a wife could be paired with him in serving the ancestors. Moreover, only a wife would stay next to him in death—her tablet paired with his on the ancestral altar, her body next to his in the grave.

LITERARY IMAGES

So far, I have focused on meanings of marriage sanctioned by the government and the intellectual elite of Confucian scholars. But literary images not closely tied to moral, ritual, or legal models were also pervasive elements of Sung culture and shaped ordinary behavior in many ways. Poetry, fiction, anecdotes, and folktales not only brought in issues like love, beauty, and destiny, but also sometimes implicitly reversed priorities, favoring the spontaneous over the controlled, the emotional over the rational.

There was such a plethora of images people could use to allude to marriage that Sung writers compiled guides to help those composing marriage letters or the couplets hung up to decorate a house for a wedding.[26] In the late Sung, one twenty-four-chapter reference work was devoted entirely to marriage-related correspondence and the phrases to be used in such communications.[27] Even though these sample marriage letters frequently allude to the classics, they do not place marriage in the context of ancestral rites, yin and yang, or the subordination of women. Rather, they allude to a variety of dimensions of marriage partially at odds with those views. For instance, the natural basis of marriage could be evoked by quoting the saying "It is right that they have wives and families," which echoed lines in the *Book of Poetry* and *Mencius*.[28] To convey the idea that marriages were predestined, people could echo passages from the classics that had become proverbs or aphorisms. Some commonly given in reference books are "There is a mate for each person," "The divination of the phoenixes," and "Heaven made for him a match."[29] The idea that women ought to be married at a certain age was commonly conveyed by the line from the *Book of Poetry*, "The plum has reached its time."[30] The association of women's brief period of beauty with that of the plum tree was evocative, leading poets and painters to juxtapose lovely women and plum blossoms with considerable frequency (Fig. 12).[31]

Letters sent to propose or accept an offer of marriage contained not only these classical lines, but also allusions to more recent stories. A reference book gave the following letter as a sample reply to a proposal for a marriage between two families from the same community:

Fig. 12. A woman beside a flowering plum branch
Sung album leaf. Harriet Otis Cruft Fund. Courtesy,
Museum of Fine Arts, Boston (37.302).

When one pays millions for a desirable neighborhood, one can benefit from its advantages for a long time. Similarly by presenting the betrothal gift of five bundles [of cloth] one promptly gains an alliance for joint happiness. This came about by chance, not by our efforts; it is truly a blessing.

We are frugal and diligent and will be able to make our preparations in a simple way. Suggestions from your great wealthy family we will take as orders, so that we learn a little of how a rich family acts. Who would ever have thought that the wealthy one of Pei-p'ing would not be ashamed of the poor one of West Yüeh?

Now we receive this letter and the pledge of a decorated bird. How fortunate that our humble house is allowed to match yours! Five generations will flourish! How can it be otherwise? Who else would make as fine a son-in-law as our neighbor with his excellent goodness? How satisfactory that we are to be united as affinal relatives of the same community![32]

The allusions in this letter come from many sources. The reference to paying millions for a desirable neighborhood came from one of the dynastic histories.[33] Calling the betrothal gift five bundles of cloth was from one of the early ritual classics, the *Rites of Chou*.[34] Joint happiness evoked the line in the *Book of Rites* that marriage was for the joint happiness of two surnames.[35] The pledge of the decorated bird refers to the goose specified as the calling gift that messengers present when conveying marriage proposals in the classic *Etiquette and Ritual*.[36] The phrase "five generations will flourish" evokes a passage in the *Tso Chronicle*, in which a divination for a marriage yielded the message "The male and female phoenix fly together singing harmoniously with gemlike sounds. The posterity of Kuei will be raised among the Chiang. Five generations [of descendants] will flourish, serving as ministers."[37]

The reference to the rich family of Pei-p'ing in this letter evokes a folktale that had circulated for centuries. Yang Yung left home as a young man after his parents' death, overcome by sorrow. He finally settled near a road and supported himself by pumping water for travelers and repairing shoes and sandals. Some years later a god transformed himself into a student and appeared before Yang. The god gave Yang seeds (in some versions, made of stone) and told him to plant them. Yang did so and before long they produced plants bearing white jade disks and coins. The student/god appeared again and suggested that Yang seek a wife. Yang demurred on the grounds that no one would wish to marry a man his age. The student/god assured Yang he would not be refused if he asked for the daughter of the Hsü family. The Hsüs were the most prominent family of the Pei-p'ing area and had already rejected many suitors. When the matchmaker whom Yang sent approached the Hsüs, they thought Yang was crazy. As a joke, they said that they would consent to the match if he presented a pair of white jade disks and a million cash. Because of his magic seeds, this was easy for Yang, so the couple was married. In time they had ten sons and founded a major family.[38] This story was often alluded to in the Sung with phrases like "the seeds become a pair of jades," "planting jade to get a wife," and "jade fields produce jade disks," all of which probably carried erotic overtones as much as intimations of predestination.[39]

Men with literary educations often wrote marriage letters much like those found in reference books. Hung Kua (1117–1184), for instance, wrote the following letter for the betrothal of his fifth son to a maternal relative:

> Marriage connections going back for three generations are old ones indeed. When there is affection like that between P'an and Yang, [betrothal gifts] of ten black silks and plans for the good [union] can be embarrassing. Yet the register at Sung-ch'eng was not an accident. The feelings of Wei-yang can be made even deeper. I humbly note that your excellent daughter will be

admonished when the sash is attached and she is sure to be respectfully obedient to her aunt. My fifth son's studies are incomplete and he cannot be compared to his maternal uncle. Therefore I have planned a grand divination to tie this alliance for happiness. It is an exaggeration to say a hundred carts fill the gate. In the beginning I was not competing to be extravagant, but the three stars [of good fortune, official salary, and long life] are at our house. Soon we will announce the date.[40]

Hung Kua's allusions are as mixed as those in the sample letter. The hundred carts, from the *Book of Poetry,* is an allusion to generous betrothal gifts.[41] Reference to tying the bride's sash calls up the classical description of the wedding ceremony: before the girl leaves home, female relatives adjust her clothing while giving her instructions on how to act in her new home. Her mother says, "Be diligent and reverent. Day in and day out disobey no rule of the household."[42]

In his letter, Hung Kua refers prominently to the fact that this was a marriage between relatives. P'an and Yang were P'an Yüeh and Yang Chung-wu of the Chin dynasty, whose families had been tied by marriage for three generations; their friendship was famous because of the moving eulogy P'an wrote for Yang, preserved in the *Selections of Literature.*[43] The term *Wei-yang* alludes to one's mother's brother's family, based on a poem in the *Book of Poetry* that commemorated Duke K'ang's meeting at Wei-yang with his mother's brother, Duke Wen, who helped him gain the throne of Chin.[44] This alliance was frequently summoned up with such phrases as "The alliance of Ch'in and Chin," or "Ch'in gave a wife to Chin," or "Wei-yang relatives."

Hung Kua uses the phrase "the register at Sung-ch'eng" to allude to a folktale so central to popular thinking that it is worth recounting in some detail. Early in the T'ang dynasty, an orphan named Wei Ku was having a lot of trouble finding a suitable wife. In 628, he was staying at an inn in Sung-ch'eng to negotiate a possible marriage with a Ssu-ma girl. One morning he set out early to meet the go-between at a temple. The moon was still bright when he arrived, and he saw an old man sitting on the steps, looking at a document by the light of the moon. Wei took a peek at it, but could not make it out. He asked the old man what it was, remarking that he could read virtually everything, even Sanskrit, but could not decipher his document. The old man laughed and told him that the document was not of this world; it was from the officials of the nether regions who control the course of people's lives. The old man, it turned out, was such an official himself, responsible for the marriage registers. Wei took advantage of this opportunity to plead his case, explaining how he had been trying to marry for ten years without luck. Would his current negotiations succeed? he asked. The old man gave him the bad news: Wei's bride was then only three sui, and they would not marry until she was seventeen. Wei asked about the bag the old man held and was shown the red cord in it. This cord, the old man told him, was used to tie the feet of a future husband and wife. "Even if their families become enemies, even if their social rank diverges drastically, even if they go to the ends of the earth to serve in office, or live in different villages in Wu and Ch'u, this rope, once tied, can never be untied." Wei learned from the old man that his future bride was the girl of the old woman vegetable seller north of the inn. Wei and the old man walked by the place together and saw the woman and child, clearly people of very low social station. Unwilling to accept such a fate, Wei asked if it would be possible to kill the girl to change it. No, the old man informed him. Because she was destined to enjoy great honors on account of her son, she could not be killed. After the old man disappeared, Wei sent his servant to kill the little girl, so determined was he not to marry a vegetable seller's daughter. The servant stabbed the baby near her eyebrows and fled, assuming he had killed her. Another fourteen years passed without Wei finding a wife. He did gain office, however, and finally a superior gave him his niece as a wife. She, of course, turned out to be the girl who had been stabbed as a child. As a baby she had been entrusted to her wet nurse, both her parents having died. Later her uncle, Wei's superior, took and reared her. When Wei saw the scar by her eyebrow, he told her the full story, which is supposed to be how knowledge of the old man under the moon spread.[45]

When talking about marriage, people could evoke this story by a dozen or more phrases in addition to "Sung-ch'eng," such as "the red cord," "the old man under the moon," or "finding a girl at the vegetable seller's."[46] Whenever people heard these phrases, they were reminded of features of marriage not much stressed in the legal and ethical models: marriage as predestined, marriage destinies as mysterious, and marriage as a physical tie binding the two parties. The popularity of stories of marriage destinies undoubtedly owed much to the widespread acceptance of Buddhist ideas of karma, but its appeal was not in any sense narrowly religious.

The image of marriage as a red cord clearly struck a note in people. A high proportion of marriage letters and marriage couplets contain a metaphor based on tying, knotting, intertwining—or the things that get knotted and intertwined: strings, cords, sashes, and vines. Marriage was imagined as a rope tying a husband and wife to each other; colloquially, one could call taking a wife "roping" her.[47] Metaphors of tying represent husbands and wives as threads—thus building on images of the patriline as a thread. Marriage takes two threads and joins them in ways that are very hard to undo. Sometimes knots, of course, prove to be stronger than the thread, and pulling knotted thread may result in tearing the thread rather than breaking the knot.

Besides the red cord of the man under the moon and the sash to be tied by the mother, two other images of marriage based on tying were common: "tying the shoulder" and "tying the hair." By Sung times "tying the shoulder" was taken as the equivalent of the ancient "asking the name" ceremony, confirming a betrothal. This meaning is based on a story about an emperor who in 273 inspected many girls from good families in order to choose secondary consorts. The girls he chose were marked by tying a piece of red silk around their shoulders.[48] "Tying the hair," by Sung times, was a common poetic term for getting married. A famous poem of Han date, "The Poem of Su Wu," has the line, "We tied up our hair to be husband and wife." Ts'ao Chih (192–232) wrote a poem with the line, "When first married, they tied up their hair and their affection was deep." Tu Fu (712–770), in his "Separating After the Wedding," wrote, "She tied her hair to be his wife."[49] Sung scholars had a variety of explanations of these literary allusions. The first occurrence of the juxtaposition of tying hair and marriage could be fortuitous: the hair was tied up to prepare for battle, not marriage. In other cases, the reference could actually be to the pinning ceremony for girls that marked their betrothal. But ordinary people—who, even if illiterate, often could recite famous poems—apparently liked the idea of tying hair as a symbol of marriage. Literally tying the hair of the husband to that of the wife, in fact, became a common step in weddings (see Chapter 4).

Marriage as predestined and marriage as a knot or tie were perhaps the most pervasive images of marriage. Later in this book I will cite stories from Hung Mai that reveal other common folk notions related to marriage, gender, and sexuality, such as the burden matchmaking can pose, the danger in being attracted to beautiful women, the miraculous powers of devoted widows, and the superhuman ferocity of jealousy. Let me close this section by citing two stories from Hung Mai that suggest some of the power of ideas about marriage destinies.

Chang Chi Takes a Wife

Chang Chi, a literatus from Chin-hua [Chekiang], while in Ch'ü-chou [Chekiang], asked to have his fortune told at Liu's shop. He was given a poem, the last line of which was "You may once more sing the song of the new groom/Old lady Wang opens her mouth, the smiling grain is ripe." Unable to understand it, he asked Liu, who responded, "I simply consulted an old divination manual, and cannot hazard an explanation. Someday you will realize what it means yourself." At the time Chi's wife was in good health, and she was not pleased with the reference to his singing again. Before long, however, she died of illness. Candidate Ch'en, of the same prefecture, married the elder sister of Ch'eng Heng. Ch'en suddenly died, and when [his widow] Miss Ch'eng was out of mourning for him, she married [Chang] Chi. Once when they were out visiting the tombs of their ancestors, they went out to the countryside with her brothers, including [Ch'eng] Heng. The topic came around to how marriages were not accidental, and [Chi] mentioned the prognostication he had been given. [Ch'eng] Heng laughed and said, "Just so. Marriage to my elder sister was foreseen." The right half of the character

Ch'eng 程 is made up of a "Wang" 王 with a "mouth" 口 above it, which was referred to as "old lady Wang opens her mouth." The left half is "grain" 禾, corresponding to "the smiling grain is ripe." The meaning was clear.[50]

Chin Chün-ch'ing's Wife

When the daughter of a certain prefect of Ch'ing-nan was eighteen, a husband was found for her and [the families] were about to choose a day for the wedding. Someone came to [the girl] in a dream and said, "He is not your husband. Your husband is Chin Chün-ch'ing." After she woke up, she did not tell anyone, but when she was embroidering a belt, every inch or so she would embroider the three characters "Chin Chün-ch'ing." Her mother saw it and was suspicious, so told her father. Her father checked and found that there was no one of this name in the prefecture, not even a lowly clerk. He questioned her, and she told him all about the dream. Before long, the man she was engaged to died.

A half-year later, the new prefect of Hsia-chou was passing through the prefecture and sent a letter to the prefect [her father]. His name was Chin Chün-ch'ing, which explained [the dream]. When Chin arrived, [the girl's father] treated him generously and hosted him for several days. He learned that Chin's wife had recently died, so told him of his daughter's dream. Chin said, "I am forty-two, six years more than twice the age of your fine daughter. I fear my death may not be far off, so as a matter of principle I could not bear [to agree to your proposal]." The host kept pushing him, saying, "It is your karma, your fate. How can you decline?" With no other way out, he married her. He died thirty years later, his wife having borne several children. Chin rose in office to director of the bureau of general accounts. He was a man from Fan-yang.[51]

This tale gives us not simply another instance of the mysterious nature of marriage destinies, but an implicit rationale for listening to the feelings of the potential bride: there may be something behind her apparently irrational ideas about whom she should marry.

―――――――――

The models and images discussed in this chapter, by and large, reinforced each other. Confucian family ethics underlay the legal principle of viewing a woman's marital status as fundamental to her identity. Ritual models also were the basis for legal restrictions concerning marriages to relatives or during mourning. Folktales about marriage destinies drew on Buddhist ideas of karma but also reinforced ancient ideas about the need to divine before settling on a match. At the same time, these sets of ideas differed in focus. The legal model imagined marriage in terms of prohibitions and focused on the limits to acceptable behavior. The Confucian model imagined marriage in terms of descent lines and highlighted obligations and virtues, particularly of wives. Literary and folk images imagined marriage in terms of unions of individuals, more than of families, and focused on the mysterious un-predictability of love. The significance of these models and images is of two sorts. They had a pervasive effect on ways of thinking and acting because most people took them for granted. Yet because of the differences among them, no one set of ideas confined thinking or acting within narrow or predictable channels.

Taken as a whole, these conceptions of marriage and women's roles in the family system both build on and complicate the more basic notions of gender differentiation discussed in the last chapter. Models of marriage pre-suppose fundamental dissimilarities between men and women. At the same time, they posit that women are never simply women: they are daughters and daughters-in-law, mothers and mothers-in-law, wives and concubines; their particular relations to others are as important to their identity as their sex. The roles women were assigned within the marriage system were gender roles, roles open only to women, but these roles separate women into opposed categories.

Although the main theme of this chapter has been the most basic ways of viewing marriage, elements that changed relatively slowly over time, one dimension of change should be noted. The Confucian and legal models, although very old, probably came to be more widely known and accepted by the general populace as the Sung progressed. As discussed in the Introduc-tion, the Sung was a period when the educated class was growing and when urbanization and denser patterns of settlement were bringing ordinary peas-ants into more frequent contact with educated men. Added to this, a major thrust of the Neo-Confucian movement was a desire to indoctrinate ordinary people more fully in Confucian values and rituals and even in current laws. Scholars decried the incursion of Buddhism into family matters like funerals and ancestral rites. Local officials tried to reform customs, and scholars wrote treatises or manuals advising on correct principles and procedures. As a result of all of this activity, it became less and less likely that anyone in the Sung would not know that the law did not allow a man to have two wives at one time, or that Confucians placed moral value on differentiation by gender and a wife's loyalty to her family of marriage. Scholars' efforts at indoctrination would have helped spread accurate knowledge of the legal model as well. Chu Hsi, for instance, in his first official appointment, issued instructions on legally correct betrothal practices.[52] Even folktales may well have circulated more widely as the Sung progressed, since urbanization, improved means of transportation, and increased interregional trade would all have added to the ease with which stories could spread through oral modes of communication. If we remember that books of all sorts were also circulating in unprecedented numbers, there is even more reason to suppose that the direction of change in the Sung was toward greater sharing of basic cultural premises across regional and class lines.

THREE

Making a Match

If we may believe biographers—and I see no reason not to in this regard—most parents in Sung China became very fond of their daughters. By the time the girl was in her mid-teens, she seemed to her parents a delight—sweet, agreeable, clever, and lovely. Families in the educated class regularly taught their daughters to read, and fathers in particular seem to have enjoyed seeing signs that they were talented (a topic to be discussed more fully in Chapter 6). Miss Hou (1004–1052), we are told, was exceptionally bright and enjoyed reading. Her father "loved her more than his sons" and liked to discuss politics with her.[1] Miss Ch'ien (1030–1081), her biographer reports, was much brighter than ordinary girls: "From the time she wore her hair in coils till she was pinned, she learned to make cloth and gained command of literature and history. As for calligraphy and composition, she mastered anything as soon as she was shown it. Therefore both her parents cherished her."[2] Su Shen (c.s. 1019) doted on a daughter born in 1031 when he had reached a relatively advanced age. "Because she was both lovely and quick-witted, he became especially fond of her. She talked while still an infant and gradually was reciting books. As she got a little older, she proved receptive to instruction in propriety. She was also capable of grasping a brush and writing her own compositions. When she came of age, he spent a long time picking a mate for her."[3]

PARENTS' BURDENS

Loving parents naturally wanted good homes for their daughters. Yet even if they liked to think that marriages were predestined, they also knew that making the best match for a son or daughter involved difficult choices. Miss

Ch'eng (1061–1085) reached twenty-five without marrying. After her death, her uncle Ch'eng I took pains to explain how this had happened:

> When young [my niece] was sedate and calm and did not speak or laugh foolishly. Her style was lofty and her interests high-minded. She was exceptionally farsighted when she discussed affairs. She could sit calmly all day, dignified and correct. She was never taught to read books, but on her own learned the meanings of texts. Everyone in the family loved and cherished her.
>
> For a husband we wished to get someone who would be her match. Her father [Ch'eng Hao, 1032–1085] was famous in his age, known throughout the realm, and men of discernment all frequented his home. And yet although we looked for a husband for seven or eight years, we never found a suitable one. Our relatives considered this sad, and our friends considered it wrong, saying that since antiquity they had never heard of a woman not marrying because she was too worthy. With no alternative, we set our sights lower. Once, we were in the process of negotiating but could not bear to let her know, for we knew the man was not up to her. Then her mother died, and she mourned her to the full extent of her grief; not one of the filial gentlemen of the past exceeded her [in mourning]. She ruined her health and died. . . .
>
> All of the others deplored the fact that she had not married; only I disagreed. Her father and I took the sages as our teachers and tried to do the appropriate thing. If we matched her to an ordinary fellow because we had not come across a worthy one, that would bring disgrace to her to the end of her life. I deplore her death, but not her failure to marry.[4]

As Ch'eng I saw matters, his brother wanted a man who would match his daughter as fully as possible but had great difficulty finding such a man because she was so exceptional. To both Ch'eng I and Ch'eng Hao, it would be a disgrace for her to be married to a man beneath her. But what constituted a match? Did Ch'eng I mean to imply that no men were as high-minded or learned as his niece? From other sources it seems that learning in a man was matched, in common thought, not with a woman's learning but with her beauty. Yüan Ts'ai assumed everyone understood such principles when he warned against trying to match a "foolish and vulgar son" to a beautiful woman, or an "ugly, clumsy, and spiteful daughter" to a superior man.[5] Thus a talented woman who was not also a beauty might be hard to match. Lovely young ladies were what men wished to have attend them with towel and comb.

Matches were not just matches of individuals; they were also matches of families, and many discussions of marriage arrangements focus on this dimension. After his father died, Tseng Kung (1019–1083) was left with the task of finding husbands for his nine younger sisters. He described himself as "very worried that they would miss their time and also scared that they would not get appropriate homes."[6] Families may have liked to think they were fussy in selecting sons-in-law because they loved their daughters so much, but it is evident that other motivations, not necessarily consciously thought through, also pushed them in that direction. Marrying a daughter down was looked on as shameful, something that could be explained only if she had some major disability (blindness, deafness, mental retardation). This sentiment forced the government to go to considerable efforts to see that suitable husbands were found for all daughters of imperial clansmen, even ones quite distantly related to the emperor.[7] Moreover, as will be evident throughout this chapter, families of both boys and girls saw affines (families linked by marriage) as potential friends and allies. Searching for a talented son-in-law or a bride from a family of good reputation, thus, was also a search for a family one could turn to for help in social and political life. But by and large, parents cast their decisions as moral ones: they saw themselves as choosing good people and good families instead of bad ones. In this way, they obscured the fact that the interests of the spouses and their families might not be identical, especially in the case of daughters marrying out. Parents did not ask whether their daughter would be disadvantaged by marrying into a prominent family far away or becoming the second wife of a man fifteen years her senior. Instead they posited an identity of her interest and their interest: both would be better off because of a marriage to a "good family."

Matches of families were conceived as matches of equals, but families looked for different sorts of things when choosing brides for their sons than when finding husbands for their daughters. If a family's concern was focused solely on their own family and descent line, it would make sense for parents to take more care with the selection of daughters-in-law, who would raise their descendants, than with the selection of the husbands of daughters who left. Yet, as Ch'eng I lamented in a different context, the general tendency was for parents to worry more about finding husbands for their daughters.[8] This preoccupation may have violated Ch'eng I's notion of what was right, but it had a certain logic. The family's son stayed home; therefore, parents did not feel anxious about his welfare. For their daughter, they were not merely choosing a spouse, but a family and a future. Her entire welfare was at stake. One of the most common lines in wedding couplets was "If you love your daughter do not give her to a mediocre man."[9] It was probably to help ease this sense of responsibility that parents sometimes turned to diviners to see if they had made a good choice.[10]

Because picking marriage partners could be so complex, some families started looking for potential spouses when the children were very young. Ssu-ma Kuang complained that people liked to engage their children as babies or even before they were born; yet ten or twenty years later the children might no longer match, thus necessitating a dishonorable repudiation of the engagement. Yüan Ts'ai similarly argued against early engagements, pointing out that wealth and honor come and go unpredictably and that the prospective son-in-law might turn out to be dissolute or the prospective bride unruly.[11]

Still, childhood engagements were commonly looked on with pride as a sign of the strength of the ties between the two families. The biographer of Miss Wang (1031–1098) reported that Fan Chung-yen (989–1052) had been a good friend of her father's and the two had engaged their children to marry when still young. She married Fan Ch'un-jen (1027–1101), while her younger sister married his younger brother. The biographer of Miss Shih (1246–1266) reported that her father was so grateful to Yüan Ssu-tao (1191–1257) for visiting him every day while he was ill that he proposed that she, then six sui, eventually marry Yüan's son, then seven. Marriages among relatives were perhaps particularly likely to be decided early. Two neighbors in Kaifeng, both officials, were related by marriage, Hsing's wife being Shan's younger sister. While Shan's son and Hsing's daughter were still in diapers, they were engaged to be married.[12]

Parents were generally well into their fifties if not sixties when the last of their children reached the age to marry. Getting spouses for all of them was considered the last burden before they could enter a carefree old age. Literati frequently referred to the task of finding husbands and wives for their children as "Hsiang-p'ing's burden" or "Hsiang-p'ing's hopes," alluding to a man in the Han dynasty who went off to wander among the mountains once he had fulfilled these obligations. Parents who suspected that an illness they suffered might prove fatal sometimes hurried to find their children spouses while they had time left. Miss Chang Fa-shan (1134–1172) married a widower and thus acquired stepchildren in need of spouses when she herself was still in her thirties. As her illness worsened, she spoke to her husband "day and night" on this subject, hurrying to get everything ready, sewing items for the dowry, determined to finish all the preparations before she died.[13]

As Miss Chang's case illustrates, deciding on spouses for the children is one area of family decision making in which authors regularly portrayed women as quite active. Miss Fan (1015–1067) not only saw to her own children's marriages, but she also arranged her husband's two younger sisters' marriages and the marriages of his dead brother's seven children, spending ten-odd years finding everyone spouses and preparing the dowries and betrothal gifts.[14] And even when women did not take the initiative, they would expect to be consulted. After Chao Huang's elder daughter died, her husband, Liu Yeh (968–1028), passed the civil service examinations. Chao then sent a matchmaker to his former son-in-law to propose that he next marry the eldest of his as yet unmarried daughters. Liu hinted that he would prefer the youngest of the girls, but Chao's wife, we are told, ruled this out, quoting the maxim that one takes the crackers from the top and arguing that even though Liu had passed the examinations, that did not give him the right to pick and choose among a family's girls.[15] Among women's common informal powers, it would seem, was the ability to initiate or reject ideas about mates for their children.

MARRIAGES BETWEEN FRIENDS AND COLLEAGUES

Among those who left written record, it seems to have been common for men to try to turn a friend into a kinsman by proposing a marriage between members of their families. Biographies abound with examples. Han Yüan-chi (1118–1187) became friendly with Chang Hsiao-hsiang (ca. 1129–1170) while both were in the capital. Han's elder brother's first and second wives had both died, leaving behind children. Chang,then approached Han and proposed a match between Han's brother and Chang's own sister.[16] Friendships did not have to be of long standing to lead to marriage. Chou Pi-ta (1126–1204) wrote that when his uncle took up a post in Yüan prefecture in 1146, he asked which of the local gentlemen were worth visiting. A certain Mr. Ts'ai was recommended on the grounds that he was descended from an official and entertained visitors with wine, poetry, music, and chess. Chou's uncle found Ts'ai so congenial that when he discovered Ts'ai was looking for a son-in-law, he proposed a match to his second son. "With a single word the families were linked by marriage."[17]

Friends could approach each other directly about marriages without using intermediaries. Liu K'o-chuang (1187–1269) confessed that at age eighty-two he said to an old friend,

> I have already handed back my tablet of office. It has taken me time, but I have finished arranging the marriages of my sons and daughters. The only one left to worry about is [my grandson] Huan. He is of pure character and moreover the first son of my first son. I took advantage of the regulations to get him a court rank, and almost at once he left, without having acquired a wife. You have a grown-up, beautiful, and accomplished daughter whose virtues are talked of in the women's quarters. Wouldn't they match?[18]

The friend, we are told, agreed, and before the day was out they had completed the engagement steps of "asking the names" and "presenting the gifts."

As several scholars have noted, officials in the Sung regularly married their children to the children of other officials, paying little attention to where their families came from. This practice was especially common in the Northern Sung.[19] Of the couples I studied from funerary biographies, in the Northern Sung only 52 percent came from the same circuit, and only 37 percent from the same prefecture. In the Southern Sung, by contrast, the figures stand at 82 percent for the same circuit, 64 percent for the same prefecture.[20] In the Northern Sung, the families of high officials were motivated to arrange marriages that would connect them to other high officials. They cared less about where the family originated or even where its present home was than about the current standing of its leading men. Because the dialects all over north China were mutually intelligible, brides would not have difficulty talking to their husbands or mothers-in-law even if they came from different circuits. And officials from remote parts of the country had many opportunities to meet each other, particularly while serving in the capital or provinces. For instance, in about 1020 Ch'en Hsi-ku, from near the capital, became friends with Li Wei, from Hopei, when both were serving as officials. Soon they agreed that their children, then only a few years old, would later marry.[21] Moreover, since a large share of the families of higher officials settled in the capital, Kaifeng, what appear to be long-distance marriages may actually have been marriages among neighbors. Even so, some officials claimed to favor matches with official families from their own region. In the Northern Sung, when Chang Chih (1070–1132), from Jao-chou, south of the Yangtze, took the examinations in the capital, Kaifeng, a high official from his home prefecture got him to agree to marry his daughter. Similarly, Ko Sheng-chung (1072–1144) wrote that when his father had been serving under Chang P'an in Kiangsu, "because they were colleagues and moreover from the same prefecture," they had arranged for him to marry Chang's daughter, Chang Hu (1074–1122).[22]

In the Southern Sung as well, officials from different circuits sometimes arranged marriages between their children. In 1147, Hu Ch'üan (1102–1180) from Lu-ling (Kiangsi) was serving in a distant provincial post under Li Kuang (1078–1159), from Shao-hsing (Chekiang). Li was impressed with Hu's twelve-year-old boy and arranged with Hu to engage him to Li's seven-year-old granddaughter.[23] Generally, though, it does seem that high officials were more inclined than in the Northern Sung to find mates closer to home. Perhaps this reflects the greater difficulties that dialect posed in the south, or the fact that the leading official families did not settle in Hangchow, as their predecessors had settled in Kaifeng. Perhaps it reflects a newfound need to strengthen ties to locally important families that had not produced officials, or the fact that the economic and cultural development of the south was such that leading families could find suitable mates nearby. Perhaps it reflects the increased influence of mothers who preferred not to see their daughters go so far away that they would never see them again. Whatever the explanation or combination of explanations, the change from the Northern to Southern Sung is further evidence that marriage practices were subject to change.

MARRIAGES BETWEEN RELATIVES

A marriage connection begun on the basis of friendship would, all seem to have hoped, be reconfirmed with subsequent marriages between the families involved.[24] Chinese exogamy rules prohibited marriages between

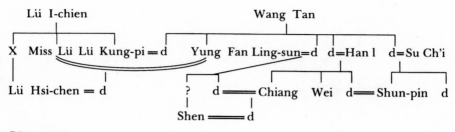

Diagram 1

cousins of the same surname, but not marriages with other relatives such as father's sister's children or mother's brother's or sister's children. There was nothing new in what was called "repeating marriages" and "marriages generations old."[25] Marriages between relatives probably occurred at all social levels. Among the educated particularly, many examples can be cited. Early in the eleventh century, for instance, the eminent statesman Wang Tan (957–1017) married his eldest daughter to Han I (972–1044), a widower twelve years older than she; his second to Su Ch'i (987–1035); his third to Fan Ling-sun; and his fourth to Lü Kung-pi (998–1073). His son, Wang Yung, he married to his fourth daughter's husband's sister, Miss Lü. Wang Tan's children remained close, and three sets of Wang Tan's "external" grandchildren married: Han I's son Chiang (1012–1088) wed his mother's sister's daughter, that is, Fan Ling-sun's daughter; Su Ch'i's son Su Shun-pin married Han I's daughter; and Su Ch'i's daughter married Han I's son Han Wei (1017–1098). Moreover, there was a match between a patrilineal granddaughter and her mother's nephew: Wang Yung's daughter married Lü Kung-pi's brother's son. In the next generation at least one marriage was arranged among Wang Tan's "external" great-grandchildren, when Han Chiang's daughter married her mother's brother's son Fan Shen. (See Diagram 1.) Her mother is said to have wanted the marriage so that she could send her daughter to care for her own mother, then rather elderly.[26]

The penchant for marrying relatives could lead to compounded connections of all sorts. Consider the case of Li Kang (1083–1140). His father, Li K'uei (1047–1121), was raised in his mother's natal home after his parents died, his mother's father apparently preferring to raise him than see him brought up by his deceased father's second wife, his stepmother. It was his mother's brother, Huang Lü, who educated him. When it was time to find a wife for his son Kang, Li K'uei settled on a granddaughter of his uncle/teacher; thus Kang married a second cousin through his grandmother (his father's mother's brother's daughter's daughter). His wife's sister married Huang Po-ssu (1079–1119), who was her mother's brother's son. Li Kang was therefore related to Huang Po-ssu in two ways: they were brothers-in-law, married to two sisters; and they were second cousins (Huang Po-ssu was Li Kang's father's mother's brother's son's son). Li Kang was

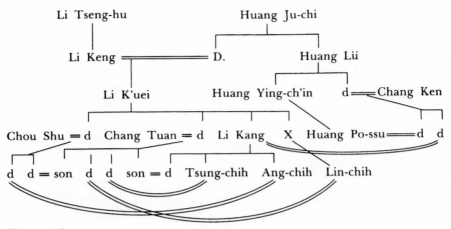

Diagram 2

apparently satisfied with his marriage to a cousin, as he married his own
children to cousins. One of Li Kang's sisters had married Chang Tuan-li
(1082–1132), and another married Chou Shu (1082–1125). These three siblings
also had their children intermarry in the next generation: Chang's elder son
married Li's daughter, and his younger son married Chou's daughter; his
eldest daughter married Li's son Tsung-chih, and his second daughter Li's
brother's son Lin-chih. Chou's younger daughter married Li's son Ang-chih.[27]
(See Diagram 2.)

In biographies it is not uncommon to find such statements as "their
families had intermarried for generations." Chou Pi-ta (1126–1204), in the
biography for his sister, wrote: "My family had old marriage ties with
the Shang family of An-yang, so when [my sister] was sixteen she 'came
home' to Ta-shen . . . to be the daughter-in-law of Tso-chün." Exactly how
closely Miss Chou and Mr. Shang were related is never stated, so one might
suppose the statement was little more than empty formula. In the biography for her husband, however, Chou Pi-ta explained the connection more
clearly (Diagram 3). Chou Pi-ta's father's elder brother's wife was a
Miss Shang, and during the Jurchen invasion in 1126 her youngest brother,
Shang Ta-shen, some nineteen years her junior, had turned to her and her
husband in Szechwan for safety. Chou's uncle Li-chien apparently liked his
wife's brother and proposed marriage to his orphaned niece "to reinforce
the good relations of the two families." One should perhaps note that
although the groom was only three years older than his bride, he was of an
earlier generation, the brother of the bride's uncle's wife, and so the taboo
on intergenerational marriages was broken. Nevertheless, because a man
did not owe mourning to a sister's husband's brother's child, such a marriage
was not illegal.[28]

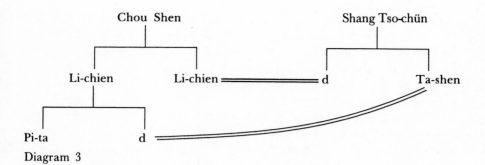

Diagram 3

In this case we have a man marrying his sister's husband's brother's daughter. The marriages among Wang Tan's grandchildren were between men and their mother's sisters' daughters; the one involving his great-grandchildren was between a man and his father's sister's daughter. All sorts of relatives were considered good candidates for marriage. Ko Sheng-chung (1072–1144) had several younger sisters. His wife, he reported, arranged to have one of them marry her brother. This, then, was a marriage with a sister's husband's sister. When Chang A-lin's wife and sister were both pregnant at the same time, the two families agreed that if one had a girl and the other a boy they would engage them to each other.[29] This was a marriage with a father's sister's daughter or mother's brother's daughter, depending on which had a boy and which a girl.

Occasionally we are told who proposed a match between relatives. In about 1095, Fan O, from Lan-hsi (Chekiang), was quite impressed with the daughter of one of his daughters who had married a Hu (also of Lan-hsi). He then went to his son-in-law (Mr. Hu) to suggest to him that the son of one of his other daughters, who had married a Chiang (also of Lan-hsi), would make an excellent husband for his granddaughter. His son-in-law could hardly refuse such a proposal. In another case a woman, eager to help her orphaned niece, proposed that the younger woman marry the aunt's second son, thus bringing the niece into her home as a daughter-in-law. In the mid–eleventh century, an elderly woman, when a married granddaughter came to visit with her young daughter, reportedly said, "What a nice girl! Can we bear to see her married into another family? No one would be better than my orphaned great-grandson." Thus the two married, linked through their mothers, who were first cousins. (The boy married his mother's father's brother's daughter's daughter.)[30]

As this evidence suggests, marriages between relatives were often favored by women. A woman would be anxious about any new woman to enter the household, whether as a sister-in-law, daughter-in-law, nephew's wife, or granddaughter-in-law. Someone from her own family, or another family connected to hers (her sister's family, her mother's family), however, would seem better than a complete stranger. Similarly, the mother of a daughter about to be married out, though of course worried about how she would fare, would feel somewhat more confident if she knew something about the family her daughter was about to enter.

A surprisingly common form of marriage between relatives was marriage with the younger sister of one's deceased wife. Indeed, often the first wife is credited with suggesting the match. For example, Han Ch'i reported that when his daughter-in-law, Miss Lü (1039–1065), was about to die at twenty-seven sui, she said to her husband: "My illness is getting worse every day. If it proves incurable, I have a young sister at home. If you would use our old connection to continue [our marriage] with her, she would surely be kind to my children. The happiness of the two surnames would persist as before and I could die without regrets." Ch'en Hsiao-piao (1014–1072), whose marriage had been arranged in his early childhood, lost his wife when she was thirty-eight. To help raise the five children she had borne, he took her younger sister as a successor wife. He apparently liked the women in this family so well that he then took his wives' brother's daughter to be the wife of one of his sons. Similarly, Yü-wen Shih-yüeh (1117–1156) married his father's sister's daughter; after she died, he married her younger sister, a woman seven years his junior. Lü Tsu-ch'ien (1137–1181), from one of the most eminent families in the Sung, married the daughter of Han Yüan-chi (1118–1187); she died after five years, and seven years later he married her younger sister. And then there was Yao Mien (1216–1262), whose first marriage, to Tsou Miao-shan (1228–1249), ended with her death a year after their wedding. When he came out of mourning he asked if he could marry her younger sister. No one in the family was enthusiastic, but her father may still have had some fondness for Yao, for during the next five years he repeatedly refused proposals for the younger daughter. Finally, when Yao Mien was picked number one in the examinations of 1253, Mr. Tsou consented to the marriage.[31] Although marriage to the younger sisters of former wives was known in all periods of Chinese history, it seems to have been particularly common in the Sung.

People had positive feelings about marriages between relatives and celebrated them in literary forms of all sorts. When families already linked by marriage were arranging another union, they wrote marriage letters that alluded prominently to the existing alliance, as seen in the last chapter in the letter by Hung Kua. Couplets found in reference books suggest that nothing could be better than such a match:

> As auspicious as the links of Ch'in and Chin
> As long-lasting as the ties between Chu and Ch'en.

> When surname is matched to surname, it can be falsely done by men.
> But when one uses a marriage tie to make a new marriage, it is
>   undoubtedly Heaven that joined them.[32]

The relations between the ancient states of Chin and Ch'in were discussed in Chapter 2 with reference to the term *Wei-yang relatives*. Chu and Ch'en is the allusion that most fully conveyed the desirable aspects of marriage between relatives. The popular T'ang poet Po Chü-i (772–846) had written a poem called "Chu-Ch'en Village," which reads in part:

> In the whole village there are only two surnames.
> Generation after generation they have married each other.
> Every house contains kinsmen, close or distant.
> Young or old always have companions wherever they go.
> With yellow chicken and white wine
> They have joyous celebrations nearly every week.
> While alive, they never are separated by great distances—
> To marry their sons and daughters they first look to their near neighbors.
> When dead they are never buried far away—
> Many graves surround the village.[33]

Even though people in the Sung wrote quite a bit about marriages involving relatives, the actual share of such marriages was probably small. Of the 135 couples in their first marriage that I studied from pairs of funerary biographies, only about 10 percent were explicitly said to be between relatives. If we could count the marriages of their siblings and children, of course, there would be a higher proportion of families in which at least one living couple had been related before their marriage. Of 27 second marriages, almost a fifth were with relatives, in all cases the first wife's younger sister or cousin.

One reason more marriages were not arranged between relations may have been that these marriages carried as many dangers as advantages. Yüan Ts'ai wrote:

> When people plan marriages they often want to "use a marriage connection to make a marriage connection" in order to show that the ties between the families are not forgotten. This is a fine element in popular customs. But there are women of narrow vision who will use their close ties to the other family as an excuse to be lax; they offend the other party, then quarreling starts, and soon no one is getting along.... There are girls who marry into their father's sister's house and are singularly despised by their father's sister; the same is true if they marry into their mother's brother's house or their mother's sister's house. These resentments arise because at the beginning the marriage was not taken seriously and the courtesies were slighted.[34]

One of the more famous cases of a marriage with a relative going sour was that between Su Hsün's (1009–1066) daughter Su Pa-niang (1035–1052) and her mother's brother's son Ch'eng Cheng-fu. She was married to him at sixteen sui and, according to her father, found herself caught in the midst of family rancor; she died two years later when no one tended her when she was ill. Su Hsün ordered his sons to break off all relations with their mother's family, a duty they kept up for forty-two years.[35]

RECRUITING A SON-IN-LAW

One consequence of the growing importance of the civil service examination system in the Sung was a change in how the politically ideal spouse was conceived. During the T'ang dynasty, leading families emphasized finding daughters of eminent pedigree for their sons. In the Sung, the symbolically most desirable catch was a talented young man for one's daughter. The best possible son-in-law, all agreed, was a man who would place well in the civil service examinations and rise to hold an important government office. How to recruit such sons-in-law was a common topic of conversation.[36] If one had a gift for recognizing talent, one could arrange a marriage with a promising young man before others realized what a good prospect he was. Some men were so perspicacious that they could detect exceptional talent even in a young boy. In 1180, for example, when Cheng Ching-shih visited the eminent official Ch'en Chün-ch'ing (1113–1186), Ch'en was impressed with Cheng's six-sui son Yüeh and offered to have him as a son-in-law. After Cheng Yüeh passed the examinations at age nineteen he married Ch'en's niece. There are two versions of how Yen Shu (991–1051) picked as a son-in-law the future chief councillor Fu Pi (1004–1083). According to one, Yen's wife had a physiognomist inspect her daughter and asked him to recommend a suitable son-in-law, and he named Fu Pi. The other is that Fan Chung-yen (989–1052) recommended two students at the Imperial Academy as being capable of rising high, one of whom was Fu Pi. People also talked about how Ma Liang spotted Lü I-chien (978–1043), another future chief councillor. Ma's wife, we are told, was surprised that he would pick a mere magistrate's son, but he dismissingly told her that the matter was beyond her comprehension.[37]

The safer way to recruit a son-in-law likely to rise was to be at the capital during the metropolitan examinations, ready to make an attractive offer to the best man not yet married as soon as the results were posted. Examiners, of course, were particularly well positioned in this regard. In 1121, when Chang Ko was in charge of the metropolitan examinations, over five thousand men took the tests, of whom five hundred were selected. Chang had a fifteen-sui daughter and looked among the new graduates for a good match for her. He asked a distant kinsman of his to approach the man he had ranked tenth, Hu Yin (1098–1156), ten years her senior.[38]

Money, of course, could be used to induce a promising young man to accept a marriage proposal. As will be discussed in more detail in Chapter 5, the value of dowries tended to rise in the Sung as prosperous families competed for the most desired matches. Chu Yü (ca. 1075–1119) remarked that those who wanted to "seize a son-in-law from under the [examination] lists" had to offer money, as much as a thousand strings of cash, ostensibly for his expenses in the capital. Hung Mai told of a high official who, when

he heard that the son of a merchant from his home area had passed
the examinations, immediately got together money and silk and went to the
capital to secure him as a son-in-law. Sometimes a rich family would make a
conditional offer to a promising young man. Hung Mai recounted the story
of Huang Tso-chih, who met a wealthy gentleman named Wang while in the
capital to take the examinations in 1180. The two became very friendly, and
Wang not only supplied Huang with expense money but promised that if he
passed the examinations he would give him his daughter as a wife. Huang
did pass and got a bride with a dowry of five million cash.[39]

Whether we look at Sung families' efforts to recruit talented sons-in-law,
to marry their children to their friends' children, or to marry with relatives,
it is clear that, in comparison to the T'ang, leading Sung families were less
concerned with the fame of ancestors than with the standing of living relatives. They took less pride in exclusive practices—in turning down offers—
and more readily offered handsome dowries. These matchmaking strategies
make sense in terms of the evolution of the ruling class. Between the mid-
T'ang and the early Sung, the aristocratic families of the T'ang lost their
ability to dominate the central government. The political situation of the
tenth century brought to the fore people who had no pedigree but who had
succeeded in building armies or staffing bureaucracies through various
personal connections. With the stabilization of the Sung government and
the rapid growth of the economy, the educated class steadily expanded.
Although the Sung is known as the period when the civil service examination
system came to dominate recruitment to office, privileges and connections
remained of great importance in a highly competitive political environment.
As the rules of the civil service system were gradually worked out, there was
a persistent tendency for those with good connections to devise ways to favor
people of their own sort (through "protection" privileges, "sponsorship,"
"facilitated" or "avoidance" examinations, and so on).[40] Thus it is not surprising that families with political aspirations were concerned to locate
useful affines and maintain ties with ones that had proved satisfactory.

MARRIAGES ARRANGED BY GO-BETWEENS

If a family did not find a good marriage prospect through personal connections, they could turn to a matchmaker, who would generally be a woman.
Lou Yüeh (1137–1213) wrote that after his elder brother died, he helped
the widow arrange marriages for her three sons and five daughters. She
especially doted on her youngest daughter. A matchmaker told him about a
certain family of imperial clansmen living in his prefecture: "The parents
are both old and live economically behind closed gates. They have reared
their sons very strictly. The sons have passed·the examinations and have

acquired good reputations. The third son, Shih-hsin, already in 1175 was granted the *chin-shih* degree and has been appointed sheriff of Lin-hai in T'ai [prefecture]." Lou Yüeh then checked on the family's local reputation, and when it matched the go-between's report, agreed to marry his niece to the Chaos' third son.[41]

Even when the two families together decided on the match, a go-between was needed for formal communication. Use of go-betweens was in accord with the classics: the *Book of Rites* insisted, "Without a go-between men and women have no contact."[42] *Dreams of Hangchow* reported that go-betweens traveled in pairs and could be recognized by the yellow ribbon in their hairknots.[43] Yüan Ts'ai noted that matchmakers were indispensable, but cautioned against putting too much credence in what they said:

> Matchmakers deceive the girl's family by saying the boy does not seek a full complement of dowry presents and in fact will help in outfitting the bride. They deceive the boy's family by promising generous transfer of goods, and they make up a figure without any basis in fact. If the parties simply believe what the matchmaker says and go through with the marriage, each side will accuse the other of dishonesty and the husband and wife will quarrel. There are even cases where the final result is divorce.[44]

Deceptive matchmakers appear often in stories. For instance, in "The Honest Clerk," a childless widower of over sixty who owned a shop sent for two matchmakers because he wished to marry again. The women were skeptical when he said he wanted a young beauty whose family rank matched his own and who would moreover bring a dowry of one hundred thousand strings, equal to his total family property. What they did manage to arrange was a match with a young concubine whose master no longer wanted her, though they deceived the woman by saying that the man was about forty.[45]

MARRIAGE AGES

In trying to select matches for their children, families paid considerable attention to their daughters' ages and some also to how these compared to the ages of the potential grooms. The families of educated men generally married their daughters off soon after puberty, a widespread practice throughout the world in premodern times.[46] The percentages of men and women marrying at various ages are given in Table 1, based on sixty-five couples whose dates of both birth and marriage are known.

The mean age at marriage for the women in this group was 19 sui, and the age span for marrying was fairly short: 54 percent married when they were from 16 to 19 sui (a four-year span); and 89 percent married when they were from 15 to 22 sui (an eight-year span). This age range is close to that found among peasants in twentieth-century China,[47] but slightly later than

TABLE 1. Ages of Men and Women at First Marriage

	Men (in percent)	Women (in percent)
12–13 sui	3	0
14–15	3	9
16–17	11	25
18–19	20	29
20–21	18	18
22–23	11	12
24–25	12	3
26–27	5	2
28–29	8	0
30+	9	2

among prosperous groups in Ming and later periods.[48] Perhaps daughters' marriages were delayed a little while families put together the substantial dowries that Sung well-to-do families expected (see Chapter 5).

Sons, however, were not so quickly married off. Their marriages spanned a much longer period, with only 52 percent falling into the six years from 17 through 22 sui, and 92 percent occurring during the sixteen years from 15 through 30. Still, the median was 21 sui.

Young women were married within a short time span because they were seen as blooming like flowers or ripening like fruit, with at best a brief period when they should be plucked. Moreover, there was a long tradition that women's marriages should not be delayed. The Book of Rites stated that women should marry between fifteen and twenty sui, and men by thirty. The law codes set only minimum ages, in the Sung thirteen sui for women and fifteen sui for men.[49] Sung scholars argued for compromises between the legal minimums and the classical preference for older ages, Ssu-ma Kuang and Chu Hsi suggesting fourteen to twenty for women and sixteen to thirty for men. Chu Hsi, in fact, delayed the marriage of his eldest son an extra year because the girl was only thirteen sui.[50] The only fully legitimate reason to delay a woman's marriage beyond twenty was mourning for a parent or grandparent. Even in this case, it bothered people to see a woman have to wait too long. If a woman reached twenty and then could not marry because of mourning, it was possible to petition the government to allow a wedding. And people would hurry up wedding preparations if they felt a death was imminent.[51]

For either men or women, having to marry late was considered a misfortune. People would cite a poem by Po Chü-i (772–846) which said that because of the disorders of the time, many men passed thirty and women passed twenty without marrying. Old age made childbirth difficult and meant that the parents would be in their decline before the children were fully grown. If a woman had to marry late, people were quick to suspect financial hardship. Writers often quoted another Po Chü-i line: "The daughter of a poor family is hard to marry out."[52] This poem laments that beauty is less important than wealth, that a rich family will need go to no trouble to find suitors for a daughter but will easily have her married by age sixteen, whereas the poor girl will still be alone after twenty and the family will have to court matchmakers actively to get any proposals at all.

In the Sung, the only sizable group of women whose marriages seem to have been routinely delayed were maidservants. In one of Hung Mai's stories, a couple realized they should do something for the maid who had served them so loyally for thirty years, so they married her out. Yüan Ts'ai sharply criticized those who kept maids in service their whole lives, never letting them marry.[53]

Since men did not "ripen" in the same way women did, families had the leeway to consider the consequences of marrying a son early or late. Some liked to see their sons married early in order to have grandsons sooner; the phrase "to see a great-great grandson" was often used to express this sentiment. But there were also men whose marriages were delayed well past thirty or who never married. Anecdotes about ordinary people, such as those collected by Hung Mai, mention old bachelors with some frequency. One man who had still not married at forty boarded with his younger brother and made a living by cutting firewood and making charcoal.[54]

Some Sung men argued in favor of postponing marriage for men. The scholar Lo Yüan (1136–1184) wrote an essay arguing that all men should wait until they were thirty to marry unless they were orphans like Confucius who had to marry to carry on the ancestral rites. "When a man reaches thirty he is knowledgeable and able to lead others." Fu Pi (1004–1083) delayed his own marriage until he passed the examinations at age twenty-eight, having asked his parents to go ahead and marry his younger brothers and sisters before him. He urged late marriage on an unmarried visitor of twenty-four, saying it allowed one to build up his energy and focus his attention on study.[55]

In exceptional cases, men delayed marrying past forty. Sun Fu (992–1057) never passed the examinations and reached forty without marrying. Finally Li Ti (967–1043) recognized his qualities and gave him his niece as a wife.[56] When Shao Yung (1011–1077) reached forty-five without marrying, two men who had studied with him came to him and said, "Of the three very unfilial acts, to have no heirs is the worst. You have passed forty without marrying. Your parents are old and you have no sons. We fear that [your behavior] cannot be considered lofty." Shao Yung responded, "I am so poor I cannot marry. It is not that I consider [my conduct] lofty." They then proposed a match with the younger sister of a fellow student, one of them offering to supply the betrothal gifts.[57]

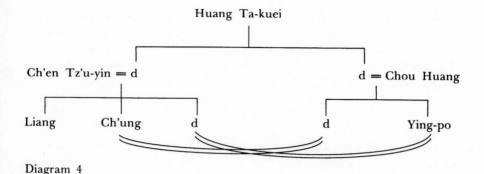

Diagram 4

For a man to delay marriage until he passed the examinations could be a strategy for mobility.[58] Hu Ch'üan's (1102–1180) father had not passed the examinations, but Ch'üan attained the *chin-shih* degree in 1127 at twenty-six sui. He then attracted the attention of Liu Min-ts'ai, a regional official in Hu's home area from an official family who was then looking for a scholar for a son-in-law. In the case of Hsü Ching-heng (1072–1128), although none of his immediate relatives were officials, after he passed the *chin-shih* examination in 1094 at age twenty-three he married a young woman from another prefecture in Chekiang whose father had been an official and who brought a dowry large enough to use for Hsü's brother's expenses at the Imperial University. Similarly, none of Chang Wei's (1112–1181) immediate ancestors were officials, yet after he became a *chin-shih* in 1138 at' twenty-seven, he married a young woman from his prefecture in Fukien who brought a dowry that helped get Chang's younger sister married. But of course, the strategy of postponing marriage had risks. One man, we are told, was so intent on passing the *chin-shih* examinations that he ended up alone at fifty.[59]

On average, grooms were a couple of years older than their brides (see Chapter 8, Table 2), but families did not rule out brides older than their husbands. When Huang Ta-kuei's two daughters arranged marriages among their children, their desire to see them wed to each other was so strong that it resulted in the elder sister's daughter marrying a cousin nine years her junior (Diagram 4). Ch'en Liang (1143–1194), that woman's brother, explained the motives in his elegy for his cousin/brother-in-law, Chou Ying-po:

> My mother had only one younger sister, with whom she had shared her orphan's fate. This sister, who married into the Chou family, was Ying-po's mother. Therefore, Ying-po's elder sister in return married my younger brother. My younger sister was older than Ying-po by nine years; the reason my mother engaged him to marry her was that she wanted the mutual marriage connections to continue endlessly and the love between us to develop to its fullest.[60]

Parents also accepted or chose women older than their sons when they were eager to get their sons married early (perhaps because they wanted grand-children quickly, or because they were worried about thir own or their sons' health). Thus boys who married at fifteen or sixteen generally were younger than their brides.

YOUNG MEN AND WOMEN WITH MINDS OF THEIR OWN

From Hung Mai's tales and similar sources, it is evident that young men and women were often willing to let their parents know of someone they were attracted to as a potential spouse.[61] Some young people went even further and opposed their parents' choices. The popular Buddhist legend of Princess Miao-shan dramatized this possibility. The pious Miao-shan, according to this legend, did not want to marry and so opposed her father's commands. Angry at her rebelliousness, the king tried to force her into submission by locking her up and starving her, but with divine help she escaped and began a new life as a Buddhist nun. Still, she never stopped loving her parents. When she learned that her father was gravely ill, she gouged out her eyes and cut off her arms so that they could be used to cure him, thus showing that she was as filial as any daughter who obeyed her parents' orders to marry. When the disfigured Miao-shan met her parents again, her body was transformed and she was revealed as a manifestation of the bodhisattva Kuanyin (by Sung times regularly represented as a compassionate woman). Miao-shan's story spread rapidly in the Sung and continued to be very popular in later times.[62]

Even children not motivated by religious esteem for celibacy might oppose their parents. The biography for Miss Hsü (d. 1170) reports that when her father died, her mother tried to get her quickly married to her father's sister's son before the mourning clothes were put on. She screamed and held her breath, frightening the family enough that they gave up the idea. After the mourning was over, her elder brother brought up the idea again, but, we are told, she insisted, "Marrying a rich man is not what I want."[63] Undoubtedly she knew her cousin from family gatherings and found him repulsive.

Some young women, in contrast, wanted to marry a relative their parents did not favor. Hung Mai related the case of Sun Yü, a young man who had his heart set on his mother's brother's daughter, who in turn was quite attracted to him. Her father, however, wanted all of his sons-in-law to be officials, and would agree to the match only if Sun Yü passed the prefectural examina-tions. After he had failed twice, his uncle married his daughter to someone else, and Sun, we are told, died of lovesickness.[64] A story with a similar beginning but a different outcome was told by Lien Hsüan. A young woman was in love with her father's sister's son, and he with her. She had had her nurse tell her mother of her feelings, but the mother, who loved her dearly, wanted her to marry an official. The woman and her nurse, therefore, made plans for her to elope. The plan was foiled when a young man, passing by, discovered her, threatened to expose her, and convinced her to come with him instead. She had no difficulty shifting her affections to him, but when his father summoned him back she was left stranded, ran out of money, and had to become a government courtesan.[65]

Young men, who got out more than young women, were often attracted to women who were not relatives. In fiction, a glance at a delicate young beauty could be enough to make a man lose interest in anything beyond pursuing her.[66] In real life also, it was accepted that men could decide on a woman solely from her appearance. Consider the case of the scholar Liu K'ai (947–1000). After his first wife died, he called on an official acquaintance while in the capital. He noticed a painting of a beautiful woman on the wall of the study. His host, when asked about it, responded that it was a portrait of his younger sister. K'ai then promptly reported that he was looking for a successor wife. His host said he could do nothing without consulting his father, but K'ai pushed his case, forcing him to accept betrothal gifts and to set a date for the wedding less than ten days away. Since he was not using an intermediary, it was difficult for his host to refuse him. The host's father, an official of some importance, complained to the emperor that Liu K'ai was pressuring him to hand over his daughter, but the emperor, we are told, was not alarmed. He told him that Liu K'ai was a man of exceptional talents who would make a good son-in-law, and even offered to serve as the intermediary.[67]

Men who flirted too readily could find themselves in trouble. Let me end this chapter by quoting a cautionary example, recorded by Hung Mai:

In 1121, Jen Chiung, the son of a wealthy family in the capital, was traveling by himself to enjoy the sights of spring. He stopped for a while at an inn outside the city, attracted by its secluded location. The old woman who managed it came out from the inner quarters of the house, glanced back, then said [to someone there], "I won't be back till late tonight. Please look after the house." After she left, Chiung peeked behind a curtain and saw a very attractive young woman. He couldn't very well express his admiration to her, but unexpectedly the girl tidied herself up and came out to see him, smiling faintly. She was lovely even without fine clothes. He beckoned her to sit and chatted with her. She said, "My mother has gone to a banquet at a relative's house in the village, leaving me alone in the house." Chiung, infatuated, flirted wildly with her. He ordered wine to drink with her, and then they made love.

In the late evening, the old woman came back and found Chiung in the inner quarters. Angrily she burst out: "My daughter is a virgin of a good family. How dare you sully her!" Chiung could offer no excuses, so tearfully he bowed and asked forgiveness. After a long time the old woman smiled and said: "Since you have offended my daughter, there is no alternative but for you to become my son-in-law. Otherwise I will tie you up and take you to the officials." Chiung was not married and did not want to be accused, so he promised to marry the daughter. The old woman told him that he did not need to go home, she would send a letter to inform his parents within ten days. Consequently Chiung and the girl were married.

Chiung and his wife got along very well, but he was under rigid surveillance. The old woman and her daughter took turns watching him. He was not allowed to step outside the door to the inner quarters. He was well fed every day but had nothing to do. One night, before he went to bed, someone knocked on the door loudly and continuously. The old woman answered it. About twenty to thirty people, high-spirited males and females of all ages, came in and said that a certain family was giving a feast that night in the city. The old woman decided to join them and take her daughter, but asked what to do about Chiung. Someone said that if he came with all the others, there would be no problem. They then departed for the city.

Chiung had strong doubts but dared say nothing. When they arrived at the city a little later, they found that the city gate had been closed for some time. After much discussion on how to enter, the old woman passed through a crack, and the rest, including Chiung, followed. They went to the marketplace, which was ablaze with lights and buying and selling, as on any other day. They found the house, where the family had just had a monk bestow three bushels of food for the Buddhist rituals. The people shoved each other to get at the food, eating it eagerly. Chiung, petrified, then realized [that this was a ritual feeding of ghosts and] that he had become the son-in-law of a ghost. He knelt before the image of a Buddha, then turned back to them, now able to see their weird, ghostly forms. The ghosts tried to get Chiung to go back with them, but he refused. The old woman and her daughter, feeling affection for him, were reluctant to leave. Regretting that they had brought Chiung, they blamed each other. Crying and cursing, they left.

At dawn, when the family came out to put away the food containers, they were astonished to find Chiung, whom they took for a ghost. Chiung [fled but] came out of hiding when they searched for him with torches. He told them the whole story, and in the morning they sent him back to his own family. When he saw his family, everyone cried. They sobbed to each other, "It has been a year and a half since you left. We thought you were dead when we could not find you." [Chiung had begun to look like a ghost himself], but he recovered his human appearance after several days' medical treatment. When he went back to see where he had lived, the area was desolate, covered with weeds and bushes.[68]

A man who allowed himself to be sexually attracted to an unknown woman, this and many other tales attest, was placing himself in danger, for anything might happen.

Much of what is described in this chapter is commonly found in status-conscious stratified societies in which parents arrange their children's marriages. Marrying children young, casting marriage decisions as moral choices of good people or good families, keeping financial considerations in mind, paying as much attention to the potential spouse's relatives as to his or her personal characteristics, and viewing the whole process as a burdensome yet rather exciting chore performed in part by older women—these characteristics of matchmaking are far from unusual. In such societies, the division of authority in selecting marriage partners does not fall along gender lines so much as along generational lines. Older men and women had considerable say about whom their children would marry, while the young people, male and female alike, had only limited ability to influence the decisions being made about their own fate. Matchmaking in Sung China also had other features—such as a positive attitude about marriages between cousins of different surnames—that are not found in all traditional societies but had a long history in China.

In addition, one can identify certain features of matchmaking in the Sung that are distinctive compared with other periods of Chinese history. Leading Sung families, for instance, were less concerned than their T'ang counterparts with the fame of deceased ancestors, but stressed instead the standing of living relatives. Unlike official families in Ming and later China, however, Sung official families still followed the T'ang pattern of intermarrying with the families of other officials of similar rank even if they came from distant parts of the country. As we have seen, these matchmaking strategies made sense in terms of the evolution of the ruling class, especially given the increased competition in the examinations and the way connections could be used to effect advancement.

Yet it would be a mistake to interpret all matchmaking decisions as motivated primarily by questions of political advantage for the men of the two families. Marriage choices were highly complex; mothers and fathers, grandmothers and grandfathers, had more goals than any one marriage could possibly fulfill. Probably mothers and fathers tended to have somewhat different agendas for their children's marriages, but compromises of all sorts were possible. A mother may, for example, have gotten her way in a couple of her children's marriages but had to yield in others.

This chapter has focused on the side of matchmaking celebrated in surviving sources and undoubtedly most frequently achieved in the better-off segments of society. As we will see later in this book, not all parents managed to make good matches for their children; indeed, some did not even try. Poverty, greed, cruelty, and misfortune could all intervene on the path toward a good marriage. A not inconsiderable number of girls were sold by their parents to be maids, concubines, entertainers, or prostitutes. Girls who had lost their fathers or, occasionally, whose parents could not afford to keep them might be sent to live with prospective in-laws as adopted daughters-in-law.[69] A young woman who had been sexually abused might find her marriage prospects ruined.[70] Orphaned daughters who stood to inherit could become pawns in family struggles, as Chapters 5, 10, and 13 will all show.

FOUR

Rites and Celebrations

In Sung China, as in most other societies, marriages began with rituals. These rituals were rites of passage that facilitated changing the status of the bride and groom by taking them on a journey: separating them from their former identity, keeping them in a liminal state for a while, then rein-corporating them as new people. Wedding rituals gave recognition, in a symbolic way, to the sexuality of the bride and groom and its importance to their relationship with each other. At the same time, wedding rituals served the social and emotional needs of the larger families. No matter how care-fully families had weighed the choice of a partner for their child and no matter how much they wanted the wedding to proceed, they could not help but worry a little about the future. Would their daughter's husband and his relatives treat her properly and prove to be useful friends? Would their son's wife upset the interpersonal relationships in their family? Weddings allowed members of both families to give expression to some of these anxieties in a controlled way that would not endanger the outcome. Weddings, as rituals, also helped make marriage more palatable. The rites and ceremonies pro-vided ways to obscure or mask aspects of marriage that people would prefer not to think about, to recast what might be thought of as a transaction in people into a celebration of love and friendship. And weddings provided the families in question with opportunities to show off their wealth, cultivation, and connections.

The steps of wedding rituals are described in several manuals of Sung date. But the fullest descriptions of Sung weddings are found in descriptions of the social customs of the two Sung capitals. Kaifeng, in north-central China, described in *Dreams of Kaifeng* (*Tung-ching meng-hua lu*), was capital from 960 to 1126; Hangchow, south of the Yangtze, described in *Dreams of Hangchow* (*Meng-liang lu*), was capital after the dynasty lost control of the north. The authors of both these works claim to describe the customs of the urban population, rich as well as poor, but clearly took most delight in the more elaborate practices of the better off.[1]

THE RITUALS OF BETROTHAL

Once a family had an interest in another family as a potential affine — whether this interest was based on a matchmaker's glowing report, a friend's advice, or a long-standing kinship connection — certain procedures had to be followed to bring about a formal engagement. The first step was for the boy's family to send the matchmaker with a card listing such information as his patrilineal ancestors for three generations, their titles if any, the son's seniority number within the family (whether he was first, second, or third son), the date of his birth, and his mother's surname. If the girl's family was interested (perhaps consulting a diviner before deciding), they returned their own "draft card" with similar information.[2] Next, "detailed cards" were exchanged. The detailed card from the man's family would list all the information given earlier but with more specifics, such as the hour of his birth, whether his parents were still living, and, if not, who would preside over the marriage. The card that the girl's family returned would likewise give such facts as her time of birth, in addition listing what she would bring as dowry, her "cases with jewelry, gold and silver, pearls and feathers, precious objects, useful items, and bedding, as well as the property accompanying her on her marriage, such as fields, houses, businesses, hills, or gardens."[3] In each case the card was delivered by the go-between. The exchange of these cards at an early stage gave either side the opportunity to withdraw if the information did not meet their expectations.

Once the cards were exchanged, the bride could be inspected, if the groom's family so desired. In Kaifeng, the custom was for a female relative of the groom's to visit the bride's family to look her over. In Hangchow, a meeting of the two families could be arranged, either at the girl's house or at a restaurant, where the groom could view her and make a final decision. In both cities, the insertion of a gold hairpin in her hair indicated approval on the man's side, whereas leaving some colorful satin behind showed their disapproval.

In both Kaifeng and Hangchow, the man's family, whether rich or poor, would send four or eight jars of wine, referred to as "agreement wine," once they had decided on the match. The wine was conveyed in gold-colored bottles covered in cloth, decorated with flowers, and carried on a red frame. Food items such as tea, biscuits, and mutton would also be sent. To accompany the gifts, the family would send four documents written on gold paper, one of which was a list of the gifts. In Hangchow the custom was to place these documents in a green box labeled "Five sons and two daughters," alluding, of course, to the hoped-for outcome of the marriage.

Confucian ritual manuals directed both families at this stage to report the betrothal to their ancestors.[4] *Dreams of Hangchow* reports that when the betrothal documents and gifts arrived at the bride's house, her family would set out incense, candles, wine, and fruit to announce the alliance "to the three directions." They would invite a couple from among their affinal relatives whose parents were still alive to open the documents—the first of several occasions when affinal relatives played a role in the ceremonies. Their presence undoubtedly underlined the truth that marriage did not merely transfer a girl but in fact created enduring kinship ties.

Before that day was over, the bride's family had to send counter-gifts to demonstrate its own wealth and generosity. These could include embroidered items and clothing of the sort men wear, plus either a quarter or a half of the tea, biscuits, fruit, wine, and mutton that they had just received. They would also fill a pair of wine jars with fresh water and put four goldfish, a pair of chopsticks, and two onions in them. That these objects were in pairs or multiples of two was seen as symbolizing marriage, also a pairing. These particular objects, moreover, sometimes became conventional because of homophones: *yü,* "fish," for example, is pronounced the same as *yü,* "surplus." In the case of rich families or families of officials, according to *Dreams of Hangchow,* the fish and chopsticks were made of gold or silver and the onions of silk.

From this point on, the prospective in-laws addressed each other as relatives, calling the other *ch'in-chia,* "affine" (literally, "closely related family"), and referring to themselves as *t'ien-ch'un* or *t'ien-ch'i,* self-deprecatory terms meaning a "relative who is disgracing you." Until the betrothal gifts were delivered, letters of greeting had to be exchanged between the two families at the beginning and midpoint of each month. Samples of these letters, different ones for each month, are contained in reference books. On holidays, the man's family sent gifts of cloth, fruit, mutton, and wine to the girl's family, who would respond with pieces of feminine handiwork, the value in proportion to their financial resources. Apparently this stage—during which the man's family assembled the betrothal gifts—was a crucial one, marked by anxiety that the other side might change its mind and by concern for the cost and quality of the betrothal gifts. Thus nearly continuous reassurances had to be made that the betrothal process was continuing.

BETROTHAL GIFTS

The presentation of the betrothal gifts to the bride's family marked the completion of the betrothal itself. The go-between would go to the girl's family to inform them of the day the gifts would be delivered, bringing wine and a goose or sheep. The term for betrothal gifts, *p'in-ts'ai,* is often translated "brideprice," but in the Sung the gifts commonly comprised mixed goods, not straight cash. The families of educated gentlemen and officials sent fancy women's clothes and head ornaments, various fine silks, foodstuffs such as jasmine tea, fruit, cakes, lamb, and wine, and paper money and silver ingots, everything accompanied by a betrothal letter and gift list. In the case of rich families in Hangchow, the betrothal gifts are said to have included the "three gold things": a gold bracelet, a gold chain, and a gold pendant. In less wealthy families, silver or plated objects could be substituted, or anything else, "for this is a matter where there are no set rules."[5] (In about 1180, a prefect was accused of extravagance for preparing several hundred lengths of various silk cloths for curtains, screens, and coverlets, plus several hundred sets of clothes, all gorgeously dyed, when his second son married.)[6] As for lower-class families, according to *Dreams of Hangchow,* they would send one or two bolts of cloth, some paper money, a goose, wine, tea, and biscuits. The girl's family then would use these gifts to help with their expenses.

In the case of rich families, once the betrothal gift was received, the girl's family made return gifts, including items such as green and purple silk gauze, printed silk, gold or jade desk objects (pens, penholders, and so forth), as well as fancy top-knot strings and feminine handiwork. These, too, were accompanied by a list.

These gifts and counter-gifts revealed much about the social and economic standing of the two families, providing ample opportunity for them to display their wealth and style. Not only could the man's family provide fine goods for the betrothal gifts, but the bride's family could show that they had no great need for so many items by returning half of them. These exchanges also, of course, served to transmit wealth, and thus had material consequences for the bride and groom and their families—a subject that will be explored in Chapter 5.

Three documents rolled into a bundle accompanied the betrothal gifts and the return gifts. These usually consisted of a rather general polite letter, a betrothal letter of the sort translated in Chapter 2, and a list of the gifts. It was with regard to this letter and the reply that the greatest literary efforts were expended; indeed, reference books often include several hundred examples, for these letters had to be tailored to the specific situation of the two families. Were the spouses still young children? Was this a remarriage for one of them? Were they already relatives? If so, what kind? (Separate forms were given if the parents of the spouses included two sisters, a sister and a brother, or some other combination of relatives.) Did they come from the same place or different places? Did they have the same occupation? (Forms were often classified by occupation, such as a farmer's son marrying a carpenter's daughter, a plasterer's son marrying a water

seller's daughter, a butcher's son marrying a fishmonger's daughter, or a
doctor's son marrying a doctor's daughter.) Also included were letters for
those taking the exams, those who had passed the exams, those in office,
and members of the imperial family.

Perhaps because both sides unconsciously wanted to deny that marriages
created inequalities, in marriage letters both sides addressed each other
respectfully and asserted their equality. Betrothal letters often referred to
the marriage as an alliance, using such phrases as "to conclude an alliance"
or "to settle an alliance." Equally common are references to specific alliances in classical history, such as that of the states of Ch'in and Chin.
Frequently authors would stress that both parties were acting in full faith
and would share in the benefits. Here, the term "orchid metal" might be
used, an allusion to the "Appended Phrases" section of the *Book of Changes*
and the passage, "When two people agree in their hearts, the profit will cut
through metal; when they speak from the same heart, their words will smell
like orchids."[7] In referring to betrothal gifts, authors would cite such lines
from the classics as "Without the receipt of gifts, there is no exchange and no
affinity."[8] They also used self-deprecatory statements when mentioning the
gifts they were giving, downplaying their value, but praised the generosity
of the other side, saying they did not deserve the gifts they received.

Why was so much attention given to the precise wording of these letters?
It would appear that those sending the letters had two slightly conflicting
goals. Each family wished to treat the other with all appropriate courtesy, to
avoid offense. As Yüan Ts'ai warned, only when "both families are careful
and complete in their etiquette" could affront be avoided.[9] A letter found in
a reference book, already tried and approved, would therefore be desirable.
At the same time, to avoid appearing too formal or distant, people wished
to recognize the particularities of their ties to the other family by selecting
a letter that matched their circumstances. Just as the nature and quantity
of the betrothal gifts had to vary according to the circumstances of the
family, so did the formal language that accompanied them.

FINAL EXCHANGES

Once the betrothal gifts had been received and the counter-gifts sent, the
two families did not need to communicate until the wedding date was set.
This could well be months or years after the delivery of the betrothal gifts.

When the time drew near, the groom's family would choose the exact
date of the wedding and inform the girl's family. Final preparations would
then be made, including issuing a great many invitations. The last exchanges
of goods took place just before the wedding. A couple of days before the
event, the groom's family sent items to "hasten the dowry" such as hair
ornaments, cosmetics, and a fan inscribed, "Five sons and two daughters."

The bride's family acknowledged this message by returning items of men's clothing, including a fancy scarf-cap. The day before the wedding the bride's family sent people to "make up the room," which involved laying out bedding, curtains, rugs, and arranging the various clothing and jewelry items in the dowry. A list would be compiled and also delivered.[10] After the room was made up, *Dreams of Hangchow* reports, a female servant or servants sent by the bride's family would remain in the bridal chamber, making sure no one entered it until the bride arrived. Ssu-ma Kuang noted that although the practice of "making up the room" was unattested in the classics, it was considered obligatory among his peers, who agreed that the man's family had to supply the furniture for the room but the woman's family had to provide all the goods made of cloth. He also noted—with disapproval—the tendency to put everything on display.[11]

Looking at the betrothal process as a whole, we find distinct patterns in the exchanges of goods. Objects were not exchanged in a single transaction, but in a long series of transactions, with the man's family sending something first and the woman's family responding by sending something in return. These separate exchanges were not balanced, however: the wife's family, after receiving the betrothal gift, sent back a smaller set of objects; and to "hasten" the dowry, the groom's family had to send only a relatively minor set of objects. The significance of these counter-gifts probably reflects the principle that gifts create obligations for further gifts; gifts that are countered with unequal gifts are therefore preferred as they keep the obligations active, thus maintaining social ties.[12]

By having objects from different categories presented at the same time, the value of the items was obscured. On display, the food and jewelry presented as part of the betrothal gift took some attention away from the money, just as clothes, bedding, and jewelry gave the dowry more visual interest than deeds to land or houses would. Moreover, having the same objects go back and forth served to obscure the sense that a transaction was taking place: each side was being generous in presenting gifts. The fact that detailed inventories were included in the first round of negotiations and each time gifts were delivered suggests that these items were indeed the objects of bargaining; still, the lists were not as public as the wine barrels, sheep, and trunks, which had to be transported through the streets. To the neighbors, it may well have been difficult to tell which side had spent more.

One can posit many possible reasons for obscuring the real transfers of property that took place at marriages. For one thing, the transfer of property through daughters was at variance with the idea of preserving family property intact to pass on to the next generation. As will be seen in the next chapter, dowry as wives' property was a source of tension within any family. Then too, the family's outlay for one son's betrothal gifts might best be obscured if it was significantly higher or lower than what had been expended for another son's marriage.

The exchange of goods and letters described above was what legally constituted a betrothal. The law code stipulated a punishment of sixty strokes if the woman's family broke a betrothal that had been sealed by the return of a marriage letter or, in the absence of a letter, by the receipt of betrothal gifts in any amount. In one legal case, the judge cited this law and noted that since the girl's family had returned an "agreement" card accompanied by a list of the items in the dowry, there could be no doubt that they had agreed to the match. In another legal case, in deciding whether a woman had actually been married to the deceased a judge asked not only about the wedding, but also about the betrothal: "Who was the matchmaker? What were the gifts that sealed it? What were the gifts given in response? Who wrote the marriage letter?"[13]

Given the penchant for early engagements, quite a few must have been broken. Ssu-ma Kuang argued that early engagements were often repudiated because "after the betrothed grow up, one or the other turns out to be unworthy or unreliable or develops a loathsome disease. Other reasons could be that his or her family is so poor that they are cold and hungry, or successive deaths keep them in mourning, or official service takes them far off."[14] Biographical and anecdotal sources are more likely to note the exceptions—the men who carried through with an engagement others would have renounced. Thus Ch'eng I said that he would not have been able to do what Chou Hsing-chi (c.s. 1091) did: Chou carried through with an engagement to a girl in his mother's family even though she had gone blind in both eyes.[15]

THE WEDDING DAY

"The Shrew," a story probably dating from the thirteenth century, contains a vivid portrayal of a wedding day. The bride and her family rose early. She was made up with earrings and jeweled hairpins. Dumplings, noodles, and other foods were set out as her family waited for three female relatives to arrive: the bride's father's sister, her mother's sister, and her uncle's wife. The bride lit incense before her family shrine and bade her ancestors farewell. Then the procession from the groom's family arrived, composed of musicians, horsemen, the go-between, the sedan chair, an astrologer, and various others. When the astrologer chanted a verse to request tips for these attendants, the bride's mother fetched money to pass out to them. The bride got into the sedan chair, and when it was lowered to the ground at the groom's home the astrologer again chanted a verse, this one the prelude to the go-between feeding her a spoonful of rice. After the bride was ushered into the house, the astrologer orchestrated the ceremony of bowing before the ancestral altar and to the assembled relatives. Then he asked the bride and groom to enter the nuptial chamber for the "strewing of the bed-curtains." There he chanted lines such as, "Scatter the grain in all directions that yin and yang mingling may increase." The groom then joined the guests, feasting until nightfall. The next morning the bride joined the work of the household, and the morning after that her mother came to call on her.[16]

The transfer of the bride on the day of the wedding was called the "great coming home," for this was to be her entry into her "real" home. Best was for the groom and other members of his family to go to her home to get her—called "fetching in person"—though sometimes the bride's family brought her. Reference books have forms for letters asking the bride's parents to bring her, and such letters are sometimes preserved among authors' writings. Chao Shih-ch'i offered to bring his daughter from Fu-chou to P'u-t'ien (both in Fukien) for her marriage to Liu K'o-chuang's (1187–1269) grandson, saying the journey took only one day by boat.[17] The ritual manual issued by the government in 1113 suggested having the go-between fetch the bride when the groom could not do it himself.[18]

On the day of the wedding, the groom's family would get up early to make their preparations. Chu Hsi, in his *Family Rituals*, describes the groom's family setting the table for two and laying out vegetables, fruit, wine, cups and saucers, chopsticks, and the "nuptial cups." The groom would be dressed in finery, including a crown of flowers.[19] In the classical ritual, the groom was to be instructed by his father before he left for the bride's house. Chu Hsi had the groom bow twice, then accept a cup of wine from the family head to offer in sacrifice. After many bowings and kneelings, his father would instruct him:

> Go to welcome your helpmate, so that I may fulfil my duties to my ancestors.
> Do your best to lead her, with due respect, for you then will gain steadiness.

The groom was to reply:

> I will. My only fear is that I am not equal to the task. I will not dare to forget your command.

At much the same time the bride's family was supposed to be giving her similar admonitions. Her father would say:

> Be respectful, be cautious. Morning to night never deviate from the commands of your parents-in-law.

Her mother would then straighten the bride's cap and arrange her cape. She would instruct her with these words:

> Be diligent. Be respectful. Morning to night never deviate from the proprieties of the women's quarters.

Her uncles' wives, her aunts, her elder brothers' wives, and her elder sisters would walk her to the inner door. They would arrange her skirt and gown and elaborate on the instructions of her father and mother:

> Pay careful attention to your parents' words. From morning to night never err.[20]

Even families that did not employ such archaic language probably conveyed similar sentiments in other words.

In Hangchow, the party sent to get the bride would include not only the groom and various attendants, but also hired singing girls on horseback, musicians, and a decorated sedan chair. The classics had prohibited music at weddings, a rule commentators related to yin-yang theories. Music leads to movement and is yang; it is therefore not appropriate for brides, who should be yin.[21] This rule was honored mainly in the breach: musicians and songs played a major part in keeping the atmosphere festive, and they also helped to mark each stage of the rituals. When Emperor Che-tsung (r. 1086–1100) was married some officials urged the empress dowager not to allow music, but she objected—"Even ordinary people, when they take a bride, engage a few musicians"—and ordered elaborate music for the ceremony.[22]

Singing girls might seem an odd addition to a wedding party, but they had a role to play. Not only could they sing the numerous songs required at weddings, but they could do it in style, dressed in brilliant colors. And although "proper" girls had been taught to avoid being seen by men and would tend to stay with the women and girls, the singing girls were used to men looking at them and would not be embarrassed to play silly games at the wedding. Moreover, the erotic overtones of the entertainment quarters were not unwelcome at weddings. One twelfth-century prefect reportedly had over forty singing girls at his son's wedding; for their clothes, he had silk specially dyed in red and purple patterns, each girl's costume slightly different.[23] That a prefect would engage so many singing girls for a wedding demonstrates that, whatever the origins of the custom, by mid-Sung times it was practiced by members of the educated class.

On arrival at the bride's house, the musicians, singing girls, and others in the party were greeted with wine, gifts of colored silk, and trinkets. The musicians then played songs intended to hurry the bride into the sedan chair.[24] At this point too, according to one source, the bride's mother might come out to inspect the groom and tease him, comparing his appearance unfavorably with that of her daughter.[25]

The bride, dressed as elaborately as the groom, wore a veil over her face. Once she was in the chair, the carriers noisily demanded gratuities. At the groom's house again, the musicians, singing girls, and attendants recited poems and made similar demands of the groom's family. Such solicitation could be a nuisance, and in 969 the government even outlawed the practice, though to no apparent effect.[26] People clearly attached an importance to the clamor associated with weddings, especially as the bride passed through gates. Gates and thresholds are, after all, highly symbolic of entry and exit, and the bride was leaving one family and social status and entering another. The *Shih-lin kuang-chi* gives several versions of songs that could be used to demand gratuities, such as:

> The gifts for those obstructing the gate—the more the better.
> This cannot compare to ordinary city traffic.
> One hundred thousand, bound together, ought to be enough.
> No one would reject a demand for three thousand five hundred.

And a response:

> From of old, gentlemen do not carry gold.
> On reflection, the implications of this are profound.
> If you wish the relatives to be generous.
> Do not annoy us by bringing in these vexations.[27]

Once the gratuities were distributed, an astrologer tossed grains, beans, small fruit, and copper cash by the gate, where children scrambled for them. This act was supposed to propitiate baleful spirits. The bride was then politely asked to get out of the chair. As in classical times, the bride was treated as especially important—a reversal of status corresponding to her liminal state. A green cloth was laid out for her to step on so she would avoid contact with the earth, and her way was led by singing girls with candles, one holding a mirror—to ward off evil spirits—and walking backwards. Two of the bride's maids supported her. Before entering the door, she had to cross over a saddle, a practice known since at least T'ang times.[28] Some Sung observers thought the rite of mounting or stepping over a saddle had non-Han origins, coming from the northern pastoralists during the Northern Dynasties or T'ang; others, however, suggested that it was a pun, the word for saddle (*an*) being a homophone for the word "peace" (*an*).[29]

Once inside the house, the bride was settled within a fake set of curtains (to fool evil spirits) or on the bed. In Hangchow, affinal relatives of the groom would welcome the bride's family, pouring wine for the guests. In Kaifeng, at about this point, outside the bridal chamber, the groom would climb on top of some furniture, from which the matchmaker and affinal relatives, such as his mother's sister, would beg him to descend with offers of wine. He would finally come down only when his mother-in-law made the request. According to Ou-yang Hsiu (1007–1072), "All of the agnatic and affinal relatives of the family celebrating the wedding and all of the male and female guests in the upper and lower rooms stand and watch, considering the 'groom ascending the high place' to be a splendid rite. Failing to perform it is considered a breach of etiquette."[30] The groom's token resistance thus is much like that of the bride, who at various steps had to be coaxed along by the musicians.

From accounts of this rite we know that the women from the bride's family who came to the groom's house for the wedding festivities often included her mother. This was uncanonical; according to the *Etiquette and Ritual,* only attendants are to accompany the bride; her parents say farewell to her in the hall, not even escorting her to the gate.

In both Kaifeng and Hangchow, soon after the bride and groom had entered the house they were tied together with a sash. As seen in Chapter 2, metaphors involving tying and knotting appear often in betrothal letters. These actions now resurface in the rites. The groom took a wooden tablet to which had been tied a piece of cloth in a double "same heart" knot. The other end would be tied to the bride's hand. Then, facing each other, they approached the family altar, the groom leading and walking backwards. At that point a female relative of the groom who had the good fortune of having both her parents alive would use a steelyard or a shuttle to remove the groom's cap, revealing his floral crown. The bride and groom then bowed to the family's gods and to the ancestral altar as well as to the assembled relatives. One reference book has a master of ceremony call out:

> May the bride bow to the gods of heaven and earth, the King Father of the
> East and the Queen Mother of the West.
> May the bride bow to the taboo dragon spirit of the family and the well, stove,
> and gate guardians.
> May the bride bow to all of the spirits served with incense in this house.
> May the bride bow to the great-great-grandfather, the great-grandfather and
> great-grandmother, the grandfather and grandmother.

After the couple went to the incense table, the master of ceremonies would continue:

> May the bride bow to all of the seniors among the agnatic and affinal relatives
> of her parents-in-law.[31]

If one wished to give special emphasis to the introduction to the ancestors, one could also read a prayer, for example:

> Today [give date] your great-grandson [give name] dares to report to [give
> ancestors' and ancestresses' names and titles], along with all the spirits in the
> ancestral temple: Senior grandson [name] has taken the daughter of [name]
> family as his wife. This morning they have performed the great coming home.
> We dare to introduce her according to ritual, with respect and reverence.
> Please enjoy these offerings.[32]

Occasionally educated men saved copies of the prayers they used for these occasions. Han Yüan-chi (1118–1187), when introducing his eldest son's bride, read this prayer:

In the hour *jen-hsü* of the twenty-seventh day, *ping-shen,* of the eleventh month of the fourth year of Ch'un-hsi [1177], the son of so-and-so, of such titles, named Hu, has taken as a wife Miss Ch'ao, the daughter of Tzu-ho, the new deputy prefect of Lu-chou, ranked *ch'ao-feng-lang,* and granddaughter of the drafter Tao. Now on this auspicious day we present her at the ancestral altar. As our connection is close, may the sons and grandsons continue it properly.[33]

The introduction of the bride to the ancestors immediately after her entry into the house was a marked departure from the classics, which specified waiting three months to make sure the woman was a suitable bride. Ssu-ma Kuang noted this deviation but said that the ceremony nevertheless could not be omitted. Chu Hsi, however, wishing to give token observance to the canonical form, proposed waiting until the third day.[34] The classics said nothing about introducing the bride to other deities, including the special guardians of the house. In Sung popular religion, ancestors were just some of the spirits of concern to people, which explains why brides also had to bow to other sorts of deities seen as protecting the family.

After bowing to all those to be honored, the bride would walk backwards, holding the knotted sash, and lead the groom back into the bridal chamber. That the groom pulled her to the larger family's altar and she pulled him to their private bedroom clearly symbolized the differences in their places in the family. At this point a poem would be recited to indicate it was time for the couple to bow to each other. For example:

> One bow must be returned by one bow.
> Why must you be stiff-necked as though holding back?
> Without any instructions the knees are bent and the mandarin drake's
>   curtain lowered.
> Still remember that in front of people you cannot take your time.[35]

Bowing to each other was not mentioned in the classics, but even the most conservative Sung critics thought it was a sensible addition to the rituals. What they did debate was who should bow first—Ssu-ma Kuang contending that the bride should bow first, Ch'eng I the groom, and Chu Hsi having the bride first bow twice, then the groom once, then the whole procedure repeated.[36]

Next the master of ceremonies would toss grain, money, fruit, candies, or the like onto the bed, a gesture undoubtedly evocative of the fertility hoped for from the marriage.[37] This scattering would be accompanied by yet more verses. One reference book gives verses for scattering grains to the four directions plus top, bottom, front, and back.[38] For instance, scattering to the east, the master of ceremonies could recite:

> In the curtained space the candles cast a red glow.
> May your youthful spirit and vigor never dissipate.
> May there be a spring breeze in the painted room day after day.

For scattering above, these lines would be appropriate:

> The mandarin ducks, intertwined, become a pair.
> It is time to have the good dream of a bear
> And see pearls fall into your hands.

The images in these lines allude to love and fertility: mandarin ducks represented loving couples; dreams of bears were believed to portend the birth of sons; and pearls symbolized pregnancy.

Even when the husband's authority was evoked, it was done in a playful way. When it was time to scatter grains behind, the master of ceremonies could sing:

> Long may husband's and wife's harmony be maintained.
> As ever, when the husband sings the wife chimes in.
> She never shouts like the lioness of Ho-tung.

The lioness of Ho-tung was an image for a bossy wife from a poem in which Su Shih (1036–1101) teased a man about his wife.[39]

After scattering the grains, the master of ceremonies would direct a singing girl to take a pair of cups tied with red and green cords in a "same heart knot" and present them to the bride and groom for the "nuptial cup" ceremony, in which they both drank wine. This ceremony had classical precedents, though the *Etiquette and Ritual* called for them to drink from the pieces of a gourd that had been split in two. The nuptial cup ceremony was also marked with a poem, such as:

> The Jade Maiden's red lips take several sips,
> And leave slight traces on the side of the cup.
> The Immortal Lad purposely leaves some of his wine,
> Unwilling to swallow all of the fragrance.[40]

That done, the cups were dropped; if one landed up and the other down, it was considered a lucky omen. Wang Te-ch'en (c.s. 1059) said it portended the birth of many children.[41]

The ceremony of "joining the hair" could come either before or after the nuptial cups. This ceremony, in which locks of hair from each of the spouses were tied into a single topknot, apparently derived from the poems that linked marriage with tying up the hair (see Chapter 2). Most Sung scholars seem to have thought the custom was ignorant, based on a misinterpretation of the verses.[42] The fact that lines from famous poems, taken out of context, could lead to their enactment in wedding ceremonies is yet another sign of the power of literary images. And of course, the popularity of the ceremony only made the images more potent. In Sung times, the phrase "joining the hair" was commonly used to refer to the beginning of married life.

In Hangchow, after joining the hair, the groom would pluck one of the bride's flowers (accompanied by verses), and the bride would untie the string holding the groom's flower crown together so that the flowers would fall onto the bed. Flowers often symbolize sexuality in Chinese imagery, as appears to be the case here. The groom then would ask that the curtains be closed. Those gathered around would hear more poems marking both the closing of the door to the room and its subsequent opening.[43]

In Hangchow, after the bride changed her costume, the master of ceremonies would lead the new couple into the main hall, where they greeted the guests and received their congratulations. (In the classical rituals the bride did not meet the guests, and did not even meet her parents-in-law until the next day.) Then the two sets of parents wished each other well, and the banquet would begin, preceded by many rounds of toasts. A wedding without a banquet was hardly a wedding at all. One judge, suspecting that a woman claiming rights to a dead man's property had never actually been married to him, questioned her thus: "On the evening of the wedding, which relatives got together, which neighbors were invited, and who was the cook for the banquet?"[44]

In Kaifeng, the morning after the wedding the bride would rise early and first bow to a mirror placed on a table in the hall, then bow to the seniors among her new relatives, giving each embroidered satin shoes or pillows. They would reciprocate with gifts of bolts of cloth. These ceremonies had parallels to the classical entertaining of the bride by her parents-in-law on the second day.

For the next month, contact between the two families now linked by marriage followed set forms. On the third day the bride's family would send some more silks and a wide assortment of food: goose eggs, oil, honey, tea, biscuits, goose, lamb, and fruit. Chu Hsi depicted the bride as using the food to entertain her parents-in-law.

> On this day, at meal time, the bride's family supplies a full meal and wine jars. The bride's followers set out a table with vegetables and fruit in the hall in front of the parents-in-law. They place the wash basin to the southeast of the ceremonial steps and the towel rack to the east. Once the parents-in-law have taken their seats, the bride washes her hands and goes up via the western steps. She washes the cups, pours the wine, and puts a cup of it on her father-in-law's table. She goes back down, waiting for him to finish drinking. Then, bowing again, she serves her mother-in-law. She brings the wine, and her mother-in-law receives it. After she finishes drinking, the bride goes down. She bows, then takes the meal up and offers it to her parents-in-law. She waits in attendance behind her mother-in-law. When they are finished eating, the bride removes the rice. Servants take away the remainder of the meal and distribute it to the other rooms. The bride eats what the mother-in-law left, her followers eat what the father-in-law left, and the groom's followers also eat what the bride left.[45]

On the first, third, seventh, or ninth day, the groom or the new couple together would visit the bride's parents. The bride's family would entertain lavishly, giving gifts to the groom and sending him back accompanied by musicians. A return visit would be made when a month had passed, with the groom's family inviting the bride's relations to a meal.

The steps followed for weddings are best known for Kaifeng and Hangchow, but all over the country people seem to have stretched their resources to put on stylish weddings. Ssu-ma Kuang observed that in Lu-chou (Anhwei) relatives would compete to give parties to congratulate a family on a wedding, these parties going on for forty days. Liao Kang (1070–1143) reported that in Chang-chou (Fukien), even ordinary people incurred great expenses for wedding banquets, since they had to invite all their relatives and neighbors, sometimes several hundred people. Chuang Ch'o (ca. 1090–ca. 1150) noted that poor people who dressed in hemp cloth all their lives would wear silk for the three days of their weddings. He also commented that the customs in the south differed from those of the central plain in many particulars, though his examples seem but minor variations. For instance, when the bride arrived at the groom's gate, rather than an astrologer tossing coins and sweets to keep evil spirits away, a medium from a local temple would burn paper money and ask the spirits to keep the bride's family away. In both cases, however, an expert is brought in to protect the groom's house from unwanted interference that might enter its gate when it is opened to admit the bride. Similarly, Chuang reported a kind of teasing of the bride that was probably comparable in function to much of the versifying in other sources.[46] One might also add that the basic structure of these rites, and even specific steps such as covering the ground with a cloth and flashing a mirror when the bride entered the house, continued into modern times.[47]

For all the sober disquisitions on the seriousness of marriage and the duties of a wife, weddings seem to have been rather raucous occasions, marked by gleeful high spirits. The young couple were swept along in a crowd, teased, and made to perform while tied to each other. No one had to quiet down to listen to them say anything: they never took vows or spoke to the group.

For the guests, weddings must have been great fun, with their brilliant colors, festive singing, erotically charged playfulness, and bountiful food. Not only were the bride and groom wearing fancy clothes, jewels, and flowers, but there were singing girls dressed in bright colors as well. Music was a part of the wedding from the time the sedan chair first set off, and special songs marked every stage of the wedding ritual. Many of these songs were probably well known to anyone who had been to a few weddings, and people likely joined in to sing them. "To sing the song of the new groom" was a common way of referring to a man getting married.

For the parents of the bride and groom, weddings were undoubtedly enormously taxing on their time, energy, and resources, but they also provided a good opportunity to demonstrate to friends, neighbors, and relatives that they were doing well: they had made a good match and were able to celebrate it with style. They had positions of honor as the parents of the couple and would be congratulated by everyone who attended. They would end up exhausted but proud that everything had gone so well.

For the bride and groom, weddings must have been as intimidating as they were exciting. The couple were treated as very special people and got more attention than they ever had before, but the attention they got was highly embarrassing. Still, it took their minds off the larger worries they faced: would they get along well? The bride, of course, had more to worry about in this regard than the groom. His only concern was compatibility. She also had to worry about whether she could please her mother-in-law and avoid provoking the others in the house.

The whole ritual sequence, from the initial stages of betrothal through the post-wedding exchanges, was full of symbols. The differences between men and women—or rather, husbands and wives—were highlighted and celebrated. The bride covered her face, rode in a covered vehicle, and stayed behind bed curtains or in a closed room while the man went out among the guests, expecting to be seen. At the same time, the distinction and separation of male and female were symbolically overcome by repeated emphasis on pairing and joining.

Rituals do not convey meanings in the same way didactic tracts do; therefore, wedding rituals were excellent occasions for giving expression to and symbolically resolving some of the tensions inherent in gender relations and patrilocal marriage. There were opportunities to express reluctance and resistance and to allude to sexuality and fertility. Confucian scholars, immersed in the study of texts that emphasized the patrilineal-patriarchal-patrilocal model of kinship, were often at something of a loss when evaluating wedding ceremonies. It was relatively easy for them to approve accretions of custom that seemed to reinforce this model—the bride and groom bowing to each other, for instance; but frivolity, allusions to sexuality, and extravagant expenditures all troubled them. Ssu-ma Kuang objected to what modern scholars would see as aspects of the liminal phase, when the normal rules for young men and women were suspended. Thus he did not like the practice of brides being carried in sedan chairs or grooms wearing flowers in their hair. He also insisted that the canonical ban on music be observed.[48]

Anxieties concerning the bride as a potentially disturbing factor in the family may explain why, in weddings, she is so passive. Although the groom does not do much, he at least goes to get her, addresses her father, and brings her back. The bride, by contrast, says not a word and never moves unless others lead her or instruct her. It is true that she is dressed in finery and carried in a sedan chair—a princess for a day. But her symbolic elevation is not matched by symbolic references to her ability to do things other than reproduce. Was this because people were afraid that wives might, indeed, do things, and not simply slip into a preassigned slot with no friction? Such would be one reading of the story "The Shrew," about a wedding that went awry. The spirited and talkative bride resisted the instructions of the go-between and the master of ceremonies, provoking the parents of the groom to exclaim, "It was earlier agreed that our son would marry the daughter of a respectable family. Who would have known it would turn out to be this ill-mannered, ill-bred, long-tongued wayward peasant girl?" The astrologer managed to mollify them and the ceremony continued, but the bride disrupted the ceremony again, provoking her new husband to exclaim, "Of the thousands of misfortunes, to have married this peasant woman!"[49] This tale is a farce, but the audience would not have laughed if they did not recognize some elements in the situation.

Little emphasis has been given here to chronological shifts in marriage rites. Although some customs evidently lost popularity (such as the "groom ascending the high place"), and the descriptions of the customs of the two capitals are not identical, temporal change seems to be of a lesser magnitude, all things considered, than regional variation and class differences. In fact, it could be that what appears to be change over time is in fact change in the class or regional basis of the available sources. But this does not mean that betrothal and wedding rituals have to be dealt with ahistorically. We can still embed them in history by placing them in the context of other aspects of marriage and other historical developments. The tensions symbolically resolved in these rituals were ones tied to basic features of the family system as well as common ideas about gender differences. Both the growing prosperity of the society and the enhanced opportunities for families to raise their prestige through good marriages clearly contributed to the celebration (and the masking) of the exchange aspects of marriage. The fashion-consciousness of the growing cities, especially the two capitals with their concentration of officials and rich merchants, must likewise have shaped the willingness of residents to spend freely to put on a good show.

FIVE

Dowries

What was in the cases that the family of the bride delivered the day before the wedding? Did their value warrant the emphasis placed on listing their contents in the first stage of marriage negotiations? Who got to use the items in the dowry? These are just some of the many questions that need to be answered to understand how marriage, in Sung times, served as an occasion for the reallocation of property from one generation to the next. Parents and grandparents carefully scrutinized potential mates for their children not only because they worried about the character of their future relatives, but also because financial considerations were at stake. A family with several sons might seek daughters-in-law with handsome dowries to cushion the effects of property division among the sons. Families willing to send their daughters well supplied would in turn expect to make good matches with families of substance. Thus, the transmission of property through daughters played a large part in the complex mechanisms that reproduced class inequalities.[1]

THE CONTENT OF THE CASES

Miss Cheng Ch'ing-i, married in 1264 at seventeen sui, brought into her marriage not only substantial landholdings (five hundred *mu*, nearly a hundred acres, probably enough for a dozen tenant families to farm) but also a trousseau composed primarily of luxury fabrics. It had a length of gold-washed tie-dyed silk, another of thin green silk for official robes, two of gauze in different patterns, two pairs of topknot strings, some fifteen pieces of embroidery, and thirty pieces of red tie-dyed cloth. It also included three sets of ritual books in "double goldfish" bags.[2]

Records of legal cases show that, even if wives rarely had as much land as Miss Cheng, landed dowries were nothing unusual. Called "trousseau land" or "land accompanying a woman on marriage," such dowries could vary considerably in size. The land set aside for Miss Chiang's dowry had been assigned a tax obligation of thirty-one piculs of grain, making it about ten to fifteen *mu* in size. Miss Ch'ü had been assigned a dowry of land by her grandfather after her father died; with a tax obligation of sixty-six piculs, it was in the vicinity of twenty-five *mu*. Miss Ch'en brought a dowry of land measured at 120 *chung,* Miss Chang, one of ten-odd *chung* (a local unit for measuring cultivated land). Miss Shih, early orphaned, was given land by her uncle for her dowry, which was later sold for over four hundred strings of cash. By contrast, Miss Ts'ai's dowry of land, when pawned, brought only twenty strings of cash.[3] Hung Mai told of a woman who, having no brothers, inherited her family's property and thus brought into her marriage land worth ten thousand strings of cash.[4]

The size of dowries was often expressed in terms of strings of cash (each containing, theoretically, a thousand coins), and dowries undoubtedly often did include ready cash. Ch'in Kuei's (1090–1155) wife reportedly claimed to bring a dowry worth two hundred thousand strings. And a minor official, after his wife died, used part of her dowry to buy a concubine and still had a thousand strings left. Feng Ching's (1021–1094) mother had silver that she gave her husband to buy a concubine, since she had had no sons. Sometimes women even had gold in their dowries. A rather unusual item in one girl's dowry was a two-foot statue of a lion carved in white jade.[5]

The other important items in women's dowries were clothing and jewelry. A well-to-do family would apparently send a daughter off with a great many sets of clothes, enough to last her many years, if not her entire life. Miss Huang Sheng (1227–1243) died the year after she married a distant member of the imperial clan living in Fu-chou (Fukien) and was buried with what probably had been her dowry. The items included 201 pieces of women's clothing and 153 lengths of cloth in various often highly elaborate designs.[6] Hung Mai told of a Miss Chou who died at twenty-one without having married; yet she had already woven thirty-three bolts of open-weave silk, seventy of plain silk, and 156 pieces of coarse silk, all for her dowry.[7] Fine silk clothes can last a very long time, especially when kept locked in trunks. Women not infrequently gave away some of the clothes and jewelry in their dowries to young female relatives, especially in their husbands' families, so that they, too, would have impressive dowries.[8] Dowries thus were composed in part of women's property, passed from one woman to another.

Jewelry did not have to find its way into another woman's dowry to circulate: it often was sold for cash. Miss Liu (1192–1249), we are told, sold her jewelry to buy books and paintings for her husband.[9] Bolts of cloth could also be sold. A dog butcher's wife had brought a dowry worth several dozen strings of cash. Years later, when her husband decided to give up butchering, she still had enough bolts of cloth left to use as capital to set him up in another business.[10]

DOWRY ESCALATION

Until the Sung period, the families of the groom generally seem to have had to spend more on betrothal gifts than the families of brides had to spend on dowries. The classics make little mention of dowries, but in other Chou sources there is scattered evidence of brides bringing dowries of clothes, jewelry, and household items. By Han times the bride's family, if rich, might well supply their daughter with a handsome dowry, and weddings of either sons or daughters could prove a financial burden for parents of any economic class. By the T'ang period, and probably earlier, among the upper class it was expected that the bride's family would use the betrothal gifts presented them by the man's family to prepare the dowry for their daughter, making no profit themselves.[11]

Pressure to provide substantial dowries grew in the early Sung.[12] By the mid–eleventh century it was taken for granted that a family needed more money to get a daughter married out than to obtain a bride for a son. Fan Chung-yen (989–1052), for example, when he set up rules for the outlays of his charitable estate in 1050, assigned thirty strings of cash for a daughter's marriage, twenty for a son's. Dowry escalation soon reached the point where families would borrow money to provide dowries for girls. Su Shih reportedly borrowed two hundred strings of cash to supply the dowry for a female relative.[13] Ts'ai Hsiang (1012–1067), while prefect of Fu-chou (Fukien) in the 1050s, posted a notice pointing out that "the purpose of marriage is to produce heirs, not to acquire wealth." Instead of recognizing this truth, people ignored family standing in choosing brides, their minds set entirely on the dowry. Once the dowry was delivered to the groom's home, "they inspect the dowry cases, in the morning searching through one, in the evening another. The husband cruelly keeps making more and more demands on his wife. If he is not satisfied, it can spoil their love or even lead to divorce. This custom has persisted for so long that people accept it as normal."[14]

Ssu-ma Kuang saw greed for dowries running rampant among prospective parents-in-law, some of whom "even draw up a contract saying 'such goods, in such numbers, such goods, in such numbers,' thereby treating their daughter as an item in a sales transaction. There are also cases where people go back on their agreements after the wedding is over. These are the methods used by brokers dealing in male and female bondservants. How can such a transaction be called a gentleman-official [shih-ta-fu] marriage?" Ssu-ma Kuang was convinced that treating marriage like a transaction was bad both for the bride and for her family. The bride would not be protected by her property; rather, she would be endangered by it:

> When the parents-in-law have been deceived [about the size of the dowry], they will maltreat the daughter-in-law as a way to vent their fury. Fearing this, those who love their daughter put together generous dowries in the hope of pleasing her parents-in-law, not realizing that such covetous, vulgar people are insatiable. When the dowry is depleted, what use will the bride be to these parents-in-law? They will then "pawn" her to get further payment from her family. Her family's wealth has a limit, but their demands will never stop. Therefore, families linked by marriage often end up enemies.[15]

Dowry, in Ssu-ma Kuang's view, was also corrupting in that "a bride chosen because of greediness for transient wealth and rank will seldom fail to presume upon them and treat her husband with contempt and her parents-in-law with disdain." Ssu-ma Kuang therefore hoped to discourage "men of spirit" from trying to get rich by using their wives' assets or to gain promotions through their influence.[16]

A century later, the dowry crisis had still not abated, for Yüan Ts'ai (ca. 1140–after 1195) could argue that if a family did not begin planning for their daughter's dowry when she was very young, they would have to "sell land or buildings as temporary expedients, or callously watch [their] daughter's humiliation in front of others."[17] Yüan Ts'ai also complained that matchmakers try to interest families in a match by exaggerating the dowry to the boy's family and telling the girl's family that they will not have to use any of their own money for it.[18] Choosing brides according to the size of their dowries was apparently common enough that one author took pains to point out that Miss Pien (1155–1203) had never acted that way. Neither did she pay any attention to dowry size when picking daughters-in-law, nor did she let the discrepancies in the size of her daughters-in-law's dowries influence her treatment of them once they had entered her house.[19]

Dowry escalation was not confined to the families of the rich and high-ranking. Ts'ai Hsiang's notice, after all, was posted for the general population. One observer commented that in the far south, poor girls of fourteen or fifteen worked to earn their own dowries so that their families did not have a single cash of expense.[20] Judges never registered surprise that families neither wealthy nor well educated would give land as part of daughters' dowries, as in a case concerning an uneducated family with sons, where a daughter's dowry nonetheless included mountain land.[21] Some Sung officials complained that the expenses associated with dowries were so high that some girls could not marry. One official even attributed female infanticide to the exorbitant cost of dowries.[22] Hou K'o (1007–1079), while magistrate of Hua-ch'eng (Szechwan), found that many girls grew old without marrying because "when people of Pa take wives they always demand property from the girl's family." His solution was to make up a schedule of the appropriate size of dowries according to the wealth of the family and to declare that anyone who exceeded those figures would be punished. Within a year, we are told, no over-age spinsters remained. Sun Chüeh (1028–1090) reportedly found a similar situation in Fu-chou (Fukien) and simply issued an order that dowries were not to exceed one hundred strings of cash, an act that promptly led to several hundred weddings.[23]

The escalation in dowry cost was undoubtedly one by-product of the emphasis the educated class put on making good marriage alliances (see Chapter 3). Dowries have often escalated in other societies, apparently for similar reasons.[24] By offering valuable betrothal gifts to the family of a prospective daughter-in-law, a man was facilitating the girl's entry into his home with a handsome dowry; he was not, however, making a contribution to the financial health of her natal family, for they would use his gift toward her dowry. Dowry, by contrast, involved direct transfer from one patriline to another and thus would substantially improve the attractiveness of the match in the eyes of the man's family. Although the groom's father was not to have any control over his daughter-in-law's dowry, and even his son was supposed to gain his wife's consent on its use, it would eventually go to his son's sons and daughters. This fact would not be trivial to a man worried about the eventual division of the family property among several sons.

Daughters' families were willing to invest in their dowries because affinal relationships were stronger when property was involved. The parents of the bride could expect more help from their daughter, her husband, and her sons when they had married her out with a substantial dowry. Yüan Ts'ai advised families with ample property to give their daughters a share, for if their sons proved incapable they might have to depend on their daughters' families, even for their funerals and ancestral sacrifices.[25] Dowry strengthened affinal ties because it created lingering claims to common property. Just as brothers were bound to each other as coparceners of graveyards and ancestral halls even after division of the household, affinal relatives were linked through mutual interest in the disposition of the dowry, and this kept their ties alive.

DOWRY AS A SHARE OF FAMILY PROPERTY

As dowries grew ever more substantial, they became an awkward element in the overall system of transmitting property. According to Chinese property law, all the men in the family (father, grandfather, brothers, sons, nephews, and so on) were coparceners in the estate, which means that they had rights to shares at division. When a father or grandfather was family head, he had nearly unlimited authority in the management of the family property, including the options of selling it or borrowing against it. When an uncle or elder brother was family head, he would need the agreement of any of those who were not his descendants before he could sell or mortgage property. When property was divided, it was done on the principle of equality among brothers. In this property regime, women were largely irrelevant. Neither daughters nor wives nor widows received shares in the same way men did. When they did receive or control property, it was by default, when suitable men were not available.

This model of property transmission is clearly not the whole story, for families regularly made substantial outlays for daughters' dowries. But dowry was not governed in any comparable way by a single, consistent set of ideas or practices. Fathers had wide discretion in deciding how much to assign their daughters as dowry. The pervasive practice of sending daughters off with dowries engendered a variety of intellectual and legal responses, ranging between two poles: one that supported daughters' and wives' claims to property, the other that minimized them. This divergence has perplexed modern scholars, whose arguments have assumed there could be only one law and one way to interpret it.[26] Yet conflicting evaluations did coexist, and indeed engendered each other. As social forces such as competition for desirable sons-in-law pushed up the value of dowries, women's claims to dowries gained greater recognition, and at the same time those troubled by the implications of the dowry system tried to change it. I see no simple chronological shift from one view to the other; rather, as dowry became better established both responses became more obvious.

Ssu-ma Kuang was troubled by dowry. His ideal was the undivided family of several generations depth. Women's dowries, if kept separate, continually threatened the survival of such families. He thus argued that wives should not treat their dowries as private property, citing with approval a passage from the *Book of Rites* which said that a daughter-in-law should "have nothing of her own, neither personal savings, nor private belongings." Even gifts she received had to be turned over to her parents-in-law, and she could make no gifts herself, not even of the things she had once received as gifts.[27] Any suggestion that daughters had rights to family property was abhorrent to Ssu-ma Kuang. He pointed to the tragedy of a contemporary who had built up his family's property but had neglected the moral education of his children and grandchildren. After he died, not only did his sons fight over the property, but also "his unmarried daughters veiled their heads, grasped the documents, and personally laid charges before the government in a struggle for their dowries," making a laughing stock of the family.[28]

How many people shared Ssu-ma Kuang's misgivings is hard to say. Most people do seem to have recognized that the fate of unmarried girls could hinge almost entirely on their dowries, and repeatedly told stories of girls who fell from high to low station when they lost access to property. Orphaned daughters without dowries—even daughters from official families—might be forced to become concubines or even maids. Liu Fu (ca. 1040–after 1113) recorded the case of an official's daughter, Miss Wang Ch'iung-nu, who was used to a life of luxury and able to embroider and compose poetry. When she was in her mid-teens her father was dismissed from office, and on the road home both he and his wife died. Ch'iung-nu's elder brother and his wife then left with most of the property, whereupon her fiancé refused to marry her now that she was poor. An old servant who remained with her finally convinced her to become the concubine of a rich official. Liu Fu then described the misery she endured, regular beaten by the wife.[29]

Probably because of the disastrous consequences awaiting daughters without dowries, Sung law provided some protection for orphaned girls from the greed of brothers, uncles, and other potential heirs.[30] Already in the T'ang, if brothers who were dividing property included one not yet married, or if they had unmarried sisters or aunts, the marriage expenses were to be set aside before the division was made. Unmarried brothers were to be given the funds for a betrothal gift in addition to their share, and unmarried sisters were to get half as much as unmarried sons.[31] This law was probably intended to codify practice in the T'ang, when the man's family gave betrothal gifts that cost more than the net outlay of the bride's family. In the Sung, the law was revised to match Sung custom more closely, for Southern Sung judges quoted rules giving unmarried daughters larger shares of family property as dowries. The basic rule was that unmarried daughters were to be assigned a share or portion for their dowries equal to half a son's share of the estate, not, as in T'ang times, half the size of the allotment for his marriage expenses. This formula would mean that when a boy and two girls survived, none yet married, the boy would get half the property and each girl a quarter.[32]

When judges supervised division of an estate, they might cite the rule that daughters get half of what sons get but apply it loosely.[33] In a case in the *Judicial Decisions,* for instance, a man died leaving two daughters, the eldest nine sui. A posthumous heir was appointed for him. Rather than giving a quarter to the heir and three-eighths to each of the daughters (as the statutes specified), the judge gave each one-third, with the daughters' property earmarked for their dowries.[34] Even so, these girls were getting sizable dowries. In another case, one of three brothers who had not yet divided their property died leaving a single daughter (his wife was also dead). An earlier official had said the daughter should get one-third of what would normally go to her father, but the judge revised this to half on the grounds that she had not been married when her father died and a girl should get half as much as a son, and in this case a son would get it all. Moreover, he ruled that all of the private property of the girl's father's branch (such as her mother's dowry) should go to her.[35]

Liu K'o-chuang (1187–1269) provides the most lengthy discussion of orphaned daughters' property rights. The case concerned the T'ien family (see Diagram 5). The father, an assistant magistrate, had adopted a son. After his wife died, he took a concubine, Miss Liu, who bore a son and two

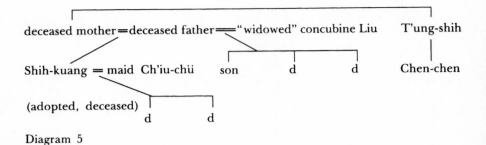

Diagram 5

daughters. His elder son died after having two daughters born to a maid, who was listed only by her personal name, Ch'iu-chü (Fall Chrysanthemum). The father's younger brother T'ung-shih wished to have his own son, Chen-chen, established as posthumous heir to the deceased elder son. Thus there were three surviving adults—the son's maid, the father's concubine, and the father's brother—each trying to maximize the shares for his or her own offspring. Liu K'o-chuang discussed this case from several angles, bringing in a variety of considerations besides the letter of the law, such as the need to get the suit settled and the awkwardness of giving the young girls shares of different sizes. He pointed out that if a posthumous heir was appointed for the elder son, that son's share of the estate should be divided in four, with one share for the appointed heir and the other three divided between the two granddaughters (each getting three-eighths of the son's allotment, in other words, or three-sixteenths of the whole). He also noted that the two young daughters of the deceased official deserved shares half the size of their brother's. However, rather than divide the property into three (one-third for the granddaughters and the adopted heir of the elder son, one-third for the younger son, and one-third for the two daughters), Liu K'o-chuang divided the property in half, one part to go to the offspring of the concubine, the other part to the offspring of the wife, now represented by the elder son's maid. In the first instance, half (that is, a quarter of the whole estate) was allocated to the son, and a quarter (an eighth of the whole) went to each daughter. In the second instance, one-quarter was apportioned to the adopted heir—assuming a suitable candidate could be found—and one-quarter to each of the girls, with the last quarter reserved for the funeral expenses of their father. The widowed concubine was left in control of the movable property, not because this was proper, but because Liu K'o-chuang wished to bring an end to the lawsuit.[36] The rights of each set of unmarried daughters to sizable chunks of the estate for their dowries were thus protected, even though there was a natural son and a potential adoptee.

Lawsuits over dowries were apparently not rare, and Yüan Ts'ai urged guardians to be careful. Men should give their daughters "dowries appropriate to their family's wealth" and keep the law in mind when taking charge of orphaned kinswomen. "When orphaned daughters have shares in the family property, marry them with as generous dowries as possible. When it is fitting that they get land, they should certainly be given it in accordance with the law. If you think only of the present and begrudge it, you will certainly be sued after the marriage."[37]

Dowries were not the only property married women might receive from their natal families. If they had no brothers or unmarried sisters and their parents died without having established an heir, married daughters would receive a share of the property under the rules for "broken lines," the proportion depending on how many sisters there were. Generally, all the married sisters were to share one-third of the estate, even if an heir was established posthumously (see Chapter 13). Even women who had brothers might get property if the parents left it to them in a will. For instance, a family's wealth might have increased considerably after a daughter's marriage, and the parents might feel that her share in the form of dowry had been inadequate. In the *Judicial Decisions,* judges upheld the right of parents to will property to their married daughters even when they had sons or adopted sons.[38] (The property unmarried daughters got in cases of "broken lines" is discussed in Chapter 13.)

WIVES' CONTROL OF THEIR DOWRIES

Giving daughters dowries has been a common practice in many societies, but married women's rights over the use and disposal of their dowries have varied considerably across place and time. In Renaissance Florence, husbands managed their wives' dowries, using them to cover ordinary household expenses. In early modern England, husbands gained full control over the cash, furniture, and other movables of the dowry. In northwest India in recent times, the bride's parents-in-law could distribute items from the dowry among family members, specifying only a certain share for the bride and groom. In modern Greece, women brought land as dowry into their marriages and retained control over it during their lifetime.[39]

In Sung China, dowry was a somewhat anomalous sort of property. It was not registered as a separate estate under the wife's name, for the government wanted property to be registered by household, under the name of the male household head whenever there was one. Nevertheless, the property was to be clearly labeled as a woman's dowry property, as this fact would continue to be relevant to its proper use, not only for as long as the woman lived but until the claims of all heirs were settled.[40] As long as brothers lived together, their wives' dowries were considered "wife's property," not subject to division. Indeed, men were sometimes accused of putting land in their wives' names to keep it out of the pool for division. One judge defended a son and daughter-in-law from his father's efforts to take the fields she had brought as dowry: "According to the law, assets acquired from a wife's family are not within the bounds of division."[41]

Wives' claims were weakest vis-à-vis their husbands. Judges occasionally cited a rule that dowry land was something husband and wife controlled together,[42] but it is doubtful that wives could easily stop their husbands from using it for ends they rejected. Husbands might simply appropriate their wives' property. The *Sung History* mentions a woman who returned to her natal home, to be supported by her brother's widow, after her husband used up all the property she had received from her parents.[43] Even in cases of uxorilocal marriage (see Chapter 13), judges do not seem to have cared whether property was listed as the wife's or the husband's. Wives could not turn to the courts for protection because they had no legal standing to bring suits against their husbands. The husband was the legal representative of his wife, or, as Chinese jurists put it, the marriage made them one unit.[44] The *Judicial Decisions* contains no case in which a wife accused her husband of selling her dowry without her permission. Thus, wives had property rights not fully backed up by more general legal rights. Even so, there were some limits on husbands' freedom. Once when a husband accused the wife he was trying to divorce of stealing his property, the judge ruled that a wife's taking the things she had brought as her dowry did not constitute theft.[45]

In biographies, women are often praised for unselfishness with regard to their dowries. For instance, in the early eleventh century Miss Chao (1008–1039), from a rich official family, was married to a man who passed the examinations at seventeen, the first in his family to have an official career. According to her biography, she felt uncomfortable having so much private property when her husband's family was poor, so contributed it all to the common pool.[46] Miss Shang-kuan (1094–1178), as we saw in the Introduction, stopped her husband when he was about to borrow money to try to redeem the ancestral graves that a relative had illicitly sold. She emptied her chests to redeem the hill and with the remainder bought more land on which she erected a building for the protection of the graveyard. The biography of Miss Fan (1143–1222), who in 1160 married into a family with less than three *mu* of land, reports that she told her husband that his property might be enough for the present but it would not be enough for their descendants. Consequently, when a neighbor wanted to sell his land, she quickly sold the land she had brought as dowry to raise the purchase price and then gave the deed to her father-in-law. Miss Chang's (1146–1195) biography records that she sold five *mu* of her dowry land to supply the money needed for her husband's brother to get a second wife after his first had died.[47]

These biographies were written by scholars who did not fully approve of wives' treating dowry as private property. They portrayed wives as willingly using all or part of their dowries for larger family purposes, such as ancestral rites, funerals, or marriages of their husbands' siblings, thus demonstrating that they were good "inner helpers" (see Chapter 6). Liu Tsai (1166–1239), for instance, noted that women by nature are stingy. Thus, Miss Chao Wu-chen (1154–1224) was exceptional, for not only did she turn over all of her ample dowry and dowry fields to her husband, but she also never asked for an accounting of the income or expenses.[48]

After a woman's death her dowry generally passed to her husband or children, but some women apparently expressed wishes about the disposition of their dowries. Miss Chao (1035–1110), for instance, reportedly told her daughters-in-law on her deathbed: "Everything in my cases is from my dowry. I never added a single item for my use. I want it to be given to all of the children and grandchildren" (that is, not her own progeny alone). When husbands took over their wives' dowries there may have been some lingering sentiment that it should not be used for purposes the wife would have disapproved. One man had to use what was left of his wife's dowry to pay for Buddhist services on her behalf when, as a ghost, she caused trouble after he used her property to buy a concubine.[49]

DOWRY AS A SOURCE OF FAMILY FRICTION

As we have seen, Ssu-ma Kuang believed that families prepared generous dowries for their daughters out of concern for their welfare. And many families clearly thought that sending their daughter well supplied would strengthen the ties between the two families. Yet dowry, like any sort of property, could easily cause friction, turning relatives into enemies. A man might marry a woman for her wealth, then turn her out.[50] And orphans with dowries did not necessarily fare well, for their guardians—uncles, brothers-in-law, or other relatives—occasionally proved reluctant to see them married and lose access to their property. One judge suspected such motives in a case concerning a man who managed the property of his deceased uncle, land that properly belonged to the uncle's daughter and granddaughter. The daughter had already reached twenty-five without any marriage being arranged, and although a marriage had been discussed for the granddaughter, nothing had been done about it. "Keeping Hsiu-niang at home," the judge observed, "is really a strategy for occupying the land."[51]

Dowries of land were sometimes promised rather than actually delivered at the time of the wedding. That, at least, seems to be the implication of a legal case in which Liao Wan-ying sued to procure the land his wife's uncle had assigned her as dowry. Unfortunately, the uncle had entrusted it to her brother to manage, and he in turn had sold it to pay his debts. The judge agreed that the brother was wrong but offered no help to the husband, telling him a real man does not marry to get a dowry and he should try not to make relations between the two families any worse.[52]

Girls with substantial dowries naturally made desirable daughters-in-law, and various ploys were used to secure them. One lawsuit concerned the daughters of remarried parents. The wife's daughter by her former husband was an heiress; the husband's daughter by his former wife could expect nothing special. The heiress had been betrothed by her father as a child, and her fiancé sued when he discovered that her mother and new husband were trying to substitute the girl with the smaller dowry.[53]

Women were often victims in these cases, but they also could be victimizers. After Li Chieh-weng died, leaving behind only a young daughter and the maid who had borne her, the local government arranged for distribution of his property, part for an appointed heir and part for the daughter, still in her mother's care. The mother, however, took her daughter's land to use as her own dowry and married before her former master was even buried. The young girl was engaged and sent to her prospective husband's relatives to be taken care of as a future bride. Later, because the government was holding her movable property (cash and silver objects), the mother and her new husband snatched her back to try to get access to it.[54]

As an example of the mixture of blessings and problems women's property could entail, consider the case of Tu Yen (978–1057), one of the most eminent men of the early Sung. In his biography of Tu, Ou-yang Hsiu (1007–1072) stressed the family's illustrious history back to eminent officials of the T'ang. He reported that the Tu family had been very rich, but when the property was divided Tu Yen let his brothers take all of his share, since they were poor. Chang Fang-p'ing (1007–1091), in his biography of Yen's wife, Miss Hsiang-li (988–1065), mentioned further that Tu Yen's father died when he was a small child and that his mother returned home, leaving him with few relatives on whom to depend.[55] A less varnished version of Tu Yen's family background is given by Ssu-ma Kuang. Tu's father, according to this account, died before Tu was born, and he was raised by his grandfather. Tu Yen's two half brothers by his father's previous wife were unpleasant to his mother, so she left to marry into another family. When Tu Yen was fifteen or sixteen, his grandfather died. His two older half brothers demanded that he turn over his mother's "private property"—meaning her dowry—which was apparently in Tu Yen's possession but which they claimed on the grounds that she had married out. When he refused, they resorted to force. One drew a sword and wounded Tu Yen on the head. Bleeding profusely, he fled to his aunt, who hid him from his half brothers, saving his life. With no paternal home to go to, he turned to his mother, but her new husband would not let him stay. Tu Yen then traveled around, very poor, supporting himself by working as a scribe. (So much for the way he selflessly renounced his share of the family property!) On his travels, Tu Yen impressed a rich man surnamed Hsiang-li, who not only gave him his daughter to be his wife but also provided means enough for him to live rather comfortably. Tu Yen was then able to take the *chin-shih* examinations, in which he finished fourth. Later, after he had reached high rank, he repaid his debt to the Hsiang-li family by using his "protection" privilege to get his wife's brother an official post.[56]

The implications of a story like this are severalfold. A man of good family without resources, like Tu Yen, could become established by marrying the daughter of a wealthy family thanks to the dowry provided for her. Yet such "women's property" could also cause enmity between brothers: it was because of his mother's property, after all, that Tu Yen was stabbed by his half brother, making it necessary for him to run away from home and thus breaking the ties of the patrilineal family. Moreover, this property had not even assured his mother a comfortable widowhood, for his half brothers were able to harass her into leaving the family empty-handed.

At least since Engels, if not earlier, scholars have identified women's rights to property as the key to their social and political position. The argument is that where such rights are limited—where, for instance, women cannot inherit from their fathers or own land in their own names if married—their power in the family and the larger society is correspondingly limited, and the cultural evaluation of their worth is narrow if not clearly negative.[57] Recently Jack Goody has shown that societies in which dowry is practiced tend to be ones with monogamy, relatively rare divorce, the possibility of women inheriting family property, and a fairly high general status of women.[58] The theory that women are better off when they can own property is today little questioned, and Western nations regularly urge other countries to revise their law codes to give women rights to property equal to those enjoyed by men.

What did dowries mean to women in the Sung? Did possessing a dowry enhance a woman's standing, her freedom of action, her ability to command respect or influence family decisions? The psychological value of entering marriage with cases full of clothes, jewelry, and deeds to land was probably as important to the wife as what she could do with the property. First, it testified to the fact that she was not a concubine: she had not been sold by her family; to the contrary, they had considered her so important that they sent her out with lots of goods. Second, it provided her with some means of pleasing others—a large part of her job as a young bride. As will be seen in the next chapter, brides often tried to win the favor of their in-laws by handing out items from their dowries. Third, a dowry gave some small measure of assurance that the woman would not be reduced to destitution. Dowries sometimes were the main means of support for widows (see Chapter 10), could be taken into second marriages (Chapter 11), and could be the basis for adoption of an heir to make sacrifices to them (Chapter 13). Fourth, dowries made wives more relevant to the prosperity of the family, thus mitigating at least slightly the devaluation of women implicit in patrilineal kinship reckoning.

Within the long course of Chinese history, the Sung seems to have been the period in which wives and daughters fared best with regard to dowries. One reason dowries were later curbed probably also goes back to the Sung, for already in that era Confucian scholars had mixed feelings about women's rights to and over dowries. Ssu-ma Kuang, for one, decried the insidious effects of women treating their dowries as their private property; yet his view of the family, focused as it was on the group that shared common property, undermined his own stance. If property was so important to the family, family heads would prefer daughters-in-law with substantial dowries, and those who brought more would have an edge over their sisters-in-law with less. Ssu-ma Kuang wished to overcome this structural problem by moral education and moral effort: parents-in-law should not be greedy; brides should not be haughty.

A more radical solution to the problem of wives' control of property was provided by those advocating the revival of ancient descent line principles (*tsung* principles). When one directed attention away from the co-resident family to the descent line, both property and women played less of a role. In the mid–eleventh century, scholars like Ch'eng I began calling for the revival of more purely Confucian forms of ancestral rites and for more emphasis on descent line principles, their motivation lying in the competition with Buddhism and the need for the educated class to develop forms of ancestral rites suited to their new social and political situation.[59]

The implications of these ideas for wives' property was brought out only slowly. In his *Family Rituals,* Chu Hsi cited Ssu-ma Kuang on guarding against wives gaining undue power because of their private property. He also, like many of his contemporaries, praised women who used their dowries for the sake of their husbands' families. At the same time, he pointed out in the *Elementary Learning* (quoting Hu Yüan [993–1059]) that it was better for wives to come from families of less standing and wealth so that they would more easily adjust to subordinate positions.[60]

Chu Hsi's disciple Huang Kan (1152–1221) went further in bringing concepts of women's property into line with descent line ideology. While an official, Huang Kan wrote two legal decisions arguing that women have weaker claims to their dowries than their husbands or sons do. The first case concerned a Miss Ch'en, the widow of a Mr. Hsü. After her husband's death she returned to her natal family, leaving behind the three daughters and one son born of this marriage but taking the two hundred *mu* of dowry fields. A Hsü family member had petitioned to try to get the fields back, but the judge had ruled against him. On an appeal, Huang Kan reversed the ruling. He wrote: "Her father gave the fields to her family [of marriage], thus they are Hsü family fields. Even though the property is called dowry, it is Hsü family property. How can the Ch'en family get it? If the Hsü family had been without children, then it would be all right for Miss Ch'en to take the fields, but she has four children and the land should be divided among them."[61] Thus Huang Kan acknowledged the claim of a widow without children to take her dowry when she returned home; but, he insisted, land that accompanied a woman on marriage was not the same as a trousseau, and the woman was not free to dispose of it as she wished when children were in the picture.

Huang Kan circumscribed women's property rights even more in the other case, which concerned a man who had one son by his wife and two by a concubine. His original family property was assessed a tax of six strings of cash, and since the land his wife had brought as dowry was similarly assessed, it was presumably of like size. After the man and his wife died, the original family property was divided among the three sons, but the son of the wife kept his mother's dowry land. At the time, the younger sons did not dispute his act. Sixteen years later after their elder brother died, however, one of the younger brothers and the widow of the other brought their claims to court, taking the case first to the county, then three times to the judicial intendant, and then twice to the military intendant. The six officials came up with three solutions. Two ruled that the concubine's sons had no claim to the legal mother's dowry land; two thought it should be divided in thirds; and two proposed that the wife's son get half and the other two a quarter each. Huang Kan, arguing that dowry becomes husband's property, agreed with those who favored dividing it equally. In the end, however, he let stand the most recent verdict dividing it in half.[62] Previous officials asked to judge this case apparently recognized that the woman would have wanted the property to go entirely to her own son and took this into account in distributing the property. Huang Kan disputed the whole idea that a wife's land was anything other than her husband's property.

In the Yüan and Ming dynasties, women's claims to their dowries were legally curbed by the explicit ruling that divorced or widowed women could not take their dowries if they returned home or remarried. This ruling naturally reduced the incentive of the bride's family to provide a substantial dowry. Reasons for these legal revisions are complex, but Neo-Confucian scholars' uneasiness about wives' control of property must have added to the forces undermining dowries.[63]

By ending this chapter with a discussion of factors that countered the escalation in the size of dowries, I wish to underline the dynamic nature of the historical processes described here. The growth of dowries can be seen as a result of economic and political changes, but it also had effects of its own. It generated not only complementary laws and institutions, such as statutes governing orphaned daughters' shares of family property, but also opposition from intellectuals and, eventually, the state. These conflicting effects interacted over time in complex ways, obscuring simple functional relations within the flux of social life.

SIX

Upper-Class Wives as Inner Helpers

Discourses on virtue, probably in all times and places, are linked in a variety of ways to issues of class. The qualities ruling classes need to cultivate in their members will depend on the sources of their power. Thus clerical elites do not honor physical strength and agility in the way that military elites do. Naturally, it is always in the larger interests of the ruling class to assert that the qualities they embody are the universally most desirable ones, the qualities that distinguish the good from the bad. In other words, they would like others generally to believe that what elevates those in power above the rest of the population is virtue, not control over political or economic resources.

The class basis of the discourse on virtue applies to the discourse on women's virtues as much as men's. In this chapter I will examine the Sung construction of the ideal wife as a manifestation of the emergence of the Sung educated class. Economically this class depended on income from land-holding, enhanced often by business activities. But it was not simply a class of the well-to-do: to acquire political power, social influence, and cultural leadership one also had to have good mastery of the literary tradition and share the ethos of the literati. The virtues most prized in both men and women, in short, were the ones that would allow a family to gain and preserve standing among the educated. In the T'ang, men and women alike were praised in funerary biographies for the eminence of their ancestry and for their mastery of ritual and correct deportment, traits closely associated with the aristocratic families. Aristocratic wives were also often praised for their beauty.[1] In the Sung, however, a rather different set of virtues got much more attention, ones closely tied, I believe, to the maintenance of upper-class status in that period.

This does not mean that class overrode or canceled gender. The good wife was not a copy of the good husband. Rather, wholeheartedly accepting differentiation by gender, she saw her role as that of an "inner helper" (nei-chü). She took care not to encroach on her husband's or parents-in-law's prerogatives, but made their lives easier by doing whatever was needed inside the home. The Confucian model of gender differentiation and kinship roles sketched in Chapters 1 and 2 underlay Sung ideals of the "inner helper." Yet literary constructions of the virtues of wives were more than products of received ideology: they were complexly related to the traits that led to the survival and success of families in the upper class of their day. The ideal upper-class wife in Sung times was not simply devoted to her husband's family; she had the managerial abilities, literary talents, and interpersonal skills to see that it thrived.

DUTIFUL DAUGHTERS-IN-LAW IN COMPLEX FAMILIES

As seen in Chapter 3, upper-class men in the Sung were married fairly young, usually in their late teens or early twenties. The younger a man was at the time he married, the more likely it would be that his parents and grandparents would still be living. (Of the men and women I studied from funerary biographies, about half were still alive at sixty and over a quarter at seventy.) Moreover, the groom in all likelihood had a brother or two. (Three-quarters of the couples I studied had two or more sons, half three or more.)[2] Thus brides regularly began married life by entering a complex family, containing one or both of her husband's parents, possibly one or both of his paternal grandparents, one or more of his brothers, their wives, his unmarried sisters, and perhaps children of his brothers.

New brides in these complex families were expected to devote their energies to serving their parents-in-law and pleasing everyone they could. As illustrated in a handscroll of the *Classic of Filial Piety*, emblematic of this service was presenting food (Fig. 13).[3] In their descriptions of a daughter-in-law's devotion, writers stressed that she sewed, cooked, and served food to her parents-in-law herself, rather than delegating such tasks to servants. A daughter-in-law, it would seem, should act as the servant to her parents-in-law. Miss Ch'en (960–1038), for example, while her husband traveled to various posts, spent the first twenty years of her married life cooking and serving for her husband's parents, who preferred to stay at home. Her contemporary, a Miss Wang (959–1038), never let the servants attend to her mother-in-law, preparing all the older woman's food herself and even fanning her pillow during the hottest weather. Miss Li (1019–1053) entered a home with a grandmother-in-law, a father-in-law, two uncles-in-law, and four brothers-in-law.

Fig. 13. A dutiful daughter-in-law helping her husband serve his parents
From Li Kung-lin's (1040–1106) illustrations of the *Classic of Filial Piety*. The Art
Museum, Princeton University (L. 1986.101).

She had no mother-in-law, but this left her with full responsibility for caring
for her ill father-in-law. For ten years she made and served all the medicines
and food. When the illness grew critical, she used her own money to make
sure nothing was left undone. Miss Yu (1077–1132) had a father-in-law who
liked to entertain guests. As the youngest bride, she dutifully served them,
never making her sisters-in-law take turns. She also had a strict mother-in-law
who never once in twenty years let her daughters-in-law sit in her presence.
As Miss Yu was the only daughter-in-law compliant enough to please her,
when the mother-in-law was ill, she would accept medicine from no one else.
When Miss Sun Ju-ching (1206–1263) married, she immediately announced
that she would take over all of the heavier tasks from her mother-in-law, who

was, she said, too old to do physical labor any longer. When her mother-in-law became ill, she nursed her, burning incense at night to pray that her own life span be reduced for the sake of lengthening her mother-in-law's.[4]

Brides might also gain the approval of their in-laws by liberally handing out items from their dowries. Miss Fang Tao-chien (1115–1191), we are told, started marriage with exceptionally rich chests, but gave everything to her mother- and grandmother-in-law, the latter someone few people could please. Miss Wang (1132–1192) entered a large household managed by the senior sister-in-law. She soon contributed some of her jewelry to cover family expenses. A Miss Tai (1161–1205) married into a family of modest means, so she sold her clothes and earrings to help, showing that she was not stingy. Her father-in-law, we are told, was delighted with her and said, "She is a true daughter-in-law of our family."[5]

Harmony was never easy to maintain in a complex family, since members' interests differed. Thus people appreciated wives who did not seem apprehensive about their husband's brothers' wives or children gaining the advantage. Miss Tseng Chi-i's (1079–1113) husband Chiang Pao (1069–1117) usually lived apart from his brothers, but they had not divided the family property. He lived on his official salary, leaving the income from the family land to his brothers. His wife, we are told, "never discussed who had what." Later, his eldest brother took his family to live in the capital but was short of funds. When Pao tried to figure out a way to help, Miss Tseng went into her room to get what she had left from her dowry and told him to offer it to his brother.[6]

COMPETENT HOUSEHOLD MANAGERS

Biographers were quite willing to describe upper-class women as intelligent and competent. As one put it, "Even though quiet concentration is the virtue of women living in the inner quarters, to sit lifelessly like a lump, ignorant of what goes on, like a clay or wooden puppet, is to be a stupid wife." Tseng Kung (1019–1083) described with approval his wife's intelligence: "She understood anything as soon as she saw it, and there was nothing she did not fully comprehend."[7]

How hard women had to toil at "women's work"—all the tasks related to clothes, food, and the interior of the house—would have depended largely on the family's wealth. Some families in the educated class were of quite modest means, and their women could not spend their days trying to make themselves look nice. Miss Fan P'u-yüan (1143–1222), although from a wealthy family, "personally did such tasks as tending the silkworms, mending, and sewing" after her husband's family suffered a financial setback. Yüan Hsieh (1144–1224) said of his sister-in-law, Miss Chao (1164–1213), that although used to the luxuries of the imperial clan, she worked harder at weaving, mending, and sewing than a poor girl. Miss Chang Yu-chao's (1146–1195) husband, the well-known scholar Ch'en Fu-liang (1137–1203), had a constant stream of visitors. Miss Chang cooked for them herself, with the help of only one maid. Yeh Shih (1150–1223) reported that in the first year of his mother's marriage a flood had swept away everything for miles around, leaving them without a house or furniture. They had to stay anywhere they could, moving eleven times. "Although she had no livelihood to manage, she still kept track of even the tiniest bit. She even collected ruined bits of hemp sacking and carefully made them into bolts of cloth."[8]

In prosperous families, too, wives were expected to work hard. Ho Tai (1153–1203) reported that his mother, Miss Tu (1133–1186), continued to weave into her old age, long after the family had become wealthy. Miss Hsia (1129–1192) was credited with helping her husband in business, building up the family property to several thousand *mu* and placing them among the leading families of the prefecture. In one anecdote concerning an official's family, after the wife died, her maid went mad and started acting just like her mistress used to, keeping close track of the payments made by each tenant and ordering one beaten because he was behind. Perhaps it was work of this sort that was implied when authors said that a wife looked after the livelihood to enable her husband to concentrate on study. Han Yüan-chi (1118–1187) made this connection explicit in his description of the merits of Miss Li (1104–1177). Her husband concentrated entirely on government affairs, "never having asked about family supplies." Miss Li took on management of their property as her responsibility, buying fertile fields and building a house by a stream. Once a peasant came into the courtyard carrying a sack of rice on his back, to the amazement of Miss Li's husband, who had no idea who he was or what he carried. She just laughed and said, "That is our rent."[9] Obviously, wives like Miss Li would be assets in landowning families where the men wanted to concentrate on literary and political endeavors.

In larger families, one of the women usually had charge of household finances and overall responsibility for managing the servants. Occasionally even a relatively new bride would have to take over these duties. Miss Ts'ui (999–1067) married into a large household of two hundred members. Her father-in-law, "worried that there was no one to manage the inside work, summoned [her] to the reception room to describe in detail all of the household affairs and entrust them all to her." She tried to decline but in the end took on the work. She proved stern on the outside but forgiving on the inside in managing servants, "and never once went overboard in beating or scolding them."[10] This sort of ability to manage servants and concubines with as little friction as possible was highly prized. Miss Fan (1015–1067) was pleasant to the concubines, but "when she was serious they did not dare oppose her." Miss Fu (1097–1148) proved a strict manager; in dealing with the concubines she never showed anger, but "everything, large or small, was done according to the rules." Miss Li Shu-ying (1196–1255) was praised for maintaining an orderly household and teaching her daughters to treat the concubines well by reminding them, "They are also someone's daughters." She also always showed the maids and concubines how to do the weaving and sewing by first doing it herself.[11]

Frugality was an important part of successful household management, for many of the families in the educated class were far from rich. Han Ch'i (1008–1075) complained that the current fashion in women's clothing and jewelry placed a premium on constant variation, so that people were always discarding their old things and eagerly seeking new ones. He thus appreciated his nephew's wife, Miss Chang (1012–1063), for her indifference to the dictates of fashion and unwillingness to spend money wastefully. Similarly, we are told that Tu Yen's (978–1057) wife, Miss Hsiang-li (988–1065), was not perturbed in the least when people laughed at her for visiting the palace in plain clothes "without kingfisher feathers or pearls." And Miss Hu (1077–1149) never wore extravagantly decorated clothes; she also had a robe that she did not discard even though it had been washed and resewn many times. A more extreme case is Miss Pien (1155–1203), who, we are told, continued wearing the clothes she brought in her dowry for thirty years.[12]

In praising women as competent household managers, the authors of epitaphs often used the sort of language we might use for efficient secretaries. These women were wonderful because they made life so much easier for their husbands, letting them concentrate on the really important things in life, such as study, scholarship, or official service. When Li Yu-chih's (1134–1199) wife, Miss Shih (1139–1197), died at fifty-nine, he recounted her virtues to the man he asked to write her epitaph. Prominent among these was her managerial competence: "I spent a long time at the Imperial Academy and often served in office. I never paid any attention to family business. Income and outlay, what we had and what we needed, the scale on which we should live, all these things she took care of, never bothering me with them."[13] Did these women view themselves in the same way—as dutifully carrying out policies set by the men? Or did they learn how to give this impression to please the men and thus make their own lives more pleasant? Without sources written by women, we can do little more than speculate that there were probably women of both sorts.

SAGE ADVISORS

Continuing in the tradition established in the Han by Liu Hsiang with his *Biographies of Great Women,* many a woman's biography emphasized how she gave wise, public-minded advice to her husband, encouraging him in his study, service to the emperor, or charitable acts. Rather than give many examples, let me relate what Li Kang (1083–1140) wrote of his wife's mother,

Miss Huang (1063–1121). After her husband was demoted to the post of magistrate of Sui-ch'ang, he wished to give up his post so that his grandfather could get one in his stead. Everyone tried to dissuade him, saying he was young and talented and should be patient; someday he would get a prestigious post that would bring honor to his family. Only his wife, Miss Huang, supported his decision. Later he got a more important regional post and had the privilege of nominating a son to office. He wished to nominate his younger uncle instead. When he told his wife, she beamed and said, "When you were in your prime you declined a post on behalf of your grandfather. Now when you have just gotten the privilege of nominating a son or grandson, you wish to put forward your uncle. No one but you could do this. It will make a major impact on improving customs. Please proceed without doubt." Li Kang commented, "Few of those who serve in office do not plan for their wives and children. What made the honorable Lung-t'u so far beyond anyone else was the inner help his wife gave him. And it is extremely difficult for a wife to be able to persuade her husband to follow the moral course the way she did."[14]

Later in the biography, Li Kang gave other examples of her sage advice. She urged her husband to be patient when he was left for a long time in the provinces, saying his post gave him the opportunity to put what he had studied into practice. Since her husband tended to be straightforward and blunt, she urged flexibility, explaining to him the Buddhist concept of expedient means. When he got into trouble, she cheered him up by saying he had not yet achieved the level of tolerance needed for the Buddhist concept of *prajñā* (wisdom). Miss Huang also aided her husband by complementing his strengths. "The honorable Lung-t'u managed the family by being strict; madame aided him by being forgiving. He took care of affairs by emphasizing the proper things; she supplemented him by emphasizing harmony. They were a couple for forty years, encouraging each other in loyalty and filial piety on a daily basis. It was owing to her help that the honorable Lung-t'u was able to establish himself and practice the Way so well he had no cause to feel ashamed even before the ancients."[15] A wife who would constantly encourage her husband to persevere in the activities valued in men of the educated class would obviously be better than one who disdained or belittled his work.

WOMEN OF LETTERS

One Sung illustrated version of the *Classic of Filial Piety for Girls* shows a woman seated by a table with books on it (Fig. 14). A model woman, the artist is asserting, filial to her parents and parents-in-law and obedient to her husband, could at the same time be a learned woman. Authors of biographies often praised women for their familiarity with books. As children they might have mastered Pan Chao's *Admonitions for Girls,* primers like the

Fig. 14. A literate woman with her books
From an anonymous Sung handscroll illustrating the
Ladies' Classic of Filial Piety. The Palace Museum, Peking.

Meng-ch'iu and the *Classic of Filial Piety,* or the standard Confucian classics, such as the *Book of Songs,* the *Book of Documents,* the *Analects,* the *Mencius,* and the *Spring and Autumn Annals.* Some also read Buddhist sutras.[16] In the educated class, literacy would seem to have enhanced a woman's marriageability. When Chang Hsiao-hsiang (ca. 1129–1170) wanted to talk a friend into a match between Chang's sister and the friend's brother, he made a point of noting that his sister was literate and could recite Buddhist scriptures.[17]

Biographers were also quick to emphasize how bright their women subjects were. Tseng Kung (1019–1083) praised Miss Wu (998–1063), Wang An-shih's mother, for "loving to study and having a powerful memory." In turn, Wang An-shih, perhaps influenced by his mother to see literary skills as attractive in women, described Miss Wang (1007–1059) as a good poet and Miss Tseng (989–1058) as an avid student of history, able to discuss historical issues as well as any famous scholar of the age. Miss Huang (1063–1121), the eldest daughter in one scholarly family, was said to have been especially bright and perceptive when young: "Each day she could memorize [passages] of more than a thousand words." In one case a maternal grandfather, finding his granddaughter, Miss Tai (1121–1192), easy to teach, gave her the same education in the classics as her two elder brothers. She also became proficient in calligraphy. Miss Ku Ching-hua (1186–1238) had a father known as a writer. Probably as a consequence, when young she "learned the books of the hundred philosophers, the historical records, even Taoist and Buddhist books. She memorized many ancient and modern essays, exceeding even the best read of Confucian scholars." Her calligraphy, we are told, was as good as any man's.[18] A woman's talents could include knowledge of physiognomy, medicine, music, geomancy, and other technical arts.[19] Miss Ting, the daughter of one official and wife of another, "was clever from childhood, and could do anything. Her skill at physiognomy must have come from natural talent." She could catch a glimpse of an official talking to her husband and accurately predict the official's fate. She could even make predictions based on handwriting.[20]

Occasionally a woman acquired a significant reputation as a poet, painter, or calligrapher, though in only a tiny number of cases has any of her output survived until today.[21] Wei T'ai (ca. 1050–1110) remarked on the number of women in his generation skilled at poetry writing, and cited the example of Wang An-shih's family: his sister, wife, and daughter all had written memorable lines.[22] By far the best known of the women writers of the Sung is Li Ch'ing-chao (1084–ca. 1160).[23] Men of her age accepted her as a poet of real talent and discussed her poems much as they did men's.[24] In her case, exceptional talent coincided with unusually favorable circumstances. Her father and mother were both writers, as a result of which she gained a solid education in the histories, classics, and poetry. After she married, her husband enjoyed discussing poetry, art, and history with her. Moreover, they had no children, so she had more time than many wives to devote to her writing. Li Ch'ing-chao frequently wrote about the lovely, sensitive, languid, delicate woman who is despondent because she is separated from her husband owing to his travels or death. Her poems were thus easily compared to those that men had long written about the unhappy beauty. That Li Ch'ing-chao wrote so well in this tradition appealed to male poets; it confirmed that the feelings men had attributed to neglected women for so many centuries were indeed the feelings a sensitive woman would have.

The success of this one women makes it all the more necessary to consider why few other wives matched her. Certainly one factor that would have discouraged many women was men's ambivalence about women who wrote. After describing how talented a woman was, biographers generally tried to make sure their readers understood that she was still modest and reserved and did not use her literary talent in an assertive way. Tseng Kung described the seven hundred poems Miss Chou (1040–1065) wrote in her short life as "calm and proper, soft and not devious, concise and careful with regard to propriety"—hardly the attributes he would have used to praise a male poet. Miss Ch'i (1011–1065), Wang An-shih claimed, wrote excellent poetry but never let other people see it. Other women declined even to learn to write poetry. Lu Yu (1125–1210) thought it worth putting in the biography of his cousin's daughter, Miss Sun (1141–1193), that when she was a teenager the female poet Li Ch'ing-chao offered to teach her but she declined, asserting, "Talent is not women's business."[25] The author of the 1182 preface to Miss Chu Shu-chen's poems began, "I have heard that writing beautiful phrases is not women's business. Yet there are occasionally cases [of women] with great natural talents and exceptional character and intelligence who come up with words and lines no man can match. Even if they wished to conceal their names, it would be impossible." He was publishing her poems some time after her death, impressed by how well they conveyed feelings of unhappiness.[26]

Why would wives decline to show their poems to others? Is it that they then would be competing with their husbands, who were trying to succeed in a world where men had to present themselves as writers? Is it that they would then somehow be revealing themselves, and the notion that wives should not be seen by anyone outside the family was overwhelming? Clearly many men and women felt that there was something unwifely about the more self-assertive sides of literary pursuits. Moreover, married women may have found it difficult to write convincing poems in the established feminine styles. After marriage, when they were busy rearing children, managing servants, and catering to their in-laws, they may no longer have been moved by images of aimless ladies, lost without their man. Unlike the women of Heian Japan and late Ming China, educated Sung women failed to create the audience or discover the literary voices that would make creative writing more attractive to them.

Did the rise of Neo-Confucianism curb women's literary creativity? By strengthening tendencies already present, I suspect that it did. It is true that all Neo-Confucian scholars approved of women learning to read and write. In his *Precepts*, Ssu-ma Kuang quoted Pan Chao's arguments that women would make better wives if they knew how to read. He added his own conclusion: "People who do not study do not know ritual and morality, and those who do not know ritual and morality cannot distinguish good and bad, right and wrong. . . . Thus everyone must study. How are males and females different in this regard?" In his "Miscellaneous Proprieties," he wrote a brief schedule for learning for both boys and girls adapted from the "Domestic Regulations" in the *Book of Rites*. Even though girls did not follow the same schedule as their brothers, they would read such books as the *Analects, Classic of Filial Piety,* and the *Biographies of Great Women.* Chu Hsi, similarly, encouraged girls to read moral tracts, specifically mentioning

Ssu-ma Kuang's *Precepts*.[27] But these men, like most of those active in the revival of Confucianism, had ambivalent views on the moral value of poetry, for men as well as women. Ssu-ma Kuang explicitly rejected teaching girls to write poems. Ch'eng I claimed that his mother felt such ambivalence herself: "She loved literature but did not write compositions. In her view it was very wrong the way some women let their writings or calligraphy circulate. Her lifetime output of poetry did not amount to more than thirty pieces, none of which has been preserved." Ch'eng I himself could remember only one of her poems.[28]

By the late Southern Sung, Neo-Confucian objections to poetry writing were probably more widely known and accepted. The poet Yao Mien (1216–1262) wrote that his wife, Miss Tsou Miao-chuang (d. 1257), was from a family with strong connections to the Chu Hsi school of Neo-Confucianism. Her mother's father, Li Shu-i, had personally studied with Chu Hsi, and her childhood home was governed on strict Confucian principles. Miss Tsou was given a literary education, reading several passages in the *Analects* and *Mencius* every day and gaining a love for T'ang poetry. She knew how to compose poems but did not write any, explaining, "This is not women's work." Yao Mien knew she was capable of clever lines, having seen her write them, yet still admired the "deep composure" that kept her from showing off her talent.[29]

PIOUS WIVES

Wives were expected to assist their husbands in ancestral rites, and many women are described as being especially careful and devout in these duties. Miss Yü (1121–1194), for instance, was praised because after she entered the house as a bride she asked what her husband's parents had liked to eat, so that she could offer it at the seasonal sacrifices. Others were praised for the attention they gave to cleaning the sacrificial utensils and preparing the food. The biography of Miss Wang (959–1038) quoted her as saying, "Sacrifices are among the most important things people do. Therefore we must carefully clean [the equipment] to manifest complete sincerity."[30]

Beyond these entirely Confucian duties, wives often had strong interests in Buddhism, Taoism, and local temples. Even men who were themselves rather cold to religious activities seem often to have admired pious women. Sage advisors, such as Miss Huang cited above, are described as drawing on Buddhist teachings to help them fulfill their eminently Confucian duties of assisting their husbands and caring for all the members of the family.

The Buddhist message probably had real attractions for women; if they were not satisfied with the state of affairs in this life, they could concentrate on attaining a better situation in the next. Women made donations to temples, much as men did, and sometimes had portraits of themselves painted below images of Buddhas or bodhisattvas that they commissioned (see Fig. 9). Religious activities also had the attraction of breaking a possibly confining routine. Religious devotions gave women a reason to leave the house, or at least let strangers into it. Women of all classes could visit temples, sometimes going in groups.[31] Temples might provide space for women to meet, such as the Dharma Propagation Temple in Hangchow, where a women's club met every month to study sutras.[32] Occasionally a woman might attain prominence as a leader of a sect. In the eleventh century a Miss Ts'ai, who refused to marry, gained followers from all walks of life who believed her to be an immortal.[33]

What is striking in women's biographies, however, is not the ways women used religious activities to escape the house, but the ways they drew on Buddhism to withdraw deeper inside. Miss Li (976–1031) frequently chanted sutras, and she abstained from meat about ten times a month. Miss Ts'ui (999–1067), we are told, had long liked Buddhist books, but when she read the *Sutra of Perfect Wisdom* she remarked, "If I had studied enlightenment earlier, these principles would already be attained." From then on she disengaged herself from worldly affairs, reduced her consumption of food, and completely prohibited the taking of life. Miss Liu (1005–1085) liked to recite Buddhist books and had accepted the five precepts (not to kill, steal, engage in illicit sexual relations, lie, or drink wine).[34] Miss Pien (1025–1093) burned incense every day and chanted sutras. She would recite the names of the Buddha, counting them with a rosary. Miss Shao (d. 1121) "recited Buddhist books all day without stop. At night she would chant secret incantations to dispel hungry ghosts. When wind, rain, or illnesses would not improve, she often got unusual responses. On the ground where one walked around the seated Buddha, she would write the five characters of the Kuanyin hymn, 'Mind, thought, no empty error.'" The bodhisattva Kuanyin, in Sung times most often depicted in female form, seems to have had particular attractions for women. Miss Yang (d. 1271), for instance, the wife of a Confucian scholar who had written studies of several of the Confucian classics, had in her tomb a small porcelain statue of Kuanyin (Fig. 15).[35]

Wives in large complex families seem to have been particularly likely to take up Buddhist devotions. Miss Chang (1074–1122) was a wife in a family of several dozen people (or, as the biographer more picturesquely puts it, of several hundred fingers). She "liked to study Buddhism, and every day would recite their sayings. She would not eat meat and was devoted in her service to Kuanyin. She repeated the Incantation of Great Compassion one billion times. Once she was ill and on the brink of death. The bodhisattva Kuanyin appeared in a white garment and necklaces. The image climbed onto her bed to wash her body with a willow branch and thorn-mustard. Soon she was wet with perspiration, and quickly recovered."[36] Miss Hu (1077–1149), in an even larger family (a thousand fingers), every morning

Fig. 15. A small porcelain statue of the boddhisattva
Kuanyin from the tomb of Miss Yang (d. 1271)
From Ch'ü-chou 1983: pl. 6.

would recite sutras, immersing herself in their study. She could not bear to
kill living things and would not eat meat.[37] Miss Chung Ling-chan (1133–
1184), wife of a Confucian scholar and official, had studied Confucian books
when young, including the tales of chaste and courageous women, but later
was more attracted to Ch'an Buddhism. She once met the great Ch'an master

Ta-hui Tsung-kao (1089–1163), who was impressed with her comprehension and arranged for her to study with a disciple of his. "Before she had reached thirty, she lived secluded, eating vegetarian food, ridding herself of worldly desires, chanting sutras by day and practicing meditation by night. She would point to the moon to illustrate her nature, saying that throughout time it has always been complete."[38]

Sometimes Buddhist devotions are explicitly said to have made a woman a better wife. Miss Wei's (992–1064) Buddhist beliefs were given credit for making her more considerate of her husband, Chang Mien (983–1060). Chang never paid attention to family finances. When he returned home to live with his parents, the household income did not always suffice. "[Miss Wei] would wear thin clothes and cut back on food so that Mr. Chang would not notice the shortages. This was probably the result of her mastery of Buddhist writings. At times of crisis she could be tranquil and satisfied with her fate, not letting outside things agitate her mind." Miss Hu (d. 1093) had a chronically ill husband whom she had to nurse. "Whenever she got a chance she would read Buddhist books to relieve her troubled mind of its worries. To avoid hurting her husband's spirits, she never let unhappy thoughts be seen on her face."[39]

Occasionally both husband and wife were equally interested in Buddhism. Ch'en Hsiao-ch'ang (1015–1082) is said to have loved Buddhist books and been able to discuss such issues as the Buddha nature intelligently with Ch'an masters. His wife, Miss P'ang (1028–1101), liked to recite Buddhist books and kept them almost constantly in her hands. Huang Kung (988–1062), who argued that Confucianism was good for decorating the body while Buddhism provided a method for managing one's nature, recited the Diamond sutra forty thousand times. His wife, Miss Hsü (987–1074), chanted 180,000 chapters of sutras in her lifetime.[40] Still, there is no mention in these cases of the husband and wife performing their devotions together; rather, it seems almost coincidental that they had the same spiritual interests.

An occasional Confucian scholar tried to talk his wife out of her Buddhist devotions. Liu Tsai (1166–1239) reported that his second wife, Miss Liang (1170–1247), came from a family that believed in Buddhism: "When she arrived she set up an image privately and would chant various things according to a yearly schedule. After I discussed with her how Buddhism and Taoism harm the Way and the true nature of spiritual forces, she wavered and, seeming to understand, gave up her practices." Ch'en Fu-liang's (1137–1203) wife, Chang Yu-chao (1146–1195), was said to have thought that her duty to follow her husband included believing what he believed and she thus did not believe in magic, Buddhism, or Taoism, nor did she fear ghosts.[41]

Wives often became serious about Buddhism in what are called their middle or late years, apparently meaning after thirty-five or so. Miss Yin (1026–1087) "in her late years liked Ch'an. She practiced not burdening her mind with things. She would sit quietly all day without thinking of anything. When affairs became confusing, she would not get upset or agitated, but accept what happened." Miss Ch'en (1039–1115) had been attracted to Buddhism since she was young, but gained higher levels of understanding in her middle years. "Every morning she would get up, fast and purify herself, and sit to recite. No matter what went on in front of her, she would not stop to look. In the midafternoon she would set out wine and play happily with her grandchildren, following the same routine every day." Miss Huang (1063–1121), we are told, became particularly devoted to Buddhism in her middle years. "As the taste of the age grew more and more superficial, she swept out a room and would sit by herself the whole day, finding her pleasure in meditation."[42] Miss Yü Tao-yung (1103–1182) in later life studied Buddhism, one morning deciding to set aside her jewelry and give up wine and meat; she then wore plain clothes and ate vegetarian food for the rest of her life. When her sons wanted to get an honorary title for her, she objected on the grounds that she had abandoned worldly affairs. Miss Tai (1121–1192), educated in Confucian texts like her brothers when young, "in her late years loved Buddhism, and read their books very thoroughly. She entrusted family affairs to her children and lived tranquilly without involving herself."[43]

Where did these women learn Buddhist precepts? Only a handful are explicitly said to have studied with Ch'an masters. Some may have received instruction from nuns who had been invited into the women's quarters for that purpose. Yüan Ts'ai warned against letting Buddhist or Taoist nuns into the home, so apparently they were common visitors.[44] But many women probably received at least their initial instruction from other lay women— their mothers, grandmothers, and aunts. Miss Hu (968–1030) had perused the entire Buddhist canon and had memorized more than ten sutras. She then, we are told, taught others in the women's quarters.[45]

In our society it is taken for granted that people may become more religious in their later years as they confront the prospect of death. We also know that many women experience crises in their forties and fifties when their children leave home. Perhaps these were among the reasons middle-aged wives of literati became interested in Buddhism. But we should note that observers did not see them as especially preoccupied with questions of death, rebirth, or salvation. Nor had their sons left home: in fact, they were often surrounded by grandchildren. Sung writers describe them as eager to save the members of their families, but also in search of personal tranquillity and insight. Confucian writers were willing to praise them because their piety seemed to them to make them better wives and mothers-in-law.

A good inner helper, as conceived by male writers in Sung times, was not passive or subservient. Intelligence, resourcefulness, and energy were all considered positive traits. A wife had a lot to do as household manager, not to mention as mother (see Chapter 9). So long as she presented herself as assisting the men rather than pursuing her own goals, she would be respected for competence and efficiency.

As best I can detect from admittedly imperfect sources, most women in the educated class internalized a large part of this discourse on the good wife. Even Li Ch'ing-chao, who was quite willing to express her bitterness about the political situation of her time and her despondency at the loss of her husband, never complained about the limitations imposed on her as a woman. Most women, it would seem, played a supporting role not only because it was expected, but also because they thought it attractive and becoming.

Conceptions of the ideal wife kept these women in subordinate positions as effectively as did laws, perhaps even more so. Because this discourse constrained women, modern writers often seem to imply that wifely ideals were propagated by men for this purpose. It is true that men were the authors of the narratives cited in this chapter. Yet a case can be made, I believe, that this discourse was not simply a creation of Confucian philosophers, nor was it perpetuated solely by men.

Let me offer two sorts of arguments. The first concerns women's involvement in shaping the discourse. Women, after all, were the ones who reared the daughters and trained the daughters-in-law. What traits would older women want to see in younger ones? Because women spent all day in the inner quarters, they had even more reason than men to wish to see peace and harmony there. Wouldn't they want cheerful daughters, agreeable daughters-in-law, and saintly mothers-in-law? Men often accused women of seeking to divide complex families, and some wives undoubtedly did try to do so. But grandmothers are never portrayed as sharing these feelings; when the family was large because it included a woman's own grown sons, she would be as concerned with avoiding division as her husband. She would want her daughters and daughters-in-law to be easy to live with.

The second argument concerns the relationship between what authors wrote about wives in biographies and what they wrote on other topics. The discourse on wifely virtue in biographies is clearly connected to the traditional Confucian understanding of the ethics of interpersonal relations, especially family relations. But the discourse does not seem to be especially closely tied to the main intellectual concerns of leading thinkers in the Sung. Writers with the strongest identification with the Neo-Confucian movement, men like Ch'eng I, Chu Hsi, Huang Kan, and Wei Liao-weng, wrote very much the same sorts of things about women as other Sung writers.[46] They do not even seem to have been more likely to praise a woman for her devotion to ancestral rites than for her Buddhist piety. The explanation, I would hazard, is that biographers did not have an entirely free hand. The family of the bereaved had their own notions of what made the woman good and wished to see these traits highlighted.

What they thought made women good was intricately tied to the nature of the Sung educated class. Women in this class should differ from lower-class women in much the same way upper-class men should differ from peasants: by exhibiting restraint, composure, and knowledge of books. Besides the traits that indicated class origin, upper-class wives needed traits that would help their families maintain class standing. Women in the upper class were lavishly praised for emanating peace, calm, and harmony because the complex families of their class were fragile and women were commonly seen as the main source of tension, division, and squabbling. Yüan Ts'ai wrote: "Many cases of family discord begin because a woman, by what she says, incites animosity between her husband and other family members of his generation. The reason for this is that a woman has limited experience and lacks a sense of the common interest or fairness."[47] Lower-class women were also commonly seen as having such traits: "Women in the streets and markets," in Hu Ying's (c.s. 1232) depiction, "often get enough to eat without having to work. Since they have nothing to occupy their minds, they gather in groups of two or three to gossip. When neighbors do not get along, it is usually because of them."[48] Good wives of upper-class men were thus not women who acted in the ways that come naturally to women, but women who had overcome such tendencies, thus making it possible for their families to thrive.

SEVEN

Women's Work Making Cloth

The thirteenth-century poet Shu Yüeh-hsiang (1217–1301) noticed how hard peasant women worked in Chekiang, picking tea, treading on waterwheels, drawing water from wells, carrying food to laborers in the fields, pounding rice, making clothes, planting grain, and selling fish and vegetables. He commemorated their labors in a series of ten poems, the first three of which are as follows:

> By the front hill the woman picking tea
> Quickly takes up her basket, revealing her take.
> The work is hard but she knows her task
> And sings and laughs without sign of sadness.
> Her eyebrows, reflected in the water, she doesn't paint.
> A flower is stuck in her hair, but she doesn't blush.
> Everyone cares about appearance,
> So why doesn't she comb her hair?

> At the edge of the field the waterwheel woman
> Draws the water to let it circulate.
> Her black hat is pushed to the side in the burning sun.
> Her blue skirt flaps noisily in the evening breeze.
> Over and over she repeats the same steps,
> Treading away on what seems to be empty space.
> I catch the sense of her work song:
> As long as you live, don't marry into a peasant family.

> The woman by the river pulling up fish
> Every morning goes to the city.
> Leaving her young child to watch the boat,
> She trades her catch for wine for her drunkard husband.
> Not one to wear fancy socks,
> The edge of her long skirt is wet with water.

Her family are drifters;
Smiling, they leave the mooring.[1]

Poets and painters seem to have enjoyed depicting women at work; there was something mildly erotic in imagining gazing on women absorbed in their exertions, unaware that they were being observed. Be that as it may, we can be grateful for the evidence they left. After all, in the vast majority of families that had to toil to feed and clothe themselves, women worked as long and as hard as men. In the more temperate regions of central and south China, women were depicted outside doing agriculture work. Lu Yu (1125–1210), in his diary, reported noticing that near Ch'ung-te county even as women worked the waterwheels with their feet, they would be splicing hemp with their hands. Fan Ch'eng-ta (1126–1193) wrote a poem about the old women, young girls, and mothers with babies sleeping on their backs going out to pick tea shortly after the end of the mulberry leaf–picking season. Ch'en Ts'ao (thirteenth century) wrote a poem titled "Peasant's Wife," in which he had a woman joke, "A husband and wife from one field get two bodies caked in mud."[2]

Yet whatever women contributed to general agriculture, in the imagination of Chinese scholars women's work largely lay elsewhere. Their work was the slow and tedious production of textiles, done largely within the confines of the home. Symbolically women were associated with cloth, and since ancient times the sexual division of labor had been epitomized by the saying that men plow and women weave.[3] Producing cloth was looked on as a basic productive activity, comparable to growing grains. Just as people needed to eat, they needed protection from the cold. When men and women each did their share, households would be self-sufficient in food and clothing. This model had long been implicit in the government's system of taxation. For many centuries farming households had owed the larger part of their tax obligation in grain, due in the fall, but a substantial amount was also paid in bolts of plain cloth, due in the summer. The government, thus, put the weight of its tax collection apparatus behind encouraging every family to produce cloth.

Sung writers, continuing a long tradition, regularly paired the work of men in the fields producing food with the work of women within the house producing cloth. In a memorial to the throne, Ssu-ma Kuang described the exertions of men who tilled, planted, and harvested through heat and cold, and of women who raised silkworms, spliced hemp fibers, tied the warp threads onto the loom, and wove cloth strand by strand. Such hard-working families, he observed, would get pressed in the summer and fall to pay their taxes and repay their debts, so that before the grain was brought in from the field or the cloth removed from the loom, they no longer owned the hard-won fruits of their labor.[4] Local officials, in urging the residents under their supervision to devote themselves to productive, agricultural work, usually made some mention of women's contributions. Chu Hsi in 1179 urged the residents of Nan-k'ang to work hard at agriculture, specifically recommending that they grow mulberry trees and ramie so that the women could raise silkworms, spin, and weave to make ramie and silk cloth.[5] In a legal judgment, Hu Ying (c.s. 1232) described how peasants who had pawned their fields struggled to accumulate the cash to redeem them: "Day and night the men plow and the women tend silkworms, not daring to eat a spoonful of grain themselves or use one skein of silk thread for their own clothes, trying to build up their savings grain by grain, inch by inch."[6]

Not all women in peasant families would have worked at making cloth. Differences in climate and soil made some areas unsuited to production of cloth, or so suited to something else like tea that the family specialized in that activity, purchasing whatever cloth they needed. The very poorest families might not be able to secure the land and equipment needed to produce cloth: families growing mulberry trees needed ladders and baskets for picking and storing the leaves; those raising silkworms and producing thread needed a room for incubation, trays and racks, large frames for reeling, reels and spools, and spinning wheels. If they wove themselves, they needed looms. Families that produced only hemp, ramie, or cotton still needed some spinning and weaving equipment, if less than for silk production.[7] To produce five bolts of hemp or ramie cloth (each bolt about 0.6 m wide and 12 m long), a family would generally have to devote one to three *mu* of land to cultivation of the fiber-producing plants. If their goal was a comparable amount of silk, they would need perhaps a thousand mulberry trees spread over several *mu*. Five bolts would be enough to provide two sets of clothes for each person in a family of five, with some left over for tax payment.[8]

Evidence of the lives of peasant women in the Sung is very thin, but we can say with some certainty that they spent a lot of time working. In this chapter I will examine what their textile work entailed. I devote considerable space to the work itself for two reasons. The first is our ignorance. Living at the end of the twentieth century, we have some idea what it meant to cook, clean, and tend to small children, even what it meant to supervise servants or pick tea; but we know much less about splicing, spinning, reeling, and all the other tasks involved in making cloth. The second reason is that because the finished product could easily be sold for cash, women's textile work raises questions about the links between women's participation in the commercial economy, their status in the family, and the more general evaluation of their social worth. Commercialization of the economy proceeded at a rapid pace from the late T'ang through the Sung period. Markets expanded, with ever more goods—including the cloth produced largely by women—being drawn into them. This commercialization had an impact on the organization of the production of cloth as more families came to specialize in certain types of cloth or stages in the production process. How did these developments affect women?[9] Did women gain more say in decisions about the allocation of family resources when the work they did had a clearer cash value? Did expanded opportunities to earn money give women more autonomy?

SPLICING AND SPINNING

Women were not the only ones involved in the production of cloth. Men grew the fiber-producing plants, helped with sericulture, managed most of the trade in raw, processed, and finished materials, and performed much of the more specialized weaving. Women and girls, however, put in long hours at the most tedious tasks. The yarns needed to weave cloth were overwhelmingly produced as a sideline activity by families that also engaged in the production of foodstuffs. The technology was simple enough that entrepreneurs did not need to set up large establishments and hire workers. Indeed, the work could be done just as well by women working in their own homes with simple equipment, starting and stopping as other demands required.

Since ancient times, everyday clothes had been made of hemp cloth, and coarse hemp cloth was used for mourning garments. Hemp, an annual plant, could be grown in most parts of China. Its seed could be pressed for oil and its inner bark (bast) could be processed to produce long fibers. Male hemp plants produced a finer fiber than female ones, so male plants were mostly used for thread, female ones for rope, sacking, and the like. Almost as important as hemp was ramie, grown primarily in south China, but also in Szechwan and Honan. Ramie had no uses outside of textile production and could not grow in the colder areas of China. On the plus side, it was a perennial plant and could be harvested three times a year. The fabric produced from it was softer and more lustrous than hemp and was particularly suited for summer clothing, as it dried easily even in humid weather. When sold, ramie cloth fetched a price several times that of hemp cloth.[10]

Processing hemp stalks involved many steps. Men would harvest the stalks and soak them in water for a day. Either men or women, but usually men, would then peel the skin from the stalk to remove the fiber;[11] this would be soaked for a night, washed and dried in the sun. Next men or women would separate the fibers by beating the dried bast and drawing it through comblike structures. They would have to smooth out by hand any lumps that remained, then soak the fibers again and split them into single strands. The next stage, splicing, was exceptionally time-consuming and was always women's work: it involved connecting these strands to make long continuous strands by manually taking two and twisting their ends together. (See Figure 16 for a rather idealized view of three women serenely performing this task.) Once yarn was spliced, it had to be twisted or doubled using

Fig. 16. Women splicing hemp
From a painting attributed to Liu Sung-nien (ca. 1150–after 1225). Collection of the
National Palace Museum, Taiwan, Republic of China (VA 35c).

spinning devices to make it strong enough to weave with. Ramie processing did not involve quite so many steps, but had to be done under time pressure. Strips containing the fibers had to be removed from the stems immediately after they were cut, while still in the fields. These strips later were soaked and the outer layer scraped off, then hung up to dry. After that women would separate, splice, and spin, still working under time constraints.

Since splicing was never mechanized to any degree, in areas where a lot of hemp or ramie was grown, splicing took up much of women's time. Fan Ch'eng-ta reported that in a town near Su-chou known for its cloth, the village women could be seen on the road splicing hemp as they walked.[12] Spinning, by contrast, could be performed more efficiently when the spinner had a better spindle.[13] In Sung times, many families used simple hand spindles. Wang Chen's *Book of Agriculture* (1313) describes a simple spindle that was suspended from the left hand and revolved by the right. Country people, he reported, found it convenient to use this simple spindle whenever they had spare time.[14] The problem with hand spindles was not simply that they produced an uneven thread; they also were slow. It has been estimated that the yarn that would be used in one day of weaving on a treadle-operated loom would take thirty to forty days to spin with a hand spindle. A family able to invest a little more in equipment could supply its women with a spindle wheel, such as the one shown in Figure 17. Here, while one woman holds the ball of yarn, the other turns the wheel. Even more efficient was a treadle-operated spinning wheel, turning three or four spindles at once, which could speed up their work severalfold.[15] To save wives and daughters this work and to help cope with the time constraints, it was apparently possible in some parts of north China to take spliced ramie to a large water-powered spinning wheel and have it spun there. Wang Chen reproduced a picture of this "great spinning wheel" and recommended that other areas copy it.[16]

Hemp and ramie were not the only plant fibers used for cloth. Fibers from the bean-creeper and the banana plant also made their way into cloth to some extent.[17] Minority groups along China's borders had also been using cotton for centuries. Cotton came originally from India and had been introduced into China both via Central Asia and via Burma and Yunnan. It was in the Sung, however, that cotton production began its dramatic rise. During the eleventh century, cotton was already cultivated in Kwangtung and Kwangsi, and by the end of the twelfth century also on Hainan Island and in Fukien. As the plants were brought farther north, their characteristics changed. The growing period was gradually shortened, and an annual variety producing few or no branches was developed. This occurred by the thirteenth century, if not earlier. It was easier for farmers to control the yield of the annual plant, thus increasing its economic potential.[18]

Cotton was not a bast fiber, like hemp and ramie, but a seed fiber. Before it could be spun, the fiber had to be loosened with big forks, dried in the sun, ginned to remove the seeds, fluffed up by bowing with a silk-string bow, straightened, and divided into slivers of equal length and weight.[19] Cotton had several attractive features: it made excellent warm padding for winter coats or quilts, as good but cheaper than silk floss. Woven into cloth, it was both lighter and warmer than hemp or ramie. Moreover, it was soft and comfortable. Wang Chen, in 1313, explained the advantages of cotton production: "Its advantages over sericulture are that one does not have the labor of picking [mulberry leaves] and feeding [silkworms], and the harvest is predictable. It is better than hemp and ramie in that one is spared the work of splicing and gains greater protection against the cold."[20] The reasons it did not spread sooner in China seem to have been the slow development of

Fig. 17. Working-class women spinning hemp or ramie on a spindle wheel From a painting by Wang Chü-cheng (eleventh century). The Palace Museum, Peking. From Chung-kuo mei-shu: hui-hua pien 3: pl. 19.

strains suited to central China and the difficulty of removing the seeds from
the fibers.

By the end of the Sung, cotton production was already of considerable economic importance in Fukien. Hsieh Fang-te (1226–1289), in a poem
thanking someone for a gift of cotton cloth, wrote that Fukien was well
favored, as cotton grew well there, and with a harvest from a thousand cotton
plants a family of eight would have no fear of poverty.[21] By the end of the
Sung, the government was collecting some of the cloth tax in the Chiang-nan
area in cotton.[22]

The spread of cotton cultivation was promoted by improved methods of
ginning. Wang Chen reported that in his day the old unsatisfactory method
of ginning by crushing raw cotton with rollers was being replaced by a gin
with two rollers that turned in opposite directions.[23] Legend has long had
it that a woman, Huang Tao-p'o, brought up-to-date cotton technology to
the Chiang-nan area. According to T'ao Tsung-i (fl. 1300–1360), a village in
Sung-chiang (Kiangsu) with poor soil was already relying on cotton as its
main crop in the late thirteenth century, with producers doing the ginning
by hand. When Huang Tao-p'o arrived from Hainan she introduced ginning devices along with better spinning and weaving equipment; she so
transformed the local economy, T'ao reported, that shrines were established
to her memory.[24] Women, in other words, could be heroes through creativity
in the very gender-specific realm of textile work.

Spinning cotton was more demanding than spinning hemp or ramie.
Instead of splicing fibers before spinning them, with cotton one had to draw
out even amounts of the short fibers as one spun so that they could be
twisted into a thin, even thread. Wang Chen illustrated the spindle wheel
women used, modeled on that used for ramie and hemp.[25]

RAISING SILKWORMS AND REELING SILK

When women worked making ramie, hemp, and cotton thread, they were
engaged in everyday tasks of a utilitarian nature. Much more romantic and
miraculous was work with silkworms. Strange little worms consumed enormous quantities of mulberry leaves and, if treated just right, would spin
extremely fine but strong fibers hundreds of meters long, fibers that could
be made into the softest, lightest, and shiniest of fabrics.

Silk had been made in China since ancient times, and techniques were
continually improved. Some scholars regard the silk produced in Sung times
as technically the best ever produced in China.[26] Threads could be spun in
many different thicknesses; they could be dyed many colors; and weavers
could weave them into light, airy gauzes, shiny satins, heavy twills, and
multicolored complex weaves, not to mention plain flat tabby.

Getting into silk production required a substantial investment in mulberry trees and all sorts of equipment for growing worms, reeling, spinning, and weaving. Sung and Yüan agricultural manuals devote considerable space to the production of silk, especially Ch'en Fu's *Book of Agriculture* (1149), the anonymous *Essentials of Agriculture and Sericulture* (1273), and Wang Chen's *Book of Agriculture* (1313).[27] There was a science to getting the mulberry trees to produce just the sorts of leaves one wanted. But that was largely men's work. When it was time to pick the leaves, however, women generally helped. The poet Tai Fu-ku (1169–after 1246) depicted such a scene, imagining he was a woman:

> Originally I was a daughter of the Ch'in family,
> But this spring I married young Wang.
> My husband's family emphasizes silk work,
> So I go out to pick mulberry leaves along the path.
> When I pick the low branches they break easily.
> The high branches are hard to reach by hand.
> I climb the bamboo ladder to get to the top of the tree,
> Thinking of the silkworms suffering from a paucity of leaves.
> When I lift my head, the mulberry branch catches my hair and lips;
> When I turn my body, the mulberry branch hooks and tears my skirt.
> Hard it is working at silkworms and mulberries.[28]

Wang Chen, in the illustrations to his *Book of Agriculture,* had a man on a ladder picking mulberry leaves, but showed a woman doing the same work on a high bench.[29]

In the north, where only one generation of silkworms was grown a year, the busy time was in the spring. In the south as well, the spring crop was the larger and more demanding one. Silkworm eggs would be saved over the winter. When the mulberry leaves had budded out, papers containing the eggs would be stored in a warm place until the eggs changed from pale yellow to green and the worms emerged. The hatched worms would have to be transferred to trays and spread out to give room for each worm to grow. These trays would be placed in a special silkworm room that could be devoted to their care and kept warm with heaters. For the next month the worms had to be tended carefully, given five or six feedings a day of chopped mulberry leaves, and kept from getting too cold. During this time they would "sleep" (actually molt) three times and grow almost one thousand–fold in weight, to about four grams each.

The worms had to be well fed to spin their cocoons, especially during their last few days of rapid growth. Feedings increased to ten times a day, some of those at night. Ch'en Fu warned that one should dry out the leaves before giving them to the worms for fear that wet leaves placed over the worms in a heated room might "steam" them.[30] If all went well, the silkworms would then spin cocoons for several days. Once the cocoons were spun, fast action was again needed because the cocoons would be ruined if the worm completed its transformation into a moth. If the family was not raising many silkworms, it could reel off the silk fibers from live worms. If they did not have enough labor to accomplish this rapidly enough, or if they needed to wait to borrow or rent reeling equipment, they would need to kill the worms in the cocoons. Generally this was done by steaming them or by packing them in baskets and suffocating them.[31]

Reeling silk meant taking up the ends of the fibers from several cocoons and drawing them out together while twisting them into a single thread strong enough to use in weaving. The cocoons had to be placed in a basin of water to turn freely while the reel was turned. Reels could be quite simple, but Ch'in Kuan (1049–1100), in his *Book of Sericulture,* described a complicated reeling frame that could allow one person to make two threads at a time.[32] Such reels are depicted from time to time in paintings, such as the one shown in Figure 18. Before using reeled silk to weave, it was still necessary to make threads by twisting several strands together on a spindle wheel, and to make warp threads by twisting some threads again on a spooling frame.

Silkworms were notoriously temperamental. Some years all the eggs hatched and spun magnificent cocoons; other years the results were disappointing. Women invested both physical and emotional energy into trying to keep the worms happy. They also wanted the silkworm spirits to be on their side. Ch'in Kuan, in his *Book of Sericulture,* treated praying to the silkworm spirits as one of the regular steps in the production process. Wang Chen and later authors included illustrations of the silkworm goddesses.[33] Hung Mai told of a family of silk producers, who normally raised a hundred trays of silkworms a year, which made them rather substantial producers. For three years their worms produced exceptionally large quantities of cocoons three times a year. The following year, however, the spring and fall batches produced not a single cocoon, and the next two years were the same. This shift in luck they attributed to an unusually large worm that had appeared on a tray the first year. Sensing that it was an auspicious sign, the wife had tended it carefully and placed it on their Buddhist altar. When its transformations seemed to be reaching their climax, they buried it under the mulberry trees.[34] Somehow, it is implied, this divine silkworm had rewarded them for their devotions for three years but thereafter lost its power.

People's anxieties about silkworms are perhaps best attested by the precautions they took when they had to deviate from their standard procedures. Hung Mai recorded a revealing story:

> In 1187, silkworms did well in Yü-chang and the price of mulberry leaves was dozens of time higher than normal, creating panic. Sometimes the whole family would weep in the silkworm room and call in a monk to chant sutras as

Fig. 18. A woman reeling silk
Detail from a thirteenth-century handscroll attributed to Liang K'ai (ca. 1200). The
Cleveland Museum of Art, John L. Severance Fund (77.5, sec. 3).

they sent the worms down the river [thus, in a sense, giving them a funeral].
Some rich families made a large box with a lattice on top, placing money in it,
and writing, "Good friends downstream: If you have plenty of mulberry leaves,
please take this money as payment and feed it to these silkworms so they will
have no reason to resent heaven or earth." Others had no choice but to dump
the worms, but none of them were happy about it.

The exception was Hu Erh, a commoner of Chung-hsiao village in Nan-
ch'ang county. He had plenty of mulberry leaves, enough to feed his worms,
but decided to sell his leaves to make a quick profit. When he told his wife
that he wanted to bury the worms, she was against it, but he paid no attention
to her. Calling to her, he took a hoe and dug a hole under the mulberry trees
and buried the worms there. He planned to take the mulberry leaves into the
market the next day. Proud of himself for having devised a great plan, he
drank wine and fell asleep drunk. At the third watch, he heard noises outside.
Suspecting robbers, he lit a torch and went to look. It was the silkworms. He
took a broom to sweep them away, but the more he swept, the more they
spread out. This went on all night, and the whole family was afraid. His wife
especially blamed him for what he had done, which just made Hu angrier, and
he decided to wash them all away.

The next morning at dawn he was determined to go ahead, resenting only that he would lose a day in reaping his profit. Suddenly he again heard a clamor and shouted, "Is it those weird creatures again?" He got up quickly and lit a lamp. As soon as his foot touched the ground, he felt an insect bite and screamed with pain. His son got up next, and the same thing happened. His wife ran to see what was going on and found that the bed was swarming with caterpillars and the father and son were writhing in pain. After a few days Hu Erh died, and the caterpillars disappeared. The son, fortunately, was all right. The silkworms in other families had by then spun their cocoons, while the Hus' mulberry leaves still filled their courtyard. They never got a single cent for them.[35]

Silkworms, it would seem, were quite capable of turning on people who did not treat them properly.

WEAVING, DYEING, AND FINISHING CLOTH

So far, I have discussed only the production of thread. With the thread prepared, women still had much work to do before they had cloth ready to make into clothes. Hemp, ramie, and cotton they generally wove into simple flat tabby weaves, using warp and weft threads of the same size. They would use looms owned by their families, the looms varying considerably in size, complexity, and efficiency. Chou Ch'ü-fei (d. after 1178) reported that in Kuei-lin (Kwangsi), people wove ramie cloth on simple looms tied to their waist, allowing them to get up to do other chores.[36] These relatively primitive back-strap looms had probably been in use since the Shang dynasty.[37] They could be used for simple weaves but also were suitable for extremely complex tapestry weaves, so their products could be of high value. In other parts of China, larger free-standing looms were standard, as they had been for many centuries. The best were treadle-operated looms that allowed the weaver to work more quickly because he or she could raise the warp threads by foot, freeing both hands to pass the shuttle back and forth quickly. Treadle-operated looms had been used for silk since the Han dynasty, and by Sung times appear also to have been used for more utilitarian textiles. Setting up treadle-operated looms was a laborious task requiring at least two people, as the warp threads had to be guided through small holes in the heddles that would lift them.

The poet Wen T'ung (1018–1079) portrayed a woman laboriously weaving her family's tax cloth on a treadle loom:

> Both hands are tired from throwing the shuttle.
> Both feet are weary from pressing the treadles.
> After three days of weaving without stop,
> She can cut off one bolt of cloth.

> The place where she weaves is exposed to wind and sun.
> When she cuts the cloth she is careful with the knife and measure.
> Everyone says the border is well done.
> She herself likes the tightness of the warp and weft.[38]

A loom could take up considerable space, so it is not surprising that in many peasant families the loom would be set up outside in the courtyard, as this poem suggests.

Ordinary households could easily weave plain silk, using treadle looms. Still, weaving silk took more time than weaving hemp or ramie because of the fineness of the yarn. Moreover, much silk was woven into special fabrics, including damasks, gauzes, and satins. To weave a bolt of gauze, about twelve meters in length, the government allowed a worker twelve days.[39] More elaborate weaves required better equipment and more experienced weavers. For complex multicolor weaves, the threads had to be dyed before they were woven, then a great many shuttles used for each of the different colors. It was best done on a draw loom, a tall structure with a place for a child to sit to raise specified warp threads, as instructed by the weaver. Thus, weaving silks of these sorts was a specialized craft, and often the weavers were men. But women could also learn this craft. One late Sung depiction of the sericulture process has a woman weaving on such a draw loom, assisted by a child (Fig. 19).

Ramie, hemp, and cotton did not require much processing after they were woven. For men's work clothes, dying was not necessary. In paintings, working men are often shown in off-white, undyed clothes, conforming to sumptuary rules.[40] Probably most of their clothes were of home-spun and home-woven cloth, perhaps bleached by a simple process, such as laying it out in the sun. One poem alludes to girls weaving white ramie cloth aboard boats (presumably ones they lived on), then laying them on the sandy shore to bleach.[41] Applying lime or certain types of ashes was also known to bleach ramie.[42] Women's clothes were more often made out of dyed cloth—or at least poets and painters liked to depict women in colored clothes.

Dyes could be prepared at home. A great many mineral and vegetable dyes were known by Sung times. Agricultural manuals described how to grow some of the most common vegetable ones, like indigo and "red flower."[43] Once dye had been prepared, it would be possible to dye more yarn or pieces of cloth than the average family would produce in a few months, so in more densely populated areas dye shops or communal dye ponds would be a convenience. Dye shops were definitely available in large cities for dying silk. One shop in Chin-hua (Chekiang) had several hundred bolts of gauze as well as several hundred pounds of red-flower dye on hand, to which over a thousand pounds of purple grass were added. One dyer in Loyang was particularly known for his tie-dying of elaborate designs.[44]

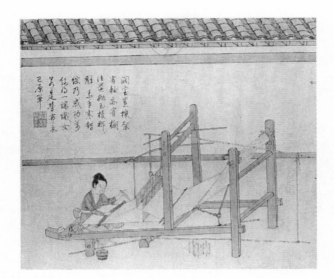

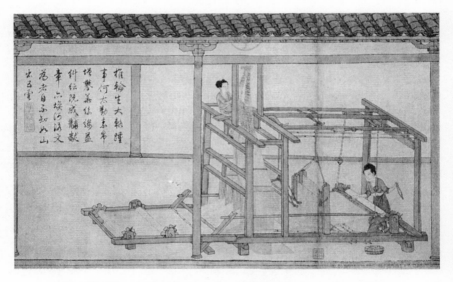

Fig. 19. Women weaving on a treadle loom and on a draw loom
Details from Cheng Chi's thirteenth-century handscroll copying Lou Shu's (1090–1162) depiction of the steps involved in making silk. Courtesy of the Freer Gallery of Art, Smithsonian Institution, Washington, D.C. (54.20).

THE COMMERCIALIZATION OF CLOTH PRODUCTION

The economic developments during the late T'ang and Sung were so dramatic that they have often been called revolutionary. The sexual division of labor could not have remained entirely unaltered in the circumstances. Cities provided women with new opportunities to make money; innkeepers, for instance, not uncommonly were widows.[45] The expansion and commercialization of textile production made it easier for families hard pressed for cash to turn to their wives and daughters for help in raising funds. At the same time, commercialization undermined the age-old principle of the sexual division of labor by fostering the appearance of male master weavers.

The sorts of labor women performed in textile production were shaped by the growth of the market for raw materials, thread, and finished cloth of all sorts. No family had to produce cloth in order to have clothes, nor did producer families have to perform all the steps. Families could concentrate on what they did most efficiently, selling any surplus they produced at local markets or to traveling salesmen.[46]

The market for cloth was huge. The government needed hemp and ramie for soldiers' uniforms and silk for officials' salaries and payments to the Khitan and Jurchen.[47] In the Northern Sung, nearly half a million bolts of hemp and ramie were collected as tax, with two circuits producing over half: Ho-tung, with 151,116 bolts, and Kuang-nan-hsi, with 105,647.[48] Considerably more was collected in various sorts of silks—almost three million bolts of plain silk, some hundred thousand bolts of gauze, and thousands of bolts of various specialty weaves.[49] A good portion of these quotas was actually filled by merchants who bought up cloth from producers and either sold it to those who owed the stuffs as tax or, when the government was willing to commute cloth tax to money, sold it directly to the government. The government also bought cloth from producers, setting the price unilaterally and thus often imposing a hardship on families forced to sell at below market prices.[50]

Families might decide to devote more of their energy to cloth production because merchants advanced them capital. Hung Mai told a story about a commoner of Fu-chou in Kiangsi, who had established a business trading in hemp and ramie cloth. At the beginning of each year he would travel throughout the prefecture lending capital to the weaving families through brokers. Then from the sixth through the eighth months he would personally collect from them. One of his brokers had received five hundred strings of cash from him to set up a store/warehouse, which he filled with several thousand lengths of cloth.[51] Families that received advances of this sort would not need to sell the bast or the yarn, for which there were also markets, but could carry the process through to produce finished cloth.

Cotton was, probably from the beginning, a frequently traded product. North China, where warm garments were essential in the winter, needed more cotton than it could produce. In some areas where cotton could be grown, it could not be efficiently processed, because lack of warmth and humidity hampered the spinning and weaving processes. Thus raw cotton was shipped to the areas that could spin and weave it best, and finished cloth was transported to areas with high demand.

Silk was if anything more deeply enmeshed in the market. Farming households that produced silk as a sideline could buy the equipment they needed to raise silkworms as well as the mulberry leaves; and they could sell cocoons, reeled silk, or finished cloth. Producing a little more silk than they needed for taxes and consumption was thus a means for a peasant family to raise a little cash. A length of plain silk, in 1066, could be sold for about fifteen hundred cash, which at that time probably bought the rice needed to feed an adult for two months.[52] Demand stimulated production so that in the major cities an extraordinary variety of types of silk were available for sale.[53]

Commercialization resulted in the rise of families that specialized in silk production. These included both rural families that raised silkworms and optionally also produced silk textiles, and urban families that bought reeled silk and used it to weave fancy fabrics. In mountainous villages in Wu-hsing, a gazetteer reported, wealthy households might raise several hundred trays of silkworms and employ workers to weave. Many of the residents of the county seat of Chin-hua, in Chekiang, made their living by weaving—so many, in fact, that they were said to "clothe the world." In one tale recorded by Hung Mai, a man introduced himself as "Eighth-Uncle Chang, a gauze weaver from Lord Fan's Bridge in Jun-chou."[54] Ch'en Fu, in his agricultural treatise, explained that a family could support itself by raising as little as ten trays of silkworms, "each tray producing twelve *chin* of cocoons, from each *chin* they get 1.3 ounces of thread, from 5 ounces of thread one gets one length of thin silk, which can be exchanged for one picul four pecks of rice." Specialized silk-producing households, however, often apparently bought all or part of their mulberry leaves on an open market, which made them dependent on market prices and led to the sorts of problems referred to above when the price of leaves rose rapidly.[55]

Not all families that raised silkworms wove with the thread they produced. Some families sold the thread as soon as it was reeled, perhaps because they did not have the capital to invest in elaborate looms. Fan Ch'eng-ta portrayed the women in a farming family busily boiling cocoons and reeling silk, the reels making as much noise as a storm, the cocoons supplying seemingly endless threads. Because they could not weave it into silk themselves, they would take it to the market the next day to sell.[56]

Government documents frequently refer to "weaving households," most of which probably made their living predominantly from silk work, either growing silkworms and weaving, or weaving alone. The government took an interest in such enterprises because it imposed considerable obligations on them to produce specified types of cloth. In 1036, for instance, Chang I reported that several thousand weaving households in Tzu-chou (Szechwan) had to turn over two-thirds of their output to the government. Once in Ch'eng-tu, when the weaving households could not meet the government's demands, eighty men from the army were assigned to weave.[57] No evidence has been found so far to suggest that these weaving households were workshops that hired outside workers to spin or weave for them; instead they appear to have been family businesses. The increase in Sung times in the number of specialized weaving households weakened the link between women and cloth production. A larger share of weaving, at least of the most elaborate fabrics, was now done by specialized male craftsmen, probably assisted by women in their households.[58]

In a family that treated silk production as its major livelihood, both men and women undoubtedly shared in the tasks. A late Sung copy of a twelfth-century painting illustrating twenty-four steps in the sericulture process portrays forty-two women, twenty-four men, three boys, five girls, and two babies. The babies are there to show that sericulture was done amid other domestic chores, such as caring for infants. The children, however, are helping. In one of the last scenes a boy is perched on top of the draw loom, raising the warp threads specified by the woman weaver seated below, a technique required for the weaving of brocades. Whether the boy is a son in the family, a servant boy, or an apprentice is unclear. (In the slightly later Freer version [see Fig. 19], the child on the loom seems to be a girl.) Men are shown tending mulberry trees, picking mulberry leaves, carrying equipment, preparing heaters, laying out the spinning frames, storing the cocoons in urns, and praying to the silkworm spirit. Women seem to have special charge of the silkworms, a pair of them tending them together. Only in one scene do more than four people appear as a group: just before the worms are ready to spin, three men and two women are busy arranging a spinning frame.[59]

Even if women cared for the silkworms while men picked leaves and moved the equipment, the men probably made the financial decisions. Such, at least, is the implication of two stories reported by Hung Mai about silkworm-raising families facing high prices for mulberry leaves, one of which was translated above. In both cases the husbands are described as consulting with their wives but overriding their advice. In the story related above, the wife is vocal in blaming her husband; in the other, when the man wants the worms dumped, his wife and daughter-in-law conspire to save some to have eggs for the next year.[60]

Not every woman engaged in textile production was working under the supervision of her family head. An individual woman might work as a spinner or weaver in another household, much as she could work as a cook,

seamstress, or scullery maid. Hung Mai told of a widow of sixty whose sons
had all died in an epidemic and daughters-in-law had all remarried, leaving
her alone with only one eight-year-old grandson. Each day she would go out
to spin and splice for another family, returning to eat with her grandson.
(Whether she kept working for the same family or moved about is unclear.)[61]
The only women working in large-scale weaving establishments in Sung times
were those in government workshops, where their labor was probably at least
partially compulsory; in 981, when the government abolished the weaving
workshop in Hu-chou, the twenty male workers were sent to the capital and
the fifty-eight female workers were released.[62]

In the Sung period, as in ages past, the preferred way for a widow to
support herself and her family, should the need arise, was to splice, spin, or
weave.[63] The social approval given to these activities undoubtedly relates to
their femininity (they were women's work) and their domestic location
(women did not need to come into much contact with men to perform them).
Supporting oneself or a family by such work may have become somewhat
easier in Sung times with the expanded market for thread and cloth. Miss
Ch'en T'ang-ch'ien, married less than two years when widowed, said she
would not remarry but instead support her infant son and parents-in-law
by sericulture. Miss Chou (1113–1174), widowed with five young children,
raised silkworms, spliced and spun hemp, and wove, starting work before
her children were up and working all day without resting. Even the widows
of officials are said to have kept their families together through such work.
Miss Ch'en's (1016–1089) husband died at his post in 1059; far from home
with young children, she got by thanks to her labors at spinning.[64] Of course,
a woman did not have to be a widow to need to support herself. The daughter
of a prostitute who had been raised by another family did not want to
obey her mother's demand that she continue the older woman's profession,
telling her that she would support her instead by weaving, claiming special
skill. Those without special skills, it should be noted, could not expect high
wages. One farmer's daughter abandoned by her husband worked for wages
as a weaver but did not make enough to provide more than the most minimal
subsistence for his mother and herself.[65]

In the postindustrial age, we tend to look on textile production as a craft
or industry, comparable, perhaps, to production of paper or pottery. In traditional China, by contrast, the manufacture of cloth was considered an
agricultural activity. Farming families raised animals and grew crops. Much
of what they produced required processing to be fully useful: grain had to be
husked, and if it was to be used for noodles, it had to be ground; vegetables
had to be dried or pickled to keep; beans had to be fermented to make soy
sauce. The task of processing plant fibers and silkworm cocoons was perhaps

more laborious, but it was not fundamentally different. Women who spent their days splicing hemp or reeling silk were peasant women processing agricultural products, not artisans.

There were slow but steady changes in the work women did to make cloth during the Sung. Stimulated by the ready market for fabrics of all sorts, producers kept improving their equipment, inventing better spindle wheels, reeling frames, and looms. Since women were active as spinners, reelers, and weavers, they undoubtedly appreciated the technological improvements, and often may have suggested adaptations to the equipment themselves. Over the course of the Sung, the profit to be made in one type of cloth or another varied, and farmers' wives and daughters switched regularly from one type of production to another.[66] Certainly, as cotton came to be better known and adequate gins were invented, more families took to producing cotton. Men were more active than their wives in marketing, but the women probably supported decisions that would lead to more income from their labors.

The commercialization of the Sung economy meant that families could see the monetary value of women's textile work: in the mid–eleventh century a finished bolt of ramie cloth was worth about five to seven hundred cash, a finished bolt of plain silk about fifteen hundred. Did these opportunities to earn cash in any way enhance the status of wives in these families? Did they gain more authority or autonomy? I see very little evidence that they did. First of all, textile production was overwhelmingly a household affair. There would be no more reason for the money received from the sale of a bolt of cloth to go to the woman who wove it than to the man who had hoed the hemp field and peeled the hemp bark. The work was done by the household, under the general direction of the family head, and any income from it was family income.

If the women who sold their textiles gained a greater sense of self-worth in the process, no literatus seems to have noticed. To them, the increased penetration of the market into household production of textiles just made the lives of women harder. Rather than worry that weaving women were becoming too autonomous, they tended to pity them for having to work so hard for so little reward. Wen T'ung (1018–1079) wrote a poem on the hardships of women who wove to pay the family tax burden. After he described the weariness of the weaver, he related what happened when the officials rejected the cloth she had just woven:

> Her parents take it back to their cottage
> And throw it at the inner door.
> Looking at each other, they say nothing.
> Her tears flow as though from a leaking drain.
> To get some cash she takes off clothes to pawn
> And buys yarn to fasten to the loom.

> She does not dare leave the loom
> Through the night, after the fire and candles are out.
> She has to finish the tax [cloth].
> How is there time to worry about her own clothes?
> She has long known bone-piercing cold.
> She willingly exposes her arms and legs.
> The local government runner is squatting at the door,
> Cursing them for handing [the cloth] over late.
> How can the feelings of the weaving woman
> Catch the attention of the officials in charge?[67]

Wen T'ung's contemporary Hsü Chi (1028–1103) wrote a poem titled "Weaving Girl," which depicts women promptly selling the cloth they weave to buy more yarn to weave some more:

> It is not that her body does not love clothes of silk gauze.
> When the moon is bright, through frost and cold, she never leaves the loom.
> Even when it is woven into gauze, she does not wear it.
> She sells it for cash to buy silk yarn to take back.[68]

Two centuries later, Wen-hsiang (1210–after 1276) wrote a poem decrying the exploitation of the girls engaged in sericulture:

> Wu people are pressed for time in the third month of spring.
> The silkworms have finished their third sleep and are famished.
> The family is poor, without cash to buy mulberry leaves to feed to them.
> What can they do? Hungry silkworms do not produce silk.
> The daughter-in-law and the daughter talk to each other as they carry the
> baskets.
> Who knows the pain they feel in their hearts?
> The daughter is twenty but does not have wedding clothes.
> Those the government sends to collect taxes roar like tigers.
> If they have no clothes to dress their daughter, they can still put the
> [wedding] off.
> If they have no silk to turn over to the government, they will go bankrupt.
> The family next door went bankrupt and is already scattered.
> A broken-down wall, an abandoned well—the sadness of out-migration.[69]

Wen's contemporary Ch'en Yün-p'ing concluded a poem by querying an experienced woman silk worker about her work. He attributed to her this response:

> From the seven days that the silkworms are on the trays,
> We get one hundred *chin* of cocoons.
> After ten days of reeling, we get two skeins of silk threads.
> Then, strand by strand, we weave it into gauze.
> A hundred people laboring hard is not enough to clothe one person.

The poet finished by describing the woman's feelings:

> She lifted her head and noticed the yellow tips of the mulberry leaves.
> She lowered her head and shed tears out of shame for her plain cloth skirt.[70]

In these poems, we might note, women's hardships are blamed on government tax collectors, not gender inequalities or anything to do with the family system. Poets added pathos to their protests against government oppression of the poor by depicting the victims as women.

EIGHT

Husband-Wife Relations

In didactic writings, the husband-wife tie was unproblematic: it was a hierarchical relationship maintained by the wife's willing submission. The *Classic of Filial Piety for Girls* had Pan Chao respond to a student's comment concerning the importance of husbands by saying, "The husband is heaven. How could one not serve him?"[1] Two Sung painters illustrated this passage by having the wife show bodily deference to her husband. In one she kneels before him, offering him a dish;[2] in the other (Fig. 20), she bows her head slightly, as if awaiting his instructions.

Other Sung sources demonstrate convincingly that submission was far from the only thing characterizing the bond between husbands and wives. Love, affection, hatred, bitterness, disappointment, and jealousy are all depicted as common elements of marital relations. Unfortunately, few husbands or wives wrote about their own marriages; first-person accounts are relatively rare. Upper-class men in Sung times, moreover, did not introduce their young wives to their friends or talk much about them. Even a man extremely happy with his wife would be embarrassed to make his feelings public. Poets wrote to express their sadness at parting from brothers or friends and showed the poems to others. They even shared poems they wrote about parting from courtesans. But they did not share (or perhaps even write) poems about parting from their wives. Even after his wife died, a man would feel most comfortable describing her as a dutiful daughter-in-law to his parents, a competent manager of their household, and a loving mother to their children, but not as the great love of his life or his strongest ally in times of trouble. He might write poems expressing his grief, but usually these poems would focus more on his emotional response to her death than on their life together.

Fig. 20. A woman paying respect to her husband
From a handscroll illustrating the *Classic of Filial Piety for Girls*, attributed to Ma
Ho-chih (twelfth century). Collection of the National Palace Museum, Taiwan,
Republic of China (SH 35).

Couples must have been as varied in Sung China as in any other place,
with some deeply in love and others barely tolerating each other. The history
of any particular couple, if somehow we could retrieve it, would certainly
show that they had adjusted to each other in major and minor ways; that is,
that husband-wife relations were not produced automatically according to
moral maxims, class position, and age, but were shaped by processes of give
and take in which each party could draw from a stock of images and ideas

to set the tone for their life together. Since husband-wife relations are so central to an understanding of marriage, in this chapter I will try to tease out what I can from the meager sources to show how husbands and wives worked out a common life.

DEMOGRAPHIC CLUES

Vital data about Sung couples provide a few clues about married life. In the upper class at least, most men and women married while quite young; as discussed in Chapter 3, nearly 90 percent of the women and 60 percent of the men in my sample were wed by twenty-two sui. Their relative youth likely increased the chances that they would feel strong sexual attraction for each other, since both would be at an age when hormones were causing all sorts of changes to their bodies and their emotions. Often the woman was two or three years younger than her husband, but not always. In about a quarter of the cases I studied, the woman was older than the man, in 7 percent of the cases by three or more years—figures not out of line with studies of well-off families in later periods.[3] It was more common, however, for the husband to be substantially older than his wife: in 31 percent of the cases, the man was five or more years older; and in fully 12 percent he was ten or more years older—even though these were first marriages for both partners. (See Table 2.)

Age differences must have had some effect on husband-wife relations. A wife as old as or older than her husband may have managed to avoid being dominated by him, at least to a degree, even if she married as a teenager.

TABLE 2.   Age Differences Between
Husbands and Wives

Years Husband Was Older Than Wife[a]	Percentage of Cases
−4, −3	7
−2, −1	12
0	8
1, 2	17
3, 4	19
5, 6	10
7, 8	6
9, 10	6
11, 12	4
13 or more	4

[a] A negative age difference means the wife is older than the husband.

When a girl of seventeen married a man in his mid-twenties, however, he may well have looked on her as a child and treated her accordingly. But this is mere speculation. Sung writers did not treat age differences as of much significance. Biographies of wives do not say that they were respectful even though older than their husbands, or that they proved competent managers despite being much younger than their husbands.

Another demographic clue to husband-wife relations is the number of children couples had. Having their marriages arranged by their parents when they were still teenagers did not prevent couples from becoming sexually compatible enough to have many children. The couples I studied regularly had four, five, six, or seven children who survived long enough to be worth recording, though some of these may have been born to a concubine rather than the wife.

Uncertainty about how long a marriage would last must have affected how husbands and wives looked on each other. Most marriages began when the spouses were young, but they did not all last until the spouses were old. Apart from the tiny number that ended in divorce, they endured only until one or the other partner died, and that could happen at almost any time. Among the couples I studied, 2 percent of the men and 10 percent of the women died by age thirty, another 4 percent of the men and 10 percent of the women by forty, and another 16 percent of the men and 13 percent of the women by fifty. Thus, even though the mean length of marriage was a little more than twenty-five years, a sizable number lasted only ten or fifteen. Indeed, marriages were disrupted at a very regular rate, with close to 20 percent ending in every decade (Table 3). When marriages ended within the first fifteen years, it was usually because of the death of the wife, in many cases in childbirth. Thereafter it was the man's death that was the more likely reason.

TABLE 3.   Length of Marriages

	Percentage of Cases
Up to 5 years	8.3
6–10	9.7
11–15	11.1
16–20	8.3
21–25	8.3
26–30	12.5
31–35	8.3
36–40	9.7
41–45	8.3
46–50	11.1
51 or more	4.2

IMAGES OF LOVING MARRIAGES

Husbands and wives who loved each other were commonly likened to mandarin ducks—beautiful, sedate birds that stay paired, floating around a pond side by side. Couples who loved each other might also be described as "bound like a bundle of firewood," an image that plays on the image of marriage as a tying together. And husbands or wives who wanted to express their love could refer to their desire to grow old together, spend a hundred years together, or share the same grave. That conjugal love was a beautiful thing and the goal of all marriages is implied in these images and sayings.

In biographies, the ideal relationship between a husband and wife was often portrayed as marked by great reserve and courtesy. It was not the wife who treated her husband like a friend, telling him at the end of the day all that she had done, whom writers held in esteem; rather, they praised the wife who out of respect for her husband's dignity did not bother him with details and treated him "like a guest," even after decades of marriage. Loving wives were like Miss Fu (1097–1148), who gave her husband some jewelry to cover his expenses when he went to take the examinations, telling him as they parted, "Go and do well to bring glory to your parents. Do not worry about family matters."[4] In other words, the loving wife was the good inner helper.

Very short marriages rarely led men to compose interesting funerary biographies about their wives. Ou-yang Hsiu's biographies of his first two wives, for example, like Tseng Kung's and Lü Tsu-ch'ien's, are remarkably uninformative. Perhaps when a woman died within the first five years of marriage she was still too much the bride, not yet enough the mother and household manager, to let her husband say anything personal about her. Longer marriages sometimes inspired more revealing accounts, however. Li Kou's (1009–1059) marriage to Miss Ch'en (1015–1047) lasted seventeen years. His biography for her concentrated almost exclusively on how uncomplaining she was. "When I traveled in the four directions, she never made any suggestions, nor did she ever ask any questions. Sometimes she had to stay home alone for several months without much money, but she never revealed any resentment."[5] Much the same image comes out in Liu K'o-chuang's 1187–1269) account of his wife, Miss Lin (1190–1228):

> During the nineteen years that she was my wife, I had to travel on official business constantly, across rivers and lakes, from mountains to seas. Despite the very great distances, she always accompanied me. Once the boat capsized at the Sung River rapids, and only ten people survived. When we were told that our baggage was lost in the water, I became very upset, but she remained as calm as usual. Another time when we were sailing on the Li River the boat crashed. As before, she showed no sign of panic in the face of peril.[6]

Because staying home to care for her parents-in-law was perfectly honorable and praiseworthy, I suspect that wives' travels were mentioned so often because they were, in fact, important to the husband-wife relationship. On these trips, there would be no sisters- and brothers-in-law, no nieces and nephews. Moreover, the journeys themselves often took weeks or months, periods when the husband and wife would spend a larger part of their days together than usual.

Yüan Hsieh's (1144–1224) marriage to Miss Pien (1155–1203) lasted thirty years. He remembered her diligence, conscientiousness, and generosity: "Preparing my food and drink, mending my clothes, these things she always did herself without letting me know. But she would invariably tell me if she spent any money or made a gift, no matter how slight. She would always say, 'My heart is like a great road with room for everyone.' She said whatever she thought with no deviousness."[7]

Ssu-ma Kuang was married to Miss Chang (1023–1082) for forty-four years. "From when she was first married until she closed her eyes [in death], she never showed anger or spoke foolishly. Even when others attacked her, she accepted it silently, never arguing her version and never harboring resentment." She was generous to the maids and concubines, sympathizing with them and never showing jealousy. "One evening she was washing her feet and a maid poured in boiling water, scalding one of her feet. All she did was rap her on the forehead a few times, even though her foot festered for over a month." She was frugal in her daily expenses, but never complained if her husband gave assistance to his relatives. Once when their clothes were stolen, he fretted that he had nothing to wear to see guests, but she gave him some perspective, saying that anything that protected their bodies would do.[8]

Hung Kua (1117–1184) grew old together with his wife, Miss Shen Te-jou (1119–1179). After forty-five years of marriage, he wrote of the ways she always willingly took on family responsibilities, such as arranging the marriages of his younger brothers and sisters and performing family rituals, even preparing the coffin, shrouds, and clothes for her own funeral. Although he generally stressed the way she enabled them to live rather separate lives, he did provide one glimpse of the pleasure he took in her company. During a stay at home, he wrote, he acquired a country retreat and built a pavilion on it; his wife "enjoyed going there with him to gaze at the stream and the mountains, staying until dark."[9]

Men's narratives of their wives are, of course, as much about their own self-presentation as about their wives. Often a man would stress how uncomplaining his wife was, and he did not mind admitting how hard he made her life—how little money they had, how many times they had to move, how many family responsibilities she had to take on. He wanted others to think of his wife as having put up with it all in good spirits. In reading through these accounts, I was left with the impression that men took a secret pride in being difficult husbands. Did they see it as more manly to be incompetent in the management of daily life, at least when their incompetence would prompt the nearest woman to take over and make life as comfortable as possible within the limits of income and circumstances? Given the aesthetic appeal of the image of the lovely handmaiden attending to the needs of the dominant man, I suspect that that was precisely the case.

COMPANIONATE MARRIAGES

For all that they praised men and women who led separate lives, writers often reveal positive feelings about marriages in which the husband and wife shared intellectual interests. Ou-yang Hsiu (1007–1072) reported that Mei Yao-ch'en (1002–1060) told him that his wife, Miss Hsieh (1008–1044), learned enough by listening to his conversations with visitors from behind the door that she could discuss current events intelligently with him. Su Shih (1036–1101) claimed to have enjoyed conversing with his first wife, Miss Wang Fu (1039–1065), who was sixteen when they married. "At first she did not mention that she could read, but when she saw me reading books [aloud] she would stay close all day. I still did not know if she understood them, but later when I forgot something, she would promptly remind me. It turned out that she had a good general knowledge of other books as well. This is how I learned she was bright but modest." She regularly asked him about his official business and gave advice. When he had visitors, she would listen to their conversations from behind a screen, afterwards warning him against people she considered untrustworthy. Hu Yin (1098–1156) reported that his young wife, Miss Chang Chi-lan (1108–1137), would keep him company in the evening, sewing while he read or wrote, and occasionally discussing things with him. She had learned the *Analects* as a child, but got her husband to explain its meaning more fully to her. When they were separated for reasons of business, as they often were, she wrote letters to him. Chou Pi-ta (1126–1204) described his wife, Miss Wang (1135–1203), as very well educated and able to discuss his work with him. In the evenings they would teach their son together, and then they would play chess, sometimes long into the night.[10]

To Chinese in later centuries the most famous companionate couple of the Sung was Li Ch'ing-chao and her husband, Chao Ming-ch'eng (1081–1129), who married when she was eighteen and he twenty-one. Childless, they had an exceptionally close intellectual relationship. What brought them together was a shared passion for collecting anything with historical, literary, or artistic associations: books, paintings, calligraphy, rubbings of inscriptions on stone slabs or ancient bronze vessels, and the ancient vessels themselves.

They catalogued their collection, the surviving inventory of their rubbings showing that they pored over them looking for any discrepancies between these texts and other historical sources. Their collection gradually grew to a huge size: in 1127, Chao took fifteen cartloads to Nanking, but the bulk of the items, over ten rooms' worth, were left behind in Shantung and destroyed in a fire when the Jurchen seized their hometown.

In the postscript Li Ch'ing-chao wrote to the annotated catalogue of their rubbings, published after Chao Ming-ch'eng's death, she described their obsession with collecting.[11] Even when newly married and still a student at the Imperial Academy, Chao would use any cash he could raise to stop on the way home to buy rubbings, which they would later inspect together. Wherever he traveled he looked for antiquities. "If he saw a painting or piece of calligraphy by a famous person, ancient or contemporary, or a rare ancient object, he would take off his clothes to trade for it." Once someone offered them a peony painting by Hsü Hsi for two hundred thousand cash. They kept it overnight, and when they had to return it because the price was so high, "husband and wife shared their disappointment for several days." She also wrote, "Whenever we got a book we would immediately inspect it together and organize our collected notes and labels. When we got a painting, calligraphy, or bronze vessel, we would view it and discuss its shortcomings, devoting to it the time it took for a candle to burn down." She also described a game they would play after dinner sitting among their books with a pot of tea. One would mention some passage, and then whoever could identify exactly where it could be found in what book got to take a sip of tea. They would often end up laughing and spill the tea. Later, through considerable tribulations as they fled from the Jurchen invaders, both Li and Chao made every effort to take as much of their beloved collection with them, but gradually lost almost all of it.[12]

Li and Chao are seen as an ideal companionate couple not only because they shared a love of old things, but also because she wrote excellent verse on the long-popular theme of the woman overcome by sadness because her lover is away. Among the most famous of her poems is the following, generally interpreted to reflect her feelings when separated from her husband:

> Thin mists, thick clouds, a long gloomy day.
> Incense burns in the golden animal-shaped pot.
> Once again it is the Double Ninth festival.
> Lying on a jade pillow, through the gauze bed curtain,
> I feel the midnight coolness penetrate.
>
> At dusk I had a cup of wine by the eastern hedge.
> My sleeves were filled with a hidden fragrance.
> Do not say I am not overwhelmed.
> When the west wind blows the curtain up
> One can see I am thinner than a yellow flower.[13]

After her husband's death she sometimes referred to their life together in her songs. The second half of one such song reads:

> We were happy together in those years,
> Our lives like incense filling sleeves.
> By the fire we made tea.
> We traveled on beautiful horses, by flowing streams, in light carriages,
> Undaunted by sudden storms,
> So long as we could share a cup of warm wine and sheets of fine paper.
> Now embracing each other is impossible.
> Can there be times like those ever again?[14]

Li Ch'ing-chao and Chao Ming-ch'en are important not because they represent a common type of couple, but because they caught people's imagination. For all the forces that worked against married women developing their talents, people still saw intellectual relationships between husbands and wives as an alternative ideal.

BOSSY WIVES AND VIOLENT HUSBANDS

It was never claimed that all couples were happy. Both husbands and wives had many opportunities to make the other's life unpleasant. Hung Mai described his wife's sister as a classic bossy wife, married to a timid husband:

My wife's father's fifth daughter, named Tsung-shu, was quick-witted from youth and knew how to read. When she came of age, she married the scholar Tung Twenty-eight of Hsiang-yang. Tung was weak and timid, Shu arrogant and overbearing. She bossed him around as though he were a servant. Unsatisfied with him, she became depressed and fell ill. In the winter of 1126, when soldiers from Kuo Ching's army raided Hsiang and Teng, [Tung] died in Han-chiang. The following year Shu followed her mother, Miss T'ien, to Nan-yang, where she ate, drank, and amused herself without any sign of grief [despite still being in heavy mourning for Tung]. She gradually recovered from her old illness and became quite cheerful. One morning, without any reason, she uncontrollably vomited over a pint of blood. She became worried and had [a medium] called [words missing in text]. [The medium] said, "Ho-chung should not remarry. If she does I will kill her." Ho-chung was Shu's adult name, not known even to people in the family. Shu recognized the voice as that of her dead husband and scolded him, "I've been burdened by you my whole life. Even after dying, you are still causing me trouble. What business of yours is it if I marry someone else?" The medium regained consciousness without saying anything more, and Shu recovered. It happened that my father-in-law came south and brought [his wife and daughter] along to Yang-chou. He proposed getting a new son-in-law for Shu, mentioning Wang

Yüeh [as a possibility]. Shu said, "I've already been troubled once in my life by a literary official and have no desire to repeat the experience. I'd be satisfied with a military officer." So she married Mr. Hsi . . .[15]

—and, of course, came to a sorry end, for the ghost of her first husband did in the end exact his revenge.

Exactly how Shu badgered her husband is not made clear in Hung Mai's account. He probably thought his readers would be able to imagine what a bossy wife was like. One of the few descriptions of an argument between spouses in fact concerns a *staged* argument. After Ch'in Kuei (1090–1155) and his wife, Miss Wang, had been captured by the Jurchen, they devised a way to avoid being split up. When Ch'in Kuei was to be sent off on an expedition, his wife yelled at him loudly enough to be heard by those nearby: "When my father married me to you he gave me a dowry worth two hundred thousand strings of cash, expecting that we would share good or bad fortune together our whole lives. Now that you are employed by the Great Chin, you abandon me on the road!" She kept yelling at him until his captor's wife persuaded her husband to let Ch'in Kuei bring his wife with him.[16] How often wives mentioned their dowries or their fathers when quarreling with their husbands, or purposely shouted within earshot of neighbors, is of course hard to say. But we might recall Ssu-ma Kuang's argument against selecting wives for their wealth or influential relatives on the grounds that they would be haughty and hard to control.

Both husbands and wives could easily go beyond mere bickering and shouting at each other. Women often directed their anger downward, taking out their frustrations with their husbands on anyone who ranked lower than them, especially maids and concubines. Men did not need to displace their anger in the same way. Rather, it was common for them to hit their wives, just as the wives would hit the maids. Hung Mai recorded several cases in which wife beating was incidental to the main story. In one, a man met a distressed-looking woman on the road. She told him, "I have been unfortunate. My husband is very bad and constantly beats me. Moreover, my mother-in-law is exceptionally hard and violent. Not one day of peace have I had. Yesterday they chased me out and I have nowhere to go."[17]

Beating a wife to death was a serious matter, but beating as a form of discipline was taken for granted. As an example of an official's talents as a judge, his biographer reported how he dealt with a man accused of beating his wife to death. Suspecting that there had to be more to the story, the official got the man to describe for him what had happened: "My mother was yelling at my wife, and my wife was talking back. I couldn't take it, and in my anger I beat her. By accident I killed her." The official assured him that he would not face the death penalty because "beating an unfilial daughter-in-law is not the same as beating a wife."[18]

SEXUAL RELATIONS

What did people consider normal sexual relations between husbands and wives? The sources provide no more than scattered hints. Sexual attraction, as a topic of literature, largely concerned men's attraction to women other than their wives, especially courtesans, singing girls, and prostitutes.[19] Girls in their teens (about eleven to sixteen years of age, Western style) clearly fascinated men. The appeal of the pubescent girl may have been her presumed innocence: she could show off her youthful good looks, smile, sing, and chat with the naturalness of a child. No one regarded her behavior as forward, manipulative, or based on real sexual desire. Yet men were seen as able to awaken her desires. Long-entrenched practices of sexual segregation, after all, were built on the assumption that sexual desires were easily stimulated in both sexes. From fictional stories that involved unrelated men and women chancing to meet, one can infer that people assumed an inexperienced girl would respond favorably to a man who approached her gently. One of the best-known stories in Sung times was the *Romance of the Western Chamber,* based on a tale written in the late T'ang by Yüan Chen (779–831). In a highly elaborated Sung version intended for oral performance, the young hero falls hopelessly in love after catching a fleeting glance of a delicate seventeen-year-old girl staying at a temple he visits. She, in time, is attracted by his ardor and good looks.[20]

Sung writers' attitudes toward the sexuality of wives seem more complicated. We should try to separate the sorts of behavior men knew occasionally occurred, the sorts they thought normal, the sorts they thought attractive, and the sorts they considered morally preferable. From men's poetry, it would seem that they found a vague sort of longing attractive in women. There was an old tradition of men writing about the feelings of the neglected woman, separated from or abandoned by her husband. Although it may have been mildly erotic for men to think about a woman being alone, the feelings attributed to the women were generally quite abstracted and generalized ones of longing, sadness, and aimlessness. The pleasure men derived from pretending to gaze on women was probably tied to their strong objection to other men looking at their wives. As we saw in an earlier chapter, Ssu-ma Kuang admonished wives not to let outsiders see any unclothed part of their bodies, to the extent that they should hold their sleeves over their faces if they had to flee a fire. Wives' bodies were very private things.

Certainly men thought a small minority of women were sexually voracious and therefore not easily confined within the bounds of monogamy. One of the most common types of folktale concerns the fox-spirit that transforms itself into a beautiful young woman, seduces a man, and, in one way or another, drains him of vitality. Stories of adultery often describe the woman as lewd and promiscuous (see Chapter 14). But I do not think that Sung writers considered such women either normal or typical. They rarely if ever worried about the effects of denying sex to young widows. They took for granted that a widow of twenty-five would have a hard time financially if she did not remarry, but did not express concern that celibacy might be a major burden as well. It should be noted, however, that Hung Mai's anecdotes contain many more cases of widows who had illicit affairs than wives who pursued extramarital affairs, suggesting that people in fact were aware that not all widows settled down easily to a celibate life.

Wives' views of their own sexuality are even more difficult to reconstruct. Girls who expected to marry one day and women already married were taught to look on rape as a violation of their personal integrity so fundamental that suicide was the most appropriate response. Examples of women committing suicide for this reason were common in didactic books like Ssu-ma Kuang's *Precepts for Family Life* and Chu Hsi's *Elementary Learning*, as well as in collections of biographies of heroic women in the dynastic histories. All wives would have known of the feelings against respectable women entering sexual unions with a second man, even after their first husband died (see Chapter 11). At the same time, wives knew that men did not look on courtesans as unclean and, indeed, often were very attracted to them. Could many wives have escaped feeling ambivalent about using their sexual attractiveness? Would seductive behavior diminish their standing as wives, or would it secure their husband's devotion?

Some men probably had a fair understanding of women's sexual responses, for a technical literature on the biology of sexual intercourse did exist, written for those who wished to practice Taoist longevity techniques. These writings encouraged men to have sexual relations with as many young women as possible, and to bring their partners to orgasm without expending any semen, instead redirecting it to their brains. Sexual intercourse itself was referred to as a battle between the man and the woman, in which each tried to take from the other without giving.[21] As interesting as this literature is, I am reluctant to make much of it. These theories appear to have had little influence outside fairly narrow circles and were likely no more important to marital sexual relations than the Buddhist literature extolling celibacy and portraying sex as vile and dirty.[22] In modern China, the average husband does not seem particularly sensitive to his wife as a sexual being, nor do women have high expectations in this regard.[23]

Another type of technical literature that may well have influenced husbands and wives was the medical literature, for literate men and women often seem to have been familiar with medical theories. Ch'en Tzu-ming, in his book on women's medicine, written in 1237, devoted a seventeen-page chapter to the topic of "seeking an heir." After an introduction which mentioned Mencius's statement that having no posterity was the worst of unfilial acts, he gave a wide variety of advice on how to avoid this outcome. One authority he quoted pointed out that although girls begin to menstruate at fourteen sui, marriages at that age often do not lead to children, or the children born are weak and do not survive. Not until about twenty sui are a woman's yin forces fully strong. Ch'en also attributed some cases of infertility to factors beyond physicians' control, such as geomancy (faulty burial) and astrology (mismatching the birth dates of the couple). Ch'en supplied information to calculate auspicious dates for intercourse for those who wished to get pregnant, as well as days to avoid. One should, for instance, shun sex on days containing the cyclical characters *ping* or *ting* (that is, the third and fourth days in each ten-day cycle) as well as the first and fifteenth days of each month; exceptionally windy, rainy, foggy, cold, or hot days; and days marked by lightning, thunder, eclipses, or earthquakes. There were also places to be avoided, such as the open air, temples, spots beside a well or latrine, or beside a grave or coffin. If one wished a boy, the best time to conceive was on the first, third, or fifth day after the woman's period ended; for a girl, the second, fourth, or sixth days.[24]

Although Ch'en quoted the theory that the date of intercourse determined the sex of the child, he also cited the contradictory theory that it took until the end of the third month for the sex of the fetus to be established. Thus a pregnant woman could affect the sex of her unborn child by such behavior as carrying around bows and arrows or riding a stallion if she wanted a boy, or wearing earrings or other women's jewelry if she wanted a girl.[25] Ch'en, moreover, provided prescriptions for medicines a woman could take to turn a female fetus into a male one.[26]

After listing many prescriptions a woman could take to treat infertility, Ch'en included a course that husbands could follow. A man whose family had not produced a son by the wife in three generations (the only sons having been born to concubines) was instructed by a monk to do good deeds and cultivate his virtue for three years. He pursued this course faithfully, and finally his wife bore him a son.[27] This prescription coincides with the message in many didactic stories illustrating the workings of karma: those who do good deeds will be rewarded with the birth of children.

Even if writers did not discuss normal sexual relations between husbands and wives, they did occasionally point out the oddity of cases of sexual aversion. Yu Chi (thirteenth century), in recounting his family history, mentioned two such cases. In the early eleventh century, Yu Shen had been orphaned as a baby when his nineteen-sui mother, just widowed, committed suicide by stabbing herself. At thirty a son was born to him, and thereafter he lived separately from his wife and never came near her. She, we are told, lived to age 104, apparently thriving on celibacy. The second case concerned the author's great-great-grandfather, Yu Liang, who, he said, "loved purity." Although he had both a wife and a concubine, he did not like to be near them. He may have been allergic; the smell of women's hair oil evidently gave him uncontrollable fits of vomiting. He remained a virgin his entire life, fulfilling his obligation to the descent line by adopting a kinsman's son.[28]

Religious motives could also lead either men or women to renounce sexual relations, in imitation of the behavior of monks and nuns. Miss Ch'en (1024–1083), we are told, became increasingly serious about Buddhism in her middle years. She not only abstained from meat and chanted sutras all day, she also dressed up a concubine to serve her husband in her place. Liang Chi-pi (1143–1208), his son-lin-law reported, became interested in the theories of conserving life forces and after forty no longer entered the inner rooms. At New Year's, when all the relatives mingled, husband and wife would treat each other like acquaintances who rarely met. Hung Mai recorded the case of a young married man of twenty-four who decided to live like a monk and took to sleeping separate from his wife. At first she tried to follow his example and practice devotions, but in less than a year gave up and married someone else.[29]

THE PROBLEM OF JEALOUSY

Without doubt, the most serious source of friction between upper-class husbands and wives was, from the wives' point of view, their husbands' doting on their concubines, and from the husbands' point of view, their wives' jealousy when they acted in this normal way. Naturally, not all men had concubines, but they were a common feature of the multi-generational households of the better off. Among members of the educated class who left written records, it seems to have been extremely common for men who lived to forty or more to take at least one concubine. Men disinclined to take concubines attracted more notice than those who kept several.[30]

Ssu-ma Kuang, like other Sung moralists, instructed wives that it was up to them to suppress feelings of jealousy, even asserting that no virtue was more important in a woman than lack of jealousy. Concubines were sanctioned in the classics, so it was up to wives to live harmoniously with them.[31] Young girls from educated families, having been taught stories of the heroines of the past, probably all expected to maintain their equanimity, generosity, and good humor when their husbands showed interest in other women. In theory at least, wives had a mistress/servant relationship with the concubines in their houses and were in no way diminished in stature by having help in serving their husbands. But even women who thought beforehand that they could handle the situation might find themselves emotionally distraught when a concubine was introduced into the household. Hung Mai told the story of Hsieh Hsün, who had managed to escape from the Jurchen only thanks to his wife's help. Later, he was rewarded with four concubines. He wished to decline out of a sense of obligation to his wife, but she urged him to accept, saying the gift was a great honor. "I'll look after them like children.

Don't turn them down." Soon, however, Hsieh Hsün started paying less attention to her. Once, when they were both tipsy from wine, she accused him of forgetting how she had helped him; he lost his temper and struck her on the head.[32]

Writers commonly looked on jealousy as a form of willfulness, one of the failings of a spoiled, self-centered, or high-handed woman. In their view, a woman who, for whatever reason, could get her husband to do what she wanted would not let him keep concubines or sleep with the maids. Jealousy was also seen as a sort of poison that could make a person sick. Once when Huang T'ing-chien (1045–1105) wrote to Ch'en Tsao, he inquired about the latter's wife's illness: "Since in your late years you have gradually sought quiet pleasures and have not brought home any new concubines, what troubles have made Miss Liu sick this time?"[33]

The perception that jealousy was like an illness or possession comes out well in the following story recorded by Hung Mai:

> The wife of Yeh Chien, the legal administrator of T'ai-chou, was by nature cruel and jealous. If the maids or concubines seemed at all human she would beat them viciously, sometimes even killing them. Yeh could not control her. Once he told her his true feelings: "I am almost sixty, so how could I be seeking sensual pleasures? It is just that I am old and do not have a son, so I want to buy a concubine as a strategy for getting an heir. Would this be all right?" His wife responded, "It would be better to wait a few years. Perhaps I will have a son myself."
>
> After the time agreed on had elapsed, she had no choice but to go along with his request. But since she was given to jealous hatreds, she made an agreement with him, "Build me a separate house where I can devote myself to religion." Yeh was delighted with the idea, and built a house behind the hill for her to live in. Family servants carried greetings back and forth every morning and evening and sometimes brought wine or food. Yeh concluded that she no longer had her old attitudes and sent his new concubine to call on her. When evening arrived and she had not returned, he took a walking stick and went to investigate himself. He saw the door locked as though no one was at home. He ordered a servant to open it, only to discover that his wife had turned into a tiger and eaten his concubine's heart and innards, leaving the head and limbs. He quickly went down the hill and got a group with torches to search for her, all without success. The year was 1149.[34]

Sung men's interpretations of the nature of jealous feelings seem, to modern eyes at least, rather simplistic. A single word, *tu,* was used to label the feelings and motivations of a woman whose behavior and attitudes changed after her husband showed interest in maids or concubines. Imagine what appears to have been a fairly common case. A woman enters a household as the young bride, perhaps eighteen years old, and has to learn to get along not only with her husband but also with her parents-in-law, brothers- and sisters-in-law, and their children. Gradually her standing improves. She has children; her parents-in-law die; her husband and his brothers divide the household. By thirty-five or forty her position is much better. She is mistress of the house, busily engaged in finding spouses for her children and expecting soon to be a mother-in-law when her eldest son gets a wife. But now her husband brings home a seventeen-year-old concubine to keep him company at night, believing this to be appropriate to his standing as family head and seeing no reason why his wife should not be satisfied with her highly honorable roles as mother of his children and manager of his household. I can imagine at least three components to the feelings that led many such women to feel hostile to the girl or seek to humiliate her husband. First, her dignity was injured. The maids and daughters-in-law who had learned to treat the wife as the mistress might now laugh at her behind her back as an unwanted woman. Second, seeing the young concubine would make her only too aware of how her appearance had changed over the years, suddenly bringing home the fact that she was growing old. And third (to post-Freudian eyes at least), there must have been an element of sexual frustration as, after many years with a fairly normal sex life, she now found herself with little if any conjugal pleasure. She probably would not have labeled her feelings toward her husband as sexual, but frustrated sexual desires surely amplified the emotional responses of such wives. Perhaps we can read something of these sorts of feelings into an album leaf shown in Figure 21: a woman, having finished her makeup and hair, gazes at her reflection in a mirror, only a few feet from where two younger women, possibly a maid and a concubine, stand, more absorbed in their own interests than in attendance on her.

However we analyze jealous feelings, there is no doubt that they could be disruptive. Biographies of wives regularly state that the woman was even-tempered and patient and rarely if ever beat the concubines or maids —suggesting that such forbearance was rare. In Hung Mai's tales, in fact, wives often beat concubines. In one, a young wife beat to death the maid she had brought with her at marriage after her husband began to have sexual relations with her. In another, a woman reported that she had run away because her mistress beat her after the master became intimate with her. Another source reports that when Li Kuan's widow remarried, she fell ill, whereupon Li Kuan's ghost appeared and accused her of three times killing maids he had gotten pregnant, with the result that he died with no heirs. [35]

Even when wives' jealousy did not lead to violence, it could keep their husbands from spending time with them. Hung Mai reported that Fan Tou-nan bought a concubine soon after passing the exams in 1175. Because his wife could not accept the younger woman, he pretended that he had to go away on business and said good-bye, whereas in fact he only moved to a temple to stay with his concubine. Hung Mai also told of a man who, after marrying an official's daughter, became enamored of a sixteen-sui concubine and "as

Fig. 21. A woman checking her appearance
Album Leaf by Wang Shen (ca. 1046–after 1100). Collection of the National Palace
Museum, Taiwan, Republic of China (VA 15H).

a consequence was constantly bickering with his wife." Yüan Ts'ai wrote
that "some men with jealous wives set up maids or concubines in separate
houses," but warned against this practice because the concubine might well
establish an illicit relationship and the master would end up raising a child
that was not his own.[36]

Why didn't these men command their wives to leave their concubines
alone? One senses that however much the men disliked the rancor in the
women's quarters, there were limits to what they could do. Although they
could remove the concubine from the wife's sphere of control, they could
not challenge her control in that sphere. This situation is parallel to that
between mother and wife. A man might love his wife and hate to watch his
mother maltreat her, but he would not challenge his mother's right to give

the orders. Rather, he might try to soften his mother's attitude or take his wife with him when he received a distant posting. Moreover, because doting on concubines was associated with self-indulgence, it gave wives some leverage in dealing with their husbands. Chou Pi-ta's (1126–1204) wife, we are told, confined his concubine without water because of the way he looked at her. When Chou passed by, the concubine begged for water, and he brought her some. His wife, observing all this from behind a screen, then made fun of him: "Look at you, a high official, fetching water for a maid!"[37]

Some men relented and got rid of their concubines. Ts'ao Jui (eleventh century) had to marry out a maid he was intimate with because she and his wife were competing for favor. Later he would visit the former maid at her new husband's house. Gossipmongers liked to tell stories of ousted concubines of prominent but disliked men, clearly relishing the idea that men who seemed so strong in public life might have domineering wives. Wang Huan, we are told, got ahead because his wife was the daughter of the high official Cheng Chü-chung (1059–1123). She "presumed on her family's influence and was jealous." When a maid bore her husband's son, she had it sent away. Wang Ch'in-jo's (962–1025) wife was so jealous that he was unable to take a concubine. When he named his study after the phrase from the classics "The three things he was in awe of," a friend teased him that in his case the four things he was in awe of would have been more appropriate: there was, after all, his wife too. Ch'in Kuei's wife, we are told, was both domineering and jealous; once she sold his pregnant concubine even though Ch'in Kuei did not yet have any sons.[38]

Stories of ousted concubines could be told to impugn ancestry. Was the concubine pregnant when expelled? Han T'o-chou (d. 1207) was said to be born to a maid already pregnant when his father acquired her from a broker after she was ousted by a jealous wife of a Wang family. Chia Ssu-tao (1213–1275) was similarly said to have been born to a woman whose husband sold her to Chia's father, but who then became pregnant and was given to another man because Chia's father's wife was jealous.[39]

Although jealousy was universally condemned, it was not unheard of for men to have some sympathy for wives grappling with jealous feelings. In the Introduction, I discussed Wang Hsing's advice to his old friend Wang Yen (890–966), whose wife fell ill after Wang had risen to high rank. He thought she might well get better if he let his many courtesan-concubines go and they lived as they had in the old days, one man and one wife.[40] Judges sometimes even criticized husbands for giving their wives cause to feel jealous, as in one legal case concerning a quarrel between a husband and wife that resulted in the man striking his father-in-law and the latter taking his daughter home. The judge reported that the husband loved the concubine who had borne him a child and neglected his wife, who was consumed by jealousy. "It is common for women not to be wise; there is no reason to place the blame there," commented the judge. He ordered the husband to apologize to his father-in-law for hitting him, to marry his concubine out to someone else, and to find a wet nurse for his child. The judge also ordered the father-in-law to send his daughter back. That way, he argued, there might be a little peace in the family.[41]

Did women share men's view of women's jealousy? How did women whom others labeled as jealous think of their own actions and feelings? Many probably saw themselves as strict with the concubines and maids because it was their responsibility to maintain an orderly household. To their mind, maids and concubines, who came from lower-class households, had all sorts of bad habits that it was necessary to curb. If their husbands were too smitten with the younger women to teach them to follow the rules, the wives would have to. Men, it might be added, were likely unaware of the ways a favored concubine could provoke a wife. Spending more of their time with the concubine, they would hear more of her side. In some cases the concubines probably did need a little discipline.

Even if many women did not see their own jealousy, there must have been some who did. If they had grown up looking on jealousy as a destructive vice, they would have been deeply troubled when they found themselves unable to suppress hostility toward the women who had disrupted their lives. Where could they go for counsel? The Confucian primers they had recited in their childhood, like the *Classic of Filial Piety*, gave no advice on how to manage such feelings or make them go away, nor did the inspirational books written specifically for girls like the *Classic of Filial Piety for Girls* or *Biographies of Great Women*. The Confucian classics such as the *Analects* and *Mencius* were just as useless, written as they were for men who never had to suppress their own feelings of possessiveness toward women or even, in most cases, their sexual desires. Sung Neo-Confucian philosophers discussed with their disciples many issues of moral cultivation, but they focused on men's moral problems. They talked of controlling desires, but the desires to be controlled were the ones problematic for men in the literati class: their ambitions for worldly success, their tendencies toward greed and self-indulgence. Philosophers did not consider at any length the problems women might have in controlling complex emotions. Given upper-class women's high levels of literacy, it is indeed striking that so little was written to meet these needs.

A woman who found herself torn by powerful emotions could turn for help to other women her own age or older—her mother, sisters, cousins, and sisters-in-law. She could also, and perhaps on these counselors' advice, turn to Buddhism. Buddhism taught that carnal desires, indeed all desires, were an impediment to spiritual progress. It also taught a valuable perspective on growing old: nothing in the world is permanent; the only permanent thing is impermanence. And it provided techniques for calming the mind and ridding it of unwanted thoughts. If a wife turned to Buddhism to gain equanimity, she would be respected by all around her for enhancing the harmony of the house. She would not be the bitter neglected wife, given to violent outbursts, but the family's saint, the one who had given up meat, recited sutras, taught Buddhist precepts to her relatives, and showed compassion to all around her. She would also be, in a subtle way, challenging the behavior of her husband, who so obviously had not freed himself from carnal desires. This, I suspect, is one reason Confucian scholars, quick to condemn Buddhism in other contexts, were generous with praise for women who took it up. Family harmony, a Confucian value, often could be attained no other way. But Confucian men did not tell women to turn to Buddhism to gain control of their lives: it seems to have been a solution they developed for themselves.

Marital relations in Sung times, as in most other times and places, were far from immutable. For all the guidance in the didactic literature on proper family roles, for all the clarity with which the legal responsibilities and duties of the two parties were set out, there was still considerable room for positioning in any marriage. Husbands and wives could conceive of many ways to act. Women and men alike knew of both doting and estranged couples. They recognized as common characters both men who beat their wives and wives who berated their husbands. Sexually compatible and sexually unsatisfied couples both existed in their imaginations. I do not wish to imply that all possibilities could be conceived; much of what we know in our society would have been beyond their ability to imagine. Still, they could see options. Some women, we have seen, asserted their authority over other members of the household, while others withdrew into Buddhist devotions. Women who wished to travel with their husband could cite his need for a household manager; those who preferred to stay home could cite their duties as daughter-in-law to his parents.

That wives had options does not mean they had power equal to that of their husbands. Legally they were virtually powerless: they could not over-rule their husbands on any family matters, nor did they have a right to punish their husbands or expel them. They could not even legally just give up and leave. Rather, women had ways—tactics perhaps—to make the best of their situations within these limits. Margery Wolf once described the successful Chinese woman as one who had "learned to depend largely on herself while appearing to lean on her father, husband, and her son."[42]

The complementary images of the jealous wife and the smitten husband conveyed powerful messages about husband-wife relations. I suspect that few wives were particularly conscious, much less resentful, of the legal inequalities in this relationship, for they had learned to think of marital discord not as a product of unequal legal rights but as resulting from husbands' attraction to young women and wives' inability to control their jealousy. Emotion was the culprit, emotion that could not be curbed by prudent calculation or devotion to duty.

NINE

Motherhood

Pregnancy, childbirth, and the care of children are features of women's lives in all societies, but women experience them in diverse ways, depending on their interpretation of the biological processes, the value they place on the birth of boys versus girls, their ideas about how best to care for children, and their ideals of motherhood more generally. Certainly in Sung China, bearing and rearing children were central to everyone's understanding of the role of wife. Wedding ceremonies openly alluded to the bride's potential fertility with such expressions as "Five sons and two daughters." "May you have many sons and a long life" was the way Miss Wang's (1212–1284) mother-in-law thanked her for patiently nursing her invalid father-in-law.[1] Across class lines and throughout the Sung, women's identities revolved very much around being mothers to their children.

PREGNANCY AND CHILDBIRTH

Most married women in Sung China were pregnant much of the time. For twenty-five to thirty years, from the time she married in her late teens until her mid to late forties when her reproductive capacity came to an end, the typical wife would be pregnant repeatedly. Of the couples I studied in funerary biographies, those who lived to forty-five without being widowed averaged 6.1 children who survived long enough to be thought worth recording (though children born to concubines may on occasion have been included as well). The actual total of live births was surely higher, for people often omitted mention of children who died in infancy or childhood. It is also likely that a significant share of pregnancies ended in stillbirths or miscarriages. Thus a great many women must have been pregnant ten or more times.

Gynecological and obstetrical problems were discussed in both general and specialized medical treatises written in the Sung.[2] One twelfth-century bibliography listed sixteen specialized titles on women's health. Chu Tuan-chang's eight-chapter treatise on women's medicine, prepared in 1184, gives prescriptions for such conditions as morning sickness, food cravings, births complicated by the incorrect position of the fetus, postpartum hemorrhaging, placentas that did not descend, sealing of the umbilical cord, and various post-partum illnesses. Ch'en Tzu-ming's 1237 treatise is even longer, comprising twenty-four chapters. It cites earlier authors more frequently, analyzes topics more fully, and includes some topics not in Chu's book, such as infertility.[3]

The Sung medical literature did not treat pregnancy as a debilitating condition until the final month. Women who had given birth before probably took pregnancy in stride, letting it interrupt their work as little as possible. After all, they still had children to nurture, parents-in-law to serve, housework to attend to, and perhaps silkworms to care for or servants to supervise. That people did not see any need to coddle pregnant women comes out in the unembarrassed account by Su Shun-ch'in (1008–1048) of the events leading to the death of his wife, Miss Cheng (d. 1035). After they had been married about seven or eight years he was appointed to an official post. He and his wife already had three children, and she was pregnant again. She suggested that he take the children with him while she remained behind to care for his mother, but family members persuaded her that it was her duty to accompany him. Two months after they arrived, his father died, and they immediately put on mourning dress and headed home, traveling day and night without regular meals or rests, even though she was in the late stages of pregnancy. She was thrown from her horse and injured her leg in three places, but insisted on continuing without pause, saying, "Once I quickly get to the front of my father-in-law's coffin to grieve, I will be able to die without regrets. It would be very unfilial to add to my mother-in-law's grief by dying [before arriving]." The night they arrived she gave birth to a child, which caused further stress and led to her death seven days later.[4]

In the last month of pregnancy, medical authorities advised extreme caution. Women were told to remain calm, not lift heavy burdens or climb to high places, and not drink too much wine or eat food hard to digest. Under no circumstances should a woman in her last month wash her hair.[5]

That last month, too, was the time to select an old and experienced midwife, perhaps one like Old Lady Ch'ü who was still attending the births in a certain Sung family when over eighty.[6] Little is known of the training of midwives. Probably most learned their profession by helping a more experienced woman for a few years before starting to practice on their own. Midwives could be expected to tell the woman when to push and to reposition babies that did not come out head first.[7]

When deliveries proved unusually difficult, male physicians might be called in. Hung Mai reported the following story, told him by Chu Hsin-chung (1097–1167):

> When Chu Hsin-chung's grandfather was living in T'ung-ch'eng [Anhwei], the wife of one of their friends or relatives was in labor, but for seven days the child did not descend. They had tried every sort of medicine and holy water and were merely waiting for [the mother] to die. The famous physician Li Chi-tao happened to be visiting Chu, and Chu asked him to examine the woman. [On seeing her] Li said, "No medicine will cure this case. Only acupuncture [offers any hope], but my medical skills have not extended that far, so I do not dare touch it," and he left.
>
> Chi-tao's teacher P'ang An-ch'ang [1042–1099] happened to pass by and visited Chu. Chu told him of the case. "The family has been unwilling to push you, but human life is more important than anything else. Couldn't you give saving her a try?" An-ch'ang agreed and accompanied Chu there. As soon as he saw the pregnant woman he exclaimed, "She won't die!" He ordered some of the family members to warm her abdomen with hot water, then he massaged her with his hands. She felt a slight pain in her intestines, then, groaning, gave birth to a boy. Both mother and child were fine. The family, overjoyed, bowed to thank him, treating him like a god. They were mystified by how he had done it. An-ch'ang said, "After the child left the womb, by mistake it grasped the mother's intestine and couldn't let go. Therefore medicine was useless. I located its hand through her belly and inserted an acupuncture needle in the 'tiger's mouth' [the space between the thumb and forefinger]. The child pulled back his hand from the pain, so was quickly born. I used no other tricks." He had them bring the child over for him to examine, and sure enough there were traces of acupuncture on the "tiger's mouth" of his right hand. This is how marvelous [P'ang] was.[8]

Childbirth was not necessarily viewed as a narrow medical matter. Religious experts could also be called in to help in cases of difficult births. Hung Mai presents many such instances. When Miss Wu could not bear the pain of labor, her family summoned a monk who chanted the Peacock Incantation. When Miss Huang's labor was unproductive, a medium was sent for who divined that the spirits were already welcoming the woman, thus predicting her death. When Miss Ch'ang's labor was not progressing and she told her family that her belly was being pummeled by a concubine she had once had beaten to death, they called in a Taoist master who administered holy water.[9] Even physicians sometimes interpreted events in terms of nonphysiological processes. Hung Mai shows this in a story much like the one above, but with a different twist:

> The wife of Mr. Lü, the county wine official, was in labor for five days without giving birth. Someone advised them that only Drunkard T'u could help, so Lü summoned him. T'u arrived drunk, went right into the room, felt beneath her

clothes, then came out and said, "Sit down. In a little while she will give birth."
Before long, they heard a baby cry. They thought that T'u had not done
anything, and that it was just coincidental that the baby was born right then.
T'u told Lü, "Look carefully at the 'tiger's mouth' of [the baby's] left hand.
There will be a small crack." When they looked, it was so. On inquiring, Lü
was told, "This is not a good child, but an evil spirit trying to take your wife's
life. Therefore, while in the womb it took hold of its mother's intestines and
would not let go, so it could not be born. I used P'ang An-ch'ang's method of
acupuncture to get it out." Lü bowed to thank him. The child soon died.

Two years later, Mrs. Lü was pregnant again, and T'u treated her by the
same methods. After she recovered, he told her, "This has already happened
twice. From now on you should lead a chaste life in a separate room to avoid
cause for regrets. Should you unfortunately become pregnant again, what
would you do? If I am not around, no one else could handle it. My life span is
near its end, and I will not be long in the world. Please think about your life;
do not neglect my advice."

The next year, T'u did in fact die. A year later Mrs. Lü died in childbirth.
Lü believed the popular theory that a woman who died carrying a child could
not be reborn and would stay in purgatory forever. He personally took a knife,
cut open her belly, removed the fetus, and threw it away.[10]

This story hinges on two common beliefs also attested to elsewhere: the idea
that certain infants are not ordinary children but evil spirits sent to cause
the parents grief, perhaps as retribution for sins they have committed; and
a view of pregnancy as so unclean or polluting that it prevented the mother's
rebirth. The origins of notions of the pollution of pregnancy and childbirth
are difficult to trace. An apocryphal Buddhist sutra (that is, one written
in China), the Bloody Bowl Sutra, describes the bloody bowl hell discovered
by Mu-lien when he entered the netherworld to look for his mother. Only
women were in this hell, and the guardian explained to Mu-lien that they
were there for such offenses as contaminating the ground spirits with
the blood of childbirth or washing blood-stained garments in rivers with the
result that those downstream inadvertently offered tea to gods brewed from
contaminated water. Several Taoist scriptures of Sung date contain similar
themes, suggesting that these ideas—quite prominent in later China—already
had some currency in the Sung.[11]

The period immediately after giving birth was a critical one for the
mother. Medical books advised staying in bed for three days. Medical authorities saw postpartum women as apt to get depressed or delirious and to
report seeing ghosts, for which treatments would be prescribed. Postpartum
women were also subject to pains, chills, and a great many other discomforts
and dangers.[12]

Dying in childbirth or a few days later as a direct consequence of the
birthing process was apparently quite common, even among the relatively
privileged educated class for whom funerary biographies were written. Ch'en

Chu (1214–1297) explicitly described how his first wife, Miss T'ung Shang-jou (1216–1252), bore four girls, none of whom survived beyond childhood. At thirty-seven sui she gave birth to her first son but died the next day. The baby died thirteen days later. Yao Mien (1216–1262) had the misfortune of losing both his wives to childbirth after only a year of marriage. The first, Miss Tsou Miao-shan (1228–1249) died twenty days after the birth of her only child, a girl, who in turn died the next year. Her younger sister, Tsou Miao-chuang, died seven days after her first pregnancy terminated in a stillbirth. When a son survived after his mother died, authors often avoided explicitly stating that his mother had died of complications from giving birth to him, probably out of sensitivity to his feelings. For instance, Yüan Ming-shan (1269–1322) reported merely that Miss Shih Ti-ch'ing (1246–1266) died "of illness" at twenty-one in the capital. Later in the inscription he mentions that her fourth child and only son was seven days old at the time.[13]

It is important to remember that although childbirth was a risky business in premodern times, it also inspired great excitement and joy for fathers and mothers, grandfathers and grandmothers, especially when the baby was a boy. The woman who used the porcelain pillow made in the shape of a baby (Fig. 22) must have gone to bed thinking of the joy of bearing a child. Shao Yung (1011–1077), who did not marry until forty-five, wrote a poem on the birth of his first son:

> I am now forty-seven.
> By begetting a son I am for the first time someone's father.
> Nurturing and teaching depend on me.
> But whether you live long or are wise or foolish depends on you.
> If I reach the long life span of seventy
> I will get to see you at twenty-five.
> I would like to see you become a great sage,
> But I do not know yet if that is heaven's intention.[14]

KEEPING BABIES ALIVE

Whatever the dangers pregnant women faced, their babies' lives were even more precarious. Infant mortality must have been high, considering that about half the daughters born to the Sung emperors died in infancy.[15] As depicted in an evocative Sung album-leaf painting (Fig. 23), death seems to have had a way of attracting babies.

Some women, of course, had worse luck than others, as yet another of Hung Mai's tales reveals:

When Liu Chiang-fu of Sui-yang and his wife were both over forty, they had just one young daughter, their sons having failed to survive, one after the other. When Liu was away in the capital on official business, the girl also died. Mrs. Liu saw to the burial, wailing bitterly. Tired, she sat down to rest and fell

Fig. 22. A baby-shaped ceramic pillow
The Palace Museum, Peking. Photograph by Wan-go Weng.

asleep. A woman with a tall hairdo appeared next to her and said, "Don't be
overly distressed. You will give birth to a high-ranking child. The official [your
husband] has already been given his appointment and will be home soon. Just
go to the wife of Wei Twelve, west of the city, and get from her an old garment.
When you give birth to the child, borrow a large silver box and, using the
garment, put the child in the box. Close it briefly, then take him out. Name
him 'Box Support' or 'Receiving Support.'" Once she finished talking, the
woman disappeared.

Five days later Liu returned, having been assigned the post of a section
clerk in Ch'u-chou. His wife told him what had happened, and the next day
they went out the west gate to search for Mrs. Wei. They went two li without
finding anyone of this surname. After they returned to the gate they stopped
at a tea shop and started talking to someone who turned out to be Wei Eleven.
When asked about a younger brother, he said, "There is a number twelve
brother whose wife has given birth to twelve sons, not one of whom has died.
They all live and eat together, too much for a poor family." Liu was excited to
hear this, and told him [of the dream]. Wei went in to tell his brother, and
brought back a silk garment from his sister-in-law to give the guest. Liu
offered two thousand cash for it, but [Wei] refused.

Later Mrs. Liu conceived, and in the fifth month [Liu] took up his post.
The year was 1120. When husband and wife were eating together, one said to

Fig. 23. Babies and the specter of death
An album leaf painted by Li Sung (fl. 1190–1230) in the Palace Museum, Peking.
From Cheng, Chang, and Hsü 1957: pl. 58.

the other, "The evidence suggests we will have a son. But where can we get a
silver box?" It so happened that [Liu] was assigned by the prefect to take
charge of the treasury and, in examining the vessels, found two large silver
boxes.... In the sixth month [Mrs. Liu] gave birth to a boy, and they named
him "Receiving Support," as she had been instructed.[16]

This boy, of course, survived and grew up to become an official.

Medical treatises offered numerous prescriptions and much practical advice on keeping newborns alive. One quoted a proverb, "Warn those rearing
little children: Protect them against drafts and dampness." It also noted that
peasant children, who were not subjected to acupuncture and moxibustion
as newborns, often fared better than those treated by ignorant doctors.[17]

In the premodern West, babies were often sent out of unhealthy cities to be cared for by wet nurses in the countryside, a practice that probably increased infant mortality. In China, wet nurses were widely used as well, but they probably did not contribute as much to infant mortality because instead of the infant being sent to the wet nurse, the woman was brought into the family as a baby nurse, in charge of tending to all its physical needs.[18] Physicians did not warn against the use of wet nurses; on the contrary, they urged selecting healthy, plump ones with white milk.[19] The common medical theory, in fact, was that nursing was like losing blood and depleted a woman's strength: "In ordinary families the wives nurse their children after giving birth to them. With childbirth their vital energies (*ch'i*) are extremely depleted. Nursing further injures the blood. Of actions that deeply endanger life and spirit, none is greater than this."[20] Those familiar with these theories might thus have hired wet nurses to protect the health of new mothers. Whatever the reasons, wet nurses were common figures in the families of the educated. Su Shih (1036–1101) wrote that Miss Jen Ts'ai-lien (1017–1088) nursed his elder sister and him, then stayed on in the family for thirty-five years, serving as a nanny for his own three sons and traveling with them as he took up posts in various places. When scholars worried about the use of wet nurses, it was because the children of the educated class might be influenced by women with undesirable habits and values, or because the wet nurse's own children might suffer if she weaned them too early in order to take the job.[21]

When a woman in the upper class nursed her children herself, it was taken as a sign of her motherly devotion. Yüan Hsieh (1144–1224) depicted his wife, Miss Pien (1155–1203), as an ideal mother. She married at nineteen and was soon caring for children, eventually four boys and four girls.

> Of the eight children, she nursed seven herself. She was extremely attentive to whether they had enough to eat or were cold or hot. Not for a moment were they out of her mind; not a sliver of a step did she fail to take for them. She would say, "My heart is attached to my baby's body." If the baby was a little uncomfortable, she would carry it all day, never leaving it in swaddling clothes or giving it to anyone else. She looked into every little thing and took care of them painstakingly. As a result every one of them grew up; we did not suffer a single early death.[22]

To Yüan Hsieh there was something very attractive in a mother tending to her infants, a feeling echoed by painters who sometimes depicted such scenes as women bathing babies (Fig. 24).

In China, as elsewhere, parents lavished love on their children and grieved when they died. Quite a few literati wrote poems about the death of an infant. Hsü Chi (1028–1103) composed one that explores how a mother might feel at the death of a somewhat older child, which reads in part:

Fig. 24. Women bathing infants
Sung album leaf. Courtesy of the Freer Gallery of Art,
Smithsonian Institution, Washington, D.C. (35.8).

Who is weeping, so distraught?
They were a white-headed mother and red-faced boy.
Then the boy suddenly discarded his mother and left.
What use is living to the mother?
On the shelf are the boy's books.
In the trunk are the boy's clothes.
The boy's voice is heard no more.
His face is seen no more.
Who is weeping, so grief-struck?
Her attachment is not severed
But her heart is broken.
A mother depends on her son for her life.
The boy is gone but will not come back.
In the morning she watches other people's boys,
In the evening she watches other people's sons.
In a day and a night
He is born ten times and nine times dies again.[23]

ABORTION AND INFANTICIDE

Before leaving motherhood in its more physical aspects, we should look briefly at how people dealt with unwanted pregnancies. It was widely recognized that children might be unwelcome. A family's poverty was the most commonly cited reason for wishing not to rear too many children: more sons would mean each share of the land would be smaller; more daughters would mean more expenses, especially for dowries.

Ingesting certain substances was believed to induce abortion, but abortion by these means does not seem to have been viewed as either safe or reliable. Chou Mi (1232–1308) reported the rumor that Emperor Tu-tsung (r. 1264–1274) was the result of a botched abortion, his mother having been a maid who accompanied Miss Li when she married a prince. "When Shao-ling [Tu-tsung] was in the womb, [his mother,] because of her low rank, took a medicine to abort the fetus. When she gave birth, the boy's hands and feet were weak, and he was unable to talk until seven."[24] A collection of didactic tales written by Li Ch'ang-ling (fl. 1233) also refers to abortion induced by taking poison. Li began by countering the argument that in the first stages of pregnancy the womb was filled only with congealed semen and blood, claiming that, even at that early phase, a spirit was already in the womb. As evidence he repeated a story Shao Po-wen (1057–1134) had reported. When his grandmother was pregnant, she took medicine prescribed by a physician. She gave birth to one healthy child, Po-wen's father, Yung; but a twin sister was also born dead, which they attributed to the medicine. Ten years later Mrs. Shao fell ill, and she dreamed that the girl visited and told of how she suffered from having been poisoned in the womb. After another ten years she returned again, saying that she would finally be reincarnated.[25]

Infanticide was undoubtedly much more common than abortion. Even those far from destitution would use infanticide as a form of birth control, and there are quite a few stories of infanticide or attempted infanticide among the educated class. In one story recorded by Hung Mai, the son of an official made an agreement with his wife that since they already had four daughters, if another was born they would drown her. In another story, a man over fifty told his grown sons in embarrassment that his concubine had gotten pregnant and asked them what to do when the baby was born: kill it, give it away promptly, or rear it for a while and then send it away (presumably to be adopted or perhaps to enter a monastery). The younger son proposed keeping it alive, but the elder threw it in a wine vat with his own hands.[26] Sometimes people changed their minds and saved babies after they were placed in the water basin. It was widely rumored that the official Shang Tun (1035–1105) was alive only because someone had rescued him after he had been left to drown. It was also rumored that when a concubine of Hu An-kuo (1074–1138) gave birth, the child was placed in water to drown, but the wife had a dream about a fish moving about in the pan, and so she saved the half-drowned boy, raising him as her own. The boy, Hu Yin (1098–1156), held the attempted drowning against his birth mother and did not wear mourning for her.[27] (One cannot help supposing that Hu Yin's legal mother told him this story when he was a small child to make sure that he looked on her as his true mother.)

Despite the evidence that infanticide was practiced by their peers, most literati treated it as a problem of ignorance, selfishness, and wickedness, most likely done by ordinary commoners, not educated families like themselves.[28] Wang Te-ch'en (c.s. 1059) reported that people in Fukien did not want more than three sons or two daughters and that if they had more they would drown them as infants. He described the efforts of Yü Wei, who, as magistrate in Fukien, had issued directives against killing children and had summoned the elders of all the villages, entertained them, then instructed them to go back and explain to their neighbors why killing infants was wrong. Those who were saved through his efforts, Wang reported, numbered in the thousands.[29] A few decades later, Chu Sung (1097–1143), while serving as a local official in Fukien, posted a placard exhorting the people not to practice infanticide. Perhaps to catch their attention, he began by reporting that a woman who had revived after dying reported being led into an area where her relatives and ancestors were lined up and where she was confronted with five blood-soaked infants and accused of murdering them. It turned out to be a case of mistaken identity, so she was returned to life. Chu then made his case: "In this area people usually rear only two children. Any more, whether male or female, they promptly drown. If the parent cannot bear to do it, then a brother, worried about his share of the property, takes [the newborn] and kills it."[30]

That people saw infanticide as sinful is evident from the many stories in which those responsible for killing a child suffer retribution. Hung Mai told of a prosperous farmer named Chiang Ssu who got angry when his wife gave birth to a girl and threw the baby into a water basin. When she did not die, he grabbed hold of her ears, pinching them off as cleanly as if he had used a knife. The baby then died. The next year, his wife again bore a girl, this time with no ears. The neighbors interpreted this as retribution and discouraged him from killing her for fear of inviting an even greater calamity. Hung Mai also recounted the case of Miss Kao, the widow of a field worker who got pregnant after an affair with some young good-for-nothing. Fearing that someone would bring charges of illicit sex against her, she drowned the baby. A few years later, she was infected with worms, and her belly swelled up. Day and night she cried out in pain. When her illness reached a crisis, she told those gathered around that it was the dead baby tormenting her. She started kicking wildly and finally died the next day. Her daughter had watched her die, yet after she was married herself, she once drowned a newborn daughter, thinking she and her husband had too many to support already. The next year when she became pregnant again, she saw a strange creature in her room. She got sick and died, suffering in the same way her mother had.[31]

Alternatives to infanticide for those who did not think they could afford to rear more children included giving them out for adoption or abandoning them in a place where they were likely to be found. Yüan Ts'ai noted that "having too many sons is certainly something to worry about," but urged waiting until children had grown up a little before giving them away.[32] In larger cities, abandoned babies were a common social problem. Local governments sometimes organized fostering systems, hiring wet nurses to care for the infants until someone could be found to take them. In rural areas, local officials might try to organize preventive measures, urging neighbors to report pregnancies in order to discourage infanticide and providing relief to those who truly could not feed another mouth.[33]

TENDING TO CHILDREN'S EMOTIONAL NEEDS AND MORAL DEVELOPMENT

The true measure of a woman's greatness, many writers seem to imply, was how well they brought up their children. The importance of childhood in human development was widely recognized,[34] and mothers were given credit for their early role in nurturing the moral and intellectual abilities of their offspring. Ch'eng I portrayed his mother, Miss Hou (1004–1052), as a major influence on him and his brother. (In the translation below, I use the term *Mother*, though like other sons writing about their deceased mothers, Ch'eng I in fact used a title closer to *Madame* or else left the subject unstated.)

Mother was benevolent, forgiving, and generous, and cared for the children of the concubines just as she did her own. She also looked after my uncle's orphans just like her own children. She was consistent in family management, organized without being severe. She did not like to hit the servants, and treated the young ones like children. If we children rebuked them, she always admonished us, saying, "Their social status is much lower than yours, but like you they are human beings. When you are older, will you be able to do these things?"

Mother often took in little children who had been abandoned on the road. Once when a petty trader was away his wife died. The children scattered, leaving with various people, all except the youngest, only three sui, whom no one took. Mother was afraid he would die, so carried him home. At the time our household included many relatives, none of whom looked pleased [when they saw this child], so she purchased food with her own funds to feed him. When the father returned, he apologized: "How fortunate that you took him in and saved his life. I would like to offer him to you." Mother said, "I have been waiting for your return; I never wanted him for myself."

Mother was good at making medicines to cure the sick. Once when it was very cold a man carrying coal passed by our gate. A family member wished to call to him, but mother persuaded him not to by saying, "You really should not do this. If you succeed [in buying the coal] you will be making the poor [deprived of the coal] suffer."

When father got angry, mother was able to get him to calm down. But she did not cover up the faults of us children. She would say, "It is because mothers hide [children's] faults from their fathers that children turn out unworthy."

Mother had six sons, of whom only two survived. She loved us to the utmost but never let up in educating us. When we were toddlers and would stumble, other family members would rush to hold us to keep us from being startled. Mother, by contrast, would admonish us, saying: "If you had walked slowly and calmly, you would not have stumbled."

Our food and drink would be set out next to her. Once when we stirred up the stew, she stopped us, saying: "If you try to satisfy your appetites when young, what will you be like when full grown?" Although she gave us orders, she never cursed us. Therefore, all our lives my brother and I have not been particular in food, drink, or clothing, and do not curse people. This is not the result of our natures, but of the education we received.

If we got into a dispute with someone, mother would not take our side even if we were right. She would say, "I am more troubled that you will not bend than that the other one will not stretch." When we were a little older, she had us study with good teachers and keep the company of good friends. Even though we were not rich, if we wished to invite friends, she happily made the preparations. In teaching her daughters, she regularly used Ts'ao Ta-ku's [Pan Chao's] *Admonitions for Girls*.

Mother routinely would instruct us, "When you notice good traits in others, try to make them your good traits also and master them together. Treat other people's possessions with even more care than you would your own." . . .

Mother was content with limited resources and economical in clothes and equipment. Seeing relatives dress up made no impression on her. When her youngest daughter was in her second or third year, she suddenly died. The wet nurses cried and wailed. Mother scolded them, saying: "Concentrate on the living. What is gone is lost. What do you gain by acting this way?" . . .

When my brother and I were young, she urged us to study, attaching to our book-strings the message, "A boy who reads books carefully," and another line, "Ch'eng Yen-shou, who will pass the palace examinations." My elder brother made a name for himself while young, and I have been called a retired scholar. When my elder brother passed the examinations, I gave up attempting them on account of my lack of talent. Only then did I realize that when we were just boys mother had recognized that this would happen. I have preserved this piece of her calligraphy to demonstrate to my descendants how perceptive she was.[35]

Reflecting back many years later on the ways his mother had reared her children, Ch'eng I found a great deal to praise. His mother lived in a highly status-conscious society but tried to instill in her children consideration for

servants, the poor, and anyone in unfortunate circumstances. She comple-
mented his father by being able to calm him down when he was angry, but
was not so indulgent that she fostered carelessness or willfulness in her
children. Rather, she "loved [them] to the utmost but never let up educating
[them]." She set a good example by devotion to others and indifference to
material goods. She was even good at motivating her boys to study for
official careers.

Ch'eng I stressed the dispassionate side of his mother's personality rather
than the emotional, noting that she took the death of her young daughter
with much more equanimity than the wet nurses. In this he was of course
going against the stereotype. Yüan Ts'ai gives us the more common view of
the emotional basis of women's child-rearing practices:

> Very often parents, during their son's infancy and childhood, love him so
> much they forget his faults; they give in to his every demand and tolerate his
> every action. If he cries for no reason, they do not have the sense to make him
> stop, but blame his nanny. If he bullies his playmates, his parents do not have
> the sense to correct him, but instead blame the other children. If someone
> tries to tell them that their child was the one in the wrong, they reply that he
> is too young to be blamed. As the days and months go by, they nurture his
> depravity. All this is the fault of the parents' misguided love.
>
> As the boy grows older, the parents' love gradually lessens. They get angry
> at the slightest misdeed, treating it as a major crime. When they meet rela-
> tives and old friends, they relate every incident of misbehavior with great
> embellishments, guaranteeing that the boy gets labeled very unfilial, a label
> he does not deserve. All this is the fault of the parents' irrational disapproval.
>
> The mother is usually the source of such unreasonable likes and dislikes.
> When the father fails to recognize this and listens to what she says, the
> situation can become irretrievable. Fathers must examine this situation with
> care. They must be strict with their sons when they are young and must not
> let their love grow thin as the sons reach maturity.[36]

In the educated class, many mothers introduced their children to the
world of books. Yüan Hsieh (1144–1224) described how his mother, Miss Tai
(1121–1192), handled the earliest stages of her children's literary education:
"She taught us characters, writing them with her hand and telling us what
they were. When we read aloud by sentences, she would correct our pronuncia-
tion." When the sons got older, her role was more to encourage and admonish
them, but she also spent long hours talking to them about the past and the
present, sharing with them her broad knowledge and good sense. It was also
not uncommon for mothers to introduce their children to a few elementary
books. Miss Kung (1052–1119), for example, personally taught her sons the
Analects and the *Mencius*. Miss Huang (1063–1121), highly literate herself,
taught each of her seven daughters poetry and ritual. In the absence of men,

mothers might go further still. Miss Yü Tao-yung (1103–1182), widowed at forty, took over charge of her sons' educations, "personally transmitting to them the classics and teachings."[37]

Daughters must also have often been taught to read by their mothers. But there was much more mothers had to teach their daughters if they were to fit comfortably within a society that stressed the differentiation of the sexes. In biographies, women are often said to have learned all aspects of women's work without needing to be taught. This turn of phrase probably reflects men's amazement at the fact that pressure had to be put on sons to get them to master the body of texts that formed the basis of their profession, whereas their sisters, merely by following their mothers about the house and gradually helping out more and more, acquired effortlessly the skills needed to cook, tend silkworms, spin, sew, and care for the young, the ill, and the elderly.

Mothers were also credited with training their daughters to be sweet, agreeable, deferential, and reserved. Naturally, Sung mothers did not look on cultivation of these traits as complicity in women's oppression. Rather, they took pride in rearing daughters whom others would praise as beautiful and feminine. The reproduction of femininity was a domain that women dominated. Fathers and grandfathers could be excused for doting on girls and encouraging in them an unseemly tendency to show off. Mothers and grandmothers, however, were expected to see that they learned appropriate demeanor. Han Wei (1017–1098) told how his wife's mother, Miss Wang (987–1041), had captivated her father but eventually learned more feminine demeanor: "When she was only a few years old [her father] was delighted with her precocity and personally taught her to recite the *Classic of Filial Piety* and several hundred of Mr. Po [Chü-i]'s satirical and miscellaneous poems. At every family gathering, she would drink a lot. But when she got a little older, she announced, 'Drinking wine and reciting books are not things women do,' then turned over her cup and never looked at the written word again."[38] One can only surmise that her mother, grandmother, or other female relatives had been making comments on her behavior that counteracted some of the positive reinforcement she had been getting from her father.

Some of the traits cultivated in daughters, such as physical modesty, seem to have been important above all as markers of respectability, indicators that the girl was no courtesan. The more attracted men were to women willing to reveal their faces to men and entertain them, the more they apparently wanted their own wives and daughters to display modesty and stay home. But mothers did not rigorously exclude the fashions of the entertainment quarters as they guided the development of their daughters, as the spread of footbinding makes abundantly clear (see Chapter 1).

For all the dangers and difficulties, rearing children must have given mothers a great deal of satisfaction. Motherhood was not riddled with nearly the degree of ambivalence as other female roles: women did not receive mixed signals on the propriety of loving their children and taking the best care of them they could. A woman who came to see herself above all as a mother to her children would find life less confusing or frustrating than one who identified herself first as a woman, a wife, a poet, a weaver, or a household manager. Mothers could throw themselves enthusiastically into tending to their baby's physical needs and spend as much time as they could spare with the older children, knowing their intentions would not be misinterpreted: whatever they did would be regarded as evidence of their love. People might criticize their specific actions, but not their motives. Motherhood was also the prime domain in which women could expect to reap rewards for their efforts; everyone thought it was only natural and appropriate that children love their mothers as much as mothers loved their young. Indeed, writers often suggested that there was no way a son could ever fully repay the debt he owed his mother.

All of this underlines yet again the importance of a woman's relations to others in shaping her identity. A woman was many things to many people: a daughter to her parents, a wife to her husband, a sister-in-law to her husband's brother's wife, and so on. But the relationship that offered her the most was the relationship with her children. Moreover, a woman's identity as a mother carried over into her other relationships: a son's wife, for instance, was not just a daughter-in-law, but the mother of grandchildren; a neighbor woman was not merely that, but the mother of a neighbor boy.

One could argue that the Chinese family values, by so honoring the role of mother, advantaged older women at the expense of younger women, fertile women at the expense of infertile women. Some women benefited, at least eventually, but the greatest beneficiaries were probably the children. By giving women every possible incentive to be good mothers, the Chinese family system encouraged attentive and affectionate child-rearing.

TEN

Widowhood

When Sun Chi (b. 1070) died in 1134, he left his fifty-six-year-old wife, Miss Ch'iang (1078–1153), with eleven children, some still young. Their finances were a mess, as he had been "careless with money and liked to make gifts. With one word he might give out several hundred thousand [cash], without keeping track of it."[1] He had accumulated a basket full of IOU's and in his final instructions told his sons to burn them all. When they wanted to obey, Miss Ch'iang stopped them, arguing:

"I will not dare take a cent of interest, and I will not send anyone to knock on people's doors to ask about how quickly they will repay. But we cannot destroy the IOU's as ordered." She instructed her sons to announce his death but nothing more.

Some nephews said there was land that had not been divided and calculated that the income from it added up to ten thousand strings of cash. Miss Ch'iang was unsure what to do. Someone advised her that no legal complaints would be accepted on property division cases after five years had elapsed, so since a generation had passed, the [nephews] had no case. She replied, "Which is better, to fight over property or to yield it?" So she paid out the whole amount, keeping nothing back. A relative through marriage heard of this and said, "If a widow and her young sons in one day lose half the family property, they will go bankrupt." But Miss Ch'iang managed the finances and took care of clothing and food for the household with diligence, frugality, and hard work. She set aside a large room on the east side of the house and invited a teacher to instruct her sons. Morning and evening they recited their lessons; she did not let them play or procrastinate. She first took care of expenses for festivals, taxes, entertaining guests, performing sacrifices, and helping kin, then set funds aside for the future, wasting nothing. Through her efforts over twenty years, her sons all got wives and her daughters all were married out. The fields and other property were slowly restored to their former state. All her relatives—inner and outer, young and old—uniformly praised her as worthy.[2]

Accounts like this one of widows with the determination to overcome adversity and successfully bring up their children are not rare in Sung sources. Such strong, competent, and selfless women were universally admired, for much the same reasons that "inner helpers" were admired: they preserved or enhanced the standing of the family of their husbands and sons.

Fifty-six when widowed, Miss Ch'iang almost surely had grown sons who could have handled many matters for her, even if she also had young children as well. Even more awe-inspiring were the widows without grown sons. Given premodern mortality patterns, it was not rare for a woman to lose her husband before her sons were grown. Of the couples I studied, 5 percent were widowed by thirty, 13 percent by forty, and nearly 20 percent by forty-five. In the ideal case, such a woman would have been living in a complex family with her husband's brothers and would simply remain with them. When the family property was divided, her sons would get what her husband would have received. Considerate brothers-in-law would postpone division until her sons were able to manage the property or otherwise support her. Even when division had already taken place before her husband died, his brothers might take in the widow and her children, supporting them as dependents if need be; this was a common act for men in the educated class, who as a rule maintained large establishments with plenty for women to do. Han Yüan-chi (1118–1187), in a prayer he addressed to his deceased younger uncle, reported that after the uncle died without an heir Han took in his widow, who had no place else to go, took care of her until she also died, and later set up an heir for them so that their line would be continued.[3]

Despite this ideal, many widows returned to their natal families, either by preference, because their brothers-in-law did not welcome them, or because they had no brothers-in-law. Widows' financial and family situations must have varied by class and also by individual circumstances.[4] Miss Wu (1035–1093), widowed after less than a year of marriage, returned to her natal home with her baby daughter and "served her elder brother and his wife" for thirty-two years. Miss Su (1031–1072), widowed twice by thirty-five sui, returned to her mother's home, where she stayed in seclusion reciting Buddhist sutras, rarely even seen by other members of the family. Even after a widow's parents and brothers were dead, survivors might take in a widow. Miss Yü Tao-yung (1103–1182), a widow herself, took in her deceased husband's elder sister, supporting her generously for fifteen or sixteen years and finding wives for her sons.[5]

Some widows without sons had daughters to whom they could turn. After Miss Chang's husband died, his daughter by his first wife, Miss Yen (1039–

1110), took her in and cared for her to the end of her life. Miss Sung, on the death of her second husband, went to live with a married daughter from her first marriage, Miss Ch'en (1155–1230). Even a sister might be called on. In about 1175 Miss Shao, old, poor, and ill, was taken in by her younger sister, already over sixty herself.[6]

THE VULNERABILITY OF WIDOWS

Widows who tried to maintain some degree of independence did not have an easy life. Normally a widow did not inherit from her husband (his sons were the heirs), but if she did not remarry she could expect to be maintained on her husband's estate. If she had no sons, she could manage her husband's property and select an heir for her husband, preferably, but not necessarily, from among his brother's sons or other close agnatic relatives of that generation. If she did not select an heir, after her death the household would be classified as heirless, and the property disposed of according to complex rules. If a widow had young sons, whether born to her, to a concubine of her husband, or adopted, she could manage the property on their behalf, but was not to sell any land or houses without getting permission of the government, for she was merely a trustee for them. If her sons were grown, she still had some claims on the property that was being used to support her; her sons were not legally allowed to sell property without getting her consent on the bill of sale.[7]

Widows in Sung China undoubtedly would have liked clearer legal claims to their dowries and to their husbands' estates. But keeping what they were legally entitled to was enough of a problem. Men would try to wrest property away from them by means they would not have used against other grown men. In Kaifeng, a neighborhood bully had tried unsuccessfully to force his neighbor to sell his house to him. After the neighbor died, the bully got the man's wife, Miss Chang, and her two sons to leave by having his henchmen throw tiles and rocks at them.[8] A reading of cases in the *Judicial Decisions* provides an abundance of evidence that men assumed widows without adult sons were easy targets. They were, after all, women; they had been brought up to be agreeable, to yield to others, to defer to men regarding "outside" matters, and to be embarrassed to be seen in public. These same cases also show that there were some pretty spunky widows, ready to fight back.

Widows needed protection from relatives as much as from bullies. Han I (972–1044) came across a widow who ten years earlier had been forcibly married out by her husband's younger brother. Her son had been given to a village woman who was bribed to claim he was her own.[9] Like Miss Ch'iang, many widows seem to have concluded the best course in disputes with relatives over property was to give in. When Miss Li was left a widow in 1045, her husband's two younger brothers divided the property and cheated her out of two hundred thousand cash. Her only son, still young, could not suppress his anger, but she advised him to forget it so as not to trouble the spirit of his dead father.[10]

Yüan Ts'ai warned that widows would often be cheated, yet he considered it inevitable because few women had the necessary skills in reading and arithmetic to manage on their own. "Such women could entrust their finances to their husband's kinsmen or their own kinsmen, but not all relatives are honorable, and the honorable ones are not necessarily willing to look after other people's business." To avoid being cheated, widows sometimes had their property listed under men's names, a strategy that could backfire.[11]

Many disputes between widows and their husbands' relatives concerned adoption. Law and custom favored close patrilineal kin as adoptees, but widows might well have reasons to prefer more distant relatives or even strangers. Above all, a widow would want to keep an adoptee who had already been set up (and with whom she already had mother-son or grandmother-grandson ties) and would resist her husband's collateral relatives' efforts to substitute their own children. Struggles between them could be drawn out, as Miss Fu, the widow of Ch'en Fu, learned. She had adopted a three-sui boy from her husband's relatives. As he was of the appropriate generation, and she had had his name transferred to her household register, everything accorded with the law. And yet, for over twenty years, Ch'en Chien, perhaps her husband's brother, sued her repeatedly, trying to get his own son appointed heir. He took the case to the county, prefecture, circuit, and ministry courts. He also illegally occupied her lands, forcing her to go to court herself to try to get them back, wearing her out, and, concluded the judge, hastening her death.[12]

Even more vulnerable were widows who had adopted children outside the husband's descent line. Miss Tseng had been married to Wu Tan. She had borne a son, Wu Chen, who died young. Since there were no suitable candidates for adoption among Wu Tan's relatives, Miss Tseng and her husband took a boy from her family and changed his name to Wu, calling him Wu T'ang. Her husband died and Wu T'ang grew up, married, and had three sons and one daughter of his own. After her husband's death, the adoption was challenged several times, first by her husband's uncle, then by his cousin. The last challenge was initiated thirty years after the original adoption, and this time the plaintiff proposed an heir to the natural son who had died young. Miss Tseng, by then an elderly widow, responded to this by stating that the adoptee's youngest son had already been made her son's heir. The judge did everything he could to defend the widow and adoptee, pointing to the selfish motives of the challengers and even noting how the disparity in the prosperity of the two lines, as measured by their tax obligations, was the real cause of the dispute. He moreover suggested that adopting from a maternal relative was much better than adopting from a stranger.[13]

A widow might need to adopt many years after her husband died. When Miss Ch'en was widowed she had a young son, Chang I-wen, but unfortunately he died at twenty-four. She then adopted an abandoned child of three as his heir (to be her grandson). When the child was eight or nine, her long-deceased husband's young brother wanted his own son to be substituted. Since the brother-in-law's son was not of the right generation to be made heir to her son, the judge let the widow keep the adoptee she had reared.[14]

Three separate judgments were preserved for the case of Miss Mao, who had married Huang T'ing-chi, the third of four brothers (see Diagram 6). Huang T'ing-chi died in 1234, when Miss Mao was twenty-three. She had borne no sons and neither of her two daughters had survived. She took an oath not to remarry, which the first judge remarked deserved respect, since she was so young and had no children. She did not adopt a nephew because the second and fourth brothers had not yet had any sons, and the oldest brother had not gotten along with her husband and did not even come to offer condolences when he died. Moreover, his sons were close to her in age. So she turned to her own aunt, asking to adopt this woman's second son, whom she renamed Huang Chen. All this was done publicly, and the two closer brothers-in-law (with whom she apparently lived) did not object. Indeed, they invited teachers for the boy and arranged his marriage. After these brothers-in-law died, however, a son of the eldest brother brought a suit asking to be made heir. The first judge was sympathetic to him, citing the standard arguments against nonagnatic adoptions: the spirits will not enjoy the sacrifices, and whatever the situation may seem like on the surface, in fact the descent line is being extinguished. Even though Huang Chen had been adopted eighteen years earlier and he and his mother got along fine, the judge wanted her to pick a second heir from among her eight nephews and assign this boy half the property. She did as she was told, taking a son of the second brother, but that just led to more trouble. The new co-adoptee's real mother, Miss Hsü, took her son back, charging that he had been mistreated. The case went to court again, and the new judge clearly thought the first had gone too far in requiring a second adoptee. If there was any more trouble about the second adoptee, he ruled, a single heir would be enough. The third judge largely concurred, and ordered the original plaintiff beaten eighty strokes for being a troublemaker.[15] Many widows in Miss Mao's situation, one presumes, simply gave in to their brothers-in-law or nephews; after all, they could not even count on judges' siding with them.

Men were undoubtedly sometimes correct in suspecting that a widow did not place a high priority on continuing the descent line of every son who lived to marry. When a widow had two or more sons and one died after marriage but before begetting any sons, she might well prefer to see all the property go to her surviving son or sons, whom she could count on to support her,

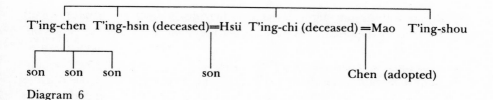

Diagram 6

than to see a full share go to an adoptee with whom her relationship would inevitably be weaker. In one such case, the judge accused the widow of being an ignorant woman, misled by the greed of her surviving son; in another case, however, a different judge strongly defended the right of the widow to decide the issue without interference from collateral relatives.[16]

Even widows who had sons might find collateral relatives trying to force themselves or their sons on them as additional heirs. Consider this case:

> According to the testimony, Fang Sen was born in 1200 and at age twenty married Miss Huang. She was born in 1204, so she married Fang Sen when she was sixteen. In 1223 she bore a daughter, Liu-ku, who was five when she lost her father and is now fifteen. Miss Huang in 1225 bore a son, Hsia, who was three when he lost his father and is now thirteen. The person named Fang Kuei claims in his own testimony that he was adopted by Fang Sen from his uncle Fang K'ai when he was eight sui and in 1217 followed his "father" when he opened a small store in the book district, two years before his "father" married Miss Huang. In 1217 Fang Sen was only eighteen. Is it likely he had already adopted Fang Kuei as a son? One adopts because one does not have a son, and either does it in old age or because one is seriously ill. Why would anyone just eighteen senselessly adopt another person's eight-year-old boy? Further, Fang Kuei does not look like a young man of twenty-eight. His empty accusations look worse and worse.[17]

Apparently when Fang Sen set up shop at eighteen, he took a young relative, Fang Kuei, to serve as his assistant. Sen died ten years later, leaving a widow with two little children. She probably let Fang Kuei continue to run the shop, but ten years later he repaid her by making a claim for a share of the property on the grounds that he had been adopted, taking the case to several judges.

A widow might have to struggle to retain property even when she gave in and made a nephew the heir. Miss Lu, an elderly widow with no sons, was pressured into accepting her husband's brother's eight-sui grandson as an adopted grandson. She gave him a share of the property and sent him back to his parents to rear. She and her daughter (perhaps also widowed) shaved their heads to become nuns and converted their house into a temple. When the brother-in-law tried to force them to turn over all the property, the case went to court. The judge declared both sides equally at fault, but in the end decided not to force the widow to renounce her decision to become a nun since she was already eighty. Irritating her any further, he thought, would simply hasten her death. He did, however, make her turn over half the property she had retained to the adoptee, instructing him to dedicate it to the upkeep of her deceased husband's grave.[18]

Adoption could even be at issue when the only property involved came from the widow's dowry. Miss Chang had married a Mr. Wu, and after both he and their only son had died she supported herself by farming the fields she had brought as a dowry. In her old age, we are told, "troubled by illness, and having neither husband nor son to depend on, she had to return to live with the Chang family." No one in her husband's family gave her any assistance, but when she was about to die, Wu Ch'en brought an accusation against the nephews caring for her, charging them with stealing title to the land and the crops growing in the fields. This claim was thrown out of court, but after her death the same man went to court again, trying to make his own grandson her heir so as to get her dowry fields. The judge, though disturbed that none of the Wus had taken care of her in her old age, nevertheless ordered that, after burial expenses were paid, whatever was left of her dowry be assigned to an heir from among the Wus.[19]

Men were well aware of the vulnerability of widows, leading some to try to arrange ways to protect their own widows and children after their deaths. After Liu Ching and his three brothers divided their property, Liu Ching prospered. When he was approaching death, he worried about what would happen to his baby son and widow. His brothers had died before him, but there were still several nephews who had considerably less wealth than he had and might make life difficult for his survivors. Therefore, in a will, he instructed his wife to give each of his four nephews ten thousand cash a year. This she did for five or seven years, but then stopped. The nephews went to a senior patrilineal relative to help them take the case to court. The judge, however, saw the case differently. To him it was evident that the arrangement had been made because Mr. Liu could not count on his nephews to take care of his orphan or widow, and so offered them money to try to buy off their hostility. Now that the widow had become experienced in the ways of the world, he ruled, she should be allowed to manage the estate on her own and keep all the income.[20]

YOUNG WIDOWS AS MORAL HEROES

Young widows who refused to remarry were widely regarded as heroic figures. People knew how hard it was for them to stand up to parents or parents-in-law who urged remarriage, how difficult it was to protect and educate their children. The woman who could hold out they viewed as extraordinary, an inspiration to men and women alike.[21]

The belief that it was morally preferable for a woman to marry only once had very old roots. The *Book of Rites* says, "Faithfulness is the basis of serving others, and is the virtue of a wife. When her husband dies a woman does not remarry; to the end of her life she does not change."[22] An old tradition, going back to the Han at least, extolled the two daughters of the mythical sage-emperor Yao who married the mythical sage-emperor Shun as wife and concubine. When he died, so it was said, they drowned themselves.[23] This story was popular enough in Sung times to be depicted in paintings (Fig. 25). The poem "Cypress Boat" in the *Book of Songs* was taken to be the oath of Kung Chiang, a widow who resisted her parents' pressure to remarry.[24] The *Biographies of Great Women,* written by Liu Hsiang at the end of the first century B.C., told the story of Kung Chiang and of other women whose primary accomplishment was determined resistance to remarriage. These women often were portrayed as citing a maxim about wifely fidelity, such as "Even if there is a sagely mate, she does not go a second time," or "The moral duty of a wife lies in not changing once she has gone [in marriage]," or "The moral duty of a wife lies in not having two husbands." Many of these women ended up sacrificing their lives rather than accepting disgrace. At the end of the first century A.D., Pan Chao (ca. 48–ca. 120) wrote that husbands had a duty to remarry if their first wives died, but no ritual text authorized women to do so. Many dynastic histories included biographies of women known primarily for resisting remarriage.[25]

Popular primers used for girls' education conveyed the same message. The late T'ang *Classic of Filial Piety for Girls* repeated the rule that men had the duty to remarry but women had no authority to take "a second dip."[26] The last item in the *Analects for Girls,* also written in the T'ang, is titled "Preserving Chastity." It describes how girls until marriage should stay in the women's quarters, keeping silent when guests are present for fear they might be heard and carrying candles if they must walk about after dark. It then goes on to discuss marital fidelity:

> When husband and wife "join the hair," the moral principles involved are as weighty as a thousand gold pieces. Should it happen that misfortune occurs and [your husband] dies first, for three years you will wear heavy mourning. You must keep your commitment and make your heart firm. Attend to protecting the family, managing the estate, and preparing the tomb, then train and educate his descendants to continue his name.[27]

The Sung government helped publicize the virtue of refusing remarriage. Sung judges lavished praise on widows who did not marry again, likening them to Kung Chiang.[28] As a way to "improve customs," the government conferred honorary banners, grants of grain, or tax exemptions on women who had been widowed young and remained unmarried for long periods. For instance, in 1094 Miss Wang was granted ten bushels of grain and ten bolts

Fig. 25. A widowed wife and concubine contemplating suicide
Detail from a handscroll attributed to Chang Tun-li (ca. 1200), showing two sisters,
consorts of the mythical sage-emperor Shun, just before they throw themselves into
the river out of grief. Archibald Cary Coolidge Fund. Courtesy, Museum of Fine
Arts, Boston (34.1460).

of plain silk because she had stayed in the home of her parents-in-law for
twelve years, rearing the posthumous son of the husband who had died
in the first year of their marriage.[29] Local officials could take the initiative in
honoring loyal widows. Ch'eng Chiung (c.s. 1163) arranged a monthly stipend
for a local widow, Miss Tu, who had pawned or sold everything in her dowry
and had nothing left to support her children, yet still refused to remarry
on the grounds that leaving her son uncared for would be disloyal to her
husband.[30] Determined widows were thus treated like the heroes of filial
piety who endured unusual austerity in mourning, sliced off a piece of their
thigh to prepare medicine for an ailing parent, or maintained an undivided
household for five or more generations.[31]

Unfeigned admiration for the fortitude of widows is evident in many
writers' accounts of widows they knew. Wang An-shih (1021–1086) wrote
that Miss Wei (987–1050), widowed at twenty-nine with two young sons, not

only taught them the *Book of Poetry, Analects,* and *Classic of Filial Piety* before they went out to a teacher, but "personally took care of the mulberries and hemp to provide their food and clothes, enduring poverty for a long time without ever thinking of changing her determination [not to remarry]."[32] Lou Yüeh (1137–1213) wrote that the widow of one of his cousins exceeded even Kung Chiang. Although Kung Chiang resisted her parents' pressure to remarry, she was not known for any other qualities. His kinswoman Miss Chiang (1117–1202), however, had been left a widow at twenty-six with five children, ranging in age from two weeks to six sui, and although her own mother tried to get her to remarry, and her parents-in-law did not discourage her, she refused, saying that otherwise the orphans' fate could not be assured. She then devoted herself to managing the family, which grew large and prosperous under her direction.[33]

Many stories of heroic widows read like miracle tales. In the popular mind, self-sacrifice of the sort exemplified by the most devoted of widows might well move the gods. Hung Mai told of a Miss Wu, the childless widow of a Mr. Wang:

Miss Wu served her mother-in-law very filially. Her mother-in-law had an eye ailment and felt sorry for her daughter-in-law's solitary and poverty-stricken situation, so suggested that they call in a son-in-law for her and thereby get an adoptive heir. Miss Wu announced in tears, "A woman does not serve two husbands. I will support you. Don't talk this way." Her mother-in-law, seeing that she was determined, did not press her. Miss Wu did spinning, washing, sewing, cooking, and cleaning for her neighbors, earning perhaps a hundred cash a day, all of which she gave to her mother-in-law to cover the cost of firewood and food. If she was given any meat, she would wrap it up to take home.

Miss Wu was honest by nature. She did not chat idly, and even if other people's things were right in front of her, she did not look at them, wanting only what was her own. Thus neighbors often engaged her, and they helped out her and her mother-in-law, so they managed to avoid dying of hunger or cold.

Once when her mother-in-law was cooking rice, a neighbor called to her, and to avoid overcooking the rice she dumped it into a pan. Owing to her bad eyes, however, she mistakenly put it in the dirty chamber pot. When Miss Wu returned and saw it, she did not say a word. She went to a neighbor to borrow some cooked rice for her mother-in-law and took the dirty rice and washed it to eat herself.

One day in the daytime neighbors saw [Miss Wu] ascending into the sky amid colored clouds. Startled, they told her mother-in-law, who said, "Don't be foolish. She just came back from pounding rice for someone, and is lying down on the bed. Go and look." They went to the room and peeked in and saw her sound asleep. Amazed, they left.

When Miss Wu woke up, her mother-in-law told her what happened, and she said, "I just dreamed of two young boys in blue clothes holding documents and riding on the clouds. They grabbed my clothes and said the Emperor of

Heaven had summoned me. They took me to the gate of heaven and I was brought in to see the emperor, who was seated beside a balustrade. He said, 'Although you are just a lowly ignorant village woman, you are able to serve your old mother-in-law sincerely and work hard. You really deserve respect.' He gave me a cup of aromatic wine and a string of cash, saying, 'I will supply you. From now on you will not need to work for others.' I bowed to thank him and came back, accompanied by the two boys. Then I woke up."

There was in fact a thousand cash on the bed, and the room was filled with a fragrance. They then realized that the neighbors' vision had been a spirit journey. From this point on even more people asked her to work for them, and she never refused. But the money that had been given to her she kept for her mother-in-law's use. Whatever they used promptly reappeared, so the thousand cash was never exhausted. The mother-in-law also regained her sight in both eyes.[34]

It would be difficult to imagine a woman more self-effacing that this Miss Wu. She was so attentive to the comfort of her mother-in-law that she never came close to losing her temper, whatever the provocation. In this way she won the goodwill of her neighbors and the help of the gods.[35]

Heroic widows were so admired that it was not at all demeaning or embarrassing for a man to attribute his family's success to such a woman. The Lo family of Ch'ih-chou (Anhwei), for instance, had an essay written in honor of their family's true founder eight generations earlier in the eleventh century. She was Miss Chang, a woman widowed at twenty-seven while pregnant with her only child. She stayed at her husband's home to rear her son and lived to see one of her grandsons become an official and to preside over a "five-generation household." By 1262, the descendants commemorating her numbered over a thousand.[36]

Given the long tradition of extolling a widow's fidelity and the widespread support for it in the Sung, it is not surprising that Sung Confucian scholars joined in the chorus. Ssu-ma Kuang wrote, "'Wife' means identity. Once she is identified with [her husband], she does not change for the rest of her life. Therefore loyal subjects do not serve two masters, and chaste women do not serve two husbands."[37] In his *Precepts for Family Life*, he cited for emulation many widows who refused to remarry. Ssu-ma Kuang did not present female self-sacrifice as emotionally or morally more satisfying than male self-sacrifice, nor did he offer as models widows who committed suicide rather than remarry. His heroes, instead, resisted their parents' efforts to have them marry again, wishing above all to continue to care for their husbands' parents or children.[38] They might mutilate themselves to discourage suitors, but did not throw their lives away.[39] He even included a widow who cut off her arm after a man touched it, feeling that she had been compromised by his action.[40] He also held up for emulation girls, wives, or widows who committed suicide to avoid being raped, but remarriage he did not equate with rape.

In later generations, it was Ch'eng I's unqualified rejection of remarriage that became most famous:

> [Someone] asked, "If a widow is alone and poor with no one to depend on, is it all right for her to remarry?"
>
> [Ch'eng I] replied, "This theory arose only because in later ages people fear freezing or starving to death. But starving to death is a very minor matter; losing one's integrity is a matter of the gravest importance."[41]

Chu Hsi included this passage in his *Reflections on Things at Hand*, which only added to its fame. He knew most people considered Ch'eng I unreasonable in insisting on widow fidelity, and when he wrote to a disciple urging him to help his sister live as a widow he used much milder language.[42] Still, his support for Ch'eng I's pronouncement helped move widow fidelity from a heroic ideal to a standard people urged on their sisters and sisters-in-law.

Much of the misogyny that modern readers see in Neo-Confucian writings on remarriage stems, I believe, from fundamentally different notions of marriage. In contemporary Western ways of thinking, marriage is about acquiring a spouse, and both men and women get married. The marriage lasts until divorce or the death of one of the spouses. Thus, to impose on a widow faithfulness to her dead husband without imposing similar faithfulness on widowers hardly seems equal treatment. To Chinese in the Sung, however, marriage was only in part about the joining of two spouses. It was primarily about how families perpetuate themselves through the incorporation of new members. A man was incorporated at birth or through adoption. His loyalty to the family into which he had been incorporated could be tested in many ways: he might have to endure a vicious step-mother, a high-handed half-brother, or deal with a wife who told tales about his brothers or otherwise disrupted the family. Overcoming these circumstances allowed the family to survive. A woman's loyalty to the family into which she had been incorporated by marriage could also be tested: she might be subjected to a nasty mother-in-law or a husband who doted on concubines, the fact of a concubine bearing sons while she did not, the death of her husband when she was childless or the mother of young children, or brothers-in-law or stepsons who made her unwelcome after her husband died or who made off with her children's property. Her heroism in meeting these tests could have just as much to do with the survival of the family as anything a man might do. For a woman, remarriage meant renouncing the family she had joined. It was comparable to a son abandoning his parents, not a man taking a new wife.

As will be seen in the next chapter, however, the glorification of loyal widows did not keep young widows from remarrying in the Sung. The extreme limits the cult of widow chastity eventually reached is a story that must be set in Ming-Ch'ing times.[43] Nevertheless, already in Sung times the honor granted the refusal to remarry was of great cultural importance, for it conveyed with great force the notion that the qualities so praised in girls and wives (agreeableness, gentleness, willingness to yield) were minor accomplishments compared to loyalty to the patriline of their husbands. It thus said something about the nature of women: a woman did not become truly great by fulfilling natural yin tendencies toward yielding, but by overcoming them. It also said much about what marriage meant to women: a woman did not marry a man so much as a family line.

OLDER WIDOWS WITH GROWN SONS

The term commonly used for widow, *kua-fu*, evokes images of the woman left in unfortunate circumstances. But the majority of those who outlived their husbands were not widowed until their sons were grown, and they did not live alone, but with their sons, daughters-in-law, and grandchildren. Their social identity was thus more that of mother-in-law and grandmother than widow, and theed; if anything, they were viewed as reaping the benefits of longevity. No one seems to have felt the need for a formal division of property between mother and sons, or a clear separation of her dowry from her sons' property, practices common in medieval and early modern Europe.

In reality, of course, there were some unfilial sons. Yüan Ts'ai spoke of "sons who falsify papers and forge signatures." In one legal case, a man who wanted money to gamble mortgaged family property without getting the signature of his mother or four brothers. There were also cases of widows who brought charges of unfiliality against their sons for not supporting them. In one, a son went so far as to sell his mother's bed.[44] But natural sons who begrudged their mothers room and board were apparently rare. Hung Mai implied that unfilial sons of this sort were popularly thought to deserve divine retribution. He told of a widow whose two sons had a silver shop in Hangchow. Knowing the waywardness of one of the sons, the widow secretly saved up for her funeral expenses. He chanced upon the money and made off with it, only to be struck by lightning not long after.[45]

Much more common, if we can believe the surviving sources, were doting sons who helped their widowed mothers enjoy their late years. Liu K'o-chuang (1187–1269) presents a good portrait of the mutual dependency of his widowed mother and her children. When his father, Liu Mi-cheng (1157–1213), was on his deathbed, he expressed great regret that he had not managed to live long enough to arrange all of his children's marriages. He asked his fifty-three-year-old wife, Miss Lin (1161–1248), to take charge of these matters, whereupon, according to her son, she set about seeing to it that the sons continued the family tradition of scholarship and the girls married educated men.[46]

Miss Lin was quite successful with her sons. The eldest, K'o-chuang, had already held office for three years when his father died, and after the mourning period was over he returned to hold a long series of posts and gain a reputation as a poet. The next two sons, K'o-sun (1189–1246) and K'o-kang (1200–1254), also eventually gained office, like K'o-chuang entering the ranks owing to the privileges granted sons of higher officials. K'o-kang was only fourteen when his father died, so the widowed Miss Lin probably deserves some credit for helping him advance. The youngest son, K'o-yung, was but seven sui when his father died, so Miss Lin educated him herself, and he always stayed closely attached to her. After repeatedly failing in the examinations, he stayed at home, devoting himself to poetry writing.[47]

During her widowhood, Miss Lin arranged the marriages of her second and third daughters and her third and fourth sons. When her husband died, she already had two daughters-in-law to serve her, but K'o-chuang's wife followed him to his posts and was not always in attendance. K'o-sun's wife, Miss Fang (1190–1259), did not accompany her husband, remaining instead in the family home. She served Miss Lin for over forty years, remaining filial in her manner, we are told, even after her own hair was white. The youngest son's wife, Junior Miss Lin (1203–1261), entered the house in 1223. She was four years older than her husband, then only seventeen sui. Probably Miss Lin had speeded up this marriage because she was already over sixty. As the youngest of the daughters-in-law, Junior Miss Lin is said to have concentrated her efforts on providing her mother-in-law a happy old age.[48]

Once she had secured daughters-in-law to manage the household affairs, Miss Lin turned her attention increasingly to Buddhism. She kept to a vegetarian diet, meditated regularly, and maintained contact with leading Buddhists at monasteries nearby. But she did not forget her family. At family gatherings, we are told, she kept trying to convert everyone to Buddhism.[49]

Miss Lin's seventies must have been a happy time for her. She was still in good health, and three of her sons were officials so that "banners always filled the outer courtyard." Moreover, at least eight grandchildren were living. In a song Liu K'o-chuang wrote on his fifty-sixth birthday in 1242, he concluded with the comment that he had no desire to become an immortal or a Buddha or assist heaven's commands; rather, he wanted his family to go on forever as they were, a fortunate family of white-haired mother and son. Indeed, her sons seem to have been remarkably devoted to her. K'o-chuang wrote that in 1237 K'o-sun suggested to him that they each find ways to be relieved of office at the earliest opportunity, as "serving in office is a way to support one's parents, but [our mother] has little concern for glory and does better with peace and quiet." Even when away from home K'o-chuang kept in touch, recording in a poem his joy at receiving a two-line letter from his mother, which told of the harvest and her hopes for his career.[50]

Miss Lin's eighties were not so joyful, but family members continued to attend to her comfort. The family was greatly dismayed when one of the grandsons, then thirty, died of dysentery in the capital, where he was waiting to take the civil service examinations. When his father, K'o-sun, died two years later, family members were afraid to inform Miss Lin, who herself was ailing. This pretense they managed to keep up for over a year. Because she was ill, her second daughter often "abandoned the work in her husband's house" to come and tend her, staying for several months at a time. Miss Lin may have specially sought this daughter's company, for she was the only one of her progeny really able to discuss Buddhist philosophy with her. As the oldest son, K'o-chuang returned home to take charge of seeing that the younger members of the family cared for her. In 1247 and 1248 he turned down official assignments to be with his mother during her last days. In his memorials requesting to be excused from office he stressed that he was the eldest son and that his mother's eyes were getting worse and worse. He also noted that since he was nearly sixty himself, he would not have much longer to care for her and could not bear to be any distance from her. Although claiming an old or ill parent was always a good way to avoid undesired appointments, K'o-chuang's wish to stay at home appears to have been genuine. He wrote to a friend that people wrongly suspected his motives: "It really is that my old mother is eighty-eight this year, and mother and son depend on each other for their life and are inseparable."[51]

The widows whose narratives have been discussed in this chapter were not primarily from the upper class. Nearly all the legal cases that reveal the vulnerability of widows concern women from ordinary families, as do many of the tales of heroic widows. When discussing the virtue of widows, lower-class examples suited writers' purposes, because the point they wished to make concerned the hardships widows endured. Even from our perspective, the idea that widows had much in common across class lines makes sense. All widows shared a key characteristic: they had no husbands to represent them. As a consequence, they did things that wives with living husbands did not do. They had many decisions to make, beginning with whether to re-marry and whether to live alone or with relatives. If their sons were young, they acted as heads of their households, not empowered to sell the family land but able to choose spouses for their children or select adoptees. They also would manage the family business, hire workers or collect rents, or go out to work themselves. They may have been bullied, cheated, or neglected, but they were more than just victims: they were actors who participated in society as honorable representatives of their families.

Widows had something else in common: they were (presumably at least) sexually inactive. The cult of widowhood in China seems to share some of the overtones of the cult of the Virgin Mary in the West. Celibate widows were mothers untainted by also being wives. They were pure and asexual, entirely devoted to the welfare of their children. Although no one denied that they had become mothers through sexual intercourse, their vows of chastity after their husbands died rid them of the uncleanness of sexuality, making them saint-mothers.[52] If their only child was adopted after a brief and fruitless marriage, so much the better. Historical sources reveal how powerful this image was for men. Perhaps it had power also for at least some women. The young widows who begged to adopt a baby so they could raise it to continue their husband's line were not necessarily coerced or cynically acting out a role to gain fame or rewards. It is quite possible that some felt asexual motherhood was purer, more saintly, and more honorable than ordinary married life and took to the role of chaste widow as they might to a religious vocation.

The main division among widows was between those with grown sons when widowed and those without. All women, as they grew older, came to be seen more as mothers/grandmothers and less as their husbands' sexual partners. A widow of sixty with a daughter-in-law to serve her and grand-children to spoil was probably, on the average, as happy as a wife in similar circumstances, though no one, of course, would ever have suggested that older women might look forward to their husbands' dying so that they could enjoy a few years as the most senior member of the family (any more than they would suggest that sons might look forward to their fathers' dying so that they could succeed them as family heads).

What should we make of a system in which young widows were held in awe and yet people were quick to take advantage of them? The explanation for the apparent contradiction is, of course, that the causal connections go the other way; it was because people knew how much young widows had to put up with that they were awed by those who managed to persevere. But I think one can go a little further and point to ways the exaltation of such widows reinforced patriliny and patriarchy. It would not do for women to fare too well without men. Exalting the courageous, stubborn, self-sacrificing widow might seem like exaltation of spunky women, but the underlying message was that women really did need men.

ELEVEN

Second Marriages

In Sung times, both men and women who were widowed young frequently remarried. The situation for women was, however, quite unlike that for men. Like divorce today, remarriage of widows was accepted as the only available course in some situations, but nothing to feel proud of. Widows who did marry again thus had to come to grips with emotional conflicts much worse than those experienced by men who took a successor wife.

THE REMARRIAGE OF WOMEN

It was perfectly legal in Sung times, as earlier and later, for a woman whose husband had died or divorced her to marry again. One judge who strongly disapproved of the remarriage of widows still defended its legality. The case in question concerned Miss Ch'ü; though she was hardly to be admired for having had three husbands, what she did was no business of her former husband's brother, the judge ruled: "Whether she marries or does not marry is up to Miss Ch'ü alone to decide."[1] Legally, the only differences between a widow and an unmarried woman in regard to marriage were that a widow was not to marry while still in mourning for her husband and was not to marry a close patrilineal relative of her ex-husband, up to second cousin. Given all the hardships poor widows were known to face, the first rule was softened in 1090, so that a widow with no one to support her could marry after a hundred days.[2]

Remarriage of widows, especially to widowers, was nothing unusual. It is referred to casually in numerous accounts of perfectly ordinary people, such as the legal cases in the *Judicial Decisions.* Hung Mai mentions dozens of widows who remarried.[3] Reference books give phrases and couplets that imply second marriages were not only acceptable, but could be worth celebrating.

For instance: "The excellent girl, her moon is not full, her shadow is short./ Happily she will be made round again like the moon."[4] In other words, a woman is incomplete without a man, so it was natural for her to marry again. Marriage letters for a woman's second marriage might note that widow fidelity was the ideal but then go on to say that marriages are predestined, thus sanctioning the match.[5]

Remarriage was undoubtedly more likely the younger the widow, the fewer her children, and the greater the difficulties posed by staying where she was. Remarriage of widows was probably more common lower down on the social scale, but it certainly was not confined to the poor or uneducated. Examples from the families of educated men are plentiful, especially during the eleventh and twelfth centuries. They include the mothers of Tu Yen (978–1057), Fan Chung-yen (989–1052), Liu Pin (fl. ca. 1000), Chia K'uei (1010–1078), and Hu T'eng-ch'uan;[6] the wives of Yao Fei-ch'en (eleventh century), Yüeh Fei (1104–1142), Chang Chiu-ch'eng (1092–1159), and Lo Tien (1150–1194);[7] the daughters-in-law of Hsüeh Chü-cheng (912–981), Ch'eng Hao (1032–1085), Chang Chün (1086–1154), and Ch'en Tse (twelfth century);[8] and the daughters of Sun Chi (1074–1134), Weng Ch'en (1137–1205), Chang Ta-yung (twelfth century), Chao Yung (1151–1209), Lin Ching-lüeh (thirteenth century), and Wei Liao-weng (1178–1237).[9] Legal cases involving remarried women included ones who married officials.[10] So do anecdotes.[11] There are fewer references to widows from educated families remarrying in the thirteenth century, which probably reflects the influence of Neo-Confucianism on what writers would mention, the sorts of writers whose collected works survive, and perhaps also on the behavior of widows in upper class families.

Not all widows who remarried were especially young. Li Ch'ing-chao was over forty-five when her husband died in 1129, yet three years later she married another official (the marriage lasted only a few months).[12] Miss Lu (1004–1067), from a scholarly family, was seventeen when she married an official. After they had three children, he died. She stayed with her mother-in-law for ten years after his death, raising the children, until her mother-in-law also died. She thus had to have been over thirty when her own mother, saying she wanted to entrust her daughter to a worthy scholar, arranged a marriage for her to a widower with two sons.[13]

All through the Sung, writers would casually mention a woman's prior husband without apology or embarrassment. The histories record that Empress Liu, consort of Chen-tsung (r. 997–1022), had been married before she entered his household. Indeed, her husband was still alive, having decided to marry her to someone else because of poverty. Emperor Che-tsung's (r. 1086–1100) mother had had "three fathers": her mother's first husband, her second one (whose name she had taken), and a relative who had cared for her for many years. After Che-tsung became emperor, he had posthumous honors conferred on all three.[14] Literati biographers of women could mention remarriage without apology. Su Sung (1020–1101), in his biography for his younger sister, openly stated that her first husband died after three years, and even though she had two sons, she married again after four years. Han Yüan-chi (1118–1187), after relating at length the distinguished ancestry of Miss Li (1104–1177), commented that she had first married Ch'ien Tuan-i but, after bearing one daughter, was left a widow and married Han Chi-ch'iu as his second wife. Cheng Kang-chung (1088–1154) wrote that his wife's grandmother was widowed shortly after bearing her mother, and four years later took the girl with her when she remarried into another family. Wang Tsao (1079–1154) claimed that Miss Shih (1055–1148) was one of the two or three most competent wives to have lived in the Sung dynasty: she had raised fifteen children and maintained harmony in a family of two hundred. He noted that this was a second marriage for both her and her husband, her first marriage to a Mr. Hu having lasted only a year.[15] If these men had found remarriage painfully shameful, they could have abbreviated their accounts of these women's early lives to omit mention of it, a tack some authors undoubtedly took.

Even near the end of the Sung in scholarly circles, where the arguments against widows' remarrying must have been well known, some authors mentioned remarriage without apology. Shih Sheng-tsu (1191–1274) had studied with the prominent Neo-Confucian teacher Wei Liao-weng (1178–1237) and was the author of more than ten books, mostly on the classics. In the funerary biography he wrote for his second wife, Miss Yang Yün-yin (ca. 1210–1271), he described her as a person who had suffered several misfortunes: first losing her mother at nine; then, after marrying her stepmother's nephew, losing both her father and her husband in enemy invasions; next having to take care of her stepmother and guard the coffins in an even larger-scale invasion in 1237 and 1238; and finally becoming seriously ill. Shih's first wife had been a close friend of hers, and after he was widowed he proposed their match. They married in 1240.[16]

An occasional man even argued explicitly that remarriage was appropriate in certain circumstances. Chao Yün-jang, the chief minister of the court of the imperial clan for over twenty years in the eleventh century, asked for permission to arrange second marriages of imperial clanswomen who were widowed young without sons. To prohibit remarriage in such cases, he argued, was at odds with human feelings.[17] The censor T'ang Hsün (1005–1064) in 1046 went so far as to charge Wu Yü (1004–1058) with selfishness for not letting his brother's widow remarry. In T'ang's view he was keeping her only to maintain his ties to her influential relatives.[18] T'ang must have assumed his audience would regard letting her remarry (even though she already had six children) as perfectly normal.

Despite all the evidence that remarriage was tolerated as a way to make do in unfortunate circumstances, there is no denying the emotional force of feelings against it. After all, the women who resisted remarriage could not all have been angling for honor as chaste widows. Many clearly felt that there was something intrinsically shameful, impure, or demeaning in leaving the family they had entered through marriage to enter a sexual union with a second man. Chang Chiu-ch'eng (1092–1159) wrote that his second wife, Miss Ma, had also been married before. After her husband died, leaving her with young children, her parents convinced her to come home in preparation for remarrying, telling her: "We are old. If you do not marry again, we will not be able to close our eyes when we die." But she clearly was not reconciled to the idea. "The day after the wedding she spent the whole day with her face to the wall, weeping. After I asked several times, she said, 'You are a determined and sincere gentleman. I will tell you the truth. My mother-in-law in the Wu family was a person of outstanding integrity who ought to be in the *Biographies of Great Women*. I had wanted to share her devotion, but now cannot, as I am already married to you.'" Miss Ma not only was troubled at having to leave people she loved (her mother-in-law and her seven-year-old son) but also distressed that she had not been able to emulate her mother-in-law's model.[19]

In another case, the woman's anguish seems to have festered for many years. Miss Ts'ai (1037–1075), the daughter of an official, was married at fourteen to a seriously ill young man who died sixteen days later. She stayed on for several years, finishing the mourning not only for her husband but also for his father, who died a couple of years later. She would not consent to remarry, so her mother and brothers got together several dozen of their kinsmen to go to her house. They argued with her that she had already done everything expected of a wife, and besides had no way to survive unless she remarried, as neither her husband nor his father had any heirs. "Although you wish to preserve your devotion, with whom will you live?" Distraught, she finally gave in to their pressure and returned home. After a year she was married to a well-to-do widower with four sons and a daughter. When her second husband died about twenty years later, she reportedly said, "To walk through two courtyards is a source of shame for a woman. How much worse to be like me! What is the use of living any longer? I am decided." She stopped eating and secretly sent an old woman to buy arsenic. Despite all the efforts of her family, she died two days after her husband.[20]

Men, too, felt there was something amiss in widows' remarrying. Han Ch'i wrote the funerary biography for his nephew's son Han T'ien (1042–1063), who died at age twenty-two, leaving behind only two young daughters, one of whom also died soon thereafter. His young wife, Han Ch'i said, "returned to her father's house," apparently as a transition for remarriage, for Han Ch'i lamented, "Your wife could not stay and returned to her family, so your coffin will be alone in the grave. What crime did you commit to deserve such punishment?"[21] Wen-ying (eleventh century) saw widows who remarried as selfish. He contrasted the case of a woman from an ordinary family who had died trying to take her husband's body back home for burial to the widows of the well-to-do and educated, who promptly packed up their dowries and looked for another husband.[22] In the Southern Sung, when Hsiao Chen passed the examinations, thus becoming a prime candidate for an advantageous marriage, he decided to marry a widow. One of his classmates wrote a song to tease him, pointedly referring to the fact that his wife had had a previous husband with the phrase, "the old store is open for business again."[23] Before the end of the Sung, men who admired Li Ch'ing-chao as a poet had begun insisting the sources that mentioned her remarriage must have been maliciously fabricated.[24]

In ghost stories we encounter another dimension to people's sentiments against remarriage. Hung Mai recorded several tales in which a dead husband returned to upbraid his wife for remarrying. In one, a talented young man named Cheng wed an attractive woman named Lu, and they became very attached to each other. One night, in bed, Cheng said to his wife, "We two are so happy together. If I die, do not marry again. If you die, I will do the same." She answered, "We ought to live to a hundred and grow old together. Why say inauspicious things like this!" Ten years passed and they had two children. When Cheng was stricken with a serious ailment, he tried to get his wife to promise in front of his parents not to remarry, but she just wept. A few months after he died, a matchmaker came, and Miss Lu discussed another marriage with her. As soon as the mourning period was over, she took her dowry and married a Mr. Tseng. On the seventh day after the wedding, Tseng had to leave on business, and Miss Lu received a letter in the handwriting of her former husband, saying:

> For ten years our hair was tied as man and wife. As long as you live, you should take charge of the sacrifices to me. From morning to night we enjoyed ourselves together. I shared with you my income and we lived together. Suddenly through the great transformation I made the long departure [i.e. died]. You yearned for another man and renounced your promise. You abandoned my lands and took my property to another household. You had no pity on my children or consideration for my parents. You lack the integrity to be a wife, the compassion to be a mother. I will accuse you in the netherworld. You can present your side in Hades.

The netherworld judge apparently found for the plaintiff, for three days later Miss Lu died.[25]

In the eyes of this ghost-husband, his wife had a duty to offer sacrifices to him as well as care for his parents, children, and property. In another case, a minor functionary came back in a dream to berate his wife for dishonoring him by marrying a mine foreman: "I had property and a two-room house, which could have supported you, yet you insisted on marrying someone else. But why did you take up with a menial? I used to associate with educated men, and we looked on his sort as slaves. You are humiliating yourself and disgracing me. Moreover, since he took you as his wife, he also started illicit relations with my maid, which is intolerable." He then promised to bring about her new husband's death within forty-nine days.[26]

Sometimes ghost-husbands were motivated by simple jealousy. In one such case, the ghost took out his ill feelings on the man who had married his wife:

Teng Tseng... married the exceptionally beautiful youngest daughter of the imperial clansman [Chao] Tzu-ch'üan... Teng died before taking up his post. The family was very poor, so Miss Chao had no way to remain as a faithful widow. As soon as the mourning period was over, she took her two children and married the son of the rich Huang family of Nan-feng. About a month later, Huang dreamed that Teng came and jeered at him: "What sort of a man are you? How dare you marry my wife! I have received a [netherworld] appointment as superintendent of the bureau of pestilence. You'd better end this marriage right away. If you do not, I will send a plague to your house. When it comes, regrets will do you no good." Huang woke up with a start, frightened. Although he was very much in love with Miss Chao, he had no choice but to divorce her immediately.

After another year, Miss Chao was even more poverty-stricken and some days could not even light a fire. She then married T'ung Chiu-chung of Nan-ch'eng. A few months later, he also dreamed that Teng came to him and warned him in the same way, adding: "I will inflict on you the same illness that killed me." T'ung was then madly in love and did not believe it. As a consequence he got the "wind labor" disease, like Teng had had, and died the next year.[27]

Widows who remarried were spared the financial difficulties of widows who remained in their husband's house, but they still found themselves with many more problems than ordinary wives. This was particularly true if they had children by their first husband, for his family was entitled to insist that the widow leave them behind, and might even refuse to let her visit them. Ch'eng I, while not approving of his nephew's widow's decision to remarry, did let her come from time to time to see the young son she had left behind.[28] Shao Po-wen (1057–1134) told of a Miss Li, widow of a county magistrate, who did not tell her new husband about the infant son she had left with his relatives. Later, when her new husband learned that the boy was in difficult circumstances, he spent freely to bring him to live with them and raised him as his own, not telling the boy his true parentage until he was grown.[29]

But taking children along was not always a good solution, for strained relations between stepbrothers were almost inevitable. A wife's sons by a former husband had no claim to her second husband's property, even if they had been supported on it and had helped work it for years. And it could happen that the father, perhaps influenced by his new wife, came to like his stepsons better than the sons by his first wife. Stepsons often seem to have taken their stepfather's family name and hence may have expected to inherit along with their stepbrothers. Yüan Ts'ai recommended taking precautions whenever marrying a widow with children: "Whether the boys will be brought into the house and whether they will share in the household economy must be declared publicly and reported to the authorities, thereby preventing disputes before they begin." Of course, disparities could also work the other way. Sons by a former husband might have inherited property from their father or might have claims to their mother's dowry not shared by their stepbrothers.[30]

Normally, a widow could not take any of the property of her former husband into a second marriage. The code stated that when there were no sons, the widow received the husband's share only if she stayed in his home.[31] She could, however, usually take her dowry with her, even if she had sons. Yüan Ts'ai argued that it was unwise for a man to put property in his wife's name (to avoid later division with his brothers) because of the danger that he might die and she remarry, taking the property to her new home. Men might even compete to marry a widow with substantial property. When a widow had sons or stepsons, they might dispute the disposition of her dowry if they did not follow her. In one case the judge did not question the widow's right to take land with her if it had come from her dowry, but considered only the possibility that it had actually been her husband's family property.[32] He probably would have been even less likely to question her removal of other types of dowry property, such as clothes and jewelry—which may in fact account for the persistent inclusion of gold jewelry in dowries. Occasional judges, however, went to the opposite extreme, seeing dowry as property that would go to a man's heirs, even when they were not the wife's children. In a case of a second wife whose husband had adopted an heir before she entered the house, Weng Fu, the judge, warned her not to try to take her dowry into another marriage: "The land a woman brings as dowry is landed property her parents give to her husband's family. If her husband's family has someone with a right to a share of the property, how can she roll it up and take it with her?"[33]

So far we have been considering cases where a widow left her ex-husband's home to remarry, moving in with her new husband. However, "calling in a husband"—that is, bringing him to live in her ex-husband's house, work his fields, and help support his children—was also not uncommon. It is mentioned in reference books and in anecdotes, such as the one cited in the last chapter about the virtuous widow Miss Wu who refused to let her mother-in-law call in a husband for her. Hung Mai also told of the widow of a local exorcist who sold his ritual implements to another specialist and then "called in" another man to be her husband.[34]

Calling in husbands was undoubtedly most prevalent among relatively poor people, such as tenants. Should a tenant die, leaving a mother, a widow, and three children under ten, the landlord could evict them all, as they were unable to work the land and pay the rent. Or he could give them time to find a new husband for the wife, to take on the work and make all of the payments. Such marriages were uxorilocal in that the man joined the woman in her house, but they did not necessarily involve uxorilocal succession: the sons of the first man could still inherit his property, and the sons of the second man, if any were born, could take their father's name (and property, if any). It seems often to have been the widow's parents-in-law who wanted to bring in a husband. If their only son died leaving a young widow and very young grandchildren, their best chance for a comfortable old age was to keep the grandchildren and the daughter-in-law and bring in another man to help support them in the short term. After Miss Yeh's son died, for instance, leaving two daughters and a pregnant wife (who later bore a son), Miss Yeh "ordered" her daughter-in-law to call in a husband "to rear the orphans."[35]

Calling in husbands was recognized in Sung law. In one case Miss Kan and her husband, Ting Ch'ang, had adopted a small child of unknown origins. After Ting died, Miss Kan called in another husband. Someone tried to get them forced from their land (perhaps a tenancy) on the grounds that the Ting line was extinguished. The first judge concurred, but the second overruled him. These were ignorant people, he said, who could be excused for not knowing the rules for registering adoptions:

> When a woman has no one to depend on and is rearing a son to continue the descent line of her former husband, to give her body to a second husband is within the bounds of reason and there is nothing in the law that clearly prohibits it.... According to the statutes, when a widow has no sons or grandsons and there is no one living with her entitled to a share of the property, if she calls in a husband, he can be provisionally assigned her former husband's lands and houses as listed in the register, so long as the value does not exceed five thousand strings of cash. If the wife decides to move to the husband's house or dies, the case becomes one of a broken line.[36]

In this case, since the property was valued at only a little over two hundred strings, the widow and her new husband were able to keep it.

Marrying a widow with property as a called-in husband could be quite profitable. In one story, a poor scholar became the called-in husband of a rich widow and lived handsomely for the next ten years, never quarreling with his wife. When she died, he was grief-stricken. Similarly, when Miss Wang's husband died, her son was young, so she invited Hsü Wen-chin as a called-in husband. "Making use of Miss Wang's former husband's property, Hsü Wen-chin prospered." Even officials sometimes married widows uxorilocally to benefit from their property, though not without losing prestige.[37]

Sometimes when a man moved in with a widow, the union was not recognized as a legal marriage; instead it was viewed as something between long-standing adultery and a common-law marriage. Hung Mai told of the wife of a clerk left widowed at thirty. She had an affair with a butcher, and soon they were publicly living together. He made her son treat him like a father, which the boy deeply resented. When the boy was grown, he confided his grievance to a brave and spirited butcher, who later found an opportunity to kill the man and his two children, an action that brought him acclaim as a righter of wrongs.[38] The implication is clearly that the son felt personally humiliated by the man who entered into an irregular union with his mother.

WIDOWERS AND SUCCESSOR WIVES

Men also suffered if they lost their wives prematurely; indeed, there was a considerable body of poetry on the theme of mourning for a wife.[39] Some of the best poems written in the Sung in this tradition are by Mei Yao-ch'en (1002–1060) who lost his wife when he was forty-three. Soon after her death he wrote:

> It was seventeen years ago
> That we "tied our hair" to become man and wife,
> Yet I never tired of looking at her.
> How I will miss her now!
> My temples have already turned grey,
> My body will not remain sound much longer.
> In the end we will share the same grave.
> Till then my tears will keep flowing.[40]

A few months later, her death was still making him contemplate his own:

> From the time you joined my family
> You never complained about our meager living.
> You sewed until the middle of the night
> And ate breakfast after midday.
> Nine days out of ten we had salted vegetables;
> Only on one might we have meat.
> For eighteen years you accompanied me as I traveled to and fro,
> Sharing the bitter and the sweet.
> We expected to share a hundred years of love,
> Never guessing you would be gone in one night.
> I still remember how, at the point of death,
> You clutched me, unable to speak.
> Although my body survives for the present,
> In the end we will become earth together.[41]

Mei Yao-ch'en's strong feelings of grief, however, did not inhibit him from taking a "successor" wife less than two years after the first had died.[42] In this he was typical of men of his age and class. Yüan Ts'ai seems to have summed up common sentiments when he wrote: "One of life's great misfortunes is to reach middle age and then lose your wife. Your little boys and girls have no one to care for them; there is no one to manage the cooking, sewing, and other work of the women's quarters. Thus you have little choice but to remarry."[43] Chang Tsai (1020–1077) explained why widows and widowers were different in this regard:

> When a husband and wife first get married, they do not agree to [the other's] taking a second mate. Thus each ought to marry only once. Today, that women should not remarry after the death of their husbands is considered a fundamental moral principle. Surely men should not remarry either. Still, if one analyzes the situation according to degrees of importance, [a wife] is essential to care for parents, manage the family, perform sacrifices, and continue [the descent line]. Therefore there is the principle of taking a second wife.[44]

Not surprisingly, the younger a widower was, the more likely it was he would remarry. Among the couples I studied from funerary biographies, 89 percent of those who lost their wives in their twenties remarried; the figure declined to 75 percent for men in their thirties and 23 percent for those in their forties. I found no case of a man remarrying when he was over fifty at his wife's death. A man who did not take a new wife could take a concubine (and of course, he could keep any he already had when his wife was alive). Fifty-seven percent of those in their fifties when widowed are known to have had concubines.

Wives who did not want their husbands to remarry after their deaths did not necessarily feel the same way about their husbands taking concubines. When Cheng Chün's wife came back as a ghost to object to his impending remarriage, he justified his action by saying, "I entrusted family matters to a concubine, but it did not work out. I had no alternative."[45]

Men who remarried did not have to marry widows; it was considered perfectly normal for them to take never-married girls as successor wives. And since many widows did not remarry, there would not have been enough available widows anyway. Thus widowers' second wives were generally considerably younger than they. The average difference for such couples was twelve years among the couples I studied from funerary biographies. As a consequence, these second marriages lasted on average only seventeen years, as opposed to twenty-six years for first marriages. When they ended with the man's death, as they usually did, the widows were correspondingly younger than other widows.

Widowers' marriages did not produce as many children as first marriages, though among my set of couples the difference was surprisingly slight, 5.0

children rather than 5.4. In more than half the cases the husband already had several children by his first wife (average 3.6), so the families of men who remarried often became quite large.

Men seem to have had little difficulty adjusting comfortably to successor wives. There was no notion that they were somehow sullied by sexual relations with more than one woman, since concubinage had always been acceptable. Many men were clearly as fond of the successor wife as of the first. Men could even rationalize the second marriage as a kindness to the first wife, since the new wife would look after the sacrifices to her and take care of her children. There does seem to have been some sentiment, however, that a man who truly loved and respected his wife would not replace her when she died but make do with a concubine. For Ssu-ma Kuang, it could be an act of loyalty to the family for a man not to remarry, because stepmothers could cause trouble. He quoted the case of Chu Hui in the Later Han who lost his wife at fifty. His brothers wished to get a new wife for him, but he demurred: "In current custom it is rare for a second wife not to ruin the family." Ssu-ma Kuang commented, "Men today of advanced years with sons and grandsons should compare themselves against this example of past worthies."[46]

In the popular imagination, deceased wives could be jealous, not unlike deceased husbands. Hung Mai told the story of Chang Tzu-neng, who had married the beautiful Miss Cheng. Stricken with an illness and about to die, Miss Cheng pleaded with her husband not to remarry and not to forget her. In tears he asked, "How could I possibly do either?" She got him to swear an oath, and he said, "Should I go back on my promise, let me be turned into a eunuch and come to a bad end." Yet three years after she died Chang was more or less forced to marry the daughter of an official. After the wedding he grew despondent, and one day he saw his former wife come in through a window. "To have made such a promise and then broken it! I had the good fortune of bearing two girls. Even though we had no sons, you could have bought a concubine [to get a son]. Why did you have to marry? The disaster will take place." She then grabbed his testicles, causing him great pain and rendering him a eunuch.[47]

One might think the obvious moral of this story was that women are wildly possessive of men and driven to uncontrollable acts at the thought that their husbands are intimate with other women; even death gives them no peace. Li Ch'ang-ling (early thirteenth century), however, drew a different moral. After summarizing the tale, he commented: "'Wife' means 'identity.' One identifies once and does not change. This is the foundation of inter-personal ethics and the rule for couples. For harmony in the home, this comes first. . . . Nowadays people only know that the other has died; they do not know that although the body is destroyed, the spirit has not disappeared and definitely has perceptions, even greater than in life."[48] Thus Li Ch'ang-ling placed all the blame on the husband for remarrying.

As Ssu-ma Kuang noted, the most likely cause of trouble in men's second marriages was poor stepmother-stepchild relations. Men seem to have easily rerouted their affections to their new wives and children. The new wife, thus, was often seen as turning her husband against the children of his first wife. While the husband was alive he could arbitrate disputes between the two sides. Even so, resentment and unpleasantness were common enough that biographers nearly always praised second wives for treating their stepchildren just like their own—which strongly suggests that such impartiality was a rare virtue. When the family head died, conflicts based on step-relationships easily led to disputes over property. At this point, a son by the first wife, older than the second wife's own sons, was in a good position to make life difficult for his stepmother, for his claim to the family property was better than hers.

One widow, on the advice of her brother, divided her husband's property into three parts: 66 percent for the son adopted before she entered the house, 12 percent for the dowry of the daughter born after her marriage, and 22 percent to support herself in her old age. The son objected, and the judge ruled that the stepmother/widow could not dispose of her share and that the son would inherit it.[49] Another case concerned an educated family in which the first wife had died when her son was seven. This boy and his stepmother did not get along, and after she was widowed she took her property and married someone else. The stepson, who promptly squandered his inheritance, tried to get back part of what she had taken. He did not dispute her right to take the fields she had brought as dowry, but claimed that the other fields registered in her name and listed as purchased with her dowry money had really been purchased with family money. The judge in this case did not believe the stepson, pointing out that a man who did not live with parents or brothers had no reason to claim fraudulently that certain property was his wife's. Nonetheless, the judge made clear his disapproval of widows who remarry and urged the stepmother, out of feelings for her late husband, to give the wastrel enough property to survive.[50]

Most people in Sung times looked on second marriages for women as an expedient—a course of action that was routine and often necessary, but less admirable than remaining a widow. Widow loyalty was not a standard demanded of all wives (as physical modesty and deference to husbands and parents-in-law were). It could be expected of older widows with children, but when a young woman chose to remain loyal to her dead husband, she deserved to be lauded. Ch'eng I, of course, clearly stated the principle that hardship was no excuse for remarrying, but there is little evidence that the proportion of widows remarrying went down as a consequence, even in the educated class. The most significant consequence of the publicity given to his dictum was probably to make widows in the educated class feel even worse about themselves when they ended up remarrying.

Successor wives whose first marriage was to a widower followed a life course different from most other women. Unless the man's first marriage had been short and childless, they married men substantially older than themselves and entered a home in which there were already heirs. Thus neither did they have the chance to be their husband's first love, nor did their first pregnancy generate the excitement and gratitude typically associated with a first birth. Their husbands seem often to have doted on them, but this may not always have been a blessing, as the difference in age may have bothered them in ways it did not their husbands. Yüan Ts'ai said that the drawback for a widower marrying a virgin was that "a middle-aged man cannot cope with the feelings of a young woman."[51] The role of mother, which usually offered women so much, was in their case highly conflicted. A successor wife was expected to treat the children of the first wife with all due maternal concern, but the children were not easily won over. Once she had borne children of their own, antagonisms were even more likely, for the children of the first marriage had every reason to be suspicious of her partiality toward her own offspring and to resent her special access to their father.

Men in their second marriages did not suffer from the problems of either remarried widows or successor wives. Indeed, life was often good to them. They could take a young wife when their friends were taking young concubines and having to cope with rancor and jealousy in the women's quarters. They could be fairly confident that their second wife would live to nurse them in their old age. And, unless they married widows with children, the problems of step-relations were not their personal problems, since they were full fathers to all the children.

TWELVE

Concubines

In China, from early times, wealth and political power were associated with accumulating lovely young handmaidens. Prescriptive texts gave formulas that matched a man's political rank to the number of concubines he could have, guidelines no one ever seems to have taken seriously. A ruler of a small state might have dozens or hundreds of palace ladies, with possession of them serving as evidence of his wealth, much like possession of horses or precious stones. The first emperor of the Ch'in (Ch'in Shih-huang-ti, r. 246–209 B.C.) is reputed to have had over ten thousand female attendants, and many later emperors had well over a thousand. Throughout the imperial period, rich men acquired maids and concubines as a form of conspicuous consumption and proof of virility; even a man of quite modest financial means might take one or two concubines who would help his wife with the housework.[1]

In large cities, another institution developed to provide men opportunities to enjoy the company and sexual services of women: houses of entertainment, staffed by women trained to please. Singing was the most common skill such women mastered, but some also played musical instruments, danced, or wrote and recited poetry. In the T'ang capitals of Ch'ang-an and Lo-yang, the pleasure quarters where these women and their proprietors lived were very popular among educated men who came to the capital to pursue their careers. A good share of the anecdotal literature from the T'ang concerns men's entanglements with such women. Writers were attracted to their talents, admired their capacity for devoted love, and sympathized with the indignities they had to endure from the owners of their establishments.[2]

With the great growth in the money economy in the Sung and the development of commercialized cities throughout the country, the opportunities for men to exchange money for women seem to have steadily expanded. In the largest cities, the entertainment quarters flourished much as they had in the T'ang capitals. But by mid–Northern Sung times the sorts of men who previously might have been satisfied to visit such quarters and have affairs with some of the women there had the means and desire to purchase women to bring home as concubines. Thus, as the upper class expanded, so did the market for women to serve as maids and concubines in their homes.

Surviving sources reveal that educated men's feelings about concubinage were mixed. There was nothing wrong with a man taking a concubine—or even three or four—but if he became too preoccupied with her, he would be looked on as self-indulgent and undisciplined. Writers took delight in recording clever exchanges between poets and their courtesan-concubines, but also portrayed concubines as lower-class women with little sense of family duty or honor. Men liked to gossip about fights between wives and concubines, especially if the man involved was prominent. They lamented the unlucky fate of women of their own social class who had been reduced to becoming concubines. They also vilified those who kidnapped girls or women to sell them into concubinage. Yet they certainly knew that few women became concubines voluntarily. These mixed feelings about concubinage reflect, and also probably contributed to, the often confusing situation in which concubines found themselves. Their world was not one of well-defined expectations. What would happen to them depended much more on their luck with interpersonal relations than on custom or law.

In Sung times, as both earlier and later, the legal status of concubine was not as clearly defined as that of wife, probably because it carried few privileges.[3] The code portrayed a three-tier system: wives ranked higher than concubines (*ch'ieh*), who ranked higher than maids (*pi*). For instance, if a man in a fight with a stranger broke his arm or leg, the penalty would be penal servitude for one year. If the victim was his wife, the punishment was two degrees lower; if his concubine, four degrees lower. Injuring one's maid carried no penalty.[4] Under no circumstance could a man promote his concubine to be his wife, even if his wife had died, but he could promote a maid who bore him a son to be his concubine.[5] In actual social life, people seem to have had a clear sense that certain women were wives and others belonged to the broad category of concubines, but this broad category stretched from women who were treated almost like wives (especially when the wife was deceased), to women who were essentially private courtesans, to women who had come in as maids but who had become sexually intimate with their masters. Although wives often became furious at maids for what they took to be efforts to seduce their husbands, neither the wives nor anyone else seems to have thought maids had any right to fend off unwanted advances from their masters. The legal code specified no penalty for illicit sexual relations with one's own maid, and even the penalty for relations with someone else's maid was relatively light (eighty strokes, as compared to two years penal servitude if she was another man's wife).[6] The low social status of maids made them sexually vulnerable, and this sexual vulnerability contributed to keeping their status low. In this chapter, women labeled as maids who are known to have borne children by their master will be included in discussions of concubines. Legally and socially, in fact, they had absorbed some of that status: sexual relations with the maid one's father or grandfather had "favored" was treated as a type of incest, two degrees less serious than relations with his concubine, but much more serious than relations with anyone else's maid.[7]

ACQUIRING CONCUBINES

The processes through which girls entered homes as concubines look different from the man's side than from the woman's. Men could acquire concubines in a variety of ways. Occasionally they received them as gifts. Wang Tseng (978–1038), to repay Ou-yang Hsiu (1007–1072) for writing something for him, is said to have given him two gold cups and two maids to drink with him. Su Ch'e (1039–1112) reported that Emperor Chen-tsung (r. 997–1022) arranged to have a concubine bought for Wang Tan (957–1017) when he learned that Wang did not have a single one. Emperor Jen-tsung (r. 1023–1063) is said to have given Sung Ch'i (998–1061) a palace maid after hearing that Sung wrote a poem about a palace woman who had called out his name when she recognized him on the street.[8] When P'an Liang-kuei (1094–1150) learned that a friend of his had no sons, P'an gave him a maid who had already borne P'an children. Hsin Ch'i-chi (1140–1207) is said to have given one of his concubines to his doctor as payment for his treatment, and then to have written a jocular verse on his action. Ch'eng Sung, gossipmongers reported, paid eight hundred thousand cash for a concubine the chief councillor Han T'o-chou (d. 1207) had returned to a broker, anticipating that Han would eventually want her back when his temper had cooled. Ch'eng subsequently presented her to Han and, as hoped, was rewarded with a better official appointment.[9]

Men also not infrequently brought home courtesans to whom they had been attracted. One case in the *Judicial Decisions* concerned a local gangster whose concubine had originally been a government courtesan, that is, a woman in the involuntary employ of the government whose job it was to entertain visitors and dignitaries.[10] Liu Chen-sun (d. 1244) was so impressed with the dancing of a young courtesan that he took her as a concubine. Later he had her help him entertain guests. Chou Mi (1232–1308) reported that after a famous government courtesan was freed, an imperial clansman took her as a concubine.[11]

Probably most concubines, however, were purchased through brokers who made a business of supplying the well-to-do with attendants.[12] The most highly specialized market was in the capitals, especially in Hangchow during the Southern Sung. The *Dreams of Hangchow,* after discussing brokers who handled male laborers, managers, and shop assistants, discussed the female equivalent: "There are official and private female brokers to assist officials or rich families who wish to buy a concubine, a singer, a dancing girl, a female cook, a seamstress, or a coarse or fine maid. They bring in and line up the girls and women and one merely points to have one of them step down."[13] Writing in the late Sung, Liao Ying-chung painted a similar picture: "A variety of names are used: attendant, helper, waitress, seamstress, front room person, entertainer, laundress, Ch'in player, chess player, and cook, all of which are kept separate. The cook is the lowest rank and yet only the very rich or high-ranking are able to employ one."[14] Hung Sun described the same market, then went on to recount the case of a prefect who had acquired a woman a little over twenty who was good-looking, able to calculate and write, and trained in fine cooking. It turned out, however, that she was used to preparing lavish banquets with no regard to expense, and in less than two months he decided he could not afford her.[15] Those who did not live in the capital or other large city might have to go to an urban center to acquire the sort of concubine they wanted. A merchant named Feng without sons took advantage of a trip to Kaifeng to buy a concubine. Yüan Shao's (c.s. 1187) father went to Hangchow to get a concubine. Visits to cities like Ch'eng-tu and Soochow also provided similar opportunities.[16]

These urban markets catered to gentlemen who sought accomplished girls. Many concubines could read, compose poetry, sing, and play musical instruments. One official in late Sung Hangchow sought a concubine both beautiful and accomplished in all the arts. After days of searching he finally found a beautiful girl who, when questioned on her accomplishments, reported that her only talent was warming wine. His companions laughed, but he tested her and was so impressed with her skill that he took her on.[17] Hung Mai told of an official in the capital awaiting assignment who convinced a friend to accompany him while he went out to buy two concubines. At the broker's, he found that the youngest and most talented girl had a price of only eighty strings, while the other two were priced at four or five hundred strings. On asking the broker about the difference in price, the men were told that these girls were available only on term contracts; the term for the youngest was almost up, only half a year remaining, whereas the other two could be taken on for full three-year contracts.[18] In other words, one did not need to buy a concubine; one could rent one instead.

It was not necessarily men who went to the brokers to pick out concubines. Occasionally a wife made the selection for her husband, considering it her duty to get a concubine for him, perhaps because she had not borne any sons or even because she thought his social standing required it. Because Ssu-ma Kuang had no sons, we are told, his wife and her sister once acquired a concubine for him and tried unsuccessfully to get him interested in her. For similar reasons, after Miss Chao Pi-shan (1188–1260) passed fifty without bearing a son she bought her husband a concubine who in time bore his only son.[19]

Concubines could even be given to wives; in one case, because a wife was burdened by household chores and her husband was poor, her brother gave her a girl of twelve to do the housework for her; this girl eventually became the husband's concubine and, at twenty-eight, bore a son. Fathers also sometimes bought maids or concubines for their daughters to accompany them when they married. This was an ancient practice, and may well have appealed to Sung men as a way to reduce jealousy. Miss Sheng (1007–1077), for instance, was raised in the home of her future mistress and accompanied her on her marriage. After her mistress died and the master remarried, she stayed on as the master's concubine.[20] To the wife there were many advantages in offering her maid to her husband. The girl was probably of very humble background and likely had never been trained in any of the arts that might make her more alluring. There could thus be no ambiguity about her social standing compared to that of the wife. Moreover, widely shared notions of the loyalty a servant owed his or her master would lead everyone to expect the promoted maid to continue to treat her mistress with all her usual deference.[21] Still, problems could develop. One young wife tried to beat to death the concubine who had accompanied her on her marriage when this woman became pregnant by the master.[22]

Brokers played a role like that of marriage go-betweens in arranging the acquisition of concubines, preparing the contract that specified the terms of the agreement between buyer and seller and then witnessing the transaction. The importance of this intermediating function is evident in the cases where an agreement was initially made between the principals speaking to each other in person, but a broker was still called in to make it fully standard.[23] Yüan Ts'ai said brokers were necessary in any purchase of a maid or concubine, but argued that the girl acquired should still be closely questioned about her background. If it turned out she had been kidnapped, the buyer should be ready to return her to her family. But most important, he should have the sense not to give her back to the broker.[24]

The contracts that brokers prepared would specify the "body price" of a concubine. This amount depended on market factors, with attractive and accomplished girls bringing in much more than others. Hung Mai mentioned figures ranging from 140 strings to 300, 400, 900, and 1,000.[25] Even the lowest-ranking official might well be able to scrape together the money for such a young woman; in his day, Hung Mai observed, even the bottommost officials (county recorders and sheriffs) earned monthly salaries of about fifty strings of cash in addition to their allotments of rice.[26]

Some masters did not pay a lump sum to the concubine's parents or broker, but rather made regular payments, somewhat like wages. The parents of

Miss Cheng, a concubine who had borne two children for Liang Chü-cheng, received thirty-five hundred cash each month.[27] Kao Wen-hu, at the age of sixty-seven, acquired a literate and musically accomplished concubine, Miss Ho, on a three-year contract with a stipulated wage of one bushel of rice a month, which her mother regularly came to collect. After the three years were over, her mother negotiated a new contract. She did not ask for an increase in the old wages, but instead of coming to collect payment every month as before, she wished to let the value accumulate, presumably toward a dowry. When the next three years were up, she again renegotiated the contract. This time Miss Ho's wages were set at one hundred strings of cash a year, an increase of about 50 percent, which Kao considered was due her because of her increased age and experience. This also was allowed to accumulate.[28]

BECOMING A CONCUBINE

From the perspective of the girl or woman, the processes that led to her entry into a home as a concubine began when she was removed from the "wife track." This could happen for any of a multitude of reasons. Parents might be tricked, desperate, or greedy; women might be misled, kidnapped, or make the choice themselves for lack of better alternatives. Some families in need of cash sold daughters to brokers or directly to masters. Even if a girl was sold as a maid or to be trained as a courtesan, she might end up as a concubine, either bought out by a patron or "promoted" after she bore a child for the master. Some parents planned all along to sell their daughters and started early to train them in the skills that would fetch the highest prices. Many girls were tricked away from their families by unscrupulous traffickers. And women often offered themselves as concubines when they had no other means of support.

The educated class professed to be shocked to learn that families sometimes trained their daughters to be concubines in order to profit from raising them. Ch'en Yu (d. 1275) wrote that poor families in Soochow would train their daughters in the arts so that they could become private courtesans and, when full-grown, be profitably sold as concubines.[29] Liao Ying-chung similarly wrote, "Lower-ranking households in the capital do not put a premium on having sons, but treasure each daughter born as though she were a jewel. As she grows up, they teach her an art in accordance with her natural talents, so that she will be ready to be chosen by some gentleman as a companion."[30]

Writers generally had sympathy for those who felt they had no recourse but to sell their daughters. Hung Mai told of an educated man moved to an act of charity when he found his neighbor weeping sorrowfully:

> The man looked around, hesitated for a long time, then sobbed and sighed:
> "I wanted to avoid mentioning it to you, but for a certain reason, I owe the

government some money; the clerks are pressing me to pay and threatening punishment. I am too poor to pay them, so after discussion, my wife and I decided to sell our daughter of marriageable age to a merchant for four hundred thousand cash. She must leave us soon, and we are dejected at losing her."[31]

The four hundred strings of copper coins that this father was getting more or less equaled the lifetime wages of a servant or worker[32] or the rent owed by a tenant family over two decades.[33] Thus a good-looking teenage daughter was a salable asset that a family in debt could hardly overlook. It was perfectly legal for a father to sell his daughter as a concubine, just as he could indenture her as a maid or marry her out. Widowed mothers could also sell daughters; indeed, it is not uncommon to find accounts of widows from once-prosperous families reduced to selling their daughters to raise cash.[34] Stepparents are, however, generally portrayed as more callous about these sorts of transactions than natural parents. Hung Mai, for example, told of a woman who took her two daughters with her when she remarried, only to have her new husband sell them both as concubines.[35]

Husbands also sometimes sold their wives as concubines, but this was not legal.[36] A story about Chia Ssu-tao's father claimed that while traveling he saw a pretty woman out washing clothes and asked her to be his concubine. She said she was already married and therefore he would have to ask her husband. This man readily agreed, getting a handsome price for his wife.[37]

Women who sold themselves appear not infrequently in Hung Mai's anecdotes. For instance, a woman famine victim who passed by an official's gate was asked if she would like to stay as a concubine. When she agreed, saying she was too hungry to walk farther, the official called in a broker to write up a contract.[38] In another story, the widow of a traveling merchant, left without means of support when he died, knocked on a door and begged to be taken in as a maid or concubine.[39] Service, however menial, was preferable to starving to death or ending up a prostitute.

Because the demand for girls as maids, concubines, prostitutes, and entertainers was so high, unscrupulous people responded by acquiring girls through all manner of deceit. A twelfth-century gazetteer of Fu-chou, Fukien, records the attempt of the prefect in 1099 to prohibit deceptive practices. This prefect reported that people from neighboring prefectures often came along and with only a small amount of capital set themselves up as "brokers in people." They would tell families that a girl was needed as a wife or an adopted child, enticing them to turn over a daughter or maid. The girl would be hidden for a few days, then packed off to some distant place to be resold. Even if the family went immediately to the magistrate when they discovered they had been tricked, a search would prove unsuccessful, and they would never learn the whereabouts of the girl, or even whether or not she was alive.[40]

Outright kidnapping is also often mentioned in Sung sources. Hung Mai recounted how the seventeen- or eighteen-sui daughter of an imperial prince was kidnapped while riding in a sedan chair on her way to visit a nearby relative, then beaten, turned over to a broker, and sold to be the concubine of a man who knew her origins and considered them part of her attraction. Hung Mai also told of a wife and concubine of an official who were both kidnapped while traveling across the city of Hangchow in sedan chairs. Kidnappers naturally were despised. In one collection of didactic tales a man who had made a living by kidnapping and "enticing" in the end suffered the retribution of an itchy wasting disease.[41]

Most of those who wrote about the market in concubines seem to have done so from a slightly voyeuristic perspective, sensing that their readers would enjoy imagining lovely young women, the attraction of the scene in no way diminished by the knowledge that these women were not there voluntarily and that many had experienced bitter sorrow. At least a few writers, however, explicitly condemned the market in concubines. The Northern Sung scholar Hsü Chi (1028–1103), for instance, tried to discourage people from willingly letting their daughters become concubines by means of a poem in which he imagined the thoughts of a girl who, through misfortune, had become a concubine in a large household.

> I originally lived by the side of Wu mountain.
> I competed with the other Wu girls in trying to look good.
> With pretty makeup on my face and two glossy topknots,
> I was the best in appearance and talent.
> At age ten I could recite the poems of Miss Hsieh.
> At fifteen, I knew the writings of Lady Pan.[42]
> After I was sixteen or seventeen things gradually got hard.
> Faced with hardships, I wandered from place to place.
> Later, alone and poor, I had even more trouble.
> I learned that there is not much one can do for oneself.
> At this time I was stupid and was deceived by someone.
> So I entered the Chu household and wore patterned gauze.
> Most of the ladies in the Chu household were jealous,
> So I learned to be careful in my behavior.
> I did not dare paint my eyebrows or raise my eyes.
> From morning to night I would drink air and swallow sounds.
> The sufferings I endured, no one knows.
> I just waited for a chance to go home, but never got one.
> Gauze clothes cover my body; emptiness grabs my tears.
> When will I get to wear my old clothes?[43]

Despite Hsü Chi's reformist intentions, his poem probably appealed to people primarily as a depiction of a sensitive, lovely young woman who had suffered at the hands of others.

MEN AND THEIR CONCUBINES

Typically, a man took a concubine after reaching middle age, perhaps by then head of the household and a bit bored with his wife of fifteen or more years. Su Shih (1036–1101), for example, was thirty-eight when he took Miss Wang Chao-yün (1063–1096), then eleven sui, as his concubine.[44] But there were many deviations from this model. Not uncommonly, young men took concubines before they were married.[45] One man, we are told, had several dozen before he reached twenty.[46] There were also men who took concubines in their seventies and eighties.[47] And men with ample wealth seem often to have kept several concubines. Chou Kao, a wealthy eleventh-century official, had several dozen courtesan-concubines, and Han T'o-chou (d. 1207) was reputed to have kept fourteen. In a story recorded by Hung Mai, a wealthy official had seven or eight concubines, who, however, were all hoping to leave when he got old and sick.[48]

How did men treat their concubines? Naturally, there was great variation, with some doting on the young women to the neglect of their wives, some treating them as little more than objects of their desires, and some eagerly showing them off to their guests. Still, certain patterns are worth noting. Men did not rename their wives, but they quite regularly renamed their maids and concubines, an act that symbolizes the social inferiority of these women. And whereas wives were normally referred to by their surnames, concubines were usually called by personal names, often ones given them by their masters.[49] The names of concubines, we find, frequently contained the character nu, "slave," such as "Soft Slave," "Lotus Slave," "Fragrant Slave," or "Slave Who Comes Forward."[50] Kao Wen-hu (1134–1212) gave his concubine Miss Ho the name Silver Flower, a literary term for snowflake. Other educated men also chose literary names for their concubines, and some made up decidedly capricious names, such as Hsin Ch'i-chi (1140–1207), who gave each of his two concubines their surnames as their personal names, so that they were called T'ien T'ien and Ch'ien Ch'ien.[51]

The training that lower-class girls received in preparation for a life as the concubine of an upper-class man was much like that given courtesans, and many men used concubines as private courtesans to entertain or amuse their guests. K'ou Chun (961–1023) was known for extravagant all-night parties, for dancing and making music with female entertainers, and for a concubine who composed and recited poetry extemporaneously. Yüan Ts'ai warned that teaching maids and concubines to entertain guests could prove dangerous: if the women were of striking beauty or superior intelligence, "there is the danger that such a woman will arouse feelings of lust in some evil guest," with disastrous consequences. Wei T'ai (ca. 1050–1110) described just such a case. One day Yang Hui had his private singing girls entertaining guests, and a certain guest, drunk, went entirely too far with one of them, greatly embarrassing the wife, who was watching from behind a screen. She summoned the concubine and beat her. When the guest demanded that the girl come back, Yang tried to break up the party, which only made the guest angrier. He started punching Yang, who had to be saved by the joint efforts of the other guests.[52]

Concubines who were treated like courtesans could be expected to act like courtesans as well. Su Shih, we are told, came to this conclusion when he discovered the favorite concubine of a recently deceased friend entertaining at another man's house. "Unconsciously he covered his face and wailed. The concubine then turned to her peers and gave a big laugh."[53] Clearly Su Shih did not wish to confront the fact that concubines were often transferred from master to master and acted like it did not matter.

Only rarely did educated men write about their concubines and their relationships with them. Liu K'o-chuang (1187–1269) claimed that he took a concubine because of his faithfulness to his wife; after she died he decided not to marry again out of respect for her. "When I was forty-two I was in deep grief—Miss Lin, who was so worthy, had died so young. I decided not to marry again. However, after her funeral there was no one to wait on me with towel and comb. Someone reported that there was an orphaned Miss Ch'en, originally of a major family, whose mother had taken her along when she remarried. The girl now had no place to go. My late mother Miss Lin acquired the girl for me."[54] Liu K'o-chuang praised the way Miss Ch'en (1211–1262), twenty-four years his junior, looked after family matters for the next thirty-five years, remembering everything and managing the family finances. He referred to her not as his concubine but as his youngest son's "birth mother." Himself he referred to not as her husband but as her "master."

The fullest account of a man's relationship with his concubine is provided by Kao Wen-hu (1134–1212).[55] In a letter, Kao reported that his wife had died in 1163 when he was thirty and that for twenty-seven years he had neither remarried nor kept a concubine, out of consideration for his children. It was only in the first month of 1200, when he was sixty-six, that he took Miss Ho on a three-year contract.

Miss Ho's duties, Kao reported, were to prepare his medicines, tidy up, and check up on him. He said she often made his morning and evening meals and took care of his clothes: washing, patching, and getting them ready for each change of season. If at night he had a coughing spell or could not sleep, she would get up, stir the fire, and decoct some medicine for him. She also could read and would help him look things up and answer letters. After she had been with him a year, Kao retired from office and went to Hui-chou, where his son was an official. He took Miss Ho with him and they spent two very agreeable years there, visiting all the local scenic spots. After that they moved to his permanent home in Ming-chou (Ningpo).

In his letter, Kao Wen-hu implies, somewhat ambiguously, that he did not make use of his rights to sexual intimacy with Miss Ho, saying that he was old and no longer interested in sensual pleasures. That Miss Ho bore no children in eleven years seems to support his claim. Other members of the family, however, clearly saw him as besotted with her and feared he would squander the family fortune on her.

Kao Wen-hu was fond enough of Miss Ho to want to see that she received money he had promised her. The problem, he reported, was that he "kept not a coin by [his] side, and for expenses made withdrawals from the family treasury. Yet [every time he asked for money] there were always excuses, complications, and refusals." To circumvent this impasse he ordered the sale of six hundred bushels of grain from one of the family's estates, but when only fifty or sixty had been sold the monk in charge of this estate informed him that Kao's son and daughter-in-law wanted to sell the grain to obtain capital for a granary. Later his son came to placate him, saying that he could get whatever he wanted from the family treasury, even the thousand strings that Kao needed. Still, every time Kao went to the treasury he was told that it was short of money. Finally, after another two years, Kao again ordered the sale of estate grain, this time bringing in a total of 1,080 strings, 800 of which were to be for Miss Ho.

According to Kao, Miss Ho wanted to stay in the Kao home as a widowed concubine after he died. Kao knew that this would not work, so in 1210 he decided it was time for her to return home. To conclude his letter, he summed up the justification for her receiving a thousand strings of cash. First, the money was his: he had earned it himself, and his son had not contributed to it. Second, she deserved it: in her eleven years of serving him she had never been sick, or received any money from the family treasury, or interfered in any way with the family finances. Even her clothes he had supplied from his own funds. Thus a thousand strings for a dowry was not excessive. Should some jealous person make a wild accusation, he wrote, Miss Ho should present his letter as evidence and hope for a wise judge.[56]

CONCUBINES AS MARGINAL FAMILY MEMBERS

Concubines were family members, but their standing in the family was insecure and their ties to their master, his children, and even to their own children were fragile.

The only place Chinese writers tried to specify how concubines were related to other members of the families in which they lived was in analyses of mourning obligations. A woman who became a wife had reduced obligations to her natal kin but mourned nearly all the relatives her husband did (such as his brothers, uncles, and cousins). These relatives all reciprocated, mourning her if she died first. Concubines, by contrast, like unmarried women, retained their obligations to their natal kin, though in practice they seldom could have fulfilled them all. Their obligations to their master's family were minimal. A concubine mourned only her master, mistress, and the master's children. Only if the concubine bore children would the master's children by other women reciprocate and also mourn her (though not to the same degree she mourned them). The master and mistress did not mourn her even if she bore children.[57]

A more complicated issue was at what level her children should mourn her. A concubine's children mourned their father's wife as the legal mother, along with her own children. There was a long tradition, however, that children honored their legal mothers at a level higher than that of any other woman attached to their father, including concubine-mothers, mothers who had been divorced, wet nurses, and foster-mothers/governesses. This is not because a child could mourn only one woman as a mother. If his mother died and his father took another wife, who also died, the son mourned each of them as legal mothers. At what level sons would mourn the concubine who bore them was a matter of disagreement in the Sung. Chang Tsai (1020–1077) said a son would observe a lower grade of mourning for his birth mother only if his legal mother was still alive. Chu Hsi told a correspondent that he was mistaken in thinking he should mourn his birth mother at the low level specified for "concubine mothers"; she was his mother, and he should mourn her for three years.[58]

A concubine's place in the family undoubtedly was very much dependent on the presence of a mistress. Even when the wife was alive, if she was incapacitated the concubine might act as the mistress of the house. In late Sung, the government ruled that men whose wives were seriously ill but who did not wish to divorce them could take another woman as a "little wife," following ordinary wedding rituals.[59] But no matter what term was used, legally if a woman was not a wife she was a concubine. Liu K'o-chuang (1187–1269), in a legal decision concerning two women who were not considered of equivalent status by family members—one managed household affairs even during her master's lifetime and looked down on the other, belonging to her master's son, as a concubine—ruled that since neither had been formally married (*fei li hun*), neither could be considered a wife.[60]

Not only did a concubine with a mistress have to be personally subservient to her, but she could also lose most of the control over her children to her. Biographies of wives often state that the wives reared the children of concubines. There is never any implication that they had to ask the concubine for permission to take over care of her children. Shu Yüeh-hsiang (1217–1301) described how his wife, Miss Wang (1212–1284), "was often generous and seldom jealous. She raised the children born to concubines like they were her own, checking if they were hot or cold, wet or dry."[61] It is easy to imagine that concubines deeply resented wives taking over their children, failing to see it as an act of maternal love and kindness.

A concubine's marginality could continue after death. Long after his father, legal mother, and birth mother had died, Han Ch'i (1008–1075) reburied them in a new family graveyard. He then took the bold step of burying his concubine-mother near the tomb of his father and legal mother as an "attending" burial. He claimed his action was not insulting to his parents because in all matters such as the quality of the coffin, the burial of his birth mother was on a level lower than those of his parents. Realizing that others would see his act as a violation of ritual, he offered as justification the principle that rituals are intended to express feelings and are not "descended from heaven."[62]

The marginality of concubines as family members comes out clearly in the following story recorded by Hung Mai:

> In 1176, Chu Ching-hsien (Ch'üan) was in charge of the tea and horse trade in Szechwan. His son Hsün bought a girl from Ch'eng-tu, Miss Chang, as a concubine, and called her Fu-niang. The next year [the son] married Miss Fan, and because of his new marriage he did not want to keep the concubine. [Miss Chang] was already pregnant and did not want to leave, but he forced her out. The next year, Chu was summoned [back to the capital] and in the sixth month left Ch'eng-tu. Fu-niang wanted to go east with him but could not. Forty days later she bore a son and gave him the baby name of "Left Behind Boy."
>
> The Chus lived in Soochow, and since that was so far from Szechwan, neither party heard anything of the other. Hsün died in 1180, his wife Miss Fan never having borne a child. Since [the father] Chu [Ching-hsien] had no other sons, he was extremely depressed. In 1185, Chu retired to mourn his mother, and Wang Wo, the man who had succeeded to his post in charge of the tea and horse trade, sent an officer to present his condolences. This officer had previously worked for Chu, and his wife had been the broker when [Chu's son] Hsün had bought Fu-niang. Casually he mentioned, "Since Fu-niang had her son, she has put up with poverty, swearing she will not marry anyone. Her son is now seven or eight and is learning to read. His appearance is impressive, and people call him 'official,' since he looks so unlike other village children."
>
> Chu Ching-hsien, while delighted to hear this, was not sure he should believe it. He questioned Tsou Kuei, who had been his clerk and had also come along on the trip, and learned that it was completely true. He then had Kuei deliver a letter to Wang and the supervising official, asking them to send the mother and child.[63]

A concubine, this story makes clear, could be used when convenient, discarded when inconvenient, and even retrieved if the children she bore later were needed by the family.

CONCUBINES AS MOTHERS

Bearing sons raised a woman's status in a family, whether the woman was a wife, a concubine, or a maid. For a wife, it eliminated one possible ground for divorce. For a concubine, it established kinship obligations to the members of her master's family. For a maid, it opened possibilities of promotion to concubine. Still, when the wife already had children, bearing children might bring the concubine into even greater conflict with the wife and her sons. Ssu-ma Kuang wrote that "when brothers do not get along, it is often because they have different mothers. When the mothers are the wife and a concubine, the emotions of hatred and jealousy [among the sons] are even worse than when [the mothers] are the first and a successor wife. Since the mothers have strong feelings, the sons become separate factions."[64]

Sons of concubines must often have found their situation confusing or stressful. A concubine's son, after all, had to show filial duty to two women who probably did not get along. Moreover, his father may have looked on his birth mother as a courtesan, and his legal mother may have looked on her as a maid. Analyzing the psychological consequences of all this is, unfortunately, not possible given the available sources. Certainly the child of a concubine could grow up suffering no obvious disabilities, social or psychological. Han Ch'i, one of the most prominent officials of the Northern Sung, was the son of a concubine. His father, Han Kuo-hua (957–1011), had four sons by his wife, the third of whom was born in 989. By that time he had probably already taken his concubine, Miss Hu (968–1030), who bore Han Kuo-hua two sons and a daughter. Ch'i's father was fifty-two when he was born and died when he was three. His concubine-mother stayed on almost twenty years longer. Han Ch'i was reared by both women, much like someone cared for by both a mother and a grandmother. Whenever his birth mother beat him, he reported, his legal mother would run to protect him, so angry at his birth mother that she would not speak to her the rest of the day.[65]

Many children, however, were not so lucky. Children of concubines seem to have been treated as more expendable than children of wives, and thus more likely to be given away in adoption or killed at birth. When Ch'en Liang's (1143–1194) father's concubine gave birth to a boy in 1160, it was given away when three months old. Similarly, one of Liu Tsai's (1166–1239) brothers, born to a concubine, was adopted out as a baby.[66] Several of the cases of infanticide mentioned in Chapter 9 concerned children born to concubines. Children whose fathers sent their concubine-mothers away also often had a bad time. It was not uncommon for officials or merchants to take a concubine to keep them company while they resided away from home, then abandon her upon their departure. They also might get rid of a concubine because of their wives' jealousy, even if the concubine had borne children. The children of such concubines frequently lost all contact with their biological mothers.

Sons' ties to concubine-mothers their fathers had rejected came to be much discussed in the late eleventh century. Officials rushed to protest when Wang An-shih's (1021–1086) protégé Li Ting (1028–1087) failed to mourn his father's concubine, Miss Ch'iu, the woman widely reputed to be his mother. She had been sent away many years earlier and had married into another family.[67] These same critics had nothing but praise for Chu Shou-ch'ang, a man who had responded to a similar situation in a different fashion. Chu's father had taken a concubine while serving as prefect of Ching-chao. She bore Shou-ch'ang, and when he was two sui she was sent away to be married into a commoner's family.[68] Chu Shou-ch'ang then saw nothing of his bio-logical mother for fifty years. As he served in office around the country, he sought her out. Finally, in about 1068 or 1069, he gave up his office and left his family, declaring, "I will not return until I find my mother." He found her in T'ung-chou, now over seventy years of age, married into the Tang family and the mother of several sons. Chu Shou-ch'ang took this whole family home with him. His story was first publicized by Ch'ien Ming-i (1015–1071), after which leading scholars, "from Wang An-shih, Su Sung, and Su Shih on down, competed to praise his actions in poems."[69] Chu Shou-ch'ang's fame was so great that Emperor Shen-tsung (r. 1068–1085) personally received him after his return with his mother.[70]

WIDOWED CONCUBINES

Because of concubines' marginal status as family members, they were par-ticularly vulnerable when their masters died. Moreover, since concubines were often over twenty years younger than their masters, they were much more likely to be widowed young than wives were. According to the law, a concubine was not to be taken over by a close relative of her former master (a somewhat narrower circle than for a wife), but when this did happen it seems to have shocked people less than when a wife met a similar fate.[71] Concubines who had never borne children had no clearly defined position in the homes of their master's widow or sons. If they had served him for many years, they might be kept on as a charitable act, much the way old wet nurses and cooks were kept on. Respectable, prosperous families would hesitate to turn people out who had nowhere to go. But even so, their life might not be very attractive. Hung Mai told of a concubine who stayed with her master's widow and his married sons only to be beaten to death by the widow.[72]

Childless concubines had no claims to property, but masters might try to make provisions for a beloved concubine. In a legal case recorded in the *Sung History*, a man wrote a will dividing his property in three, one part each for his two sons and one for his concubine. When the sons took the matter to court, saying concubines had no property rights, the judge pointed out that sons had an obligation to follow their father's wishes, so as a compromise they should allow her the use of the property if she stayed on without remarrying; on her death, however, the property would become theirs.[73]

Concubines who had borne children might be kept or might not. We have already seen several instances in which concubines who had borne children were sent away by their masters. Widows and sons were undoubtedly at least as likely to wish to see them leave as masters who had lost interest in them. One woman who had entered the Wang household as a kitchen maid at age twelve bore a son when she was twenty-eight. Three years later the master and mistress died, and their sons divided the property, leaving her to raise the boy on his share.[74] Naturally, maids and concubines whose masters had died often wanted to leave in order to marry. One maid stole her young daughter's inheritance to use as a dowry so she could get married herself.[75] Some concubines who left to marry took their children with them, a practice that may have seemed the kindest to the child at the time, but that could weaken later claims to his or her father's property.[76] After Kao Wu-i died, leaving only a baby daughter born to a maid, a nephew was established as heir. He was assigned three-quarters of the property, and the girl one-quarter. The income from her quarter was to be given to her mother, who had left the household, but in fact very little was ever delivered.[77]

Concubines who stayed behind to raise their children faced all the problems of widows, and then some. One concubine who had borne the master's only two surviving children had to go to court to defend their property from a greedy relative who had simply tried to appropriate it. She was afraid to admit she was a concubine and so in requesting a court settlement falsely claimed to be a wife. In another case, one of the parties in a dispute questioned a concubine's claim of having some standing as a "birth mother" on the grounds that she had borne only daughters.[78] If a concubine's sons were grown, of course, the situation would be different, and would depend very much on whether they were willing and able to take care of their mother.

Some of the troubles that could beset a son's relationship with his widowed concubine-mother are made evident in an account written by Fang Hui (1227–1306). Fang Hui's father, Cho (1174–1229), had a daughter by his wife, but even after she was grown and married he had no sons. In 1221, therefore, he adopted a neighbor's child to be his heir. Three years later Fang Cho was banished to Kwangtung. He left his wife behind and on arriving in Kwangtung took a concubine, who later bore Hui. Hui never met his legal mother, for she died when he was two sui. His father died later that year. The next year a friend of the father sent the concubine and her son back to the Fang home, where an uncle took them in. This uncle also died within the year. Another uncle, who had taken in the adopted son, then set up the concubine, the two boys, and a single male servant on a thirty-mu plot, where they just managed to get by.

When Fang Hui was fifteen, his concubine-mother was forced to leave and go elsewhere as either a wife or concubine (the phrase used literally means she was forced to give up her desire to remain a chaste widow). Hui, writing decades later, recalled the bitterness he felt when he was unable to stand up to his uncle in this matter. Although Fang Hui does not say so explicitly, it is probable his uncle received money in exchange for the woman. Whether in part because of these experiences or not, Fang Hui was unusual among Chinese men of his social class in never taking a wife, though according to his own report he begot seven sons and four daughters by a succession of concubines. His predilection for concubines and maids in fact led contemporaries to criticize him as dissolute.[79]

This chapter is just one of several that shows how women's fates were tied up with issues of property. A family that could provide a daughter with a dowry assured her a suitable marriage as a wife, gave her some freedom to make gifts to others, and provided her with some resources to use for her own needs. Girls most often became concubines because their families not only could not provide dowries for them, but felt compelled to raise money by selling them. Although a concubine might acquire personal property through gifts, her claims to family property were exceptionally weak. A much more marginal family member than a wife, she did not even have to be supported her whole life. All she could depend on was affection: she had to hope that her master and her sons would continue to take care of her because they loved her. And it would be best to alienate as few other members of the family as possible, because they might be able to thwart even the best-intentioned sons or masters.

The system of concubinage can be seen as a dimension of class domination. The ruling elite would not have been able to extract as much surplus from the peasants if the peasants in turn had not been able to raise cash by selling their daughters to the rich as maids or concubines. At the same time, appropriation of the "surplus" daughters of the poorer strata in these ways kept the upper and lower classes in intimate contact, thus assuring that the elite stratum was never cut off entirely from the mores, values, and experiences of ordinary people. If they bore and reared sons, poor girls who had entered wealthy families as maids or concubines could come to have considerable influence on the next generation.

What were the psychological consequences to the girl of being treated like chattel—of being sold by her parents, kidnapped and forced into submission by a broker, or given away like a trinket? What was it like to live among people who were openly hostile to her? If she had been raised to think women were sullied by sexual relations with more than one man, how did she respond if resold to a second master? It is easy to imagine that such experiences would distort concubines' personalities. Wives saw concubines as schemers. Perhaps they often were, having no faith in other human beings. What was left for them but to try to secure personal advantage?

The psychological consequences of concubinage, further, were not necessarily confined to the women who became concubines. A girl in a peasant family who saw her friend next door or her elder sister sold to a broker to repay a family debt is unlikely ever to have felt as secure again. Everyone knew that women were dependent on men and that their happiness was a matter of chance. Concubinage brought home the truth of this fact in extreme form.

Although in this chapter I have tended to paint concubines as victims, it should not be forgotten that some women saw concubinage as preferable to their other alternatives. Women in unfortunate circumstances might well have preferred to become the concubine of a rich man than to work as a courtesan, prostitute, or servant, or even to become the wife of a poor man. Some had surely seen their mothers worn down by drudgery. A chance at a pampered life no doubt appeared to them much better than the certainty of a dreary one.

THIRTEEN

Continuing the Family Through Women

In the Confucian model of the Chinese family, the meanings of family, family duty, and family honor were all tied up with the concept of the patrilineal line from father to son to grandson. Families persisted through time because sons succeeded their fathers. Parents brought in wives for their sons not because the women themselves were important but because they could bear patrilineal grandsons. Should family succession through these means prove impossible—because the parents had no sons or their sons died before having sons of their own—parents were expected to adopt a nephew or other close patrilineal relative as the best possible substitute for a natural son.

This model of patrilineal succession underlay the government's laws on succession to property, giving families every incentive to adopt. Still, it is quite evident that not everyone in Sung society accepted all the implications of the patrilineal model. When families did not have a son, many men, and perhaps even more women, preferred to continue their family through a man related to them through a woman (through a daughter, sister, mother, wife, and so on). They did this either by keeping a daughter at home and bringing in a husband for her to join their family (a uxorilocal marriage) or by adopting a boy related to them through a woman who had either married out from their family or married into it. Sometimes families kept daughters at home and took in sons-in-law even when there already were sons, usually either because these sons were too young to work or because they had ample resources and wished to expand their families.

These alternative ways of continuing families brings us back to the issue of women as property holders. Men were willing to become uxorilocal sons-in-law because women could hold property. They could be given dowries, and, if they had no brothers, they could inherit property upon their parents' death.

Looked at in terms of the transmission of property from one generation to the next, the property that a daughter without brothers received as inheritance had much in common with the dowry assigned a daughter marrying out.

KEEPING A DAUGHTER AT HOME

Uxorilocal marriages had been known since ancient times but seem always to have been looked on as an expedient, an inferior alternative that might be the best a family could do in certain circumstances. In Sung times, references to uxorilocal marriage in the classics were read as condemnations. To point to the dangers of such marriage one could cite the phrase "The men of Chü destroyed Tseng," from the Kung-yang commentary to a passage in the *Spring and Autumn Annals* on the succession in the state of Tseng going to the offspring of a uxorilocal marriage between the daughter of the duke of Tseng and the son of the duke of Chü.[1]

Keeping a daughter at home was prevalent enough in Sung times for there to be common understandings of how her marriage should be handled. The *Dreams of Hangchow* reported that "the detailed cards" for uxorilocal marriages would specify that the marriage was uxorilocal and list what the man was bringing with him, much as a woman's card in a patrilocal marriage listed the property she would bring. Reference works regularly included sample betrothal letters (thirteen in one such book) suitable for uxorilocal marriages. Occasionally even the sorts of well-educated men whose writings have been preserved kept copies of marriage correspondence they composed for uxorilocal marriages.[2]

Hung Mai often remarked in passing that a man was a uxorilocal son-in-law.[3] Anywhere in the country families without sons might take in a husband for their daughter. Seen from the perspective of the young man, becoming a uxorilocal son-in-law to an heiress could be a way to get ahead. Hung Mai told of Chan Ch'ing, a poor villager trained as a musician. Tired of being the extra mouth in the home of his elder brother, he went off in search of better prospects, begging along the way. In the city, he found work as a musician and was able to marry uxorilocally. In time he grew rich and had his sons taught to read and to cultivate the demeanor of scholars.[4] The problem with this strategy was that the man often felt humiliated by the way his wife's parents treated him. In 1186, we are told by Hung Mai, Chieh San-chih took Shih Hua as a uxorilocal husband for his well-educated daughter. Some time later, while away on business, Shih Hua wrote to his wife about his discontent: "When I am at your house, I am humiliated by your mother and father in a hundred ways every day. Now that business is not going well, things would only be worse. I will stay in Ju-ning a while longer. Put up with being alone and do not think about marrying someone else. As soon as business improves, I will return to get you." His wife must have loved him, however her parents treated him, for after she received this letter she grew despondent, would not eat, and died within four months.[5]

Families with sons who kept a daughter home could have had any of a number of motives. In an ordinary peasant household needing more labor, a young boy was of little use, but a teenage girl could be used to attract a man strong enough to work. In the early Northern Sung, a man whose only son was three sui wrote a will leaving 70 percent of his property to his son-in-law and only 30 percent to his son, with the son-in-law to manage it all until the son was grown.[6] Families also sometimes kept a daughter home to indulge a mother. The eminent official Fu Pi (1004–1083) had two of his daughters and their husbands and children live with him and his son. Su Hsien (1118–1183) indulged his widowed mother by allowing a husband to be brought in for the daughter she loved, and they all lived together for thirty years.[7]

Families with ample land or with businesses they wished to expand might also take in sons-in-law to enlarge their family enterprises. In 990, Kuo Tsai (955–994) reported that when he served in southern Szechwan he observed that rich people there often recruited uxorilocal sons-in-law whom they ranked with their own sons and assigned shares of the property. He wished to have the practice outlawed on the grounds that it led poor men to abandon their parents and also often gave rise to lawsuits. Other areas where uxorilocal marriage was described as prevalent may have been similar. Fan Chih-ming (c.s. 1100), himself from Fukien, reported that in the Hunan area uxorilocal marriage was commonplace, with uxorilocal husbands, often migrants, willing to work hard for their wives' families because they would in time take control of the property. Liu Ch'ing-chih (1130–1195), while serving as vice prefect of O-chou (Hupei), found that the local people saw nothing wrong with the sons of poor families leaving home to become uxorilocal sons-in-law.[8]

The prevalence of uxorilocal marriages in areas like these probably can be accounted for by frontier conditions, where there was little population pressure and land was relatively plentiful. In-migrants without resources were apparently often willing to take advantage of such opportunities by marrying into an established, prosperous family. Added to this, in most such frontier areas there were long-settled non-Han groups with their own marriage practices. Han observers would probably mistakenly describe a matrilineal system as one with uxorilocal marriage, promiscuity, and easy divorce. Relatively cognatic systems might also be classed as ones with frequent uxorilocal marriage, as might ones in which groom service (as a substitute for brideprice) led to the groom living with the bride's family for a fixed number of years. Han settlers to the area could have found what they called uxorilocal marriage convenient in interethnic unions with non-Han partners who saw nothing inferior in it.

References to individual cases of uxorilocal marriage sometimes suggest links to migration. In southern Szechwan, Chao Chih-ts'ai, the son of a recent migrant, married into the family of Mou Li-jen, getting a share of Mou's estate equal to that of Mou's son and establishing an enduring tie between the Mou and Chao families. Chao Chih-ts'ai's two daughters also married Mous, sons of their mother's brothers.[9] The gazetteer for K'un-shan (Kiangsu) shows that uxorilocal marriages must have been quite common there, especially in the twelfth century after the loss of the north, when many northerners resettled in the south. Six of the nine men given biographies as eminent figures from this period had become residents of the area because of a uxorilocal marriage, their own or an ancestor's.[10] Accounts of the founding of descent groups sometimes mention that an early ancestor had moved to the area as a uxorilocal husband. The Changs of Chin-hua (Chekiang), for instance, recorded that the first ancestor to settle there had come in order to be a son-in-law of a P'an family.[11]

Sometimes it was the family of the man who decided a uxorilocal marriage would be best. Tai Piao-yüan (1244–1310) reported that Tais had been living three li south of the seat of Feng-hua county (Chekiang) for six generations. His great-great-grandfather had had six sons and twelve grandsons. Of the grandsons, Tai Piao-yüan's grandfather, Tai Ju-ming (1176–1254) was notable for his dullness. His brothers decided that since their house was so small, Ju-ming should marry out, and they arranged that he move to the county seat to join the family of Miss Cheng (1190–1274). (It had probably been no easy task to find him a wife, for he must have been around thirty; he was fourteen years older than his wife.) The Cheng family took in a uxorilocal husband not for lack of sons; Miss Cheng had an elder brother who worked as the local teacher and who in time educated his sister's sons. Miss Cheng, perhaps because it was her home, made a better impression on her grandson than her husband did. Tai Piao-yüan remembered her as intelligent, good at keeping records, and a strict family manager.[12]

The ideas and feelings that might lead to keeping daughters at home are portrayed sympathetically by Sung Lien (1310–1381) in his account of a family that brought in its first uxorilocal husband in the Southern Sung. As best I can reconstruct, the Lou-Wang-T'ai family was connected in the ways shown in Diagram 7. Lou Yüeh and his wife, Miss Wang, residents of Wu-chou (Chekiang), had at least one son, but still they kept a daughter, Miao-ch'ing, at home, taking Miss Wang's brother's son, Wang Yeh, as a uxorilocal husband for her. Miss Wang had entered marriage with an ample dowry, and this formed the basis of the property she gave her daughter and son-in-law. Because this property had originated with the Wangs, it was, in a sense, returning to them. "Miss Wang loved [her daughter] Miao-ch'ing very much, so built a seventeen-room house for her on the lake and gave so-many *mu* of forested hills, vegetable plots, and fertile fields. She told Miao-ch'ing and her husband [Wang Yeh], 'This is entirely from my dowry. I have not used a hair from the Lou family. Now I give it all to you to own. You be careful

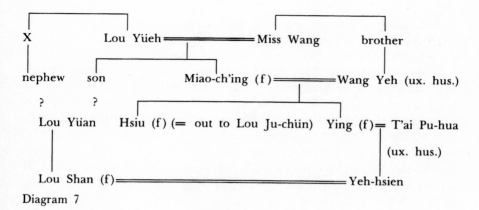

Diagram 7

with it.'" Miss Lou Miao-ch'ing and her husband had two sons, both of whom died early. They married out their oldest daughter to Lou Ju-chün, of the same prefecture and thus probably a distant relative of Miao-ch'ing's. This daughter apparently had not taken her mother's surname, for if she were a Lou it would have been strange to marry a Lou. Miss Lou Miao-ch'ing and her husband, Wang Yeh, kept their younger daughter, Ying, at home. By the time she was grown Chekiang had fallen to the Mongols, and a Mongol, T'ai Pu-hua, became her uxorilocal husband. Ying had one son by him, Yeh-hsien. Nothing more is said of T'ai Pu-hua. (Indeed, it is possible that describing this as a uxorilocal marriage was to cover up the fact that their daughter became pregnant after being raped by a conquering soldier, or after being kept as his mistress for a time and then abandoned.) Ying's mother, Miao-ch'ing, remained the dominant person in the family, for we are told:

> Miao-ch'ing doted on [her daughter's son Yeh-hsien] to a great degree and saw that he had a full education, no less than if he had been her own son. When Yeh-hsien grew up, they again consulted the family and ordered [Lou] Yüeh's grandson/grandnephew [Lou] Yüan to marry his daughter [Lou] Shan to [Yeh-hsien]. Miao-ch'ing said to [her husband, Wang] Yeh, "We two are getting old and unfortunately have no sons. Now, our daughter's son, Yeh-hsien, is cultured and well-mannered, and moreover has married my nephew's daughter. If he is not closely related, then who is closely related? All the property my mother gave us we should give to him. We should convert the house to an ancestral temple to make the seasonal sacrifices to my parents and your parents as well as Yeh-hsien's ancestors [the T'ais]".[13]

The account of this family touches on themes that recur in other references to uxorilocal marriage in Sung times. There had to be some wealth for it to work; it was linked to women's property and dowries; it was associated with women making decisions; it did not always lead to a change in surname; it might be repeated in successive generations; those arguing for it claimed it was based on kinship closeness; and it might involve the blurring of boundaries between two lines.

As in this example, there seems to have been little sense that uxorilocal sons-in-law themselves could continue the descent line. Uxorilocal husbands were not equated with adoptees. What they could do was work a family's property, support the old parents, and receive shares of the property in compensation. Sung authors do, however, refer to daughters or daughters' sons acting as heirs. Yüan Ts'ai warned families to treat their daughters well, as they might have to entrust their funerals and sacrifices to them. Neo-Confucian scholars such as Chu Hsi and Ch'en Ch'un (1159–1223) objected to the casualness with which men would take their daughters' sons as heirs.[14] The judge Wu Ko agreed to let a uxorilocal son-in-law redeem land his father-in-law had pawned many years earlier, but ordered that he not sell it. "Since Yü Liang had no sons or grandsons, he could rely only on [his daughter] Yü Pai-liu-niang to continue the sacrifices. If [she and her husband] redeem this land it should be permanently preserved to supply the expenses of the seasonal rites and registered with the government as [land] that cannot be sold to outsiders." Sacrifices are here deemed relevant, but the judge refers to the daughter carrying them on rather than her husband or son. Other Sung sources also refer to daughters, in the absence of sons, performing sacrifices.[15] In the case of Lou Yüeh, described above, the issue of continuing sacrifices seems to have been delayed until a grandson of the first uxorilocal husband was grown. The grandparents may well have thought of themselves as adopting him, though they also saw him as carrying out sacrifices to two other lines. Uxorilocal marriage was a good way to give parents a claim to one of their daughter's sons.

TRANSMISSION OF FAMILY PROPERTY
WHEN DAUGHTERS STAYED HOME

As seen in earlier chapters, during Sung times there was nothing illegal about a family transmitting property, including landed property, to a daughter as her dowry and through her to grandchildren of other surnames. Moreover, the law had long provided that if a line was "broken"—that is, if there was no patrilineal heir, natural or adopted—daughters of the family head would have first claim on the property. Yet Sung law did not explicitly provide for uxorilocal marriages to be treated differently than patrilocal marriages. Many a prospective father-in-law probably tried to convince a young man to join his family by giving verbal assurances that he would be set for life, able to take over the family property in time. But these assurances conflicted with Sung enacted law, which did not recognize agreements of this sort.

According to the Sung code, if there were unmarried daughters (literally, "daughters at home," tsai-shih) at the time a line was broken, they were entitled to all of the property. If all surviving daughters were married out (*ch'u-chia*), they were to be given only one-third of the property, the rest to be confiscated by the government. If an heir was established posthumously, the married daughters would still get their third, the heir would get one-third, and the final third would be confiscated.[16]

There was a fundamental ambiguity in applying these rules in the case of uxorilocal marriages. Was a daughter who had stayed home and had a husband brought in for her a "daughter at home" (which normally meant a never-married virgin) or a daughter married out (even though she had actually married in)? If she was classed as a daughter at home, she would get all the property or share it equally with any other sisters at home. If she was classed as married (which seems to have been the more common course), somewhat odd consequences could ensue. Imagine a family that had two daughters, one much older than the other. Suppose the parents took in a uxorilocal son-in-law for the elder and he worked the land for a dozen years, supporting his parents-in-law and young sister-in-law as well as his wife and children. The strict letter of the law said that when the parents died, if they had made no will, all the property would go to the unmarried daughter; the uxorilocal husband and the older daughter and their children would get nothing. Or imagine a similar case in which one daughter married out and one had a uxorilocal husband brought in for her. No matter how long or hard the uxorilocal husband had worked, the two daughters would each get the same share, one-sixth of the property. Or what if there was only one daughter, married uxorilocally, but she died before her parents and her husband stayed on to raise their children and support her parents? He and his children would be entitled to nothing when the parents died and the line was broken. Finally, suppose that many years after they had taken a uxorilocal husband to work their land and support them, the parents adopted a young nephew as heir. The adoptee would get everything because the family would then no longer be one with its line broken.

Over the course of the Sung, efforts were made to emend the rules on broken lines to reduce these anomalies. The tendency was toward granting uxorilocal sons-in-law slightly more claim to family property. Particularly notable are the rules that a family head could leave property to a son-in-law after his daughter had died; that even if an adoptee was later established, a son-in-law could get half of the family property (up to three thousand strings) if it was left to him in a will; and that in the case of broken lines a uxorilocal son-in-law could get a third of the property if he had increased its value.[17]

From cases in the *Judicial Decisions* it seems that neither ordinary people nor judges worried a great deal about the exact provisions of the statutes on transmission of family property with respect to uxorilocal marriage. A family without sons may have avoided stating explicitly whether the son-in-law would get a share of the family property or be expected to continue the

Chou Ping (deceased) = (wife, deceased?)   = concubine?

          | |

    Hsi-i-niang (f.) = Li Ying-lung (ux. hus.)   infant son

Diagram 8

sacrifices because they still hoped for the birth of a son or because they were afraid that the son-in-law might prove incompetent or otherwise undesirable and were keeping open the possibility of expelling him. The young man coming in probably knew that, whatever the law, families were often able to leave their property to a daughter and her uxorilocal husband. In one legal dispute over property, transmission from the man to his daughter and her husband was central: "Hung Kuang-sheng had no sons. He passed all of his family [property] to his daughter and son-in-law."[18] Many years had passed since this act, and the judge did not question that the daughter and her husband were now the owners of this property.

When a dispute arose between a uxorilocal husband and his wife's brother, judges rarely seemed to care what a son-in-law might have been led to expect when he joined a household. Liu K'o-chuang (1187–1269), for example, wrote a ruling in a case concerning the Chou family (see Diagram 8). Chou Ping brought in Li Ying-lung as a son-in-law for his daughter, having at that time no sons. But after Chou died a son was born posthumously. The son-in-law tried to secure his claim to much of the property by saying it had been given to him as dowry, but Liu K'o-chuang objected:

> According to the law, when both parents are dead, sons and daughters divide the property and daughters get shares half as large as sons. A posthumous son is still a son. If, after Chou Ping died, his property had been divided into three, with the posthumous son getting two shares and [his daughter] Hsi-i-niang getting one share, it would have been in accord with the law. Li Ying-lung became a son-in-law. When he saw that his wife's family had an orphaned son, he neither paid attention to the provisions of the law nor took care of the child. Rather, he took the best of his wife's father's fields and gave them to his own relative, falsely claiming they had been assigned [as dowry] by his wife's father and mother. Where in the world does he get the idea that sons-in-law get a share of their wives' family property? The county sheriff cited the example of Chang Kuai-ai [Chang Yung, 946–1015] to give the son-in-law 30 percent,[19] which matches the idea of the statutes that daughters get half as much as sons.[20]

Liu K'o-chuang then ordered a scrupulous examination of all of Chou Ping's property, movable and landed, so that it could be fairly divided into thirds.

Although Liu K'o-chuang wrote as though he were applying a strict interpretation of the law and dealing severely with the son-in-law, he still did not leave him and his wife out altogether. Li had apparently married into the Chou house before Chou Ping died. Technically, a married daughter who

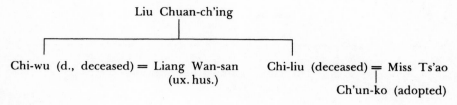

Diagram 9

had a brother had no claim to any of the family property. Liu K'o-chuang must have felt that giving her and her husband nothing was not reasonable, since the parents had apparently made no legally binding provision of dowry for her, as they would have if she had married out. He thus treated her as a "daughter at home." He may also have had some sympathy for the fact that Li had undoubtedly been recruited with the understanding that he would gain control of the property, which he would have had no son been born.

The judge Wu Ko took a considerably harsher stance against a uxorilocal husband in a somewhat similar case (see Diagram 9). Liu Chuan-ch'ing had had both a son and a daughter, the daughter older than the son. A uxorilocal son-in-law had been taken for the daughter, and, probably quite some time later, the son had married. At the time the case came to court, the father, son, and daughter had all died, the only survivors being the son's widow and the daughter's widowed uxorilocal husband. The husband was attempting to continue to manage the property and even to sell it. Outraged, the judge insisted that all of the property be assessed and held for the widow and the son she had recently adopted. The widowed uxorilocal husband was judged entitled to nothing.[21]

Possible ways to get around the legally stronger standing of unmarried daughters, as compared to their uxorilocally married sisters, are revealed in the case of a Wu family with four daughters but no sons (Diagram 10). The father had taken uxorilocal husbands for the first two daughters (Twenty-four and Twenty-five) and also adopted a boy of another surname. In sorting out the situation, the judge commented: "Shih Kao and Hu Yin are uxorilocal sons-in-law. In principle they are like half sons. But if Wu Ch'en had considered his two sons-in-law to be trustworthy, would he, while alive, have set up a boy of the Lü-ch'iu surname, giving him the name Yu-lung, to continue his line, and also taken Miss Li as the boy's wife?"[22] This adoptee lived to mourn his adoptive father and sire a son of his own before dying. At that point the two sons-in-law wanted to force a division of the family property. In the judge's words,

> Hu Yin also claims that the Wu family property has been managed and expanded by the two sons-in-law, using their wives' family assets, and so they wish it to be divided among the four daughters. But the law is not like this.

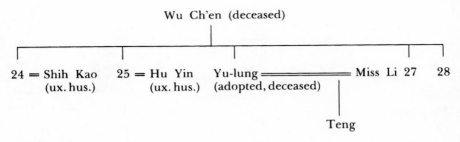

Diagram 10

> According to the law, uxorilocal sons-in-law who have managed their wives'
> family property and added to it, may, if the line is broken, be given 30 percent.
> Now, however, Wu Ch'en has descendants, so the line is not broken. How can
> one rush to divide according to the rules for broken lines?[23]

The sons-in-law cited as evidence a will, but it had not been submitted to the
court, and the judge noted that if they were relying on an oral will it would
be of little use. There was also contradictory evidence submitted on the age
at which the adoptee had been established. Then there were questions
about why the two younger daughters had not been married. The judge
realized that their presence was crucial to any division.

> Have [the two elder sisters] not realized that there are no explicit provisions
> for married daughters to receive shares, but there is established law on un-
> married daughters getting equal shares? When property is divided, unmarried
> sons get betrothal gifts and unmarried aunts and sisters, or ones who returned
> home, get dowries. Unmarried ones get separate shares of the property not to
> exceed the amount of the dowry. Also, the law says in cases of broken lines
> that all the property goes to unmarried daughters, or half that amount to
> returned daughters.[24]

There were two views on the third daughter. Some said that she had already
been married, but the fourth daughter charged that she had been sold to be
an adopted daughter. If the latter was true, it would indeed seem that the
elder sisters or their husbands were acting unscrupulously. There were also
suspicions about the delay in marrying the fourth daughter. Because of
these uncertainties, all the judge could do at this point was disallow the
lower court's consent to giving shares to the daughters under the rules for
broken lines, urge the widow of the adoptee to work hard at finding a
husband for the fourth daughter, and tell the sons-in-law to stop bothering
the court. Note that the judge granted the widow of the adoptee higher
standing in the family than either her sisters-in-law (the daughters of the
former head) or their husbands, the only adult men in the household.[25]

The ways collateral relatives could interfere with uxorilocal marriage are
revealed in the case of a Ts'ai family, which took in three uxorilocal sons-in-law

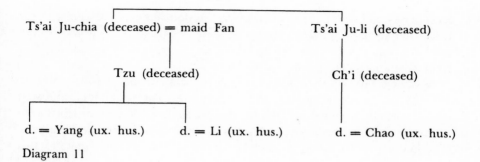

Diagram 11

(see Diagram 11). Still living in this family were the maid, Miss Fan, who had borne children by her master, Ts'ai Ju-chia; her two granddaughters and their uxorilocal husbands, Yang and Li; the granddaughter of Ts'ai Ju-chia's brother Ju-li and her uxorilocal husband, Chao. They all lived together, the property never having been divided. This Ts'ai family was from branch three of a large local descent group with four branches. Ts'ais from other branches began to pick fights with the uxorilocal husbands, wanting posthumous heirs to be established for Tzu and Ch'i, the deceased fathers of the Ts'ai women who had taken uxorilocal husbands. In other words, they wanted the property to be controlled by Ts'ais, not men of other surnames. The uxorilocal sons-in-law made the mistake of going to court to try to get protection. The grandmother did not want an heir established for her son, content to depend on her two granddaughters and their husbands. That she was a maid weakened her ability to deal with agnatic kin, however. Wu Ko, as judge, sided with the Ts'ais and ordered heirs to be established to keep the disputes from growing worse. After selecting adoptees from among the various candidates, he ruled, the property should first be divided in two (half for the descendants of Ju-chia and half for the descendants of Ju-li), then each half split between the posthumous adoptee and the uxorilocal husband or husbands. Wu Ko justified giving half to the uxorilocal husbands on the grounds that "the daughters were [the men's] natural issue and the sons-in-law have been there a long time."[26] Half could be considered generous, since the law stipulated that only one-third go to married daughters, but of course it was only half as much as they probably would have gotten if the uxorilocal husbands had not gone to court.

This case illustrates the potential conflict between families who kept daughters at home and their kin. In many areas of the country, especially in Chiang-nan and Fukien, descent groups were becoming increasingly active in local affairs from the twelfth century on. These groups might consist of dozens or hundreds of households linked by common descent to the first ancestor who moved to the area. Joint ancestral rites, often conducted at the grave to this ancestor, strengthened understanding of the nature of the kinship ties that bound them and their perception of themselves as a group.[27] It was not surprising that members of such a descent group would oppose any kin who allowed sons-in-law to inherit property, especially when a widow (that is, not one of them) made the choice.

As these legal cases show, judges associated uxorilocal marriage with women, ordinary people, local norms, and compromise, not with men, educated individuals, and national or absolute standards. How could an institution so culturally disadvantaged gain a strong hold in Chinese society, especially in a period when Neo-Confucianism was gaining in strength? How did this form of marriage come to be granted greater legal protection than before? The best explanation I can offer is that officials' commitment to more ideal family forms came into conflict with their equally strong desire to extend the reach of the state and of Confucian teachings. A major underlying reason for compromises was the shift southward of the center of China, which forced officials to come to grips with practices less common in north China. Already in the Northern Sung many leading figures came from central China, as did much of the wealth. In the Southern Sung, of course, this was the core region. In an unplanned way, local and national officials, as they dealt with particular cases or proposed revisions of the law, modified what they defined as the "Chinese" family system, giving more tolerance to what in the early Sung one official had proposed simply banning.

ADOPTION OF NONAGNATIC RELATIVES

Parents who had let their daughter marry out, assuming that they could continue their family through a son, might suddenly be left heirless if he died. They could then continue their family through their daughter by adopting one of her sons. Children of sisters and daughters were seen as closer than other relatives of different surnames; they were said to share the same substance (*ch'i*). But people would also adopt children more distantly related, such as children in their mother's or grandmother's families, or even from their wife's family, where no biological connection to the patriline existed.[28]

Sung law did not distinguish adoption of nonagnatic kin from adoption of totally unrelated people. The law specified that babies three sui or younger could be adopted even though they did not have the same surname as their adoptive parents. In the *Judicial Decisions,* adoption of babies of other surnames was not encouraged or ordered posthumously, but it was upheld when done during the lifetime of the father or mother. Moreover, judges were seldom fussy about the three-sui rule when the adoption had clearly been the parents' choice and had been in effect for years before the dispute.[29]

Adoptions of this sort occurred among officials and educated families as well as ordinary people. One of Wei Liao-weng's (1178–1237) uncles, for example, was adopted out to his mother's brother. In much the same period,

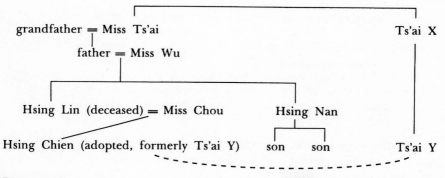

Diagram 12

Miss Huang, the wife of a magistrate, was able to adopt her brother's child. Ts'ai Yüan-ting (1135–1198), one of Chu Hsi's closest disciples, allowed his second son to be adopted by his cousin through his father's sister, a Yü. Later, after Ts'ai Yüan-ting's death, his widow asked her son to "return to the line," but he left one of his own sons to continue the Yü family line. All through the twelfth and thirteenth centuries, the Ni of Kuei-hsi and the Fu of nearby Ch'in-hsi had intermarried, so when one Ni branch had no descendants, they adopted a Fu.[30]

People turned to relatives in part because it was easy to ask them for favors. When Mr. Ch'eng was seventy, he was troubled by the fact that one of his younger sons had no heir. In 1274, when his married daughter came for a visit bringing her son, Cheng Yüan-hsien, he asked her for the boy on behalf of the son, saying that although she had married into the Cheng family she should not forget the Ch'engs. She did not agree to the adoption right away, and the next year she died, as did her brother's wife. Her father and mother then went to her husband's family to beg for the boy. The Chengs consented, and the young Yüan-hsien came and performed the mourning for his recently deceased adoptive mother, then stayed with the Ch'eng family, taking their surname. Many years later he arranged for joint commemoration of his two mothers.[31] Adoption of a daughter's child, as in this case, resembles uxorilocal marriage in terms of the final consequences for the descent line.

Adoption of affinal relatives over three sui had no legal basis, but seems to have been looked on with more toleration than adoption of strangers of similar age. Wu Ko wrote a decision for a case concerning the Hsing family (see Diagram 12) as follows:

Hsing Lin and Hsing Nan were brothers. Hsing Lin had no sons. Although Hsing Nan had two sons, he was unwilling to let one be Lin's heir. So after his elder brother's death [Hsing Nan] obeyed his mother, Miss Wu, and his sister-in-law, Miss Chou, and established as heir a nephew through the family of his grandmother Miss Ts'ai. This is Hsing Chien. Now, to establish a boy of the Ts'ais as an heir to the Hsings is definitely not the intent of the law, but at the time it was done because of the feelings of [Hsing Chien's adoptive] grandmother Miss Wu and mother, Miss Chou, and [his adoptive uncle] Hsing Nan personally arranged it. If this violated the law, it is not Chien's fault. It would have been all right if, when Hsing Nan first arranged it, someone among his agnates who understood moral principles had wanted to dispute it as contrary to law. But it is not all right to try to change the succession after eight years have gone by.[32]

Judges did not praise adoptions like these. To the contrary, they usually made some deprecating remark about how they violated patrilineal succession, perhaps citing the classical case of Chü destroying Tseng by heirship passing through one of their line.[33] Nevertheless, judges did not make a practice of overturning such adoptions.

Adoption of affinal relatives under three sui posed all of the problems of uxorilocal marriages if there were other potential claimants to the property. In one case, a widow of twenty-three with no surviving children wished to remain with her husband's family and adopt an heir. Her husband had three brothers, but one was not yet married and one had no sons. The eldest had not gotten along with her husband, and moreover, his sons were close to her in age. So the widow asked for a young boy in her father's sister's family. Eighteen years later, after the two younger brothers-in-law had died, the eldest took her to court, trying to upset the nonagnatic adoption. The judge sided strongly with the widow and adoptee, noting how difficult it could be to keep to the principle of adopting an agnatic relative.[34]

This chapter has dealt with two of the most common ways families handled a shortage of male heirs. The two strategies—keeping a daughter at home and adopting children related through women—show that women were not totally useless for family continuity; they were just not as good as sons. How inferior they were was an issue of considerable disagreement in Sung times across class, gender, and perhaps regional lines. Women apparently tended toward different views than men. In the fourteenth century, Wu Hai wrote that "nowadays there is no limit to those who ignore ritual and the law and make a son-in-law, a sister's son, or a daughters's son their heir. They destroy themselves because they cannot overcome a woman's viewpoint."[35] Wu Ko, in a legal decision discussed above, overruled the widowed concubine who was content to let her three sons-in-law support her, saying, "What do women know about principles or law?"[36] One senses that it was more acceptable for women to look on daughters as close relatives than for men to do so, and so men attributed such decisions to the women.

Class differences come into play here as well. Those who proposed rules on succession to property and those who enforced such rules as local officials were invariably members of the educated class. There seems little doubt that for them uxorilocal marriage and adoption of nonagnatic relatives carried greater stigma than they did for ordinary peasants, because among the elite, family name and ancestral rites were more crucial to personal identity. When judges labeled uxorilocal husbands as nefarious interlopers, they were applying upper-class standards to people who did not necessarily view continuing the sacrifices as more critical than being supported in old age.[37] Those who adhered to the teachings of Ch'eng I and Chu Hsi would have the greatest difficulty valorizing uxorilocal marriages and nonagnatic adoptions, but other educated men, committed to Confucianism but not necessarily to this strand of Confucianism, also were probably less comfortable with these strategies for continuing the family than most peasants.

Women often played active roles in arranging to continue a family through women, but there is no evidence women were happier or better off in families that adopted these courses. Not only did women share at least some sense that they were inferior second choices, but they suffered along with men from the legal weaknesses of these types of marriages. Both mothers who kept their daughters at home and widows who adopted children from their natal families would undoubtedly have wished greater guarantees that other relatives could not challenge the arrangements they had made. Women were actors, to be sure, and the cumulative effect of their actions contributed over time to greater acceptance of nonstandard family forms. But that was not necessarily a comfort to individual women who found their actions legally challenged.

FOURTEEN

Adultery, Incest, and Divorce

Marriages did not always work out as hoped. In extreme cases, the marriage might break up, the husband expelling his wife or either party simply leaving. Even when a marriage was not particularly bad, circumstances might lead to sexual transgressions that destroyed it. The Chinese did not have a concept comparable to original sin; that is, they did not conceive of sexual temptation and transgression as the prototype of all human iniquity. But they did have feelings of horror, shame, and anger about certain sorts of extramarital sexual relations. Incest and adultery could lead to criminal prosecution or simply to divorce. Divorce for any reason was a source of shame and embarrassment, particularly for the woman.

ADULTERY

Sexual relations between a married woman and a man other than her husband was a serious legal offense, and both individuals could be punished by two years' penal servitude.[1] In labeling an offense adultery, the man's marital status was irrelevant; after all, there was nothing illegal about a married man having sexual relations with women other than his wife so long as the women were neither virgin daughters of good families or wives—in other words, relations with courtesans, singing girls, prostitutes, or his own maids or concubines were perfectly acceptable.

Stringent laws do not necessarily keep people from committing adultery. Chuang Ch'o (ca. 1090–ca. 1150) reported that poor families might accommodate extra (paying) "husbands" to make ends meet, monks being particularly common "extra" (adulterous) husbands for poor families that lived near temples.[2] Readers of Hung Mai's stories, it would seem, accepted that adultery might occur in many circumstances. Guests might seduce their hosts' wives or concubines. Monks, especially monks offered hospitality in people's homes, were frequently suspected of seducing wives. One man of fifty had a beautiful concubine less than half his age, and she had an affair with his strong young servant. Then there was the story of a woman only half the age of her sexagenarian husband who bullied her husband into inviting a seventeen- or eighteen-year-old orphan into their home as a foster son, then began sleeping with him, making no effort to conceal the affair; her husband was driven to hang himself to avoid the ridicule of his neighbors.[3] In these tales, women are portrayed as just as likely to initiate adulterous affairs as men, especially women matched to men much older than they.

From surviving legal cases, one gets the impression that magistrates preferred not to handle adultery cases. Huang Chien was a tutor in the home of T'ao Tsen, and lived there with his wife, Miss Chu, and their baby son. Also living there, probably in a family temple, was the monk Miao-ch'eng. Someone accused Miss Chu and Miao-ch'eng of adultery, and the court ordered all three men (the monk, the husband, and the host) beaten sixty strokes. The penalty for the wife was transfer to the convict armies, where the soldiers could draw lots to see who got her as a wife. When the husband objected and appealed to a higher court, the next judge was outraged at the punishment for the wife, saying that although the penalty was on the books, it was meant for women of low-status households, or ones without husbands, or ones whose husbands did not want them back, not for cases in which the husband wanted to keep his wife. Indeed, the judge argued that adultery cases should be heard only when the husband brought the charge, pointing to the potential for false accusations. In the end he gave the woman back to her husband on the understanding that they leave the town.[4]

In China, as probably everywhere else, many husbands preferred to cover over evidence that their wives had committed adultery. Rather than bring his wife and her lover to court for punishment, a man would try to deal with the situation himself. In a case that did eventually come to court, a man claimed that he had found his wife with a government clerk, then went to get the local constable; in the meantime, however, the clerk escaped. The husband decided not to press charges, but, fearing that his son's wife had observed her mother-in-law, he had his son divorce her. Later he also decided to divorce his own wife. Some months later he and his son apparently regretted their actions and went to court to try to get their wives back. The judge was willing to have the clerk beaten one hundred strokes for adultery, but did not reinstate either marriage. The daughter-in-law had already married someone else, and the wife claimed that she had been driven out because her husband now had a maid to care for him.[5]

INCEST

Penalties even heavier than those for adultery were imposed in cases of illicit sexual relations between relatives, the penalties graded according to degree of kinship. The death penalty was prescribed for sexual relations with a father's or grandfather's concubine, the wife of one's father's brother, one's own or one's father's sister, a daughter-in-law or granddaughter-in-law, and a brother's daughter. The penalty was one degree lower (exile to two thousand li) when the woman was the man's mother's sister, his brother's wife, or his brother's daughter-in-law, and lower yet (penal servitude for three years) when she was a stepdaughter or half sister (wife's daughter by a prior husband or mother's daughter by a different father).[6] In cases of incest, if force was used the man's penalty was one degree higher and the woman was not punished. Sexual relations between a man and his mother, his full sister, or his daughter were apparently so unthinkable they are not even listed in the code; if discovered, however, they could be punished as one of the ten abominations.[7]

Of all the possible combinations, only two are mentioned with any frequency in Sung sources, probably because they were the ones people most often suspected: relations between a man and his father's concubine or his son's wife. Legally, both were among the most serious possible offenses, punishable by death for both parties if no coercion was involved, for the man alone if he forced the woman. Given Chinese family living arrangements, it is not surprising that people would have suspicions of these sorts. Because men often brought in concubines younger than their own sons, outsiders readily imagined that the concubines would have preferred the son to the father. And because men in their forties and fifties so often expressed open attraction to girls in their teens and early twenties, neighbors no doubt wondered about how they looked on the young brides brought in for their sons. Incest with one's father's concubine was legally as serious as incest with a daughter-in-law, but clearly did not stir up such strong feelings. Su Ch'e (1039–1112) even argued that officials should avoid probing into such matters, as it was so common it was not really fair that some got caught and others did not.[8]

Father-in-law/daughter-in-law incest was more troublesome. Even though brides were generally expected to avoid unnecessary contact with their fathers-in-law, they could not avoid them altogether, and were expected to serve them food and nurse them if ill. The possibility of indecent relations was therefore ever present. The standard allusions were to "the affair of the New Tower" or "the demands by the banks of the river," both based on a poem in the *Book of Poetry* long interpreted to be a criticism of Duke Hsüan of Wei who built a tower by the Yellow River, took his son's new bride there, and forced himself on her.[9]

Several cases in the *Judicial Decisions* show how difficult it could be for a daughter-in-law to do anything about unwanted attentions from her father-in-law. The judge Hu Ying (c.s. 1232) seems to have been quite unsympathetic to those who brought charges in such cases:

Even if a father is unfatherly, a son may not be unfilial. Huang Shih is Huang I's son. Even if in fact there was a "New Tower" affair, it would be up to Huang Shih to conceal his father's wrongdoing. Sending his wife away [i.e., divorcing her] would be enough. How can he go around telling outsiders, especially when the facts are obscure! He believes his wife and brings charges against her father-in-law. Worrying only that he will not defeat his father, he accuses him of one of the greatest sins. Such behavior utterly destroys all morality![10]

Hu Ying then had the son beaten one hundred strokes and his wife sixty.

In another case, it was the daughter-in-law herself who brought the charge, but Hu Ying applied similar principles.

A daughter-in-law's relationship to her parents-in-law is like a son's to his parents. A filial son broadcasts his parents' qualities; he does not tell about their sins. If Chiang Pa in fact made the "demands by the river bank," it would be all right for Miss Chang to resist him, but for her to tell other people about it violates her duty to respect elders. Moreover, Chiang Pa is [an old man], his grave trees are already planted, and his energy is in decline. How could he have unworthy thoughts?[11]

The son, in this case, had taken his wife and moved away from his father. To Hu Ying, the son's act was a much worse offense than anything his father might have done. Hu Ying ordered the son beaten sixty strokes and sent back to support his father. His wife Hu Ying ordered sent to a convict army, where she would be given to a lucky soldier.

In a third case, while Hu Ying did not doubt the accusations, still he could not bring himself to punish the man. After he had questioned the parties involved, he thought it probable that Li Ch'i-tsung was guilty. He decided not to have the principals tortured into confessions because he knew a woman could not hold out as long as a man. But he also thought it totally inappropriate to spread such grave accusations. Since a son was obligated to divorce a wife his parents did not like, the son should forget his desire "to grow old together" with his wife and send her away. He ordered the woman's father to marry her to someone else.[12]

Seeing how hard it was for an abused daughter-in-law to get justice from the courts, an abused woman's relatives probably often dealt with the situation themselves by removing her from her husband's house—which was, after all, the best they could hope for from a judge like Hu Ying. In one such instance, an abused woman's father had secretly married her to someone in another district, then claimed she was lost. When the father-in-law demanded his son's wife back, the judge (in this case not Hu Ying) refused, saying:

> Hu Ch'ien-san fooled around with his son's wife. Although his actions did not reach incest, they were extremely depraved. Miss Wu found this hard to bear and twice returned to her own home. But according to her own testimony, she never brought her complaints to the officials. And yet her father, Wu Ch'ing-i, acting on the instruction of his elder brother Wu Ta-san, hid Miss Wu, then married her to someone in another prefecture. Next they went to the authorities and falsely charged that their daughter could not be found. If the truth had not been discovered, would this not have meant bringing further disaster to [the father-in-law] Hu Ch'ien-san? If we consider the case according to the law, it would be reversed, and [the woman's father] Wu Ch'ing-i would get one hundred strokes and be registered in a neighboring prefecture. If the false accusation was on the instruction of Wu Ta-san, then Wu Ta-san should be beaten and registered, and Wu Ch'ing-i would get off. I rule that the county should interrogate Wu Ta-san, and the case be handled there. If Miss Wu returns to Hu Ch'ien-san's home, she will certainly drown or hang herself or run away, so how can she be returned there? When people do not act in ways appropriate to their status, then their word is not to be believed. For the county [officials] to give her to the government broker to remarry her again as they ruled is appropriate, and [their decision] can be left as it is. Hu Ch'ien-san has not been interrogated, so it is difficult to set a penalty. If he brings another complaint, the county authorities should send him to the jail to investigate his depravity. They should deal with him harshly in order to serve as warning to fathers-in-law who fool around.[13]

Just as it was hard for a woman to prove that she had been abused, it was difficult for a man to prove that he was not guilty. In 1045, the prominent scholar and official Ou-yang Hsiu's (1007–1072) sister's stepdaughter accused him of incest, which landed him in jail and led to two trials in which the only substantial evidence was her testimony against his. He was cleared, but naturally not everyone gave up their suspicions. Over twenty years later, in 1067, when he was sixty-one, Ou-yang Hsiu was accused of carrying on with his eldest son's wife, Miss Wu. Again he was cleared, but only after having to declare publicly that the imputed offense was despicable and to demand that the accuser come up with better evidence.[14]

Hung Mai recorded a story of trumped-up charges affecting someone much lower in the social hierarchy.

> Ning Liu of South Meadow village, in the southern suburbs of Chien-ch'ang [Fukien] was a simple-minded man who concentrated on his farming. His younger brother's wife, Miss Yu, was a little sleeker than her peers. She was also ruthless and licentious, and had an adulterous affair with a youth who lived there. Whenever Ning looked askance at her she would scold him, and there was not much he could do.

Once Miss Yu took a chicken, wanting to cook it. When Ning learned of her intent, he went into her room, demanded that she give [the chicken] to him, then left with it. Miss Yu quickly cut her arm with a knife, then went to the neighbors screaming, "Because my husband is not home, brother-in-law offered me a chicken and tried to force me to have sex with him. I resisted, threatening to kill myself with the knife I was holding, and so just managed to escape."

Ning at that time had no wife, so the neighbors thought she might be telling the truth. They took them to the village headman, then the county jail. The clerks at the jail reviewed the evidence and demanded ten thousand cash to set it right. Ning was poor and stingy, and, moreover, knew himself to be in the right, so stubbornly refused. The clerks sent the dossier to the prefect Tai Chi, who was unable to investigate the case but who noted that it involved an ordinary village wife who was able to protect her virtue and her body and not be violated. The administrative supervisor, Chao Shih-ching, concurred with Chi, and they sent the case up [to the higher level] making [Ning] look guilty. Ning received the death penalty, and Miss Yu was granted one hundred thousand cash, regular visits from the local officials, and a banner honoring her for her chastity. From this, she acquired a reputation as a chaste wife. The local people all realized Ning had been wronged and resented how overboard she had gone.

In the end Miss Yu had an affair with a monk at the nearby Lin-t'ien temple. Charges were brought, and she received a beating and soon became ill. She saw Ning as a vengeful demon and then died.[15]

The two officials involved, Hung Mai reported, also suffered retribution for their miscarriage of justice.

DIVORCE

Divorce carried rather different sets of associations in Sung China than it does today. The most powerful image was not of a couple who grew apart, bickered too much, or discovered that one partner had fallen in love with someone else; rather, the image that captured the tragedy of divorce was that of the loving couple forced to separate because the man's parents found his bride unacceptable. A poem written on this theme in the Han was well known. A comparable case from the mid-Sung also came to be widely discussed. The poet Lu Yu (1125–1210) married his mother's brother's daughter, Miss T'ang, but his mother was not pleased with her niece as a daughter-in-law. She sent the girl back, very much against Lu Yu's wishes, and Miss T'ang was then married to an imperial clansman. Some years later she and Lu happened to meet in a garden. With the approval of her husband, she sent Lu some food and wine. Moved to recall his old pain, he wrote a song on the wall of the garden, imagining her feelings. The song included the lines, "The east wind is evil, his feelings thin. All I have is sadness, parted all these years. Wrong, wrong, wrong!" In later years Lu Yu wrote other poems also generally interpreted to express his feelings on being forced to divorce his wife.[16]

Divorce could be referred to as separation (*li*) or as expulsion (*ch'u*). Normally, a man did not have to go to a judge or any other official to get approval for a divorce. But to establish clearly that he had divorced her, it was best for him to write out a divorce document, stating his intention.[17] An early Sung divorce document, dated 977, was accidentally preserved among the papers sealed up in a cave at Tunhuang. The beginning is missing, but seems to have concerned the innocence of the woman's parents.

> ... They gave birth to a girl who was gentle and sweet to all. Her relatives loved her, much as if she had been their own child.... Why, then, when they became husband and wife, did the relatives all become enemies, forming hatreds whenever they met? When fermenting agents are mixed with milk, the top separates and flows away; cats and mice cannot share the same nest for long. Now each party has consulted with his or her relatives. No more will they be allowed to call themselves husband or wife. As soon as the wife leaves, she may select a good husband—even a high official—to share her life with him as harmoniously as two instruments playing music together. May the man and woman each enjoy a thousand or ten thousand years of happiness. Food and clothing will be supplied for three years.[18]

This document was signed and dated.

Divorce documents were not mandatory. Simply sending a woman away was also accepted, legally and socially, as a divorce. A line was, however, drawn at a husband divorcing his wife and then promptly arranging for her to marry someone else, for that smacked of his selling her, something prohibited in the law but not unheard of in real life.[19]

In legal theory, a man could divorce his wife only if she agreed or if he had cause, though the classically specified causes were vague and difficult to disprove (including, for instance, talkativeness and jealousy). Moreover, he was not to divorce her if she had mourned his parents or had nowhere to go.[20] Neither the grounds nor the restrictions seem to have been prominent in people's thinking in the Sung, however. In the story translated in the Introduction, Wang's wife said she had nowhere to go, but still he was able to divorce her.[21] And as we saw above, judges ordered divorce even when a wife's only offense was the unfilial act of reporting the improper advances of her father-in-law. Moreover, wives could, and often did, resist being divorced. In one legal case, when his wife would not consent to a divorce, the husband falsely accused her of adultery. Hu Ying ordered the man beaten eighty strokes for the false accusation, but still granted the divorce, saying that he was amazed the woman would want to come back after being slandered in that manner.[22]

Divorce was certainly shameful for a woman, but not necessarily for a man. Ssu-ma Kuang reiterated several times that a man's obligations to his parents and to his family could make it imperative that he divorce a wife who was disrupting family harmony. Ssu-ma Kuang did not merely urge husbands to accept the necessity of divorcing their wives; he also urged wives' parents to assume that their daughters were the guilty parties and work to reform them. As an example he cited a case from ancient times of a woman who had married out her daughter three times, only to have her sent back three times. The third time when she asked what had happened, the daughter spoke contemptuously of her husband. The mother then beat her on the grounds that wives were supposed to be submissive, not haughty, and kept her home for three years. On the fourth try, the daughter made an ideal wife. By contrast, in his day, Ssu-ma Kuang observed, parents were more likely to sue the families of their sons-in-law than to blame their daughters.[23]

Ch'eng I held similar views. Once he discussed the ethics of divorce with a disciple:

Someone asked, "Is it proper to divorce a wife?"

[Ch'eng I] answered, "When a wife is not worthy, there is no harm in divorcing her. For instance, [Confucius' grandson] Tzu-ssu once divorced his wife. The current custom is to look on divorce as something ugly, so people are reluctant to engage in it. The ancients were different. Wives who were not good were sent away. It is just that people today make this into a big thing and bear it silently without revealing it. Sometimes there is some hidden sin, which is handled quietly, or even tolerated, which just fosters wrongdoing and thus obviously is bad. Cultivating the self and disciplining the family are the most urgent tasks for men. Best is to first cultivate oneself and then discipline one's family."

[The disciple] also said, "What about the cases among the ancients of divorcing wives hastily for something not very bad like scolding the dog in front of one's mother-in-law, or serving a pear that wasn't ripe?"[24]

[Ch'eng I] answered, "This was the way the ancients practiced generosity. In ancient times if someone severed a friendship, he did not say anything bad [about the former friend], and a gentleman could not bear to expel his wife for a great sin, so sent her away for a minor fault. Consider the one who scolded the dog in front of [her husband's] mother. There was nothing so serious in this incident, but some other day there [must have been] a major reason, so [the husband] used this pretext to divorce her."

Someone asked, "If she was expelled for this petty reason, how could there have been no objections? What about the fact that outsiders would not have been able to tell who was right and who was not?"

[Ch'eng I] replied, "She would know her own faults. If she can correct them herself, fine. Why must other people know? Those with insight will understand. Anyone who must expose his wife's wrongdoing is simply a shallow fellow. A gentlemen is not like this. Most people when they talk try to make the other party look wrong and themselves look right. Gentlemen have a forgiving attitude."

Someone commented, "There is an old saying, 'In divorcing a wife, make it so she can remarry; in severing a friendship, make it so he can make new friends.' Is this the idea?"

[Ch'eng I] said, "Yes."[25]

Divorce was probably more common among lower-class families, for whom taking a concubine was not a practical solution to either childlessness or incompatibility. A wife who did not work out was simply sent back. Hung Mai told of the daughter of a mat maker who had married a fisherman but was divorced because she did not know how to sew. Her parents were already dead, and, having nowhere to go, she became a beggar.[26] Hung Mai also told of an heiress who was divorced because of illness, perhaps epilepsy.[27]

Clearly people at all social levels found divorce unpleasant. Ssu-ma Kuang complained that men did not divorce their wives when they should because people looked on divorce as embarrassing even to the man.[28] Friends and relatives would try to talk men out of divorcing their wives. Hung Mai told of a prefect, Kuo Yün, who became fearful after a dream that portended a short career, and wrote out papers divorcing his wife, Miss Yang, with whom he had gotten along well for over ten years and who had given birth to three or four children. He moved into a separate building, and for several months friends and relatives tried to talk him into returning. Miss Yang's elder brother visited between assignments and burned the divorce papers. Yet Kuo still slept in a separate room.[29]

Divorced women did not always fare poorly; indeed, remarriage seems to have been very common. One woman, divorced from a county registrar, was later married to a county magistrate.[30] And in the story above, Lu Yu's first wife married an imperial clansman. Although a divorced woman usually left without her children, there were exceptions. The eminent official Lü Meng-cheng (946–1011), for example, had grown up in poverty after his father, enamored of a concubine, had expelled him and his mother. His mother refused to remarry, and when Lü became an official, he reunited the family by inviting his father to his home, having his mother and father occupy different rooms.[31]

Legally, women could not initiate divorce. As Liu K'o-chuang (1187–1269) bluntly put it, there was no grounds on which a wife could divorce her husband. The law code even specified a punishment of two years penal servitude for a wife leaving her husband without his permission. Wives could talk their husbands into divorce (divorce by mutual consent), however, and this sometimes happened. Chang Yüan-pi (eleventh century), we are told, married Miss Ch'en, his very beautiful cousin. He was ugly and read all night, so she told him she wanted to leave and he divorced her.[32]

In real life, some wives ran away, and some families took their daughters back because their husbands did not treat them well. Miss Meng (1078–1152) was married young to a man who proved unreliable, so her mother took her and found her a job as a wet nurse in a well-to-do family. Hung Mai told of a woman who initiated a divorce because her husband beat her and drove her son away. In another of his stories, a man couldn't stand his son-in-law's rudeness and drunkenness, so took his daughter back against her will. Later he married her to someone else.[33] Li Ch'ing-chao petitioned the court for a divorce from her second husband after a brief marriage, charging him with official malfeasance.[34] An official petitioned the court to allow his granddaughter to be divorced from her husband on the grounds that he was mentally ill. He also asked to have her dowry returned. The judicial officials pointed out that a husband's illness was not a ground for divorce, but the emperor allowed it as a special favor. In a similar case involving ordinary people, the judge, Hu Ying, first berated the wife for not being more loyal to her husband: even if he was an idiot, as she claimed, he was still alive and could see, hear, and move. The wife had also claimed that her father-in-law made unsuitable advances toward her, which the judge called slander. He ordered her beaten, but allowed the divorce that she wanted. In another case, a mother brought a charge because her daughter's husband had indentured her out as a maid. The judge ruled that if the husband could not support his wife, her mother could take her back and marry her to someone else.[35]

Often, of course, judges disapproved such requests. When a man wanted to obtain a divorce for his daughter because her husband of nineteen years had been exiled as punishment for a crime, the judge allowed him only to take her home, so as to avoid suspicion concerning her relationship with her father-in-law; she was not permitted to marry anyone else, though, perhaps in part because she herself did not want to be divorced. And one judge sentenced a woman who had left her husband to two years penal servitude and registration as a government courtesan.[36]

In rare instances, the government mandated divorce when no one wanted it. One woman was divorced from her second husband against both their wills because the judge had discovered that this man was a second cousin of her former husband, a prohibited relative. The judge cited the rule that unless the marriage had been in existence twenty years or longer, spouses illicitly joined had to be separated.[37]

In China, as in most other societies, the state took an interest in sexual behavior, especially of married women, and its laws on sexual conduct helped create and reinforce patriarchal structures.[38] These laws were also complexly related to emotions. People had strong feelings that certain types of sexual behavior were reprehensible, their feelings shaped by and reinforcing the laws. Still, passion, lust, cruelty, and probably a great many other emotions and circumstances led people to violate the norms. Sexual misbehavior was different from most other sorts of misbehavior in that those who were sure it had occurred often preferred to keep quiet, and those who heard rumors or accusations of it never knew how much to believe.

Much in this chapter is commonly found in other societies, but a few attitudes seem to have been more particularly associated with features of the Chinese family system. The problem of father-in-law/daughter-in-law incest has, I think, a distinctively Chinese cast. Naturally, the potential for such an offense was greater when married sons lived in the same house as their parents, often a rather small house, and when men married young, so that a recently wed seventeen-year-old son might well have a forty-year-old father. Then, too, the difficulties a teenage bride might face in interpreting and then fending off the advances of her father-in-law were undoubtedly compounded by the characteristically Chinese insistence that she treat her parents-in-law with all the respect and obedience she owed her own parents.

The evidence in this chapter also provides a perspective for viewing the legal model of marriage outlined in Chapter 2. When judges decided cases involving adultery, incest, or wives' abandoning their husbands, they rarely applied the letter of the law. Often they meted out lower punishments or even gave no punishment at all, merely separating the parties. And in not a few cases they reversed the prejudices of the law, for instance authorizing a woman to leave her husband or giving a divorced woman custody of a child. Legal institutions were a crucial element of the social context in which women fashioned their lives, but it was the law as practiced rather than the law as written that mattered most.

The incidence of adultery, incest, and divorce also underline once again that families were not always harmonious unions of people who thought and acted as one. When people referred to the family as a unit with its own goals, needs, or interests, they were, consciously or unconsciously, identifying the family with the men of the family, and particularly the senior men. That certainly was the assumption of the judges who preferred to expel a daughter-in-law rather than reveal that the family head had treated her indecently.

FIFTEEN

Reflections on Women, Marriage, and Change

Three main goals have shaped the way I approached Sung women's lives in this book. I have tried to reveal the complexity of the context in which women fashioned their lives by viewing marriage as a cultural framework encompassing diverse images, ideas, attitudes, and practices. I have tried to present women not solely as the objects of actions by men, but also as actors who helped create, interpret, manipulate, and contest the conditions in which they lived. And I have tried to embed women's history in the overall history of a particular period, the Sung dynasty, by relating what was happening to women to other developments of the time. By way of conclusion, I shall attempt to pull together some of what has been learned in these regards and point to questions that remain.

IMAGES AND EMOTIONS, ACTIONS AND SATISFACTIONS

Marriage and family life in the Sung were constructed around a great variety of partly contradictory and often ambiguous symbols, images, and notions. Ideas found in Confucian writings, such as women as inner and yin versus men as outer and yang, were certainly potent, even if not all-encompassing. Equally powerful were erotic images of dominance and submission, such as that of the deferential woman attending the man, "waiting on him with towel and comb." Images of determined widows, however, carried with them notions of both female sexuality and female achievement partly at odds with these images of lovely handmaidens. So did representations of mothers, from the indulgent mother tending to her babies to the older mother as family saint who put all of her love for her family into efforts to gain them spiritual merit. The common images of the jealous wife and the smitten husband, when juxtaposed, conveyed the notion that emotion is central to marital bonds, that discord is a product of men's weakness for women and of women's inability to control their jealousy. These ideas of the centrality of emotion competed with ethical models that identified marriage with duty. The notion of marriage as predestined undermined the equally strong view that matchmaking had to be taken very seriously, for an individual's or a family's very fate could depend on the choice of a partner. If we knew more about women's conversations out of the presence of men, we could undoubtedly point to many more cases of inconsistency, tension, or ambiguity. In such a cultural environment, women had room to appropriate parts of the general culture to their own benefit and to fashion ways of thinking and acting that gave them some real sense of purpose and self-worth.

How often did they do so? We certainly find evidence of resourceful women, but unfortunately there are no first-person accounts of women actually mulling over the meaning of common maxims or the choices available to them. In this book, women's voices are barely heard. Educated men give us their opinions about how women's viewpoints differed from men's. They portray women as worrying about their mothers and daughters, not just about the patriline of their husbands and sons. They credit women with favoring marriages with relatives and being the first to suggest bringing a son-in-law in for a daughter. They also depict women as being more inclined than men to Buddhist piety and to acting on emotion. Many of the differences between men's and women's viewpoints that Sung writers indicate seem plausible given the different position men and women occupied in the family system; we need not dismiss them as baseless male stereotypes.

In cases where gender differences were not noticed by writers, it could well be that men and women shared common understandings. I have discovered no reason to doubt that women accepted yin-yang cosmology or the belief that patrilineal ancestors were important. Women as much as men seem to have looked on others in terms of the roles defined in the Confucian didactic literature. I found no sign that women had some alternative vision, for instance privileging a common gender identity between maids and mothers-in-law over the status difference in their roles in the family. And both men and women seem to have looked on motherhood in very positive terms.

But agreement did not extend to all dimensions of life. Sexuality is one of the most crucial areas in which husbands' and wives' feelings and opinions clearly differed. From the images found in narratives ranging from gossipy anecdotes to funerary biographies, we can tease out some of the emotions that entered into their relations. Whereas men could openly celebrate taking a new young wife after their first had died, women who remarried often felt bad about themselves for entering into a sexual union with a second man. Similarly, while most men viewed the taking of concubines as one of life's pleasures, wives typically saw it as a trial. Men viewed women's intense jealousy as a mental aberration, like illness or possession; the women, however, were more likely to focus on their husbands' blindness to the manipulativeness of the concubines. Differences of these sorts in husbands' and wives' feelings about sexuality—their own and their spouses—must have had much to do with how both men and women perceived themselves and their relations with each other.

Such differences did not, however, keep Sung women from working hard to keep their families going. Why were they so devoted? Gradually, as I worked through the evidence presented here, I came to think that actions and satisfactions were closely linked: because there was almost always something a woman could do that would help her attain a happier, more comfortable, or more secure position, there were always real incentives to work within the system, thus gradually gaining more of the benefits it had to offer patient and persistent women. Despite the constraints women faced, rarely were they in situations in which making their lives a little more pleasant or comfortable was totally impossible. They might never have what men had, but they could work at making the next year better than the last. Young girls could concentrate on securing the love and favor of their relatives. Wives could help themselves as well as their families by throwing themselves energetically into useful work like spinning and weaving or careful management of the family's assets and servants. Many wives probably found it worthwhile to take pains to make themselves more attractive to their husbands. Certainly virtually every woman had much to gain by putting effort into rearing children, especially sons. If she could bring up filial and devoted sons, she would feel loved, respected, and secure.

Opportunities to improve their situations were not limited to the women who had the luck to become wives in respectable families. Maids could take advantage of their youth to attract their master's attention and perhaps be promoted to concubine. Concubines could focus on winning and holding their master's favor, so that he would give them gifts and privileges; or they could try to make allies of his mother, wife, or maids, to secure a better situation in the household; they could devote their energies to being good mothers, hoping that their children would eventually take care of them.

Above all, the satisfactions to be had from rearing children should not be underestimated. The job was known to be demanding. Keeping children alive was in itself a major achievement, and getting them educated and married off all took a great deal of time and attention. Mothers could make use of many talents and skills in this work: they could use their literary training to teach their children to read; they could employ their knowledge of human nature and social relations to teach them basic moral principles and techniques for pleasing others. When women excelled in these regards, they could anticipate the appreciation of their children and the respect of all those who knew them.

MARRIAGE AND THE DYNAMICS OF CLASS INEQUALITY

Whether a woman would spend her days splicing hemp or teaching her children to read depended largely on the social and economic circumstances of the family into which she married, and nothing predicted that so well as the circumstances of the family into which she was born. Still, the connections among women's lives, marriage, and the class system go beyond this simple and obvious observation. Marriage was, in fact, one of the major mechanisms for creating and maintaining class inequalities.

The class structure as a whole was built in part on the fact that women had a cash value, which gave flexibility to peasant families in need of cash to pay taxes or repay debts; the ruling elite would not have been able to extract as much surplus from the peasants if poor people had not had this capacity to raise cash under pressure. The more respectable way to do this was to engage the women in spinning or weaving for the market, but peasants who needed to meet payment deadlines could also sell their daughters to the rich as maids or concubines. Appropriation of the daughters of the lower classes in this way can be seen as a form of class domination. At the same time, it assured that the elite stratum was never cut off entirely from the mores and values of ordinary people, since women from poor families bore and reared many of their sons. The existence of concubinage also exerted strong pressure on upper-class families with daughters, for it compelled them to see that their daughters got dowries and proper educations, thus ensuring that they would never end up sold as concubines themselves.

Status consciousness at all social levels was constantly renewed as families made choices about spouses for their children. Contrary to the modern Chinese proverb that daughters are "goods on which one loses," a daughter did not have to represent a loss to her family, since arranging her marriage provided an opportunity to secure a new kinship link. Parents chose spouses for their children mindful of what their decision would mean for their family's prestige and economic circumstances. Weddings offered chances for families to confirm their standing and connections by bringing together friends and relatives to celebrate a new alliance. Marriage also affected families' wealth. Through marriage, property was passed from one group to another via dowry, generally in ways that favored those who already posssessed ample assets in wealth, official rank, or family reputation.

Class and marraige were also related at the level of discourse. The discourse on women's virtues valorized the qualities needed in the wives of scholar-official families, such as the managerial and interpersonal skills suited to keeping large, complex families functioning smoothly. Many of the practices held up as evidence of virtuous commitment to the larger family, such as refusal to remarry and consenting to adoption of agnatic relatives rather than keeping a daughter home, were easier for the well-to-do to perform.

The separation of the sexes too was practiced more thoroughly among the elite; keeping wives and daughters from public spaces was a way the elite could claim moral superiority.

Because gender conceptions and marriage practices were so closely linked to honor and status, women played a major role (or bore a heavy burden) in maintaining the honor of their fathers, brothers, husbands, and sons. Those women who, for whatever reason, were of no help in these regards (those, for instance, who had been raped, sold as a maid or concubine, or remarried) might best be treated as if they were no longer part of the family. The connections between women's behavior and class standing thus was double-edged: it made some women greater assets to their families than they otherwise would have been, other women greater liabilities.

WOMEN'S ROLES IN CHANGE

Both marriage practices and the class system underwent significant transformations during Sung times. If women were actors, can we see them as participating in the processes that led to change? To examine women's roles in these processes, let me review some of the ways women's situations changed.

GENERAL CHANGES IN WOMEN'S SITUATIONS

1. Increased commercialization of textiles
2. Increased literacy among women
3. Growth in the market for women as maids, concubines, courtesans, and prostitutes
4. Revised notions of both masculinity and femininity
5. The spread of footbinding

CHANGES IN THE RHETORIC ON FAMILY, MARRIAGE, AND GENDER ASSOCIATED WITH THE GROWING IMPORTANCE OF NEO-CONFUCIANISM

1. More attention to the segregation of the sexes
2. Higher evaluation of women's roles as family managers
3. Encouragement of women's literacy when used to educate their sons, but discouragement of it for writing poetry
4. Increased emphasis on patrilineality
5. More stringent questioning of widows' remarrying

CHANGES IN MARRIAGE PRACTICES FROM T'ANG TO NORTHERN SUNG

1. More emphasis on choosing sons-in-law for their likelihood to rise in the bureaucracy and less on their ancestry
2. Escalation in the size of dowries

   3. Increased evidence of sororal marriages (to deceased wife's younger
      sister)
   4. Increased evidence of uxorilocal marriage

   CHANGES IN MARRIAGE PRACTICES FROM NORTHERN TO SOUTHERN SUNG

   1. Decline in cross-regional marriages among the families of higher officials
   2. Greater legal recognition of daughters' claims to dowries
   3. Some questioning of widows' claims to dowries
   4. Greater recognition of the property claims of uxorilocal sons-in-law

Some of the changes listed above are more convincingly documented than
others, but here, for the sake of discussion, let us take them as given.

If the question were simply whether women participated in the processes
that led to change, the answer would have to be yes. Women may on the
whole have disapproved both of concubinage and of treating maids like concubines, but they clearly participated in furthering these practices. Mothers
trained daughters to occupy certain statuses in this system, fostering in them
the modesty expected of upper-class wives, the charm expected in courtesans,
the obedience expected in maids. Women purchased most of the maids and
many of the concubines. A wife whose husband took a concubine could to
some degree limit or shape her husband's behavior by arousing fears of
what she might do to the other woman if sufficiently provoked. And women
who became concubines and maids were of course also actors. Not only did
some women choose an economically secure position as concubine over a
life of hardship as a poor man's wife, but even the majority who had been
sold quite against their will made choices and took actions. So long as there
were chances to improve their situations, they could strive to win the favor
of their master or mistress, working within the system for their own benefit
and thereby also helping to validate it and reproduce it.

   Footbinding is another instance where we must posit women's active
participation in bringing about change. The spread of footbinding was very
much tied up with issues of women's attractiveness. Women were the ones
who spent time trying to make themselves, their daughters, or their mistresses
look appealing, but their notions of beauty were based in no small part on
their interpretations of what men liked. Men attracted by elegantly dressed
courtesans who sang for them might not want their wives or daughters to
evoke similar feelings in other men. Wives of men attracted to courtesans
had to decide whether to compete in appearance or talents or to maintain
instead a distinctly wifely demeanor, reserved and physically modest. In
rearing their daughters, they had to decide how much to stress modesty over,
say, musical accomplishments. When they decided to bind their daughters'
feet, they were accepting the need to copy some of the techniques courtesans
used to make themselves attractive to men. Once footbinding had become
the established custom, mothers could simply say they bound their daughters'

feet because otherwise no one would want to have them as wives. But the custom did not spread instantly, and for some time mothers had to make active decisions on the matter.

Did women play much of a role in shaping changes that we would class as more to their benefit? They were, of course, involved in all the decisions related to marriage strategies, such as whether to keep a daughter home and call in a husband for her rather than marry her out. They must have played some role in the escalation of dowries, since they are so often portrayed as helping put together the dowries of their husbands' younger sisters and their own daughters. Women, who like their husbands would depend in their old age more on their sons than their daughters, were willing participants in the decision to see more of the family's resources go to their daughters, though their reasons may have been different. Possibly they saw putting together a daughter's dowry not so much as a way to secure an advantageous ally, but as a way to help the young woman through a difficult transition. Since women were active in selecting spouses for their children, they probably also had something to do with the gradual decline in cross-regional marriages. Were they more inclined than their husbands to want to see their daughters occasionally and therefore more eager to keep them within a few days' travel? Could the decline in long-distance marriages among the highest-ranking families be a sign that wives were gaining influence in family decisions in line with the increase in the wealth they brought with them as dowries?

It is hardest to demonstrate much role for women in changes in rhetoric and values. The men who wrote on ethical issues, it must be admitted, attributed their ideas to their readings of the classics or their understandings of cosmic principles, not to the influence of their wives or mothers. Whether women came to evaluate their daughters-in-law or mothers-in-law by different criteria, and whether their ideas influenced their husbands or sons, is impossible to gauge from surviving sources.

Women's roles in these changes, like men's, involved many little acts that had cumulative consequences. The overall impact of their participation should not be overestimated. In none of the domains discussed above did women bring about change by working consciously against the perceived interests or desires of men. Women, even more than men, could not act as though the other did not exist. In many realms their actions were based almost wholly on judgments regarding the men around them, considerations of what would be tolerated or opposed, succeed or fail, please or displease, attract or repel.

THE HOLD OF PATRIARCHY

Listing the features of marriage and women's situations that changed in the Sung brings to the fore a fundamental question about the history of women in China. Why did changes that can be classed as adverse to the interests of women take hold fairly easily, while those that promised some improvement did not last or have the anticipated effects? Of those that portended improvement I am thinking of the increased transmission of property to daughters as dowry, the emphasis on affines as allies, the widespread tolerance of uxorilocal marriage, the enhanced opportunities for women to earn money through the commercialization of textile production, and the recognition among many educated men that girls ought to be taught to read and write. On the adverse side I have in mind the spread of footbinding, the expansion of the market in women, and a certain hardening of attitudes toward women's virtues and sexual segregation on the part of key intellectual leaders.

Since Chinese patriarchy survived many other historical changes before and after the Sung, part of the answer must be found in factors in no way peculiar to the Sung. The Chinese family system was remarkably adaptable, so that changed ideas and practices could be incorporated without disturbing the patrilineal, patriarchal, and patrilocal principles of the dominant ethical and legal models. Thus the household mode of production was not at all shaken by women selling the thread they produced. Nor were basic notions of family property dislodged by channeling more property into dowry. Added to this was the deeply rooted cultural assumption that family relations are ethical relations, based on universal, unchangeable moral principles; people, in short, did not look for change. In the Han dynasty there were dowries, concubines, literate women, and women who wove to make money. Because these phenomena were not unprecedented, writers seldom noticed differences in degree or scale. Those unaware of the extent to which circumstances had changed would not look for opportunities to refashion social arrangements.

But even if these long-term social and cultural features helped limit the impact of social and economic change, they do not explain why some changes took stronger hold than others. To account for this result, we must see the way changes impinged on each other. My hypothesis is that whatever authority or autonomy upper-class women inadvertently obtained by the forces that escalated dowries and enhanced their education, and whatever authority or autonomy lower-class women gained from the growth of the economy, were counteracted by the growth in the market for women as maids, concubines, courtesans, and prostitutes and a general tendency toward the strengthening of patrilineal principles.

Why should the large market for women have such negative effects on upper-class women's lives? A wife's ability to get her husband to accommodate her needs and desires was surely circumscribed by the knowledge that if he found her tiresome he could keep her on as housekeeper and mother to his children and bring in a concubine for companionship. The more real this possibility—the larger the numbers of friends and relatives who had taken concubines and the younger the men were when they did so—the greater the effect on the wife would be. This is not to deny that many wives coped successfully with concubines, and some even seem to have enjoyed the prestige that came with the increased numbers of women subservient to them. But the overall effect, as every observer noted, was to set women against each other and to absorb much of their energy in jealous friction.

The effects of the expansion of this market in women on lower-class women was rather different. Farmers' wives would not have been hampered by the dread that their husbands might take concubines, and although kidnapping and wife-selling did occasionally occur, they were not major worries. However, the uncertainty any unmarried girl in a poor family must have felt about the arrangements her parents would make for her may well have carried over into insecurity in later life.

The increased prominence of the market in women also, I believe, shaped intellectuals' thinking about gender differentiation. Sung scholars' views on women and marriage must be understood as the response of people vaguely aware that the nexus of women and money confused class and kinship solidarities and created ambiguous and often fragile kinship links. The boundaries between the world of educated families and the marketplace in women was highly permeable. Families purchased maids, negotiating their entry into the family as a purely financial matter; men brought ex-courtesans home as concubines and had them entertain their guests; officials fathered children by concubines, then left the concubine behind when transferred. To establish a firmer sense of security in such a negotiable world, Confucian scholars wanted to fix people in well-defined roles. To protect their sisters and daughters from the market in women, upper-class men had to see that they were taught rigid notions of modesty and given educations untainted by any suggestion that they were playthings. Men and women alike had to exert moral effort to keep distinctions of rank, function, and role in place. Uneasiness about the fragility of ties to and through women coincided, it would seem, with other forces strengthening patrilineal principles in Chinese kinship, such as the growth of descent groups and the efforts of scholars and officials to adapt ancestral rites to fit the needs of their class.

The cruder charges of misogyny that are often brought against Sung Neo-Confucianism do not hold up to scrutiny. In the chapter on widows we saw that Sung Neo-Confucian scholars went only a little further than their peers or predecessors in praising the ideal of widow fidelity. It is not worth belaboring the point that no Confucian scholars advocated either female infanticide or footbinding. Infanticide, as we saw, certainly existed, but educated men wrote about it only to condemn it. Footbinding was associated with the pursuit of beauty, not self-control or sexual segregation, and was never associated with Confucian descriptions of virtuous wives. Girls were not said to have been modest, gentle, well read, *and* content to bind their feet. Nor were mothers praised for the skill with which they bound their daughters' feet.

At the same time, it would be hard to deny that among all the ideas and images current in Sung culture, the ones Neo-Confucian scholars focused on were ones that tied wives as closely as possible to the patrilines of their husbands. Leading scholars such as Ssu-ma Kuang, Ch'eng I, Chu Hsi, and Huang Kan were quite explicit in rejecting those elements of current culture that seemed to be at odds with the patrilineal-patriarchal model, such as women's literary creativity, their claims to property, and their involvement in affairs outside the home. Because they wished to enhance patrilineal principles in general, and because they saw connections through women as fragile, they tried to mark the family off as a sphere into which marketlike relations could not enter, where interpersonal ties would be based on eternal —and patrilineal—principles.

The growth in the market in women and the resurgence in patrilineal principles in descent group organization and philosophers' rhetoric may not be the only developments that curbed improvements in women's situations. More research needs to be done on what was happening in the Yüan and early Ming with regard to dowry, marriage strategies, literacy, and the like. The Mongol conquest had an impact on Chinese law, concepts of cultural identity, and intellectuals' concerns with orthodoxy and stability that needs to be more fully understood. Still, part of the explanation for the failure of women's situations to improve undoubtedly lies in the dynamic interactions of developments begun in the Sung.

WOMEN'S HISTORY AND CHINESE HISTORY

Women's history, at its best, does not just inform us about women in the past; it challenges us to reexamine our understandings of history and historical processes. If I have been successful in these regards, readers of this book should be ready to look on familiar topics in Chinese history like commercialization, Neo-Confucianism, the legal system, and the class structure with new questions in mind. They should stop to think whether major social or economic changes would have had consequences for women similar to or different from those for men. When reading disquisitions on virtue, beauty, cosmology, or equity, they should be more sensitive to messages about gender. When considering men's lives or thoughts, they should more readily keep in mind their relations with women and children and be more open to signs of ambivalence, ambiguity, and emotions. They may even begin to expect more of historians on topics other than women and gender that are difficult to research because of the paucity or biases in the sources.

For my part, I found that trying to see women in historical context made me question my basic understandings of Chinese culture and history. For instance, I found it necessary to present the cultural matrix of ideas about women, sexuality, and affinity as an unintegrated assemblage communicated through a wide variety of media, ranging from didactic texts, folktales, and clothing styles to housing layouts. I came to think that these ideas were expressed in fragmented ways, often through images that carried ambiguous meanings, in large part because the feelings or ideas people were struggling with were ones that fit uncomfortably with rationalized and moralized views of Chinese society. As I see it, the coexistence of these partially contradictory ideas went largely unchallenged, but the assemblage was not synthesized into an overarching system.

I am beginning to suspect that this model has validity in other domains of Chinese culture as well, such as popular religion. By means of an expansive pantheon of quite variable gods and an equally diverse set of demons and evil spirits, Chinese could come to grips with feelings considered socially undesirable, such as lust, greed, hate, and loathing. Perhaps there are similarities in the ways these relatively unorganized bodies of ideas were transmitted or reproduced. To gain a more satisfactory understanding of Chinese culture and its connections with social behavior, we thus need a conceptual framework that encompasses both the articulated, moralized, rationalized ideas and the ones that had to be expressed in more fragmented and ambiguous ways.

In a similar fashion, pondering the hold of patriarchy made me reconsider other continuities in Chinese history. Although all historians today reject the old view of a "changeless" China, we should not overcompensate for past failings and deny that, in comparison to other major civilizations, Chinese history is marked by some rather remarkable continuities and a tendency to return to an equilibrium after some deviation. Throughout Chinese history, for example, certain basic cosmological principles were widely taken for granted, such as the existence of a link between the living and the dead. And during the long imperial period, the government worked again and again to reestablish patterns of land tenure giving the individual peasant household considerable leeway over how it organized its work. The imperial period was also marked by regular returns to a monarchical-bureaucratic form of government, with the dynasty maintaining centralized control by appointing civil servants to govern regional units and transferring them frequently. Were similar mechanisms involved in all of these persistent features? Do our efforts to understand the hold of patriarchy contribute to our efforts to understand other continuities and recurrent patterns? Are these continuities linked, the continuities in one fostering others?

Chinese history and culture, in other words, look different after we have taken the effort to think about where the women were.

NOTES

INTRODUCTION

1. Kracke 1954–55; Shiba 1970; Elvin 1973; Hartwell 1982; K. Chao 1986; Hymes 1986a.
2. Gernet 1970; Kracke 1975; Finegan 1976; Clark 1991.
3. Twitchett 1983; Edgren 1989.
4. Johnson 1977; Ebrey 1978; Chaffee 1985; Hymes 1986a; Bossler 1991.
5. De Bary 1953; Kassoff 1984; de Bary and Chaffee 1989; Ebrey 1984a, 1991b; Bol 1992.
6. Twitchett 1959; Ebrey 1986b; Hansen 1990.
7. See, e.g., Klapisch-Zuber 1985; Gold 1985; Rose 1986; Ferguson, Quilligan, and Vickers 1986; and Erler and Kowaleski 1988, to list only some very recent studies.
8. See Guisso 1978; P.C. Chung 1981; Holmgren 1981–83, 1983, 1991; Chaffee 1991; Rawski 1991.
9. E.g. Swann 1932; O'Hara 1945; Ames 1981; Guisso 1981; Sangren 1983; Paul 1985; Martin-Liao 1985; Black 1986; Barnes 1987; Kelleher 1987; Reed 1987; Martin 1988; Birge 1989; Murray 1990; Carlitz 1991; Rowe 1992.
10. See Levering 1982; S. Cahill 1986, 1990; Waltner 1987; Weidner 1988.
11. See Levy 1958, 1962; van Gulik 1961:170–82; Schafer 1984.
12. See Ropp 1976; Weidner et al. 1988; Weidner 1989; Widmer 1989, 1992; Robertson 1992; Ko 1992; Mann 1991, 1992; Zurndorfer 1992.
13. See Hsieh and Spence 1980; Waltner 1981; Holmgren 1981, 1985, 1986; Elvin 1984; Mann 1987; T'ien 1988; Tao 1991.
14. See especially Croll 1978; Stacey 1983; K. Johnson 1983; M. Wolf 1985; Honig and Hershatter 1988.
15. See Levy 1962; Chao Shou-yen 1963; Chang Hsiu-jung 1976; Wong 1979; Liu Tseng-kuei 1981; Niu 1985, 1987; Chao Ch'ao 1987; Kao 1988; Jay 1990.
16. See especially Lee 1981; Gronewold 1982; T'ien 1988.
17. E.g. Liu Jun-ho 1967; Tan 1978; Li Ao 1980; P'eng 1988; Chang Pang-wei 1989; Linck 1989; Liu Li-yen 1991; Birge 1992.

18. Ch'en Tung-yüan 1928:139.
19. Lin 1939:165; Yao 1983:91; D.J. Li 1971:364.
20. See especially Niida 1962:381–92; Shiga 1967:401–9; Ebrey 1981b, 1991d; Yüan 1988; Yanagida 1989.
21. Cf. Ebrey 1990.
22. Cf. Tilly 1987 for a review.
23. For good studies of women in the modern Chinese family, see M. Wolf 1972; Cohen 1976:149–91; A. Wolf and Huang 1980; R. Watson 1981; and Ocko 1991.
24. Cf. Ebrey 1984b; 1991b:49–50, 59–61; 1992b.
25. See Ebrey 1984a; 1991b:52–53, 58–59, 80–85, 102–44.
26. ICC ping 14:484–85.
27. On this source, cf. Chang Fu-jui 1964, 1968; and de Pee 1991.
28. For translated examples, see Djang and Djang 1989.
29. KHTC hsü 2:209–10.
30. SS 252:8849.
31. More than half of these cases have been translated into Japanese (Umehara 1986). On this casebook, see also Ch'en Chih-chao in CMC 645–86; and Birge 1992:98–104.
32. Cf. Bossler 1991:22–43.
33. For this last use, see Walton 1984; Hymes 1986b; and Bossler 1991.
34. See Ebrey forthcoming.
35. NCCIK 22:458–60.
36. Judd 1990.

1. SEPARATING THE SEXES

1. Cf. Rorex and Fong 1974 for the story and another version of this scroll.
2. SMSSI 4:43.
3. CF 1:468 and 6:591.
4. CF 1:464.
5. YSSF 3:49; Ebrey 1984b:286.
6. KCTSCC tse 395:9b.
7. CL 28a–29b; Ebrey 1991a:87–90.
8. HH 2:35.
9. HH 5:118.
10. SCCC 7:150.
11. SHY hsüan-chü 12:38b–39a.
12. TSC 16:186; PCC 39:512; FJC 20:8a.
13. For other examples, see Kuo-li ku-kung 1973:19; J. Cahill 1960:53; Fong 1973:77.
14. Cf. Black 1986; Pao 1987; Anagnost 1989:319–22.
15. FJLF 1:1a–3b, chüan 4.
16. KCTSCC tse 395:11a.
17. CF 8:659–60.
18. HH 2:33.
19. ECC Chou I Ch'eng shih chuan 3:884.
20. Ibid., 977, 854, 864, 972, 982.
21. YSSF 1:5, 20; YSSF 3:5a; Ebrey 1984b:189–90, 224–25, 290–91.

22. Cf. Birge 1989; Mann 1991; Ebrey 1992b.
23. Cf. Fong 1973:29–36; Barnhart 1983:58–66. For other Sung paintings of women attending men, see Kuo-li ku-kung 1970:14; J. Cahill 1960:60; Speiser, Goepper, and Fribourg 1964:19; Ho et al. 1980:54; Ku-kung 1978:36. This last shows a T'ang emperor carried on a platform by a group of young women.
24. Hightower 1981:348, 350.
25. Huang 1988:141.
26. CL 4b, 9b; Ebrey 1991a:12, 26.
27. Cf. Ebrey 1991a:36–45.
28. Cf. the paintings cited in note 13.
29. Yü 1990.
30. LCCC 11.
31. Cf. Barmé 1992:119–30.
32. Cf. Dworkin 1974:95–116; Brownmiller 1984:33–34.
33. See Naka 1898; Chia 1925; Li Jung-mei 1936; Levy 1966; Chu 1986:141–45.
34. HJCYT 2:10a–b.
35. ChiehHC 14:7a.
36. MCML 8:89.
37. E.g. ICC i 3:206, chih-ching 2:892, san-jen 5:1505; SS 65:1430; Li-li Ch'en 1976: 25.
38. Chu 1986:144.
39. Ch'ü-chou 1983:1007.
40. Fu-chien 1982:8, 19, 83–84.
41. Chiang-hsi 1990. What is particularly notable about her case is that her body was also well preserved. The published photograph of it seems to show that the large toe on each foot bent upward, matching the shape of the shoes found in the other tombs and the literary description of bound feet as curving upward like new moons. Thus it seems that in Sung times referring to bound feet as "bowed" may have meant that the large toe was bent up, not down as in later periods. The width of the shoes, however, indicates that, as in later practice, the small toes must have been turned under.
42. SLSMCT 1:14; trans. in Levy 1966:47; HJCYT 2:10b; LCT 7b–8a; HPC 44:14b.
43. HCC 3a; CLC 20:273.
44. ChiaoCC 1:22a.
45. CYCY 1:1.
46. CKL 10:158. Levy 1966:38–40 mistakenly attributes all of these comments to Chang Pang-chi two centuries earlier.
47. See Workman 1976; Frankel 1976; Fusek 1982; Birrell 1985.
48. See Ortner and Whitehead 1981 for a review.
49. See Sanday and Goodenough 1990; Kondo 1990.
50. Mandelbaum 1988:43–53, 102–8.

2. MEANINGS OF MARRIAGE

1. LC 61:4b; cf. Legge 1885 2:428.
2. EY 4:19a. On marriage-related terminology, see also P'eng 1988:1–4, 26–36; and Ch'en P'eng 1990:1–5.
3. SWCTC 12B:10.

4. SWCTC 12B:9; Cheng Hsüan in LC 26:19a.
5. On legal aspects of marriage in China, see Lü 1935; T'ao [1935] 1966; Ch'en Ku-yüan [1936] 1978; Niida 1942:537–54; Shiga 1967:415–37; Ch'ü 1965: 91–127; McCreery 1976; Dull 1978; Tai 1978; Li Ao 1980:187–282; Meijer 1981; Ng 1987; Yüan 1988; Linck 1989; Ch'en P'eng 1990; Ocko 1990, 1991; Birge 1992.
6. SHT 13:14b.
7. SHT 13:15a.
8. SHT 13:16a.
9. SHT 13:13a.
10. CMC 9:349.
11. SHT 14:1b, 26:19a–b.
12. SHT 14:2a, 3a. Cf. LC 51:25a–b; Legge 1885 2:297–98.
13. SHT 14:1b.
14. CMC 4:107.
15. SHT 14:11b–12a, 14:6a.
16. SHT 14:6a–8a.
17. SHT 22:11b–12b, 23:8b.
18. SHT 26:18b–19a, 21a.
19. See D. L. Hsü 1970–71; K.-C. Liu 1990.
20. HH 2:33, 35, 4:81–82, 5:115–20, 6:161–64. See also Kelleher 1989.
21. CF 8:675–76, based on SuiS 80:1806.
22. See Ebrey 1991b; Linck 1989.
23. CL 28a–31b; Ebrey 1991a:89–95.
24. CTC 300.
25. CL 4b–5b, 50a–54b; Ebrey 1991a:12–17, 155–66.
26. These are found in such reference books as SLKC, HMCS, CCCC, CCCCK, and CSLPKS.
27. HLPY.
28. SC 1B:15b; Waley 1937:106; MT 3B.3; Legge 1893 2:268.
29. From TC 6:21a, 9:23b–24a; Legge 1893 5:47, 103; SC 16B:3b; Waley 1937:262.
30. SC 1E:2a–3b; Waley 1937:30.
31. See Frankel 1976:1–6; Neill 1982:103; Bickford 1985:47–49.
32. HMCS i 11:11b.
33. NanS 56:1397.
34. ChouL 14:16b.
35. LC 61:4b; Legge 1885 2:428.
36. IL 4:1a; Steele 1917 1:18.
37. TC 9:23b–24a; Legge 1893 5:103
38. TPKC 292:2325. Another version is in SouSC 11:137.
39. E.g. CHWHK ch'ien 18:6b; SLPY ch'ien 61:2b, 13b; HMCS i 4:9b; SYKS 1:28b.
40. PCWC 64:16a.
41. SC 18.4:8b (Legge 1893 4:549). See also SYKS 1:33b–34a.
42. IL 6:12a. Cf. Steele 1917 1:39.
43. WH 56:1225–26.
44. See ShihC 5:185–96, 39:1660–62; see also SC 6.4:10–11a; Legge 1893 4:203; SYKS 2:2a.

45. TPKC 159:1142–43. A slightly different version of this story is translated in Kao 1985:271–74.
46. E.g. CHWHK ch'ien 18:5b–6a; HLPY ch'ien 7:1a–b; CSLPKS 8:2a–b; SLPY 61:2a–b; HMCS i 4:2b; CCCC pieh 2:3a; SYKS 1:31a–32a.
47. PTL 9:114.
48. ChinS 31:962
49. WH 29:638; TTTP 36; TSLC 4.7, p. 5.
50. ICC pu 18:1720.
51. ICC ping 13:477. See also Ch'en P'eng 1990:16–20.
52. See Ebrey 1991b:45–144; R.-G. Chu 1989.

3. MAKING A MATCH

1. ECC wen-chi 12:653.
2. SWKWC 62:953.
3. SWKWC 62:951.
4. ECC wen-chi 11:640–41.
5. YSSF 1:19; Ebrey 1984b:222–23.
6. TKC 46:636.
7. Chaffee 1991.
8. ECC i-shu 1:7.
9. Said to be from Han Yü's account of Wang Shih's marriage. See CTW 564: 11a–12b.
10. E.g. CWCW 5:118.
11. SMSSI 3:29; YSSF 1:18–19; Ebrey 1984b:221–22.
12. HsiTC 14:223; CHC 5:42a–b; CCTS 22b–23a.
13. NCCIK 22:458.
14. PCC 39:512.
15. CHTC 23–24.
16. NCCIK 22:457.
17. WCC 31:3a–b.
18. HTHS 140:10b–11a (trans. 10b). Cf. Ebrey 1984c:433.
19. Ihara 1971; Hartwell 1982; Hymes 1986b; Bossler 1991.
20. A marriage was classed as a Northern Sung marriage if the husband was born before 1100.
21. CSC 14:205.
22. FHC 28:365; TYC 14:21b.
23. Ch'engCC 129:17b–18a.
24. Cf. Chang Pang-wei 1989:46–50.
25. Cf. Ch'en P'eng 1990:69–124.
26. SSCC 14:173–76, 15:190–91; PCC 39:512–13; OYHCC 22:159; LCC 36:9b. Cf. Aoyama 1965; Bossler 1991:183.
27. LHHS 168:2a–5b, 169:2a–6b, 170:4b–6b; FHC 24:282; K'ueiSC 32:1a–11b.
28. WCC 36:7b, 34:7a. Chou Pi-ta's uncle could not legally have proposed a match to his own daughter, since a man owed fourth degree mourning to his sister's children.

29. TYC 14:21b; TWTL 2:6–7.
30. FHHWC 22:4b; Ch'engCC 130:20a; SungSWC 20:9a–b.
31. AYC 48:8b; CSC 14:199, 205; KKC 109:1541–44; TLC 10:10b–11a; HPSJC 50: 7a–11a. For other examples of men marrying their dead wives' younger sisters, see FCHC 17:26b–27a; FHC 25:292, 301; WLCC 91:579; HCCS 40:11a. See also Bossler 1991:184.
32. CCCCK ping 3:4b–5a.
33. PHSC 3:11–12; cf. Waley 1941:157–58.
34. YSSF 1:19–20; Ebrey 1984b:223–24.
35. Tseng 1986:238.
36. HLPY ch'ien 7 and 8; cf. Chang Pang-wei 1989:145–64.
37. ICC chih-wu 2:1064; HLPY ch'ien 7:12b; SLYY 9:139; SS 298:9917; SKTP 3:8a.
38. FJC 20:7a–b, 26:14b–15a.
39. PCKT 1:16; ICC san-jen 4:1497, chih-chia 7:767.
40. Chaffee 1985:101–5; Umehara 1985:423–500; Chang Pang-wei 1986; Ebrey 1988, 1991d.
41. KKC 104:1468.
42. LC 51:24b (Legge 1885 2:297 omits this sentence).
43. TCMHL 4:30.
44. YSSF 1:19; Ebrey 1984b:223.
45. CPTSHS 13:43–46; Yang and Yang 1981:17–19.
46. Hajnal 1965; Wolf and Hanley 1985:1–12. See also Fang 1985:158–59.
47. E.g. Wolf and Huang 1980:134–35; Coale 1985.
48. See Hsü Hung 1989; T.-J. Liu 1985:23; Sa 1985:279–99; Gamble 1954:41–43; Telford 1992.
49. LC 28:20b–21b; Legge 1885 1:478–79; Niida 1937:548–51.
50. SMSSI 3:29; CL 17b; Ebrey 1991a:49; CWKWC 33:27b–28a.
51. CWCW 5:118; HCCS 40:9b; HTHS 140:10b–11a; MTC 26:15b–16b.
52. PHSC 2:23, 19.
53. ICC pu 3:1568–69; YSSF 3:55; Ebrey 1984b:298.
54. HMCS i 4:8a; Chang Pang-wei 1989:170–76; ICC chih-wu 1:1052.
55. CCPP 21:13b–16b; SSWCL 18:200.
56. CP (Ch ed.) 138:3325. Cf. HLPY ch'ien 8:1a–b.
57. SSWCL 18:193.
58. Cf. Chaffee 1985:11–12; Chang Pang-wei 1989:171–72.
59. WCC 30:10b–21b; LHWC 42:8a–10a; FJC 26:1a–7b; HTC 20:8b–10a; CWKWC 90:15a–16a, 93:13b–20a; KuanYC 18:8b–10a.
60. CLC 23:362. Cf. CLC 30:434–35.
61. See de Pee 1991:37–38.
62. Dudbridge 1978.
63. YSC 16:313.
64. ICC ting 4:564–65.
65. CTL 1615–17.
66. Cf. Li-li Ch'en 1976.
67. MKHH 4:2b–3a.
68. ICC pu 16:1698–99.

69. CMC 7:230–32;
70. CMC 12:441–42.

4. RITES AND CELEBRATIONS

1. TCMHL 5:30–32; MLL 20:304–7. Unless otherwise noted, the material in this chapter comes from one or the other of these two books. On Sung weddings, see also Ma 1981; Fang 1985; Chu Jui-hsi 1988; and Wu Pao-ch'i 1989.
2. CCCC pieh 2:5a; SLKC ch'ien-chi 10:5a.
3. MLL 20:304.
4. CL 18b; Ebrey 1991a:51–52.
5. MLL 20:305.
6. CWKWC 18:24b.
7. CI 7:18a; cf. Wilhelm 1967:306.
8. LC 2:13b; Legge 1885 1:78.
9. YSSF 1:20; Ebrey 1984b:224.
10. HLPY hou 1:16a–b.
11. SMSSI 3:33.
12. Mauss 1967; L. S. Yang 1957.
13. SHT 13:13a–14a; CMC 9:346–47, 5:144.
14. SMSSI 3:29; Ebrey 1991a:50.
15. SMCYHL wai 9:13a.
16. H. C. Chang 1973:32–47.
17. HLPY hou 12; HTHS 140:10b–11a.
18. CHWL 179:3a.
19. CL 19b; Ebrey 1991a:56; SMSSI 3:34.
20. CL 20a–b; Ebrey 1991a:57–58.
21. LC 18:16b, 26:20a; Legge 1885 1:322, 442.
22. CPTC 1:5.
23. CWKWC 18:24b–25a.
24. For some T'ang wedding songs preserved at Tunhuang, see Waley 1960:189–201.
25. CPTC 8:72.
26. CP (CH ed.) 10:230.
27. SLKC ch'ien-chi 10:6b.
28. SSYI 1:8; YYTT hsü 4:421.
29. SWCY 9:355.
30. Ebrey 1989:284.
31. SLKC ch'ien-chi 10:6a.
32. CCCCK ping 1:5b.
33. NCCIK 18:361.
34. SMSSI 3:36; CL 22a; Ebrey 1991a:63–64; cf. CTYL 89:2273–74.
35. SLKC ch'ien chi 10:8a.
36. SMSSI 3:36; ECC wen-chi 10:622; CTYL 89:2274.
37. Cf. Fang 1985:167–68.
38. HMCS i 18:5b–6a.
39. JCSP san 3:447–48; SYKS 2:17b.

40. SLKC ch'ien chi 10:8a.
41. ChuS 3:3a–b.
42. E.g. ECC i-shu 10:113.
43. SLKC ch'ien-chi 10:7b–8a.
44. CMC 5:144.
45. CL 21b–22a; Ebrey 1991a:63.
46. SSCW 3:52; KFWC 5:10a; CLP 3:91, 1:7.
47. See Martin C. Yang 1945:106–13; Freedman 1979:255–72; Ahern 1974; Cohen 1976:149–91; R. Watson 1981; Weller 1984.
48. SMSSI 3:34, 35, 37.
49. H. C. Chang 1973:42, 44.

5. DOWRIES

1. Cf. Ebrey 1991c.
2. STJC 8:4a–5b.
3. CMC 5:141, 13:502, 6:184, 5:140, 8:248.
4. ICC san-pu:1806.
5. SCPMHP 142:9b; ICC chih-ching 5:918; HLYL i 4:192; HSC 80:24a–b; KHTC hsü 2:166.
6. Fu-chien 1982:9, 81–82; cf. Sheng 1990:109–12.
7. ICC pu 10:1642.
8. E.g. HTHS 153:1a–b.
9. HTHS 157:3a.
10. ICC pu 3:1574–75.
11. Thatcher 1991:36–37; Yang Shu-ta 1933:17–19; Dull 1978:45–48; THY 83: 1528–29.
12. See Ebrey 1991d.
13. Twitchett 1960:9; SSCC 14:175; Ch'en P'eng 1990:141.
14. SWC 108:1439.
15. SMSSI 3:33.
16. SMSSI 3:29.
17. YSSF 2:39; Ebrey 1984b:266.
18. YSSF 1:19; Ebrey 1984b:223.
19. ChiehCC 21:357.
20. CLP 2:52.
21. CMC 5:140, 6:197–98.
22. SHY hsing-fa 2:154–55; CYIL 117:1889.
23. ECC wen-chi 4:504; SS 344:10927.
24. E.g. Hughes 1978; Harrell and Dickey 1985.
25. YSSF 1:20; Ebrey 1984b:224
26. E.g. Niida 1962:381–92; Shiga 1967:401–9, 447–49; Yüan 1988; Yanagida 1989. Birge 1992 is an exception.
27. SMSSI 4:42; cf. Legge 1885 1:458.
28. CF 2:488–89.
29. CSKI 3:35–38. For other cases of daughters of good families reduced to becoming concubines, see LCC 36:41b; SS 415:12452, 298:9906.

30. Cf. Yüan 1988:287–96. Birge 1992:105 et passim writes as though daughters were true coparceners, guaranteed a half-share even if married out during their parents' lifetime.
31. SHT 12:12b.
32. CMC 8:290; HTHS 193:7a, 14a; Burns 1973:259–81.
33. E.g. CMC 8:277–78, where it was used in a case in which the daughter was already married.
34. CMC 7:215.
35. CMC 8:280–82.
36. CMC 8:251–57; HTHS 193:10a–17b.
37. YSSF 1:20, 17; Ebrey 1984b:224, 218.
38. CMC 7:237–38.
39. Klapisch-Zuber 1985:118–21; Macfarlane 1986:272–73; Sharma 1980:49; Friedl 1967; Goody 1990.
40. CMC 4:115; WHTK 13:138–39; CMC 8:248–49, 9:319–21, 10:365–66, 13:501–3.
41. Ebrey 1984b:101–20; CMC 10:365, 5:140.
42. CMC 5:140, 9:315–17.
43. SS 460:13485.
44. Cf. Shiga 1978:120.
45. CMC 10:380–81.
46. KSC 53:646.
47. NCCIK 22:459; ChiehCC 21:354–55; YSC 14:263. See also Birge 1992: 205–35.
48. MTC 34:25a–b.
49. LeCC 28:14a; ICC chih-ching 5:918.
50. E.g. SS 299:9928.
51. CMC 8:288. Cf. CMC 7:215–17.
52. CMC 6:184–85.
53. CMC 9:349–51, 353–56.
54. CMC 7:230–32.
55. OYHCC 31:217–19; LCC 39:54b–57a.
56. SSCW 10:184; SSWCL 8:84; SLYY 10:150.
57. Cf. Comaroff 1980; R. Watson 1984.
58. Goody 1990. See also Goody 1973, 1976a, and 1976b.
59. Ebrey 1991b:45–67.
60. HH 5:117.
61. CMC fu-lu 2:603–4; MCC 33:31a–b. Cf. Birge 1992:239–51.
62. CMC fu-lu 2:606–8; MCC 33:34b–37a. Cf. Birge 1992:251–57.
63. Cf. Holmgren 1986; Birge 1992:263–70.

6. UPPER-CLASS WIVES AS INNER HELPERS

1. Cf. Bossler 1991:22–40.
2. Ebrey forthcoming.
3. Cf. Barnhart 1983:53–57.
4. FWCKC 12:11b; WHC 19:26a; CSC 14:205; CWKWC 91:14a; CHCCHC 22: 14b–15a.
5. Ch'engCC 129:12b–13a, 130:19b; ChuHC 12:17a.

6. PSC 31:17b.
7. HCCS 40:10b; TKC 46:633.
8. ChiehCC 21:354–55, 358; YSC 14:263, 25:509.
9. CLC 30:436, 440–41; ICC pu 16:1701–2; NCCIK 22:461. For Ch'ing examples of women managing family finances, see McDermott 1990.
10. PCSCS 103:23a–b.
11. PCC 39:512; HCCS 40:7a; HsienTC 10:3b.
12. AYC 48:5b; LCC 39:55b; FHHWC 22:5b; ChiehCC 21:357.
13. ChuHC 12:15a.
14. LHHS 170:9b–10a.
15. LHHS 170:12a–13b.
16. E.g. CWKWC 91:14a; YSC 14:249; HLWC 12:13a; Ch'engCC 130:20b; MengCC 18:259; FTSC 47:10b; HTHS 151:8a.
17. NCCIK 22:457.
18. TKC 45:610; WLCC 100:633; LHHS 170:9b, 13b (quotation 10b); ChiehCC 21:353; HTHS 156:1a–b.
19. CSC 14:205; CWKWC 91:14a; TKC 45:610–11.
20. PCP 4:26.
21. Cf. Weidner 1988; Hu 1985:40–69.
22. Hu 1985:41.
23. See Hu 1966; Rexroth and Chung 1979; L. Chung 1985.
24. LCCTL 1–25.
25. TKC 45:613; WLCC 100:635; LFWCC Wei-nan wen-chi 35:216.
26. Hu 1985:42. For an example of Miss Chu's songs, see Huang 1988:275–76.
27. CF 6:594–95; SMSSI 4:45; CTYL 7:127. Cf. Chan 1989:548–58.
28. ECC wen-chi 12:655.
29. HPSJC 50:10a–b. On women writers and artists in later periods, see Weidner et al. 1988; Rossabi 1989; Widmer 1989, 1992; Robertson 1992; Ko 1992.
30. KKC 103:1450; WHC 19:26a.
31. E.g. ICC chih-ting 8:1034, pu 9:1627.
32. TCCS 98; Ebrey 1981a:104.
33. ChiLC 64:19b.
34. CWC 60:813; PCSCS 103:23b–24a; SSWC 15:471.
35. TSC 16:186; PLC 14:205; Ch'ü-chou 1983.
36. TYC 14:22b.
37. FHHWC 22:6a.
38. YSC 13:233. On Ta-hui's relations with women believers, see Levering 1987.
39. HHWC 3:54b–55a; Ch'ienTC 16:32a.
40. CSC 14:200, 202; HIC 8:105; WHC 19:28a.
41. MTC 32:18a–b; YSC 14:263.
42. FTSC 39:4a; FHC 24:287; LHHS 170:12b.
43. CWKWC 92:14a; ChiehCC 21:353.
44. YSSF 3:58; Ebrey 1984b:304.
45. AYC 46:11b.
46. Cf. Birge 1989.
47. YSSF 1:12; Ebrey 1984b:206.
48. CMC 13:506.

7. WOMEN'S WORK MAKING CLOTH

1. LFC 3:7a–b.
2. LFWCC Wei-nan wen-chi 43:266; Chang and Smythe 1981:44; Tan 1978; LHC 1:17b.
3. Not uncommon elsewhere; see Weiner and Schneider 1989.
4. SMCC 48:615.
5. CWKWC 99:8a–b.
6. CMC 9:317.
7. Cf. WCNS 16:369–431.
8. Sheng 1990:55–59, 68–69.
9. Cf. Gates 1989.
10. Kuhn 1988:30–38; Sudō 1962:328.
11. Sudō 1962:341.
12. WCL 1:12b–13a.
13. See Kuhn 1988:60–236.
14. WCNS t'u-p'u 20:431; Kuhn 1988:76–77.
15. Kuhn 1988:201–2.
16. WCNS t'u-p'u 20:424–25.
17. Kuhn 1988: 39–57.
18. Kang Chao 1977:4–13; Hsia 1987:139–45; Liu and Ch'en 1987.
19. Kuhn 1988:188–96.
20. WCNS t'u-p'u 19:414.
21. TiehSC 3:1a.
22. YTC 24:2b (p. 1144).
23. WCNS t'u-p'u 19:415.
24. CKL 24:354.
25. WCNS t'u-p'u 19:417.
26. Kuhn 1988: 385–87, citing the work of Nunome Junrō in particular.
27. NS chüan 3; NSCY 3:31–4:72; WCNS t'ung-chüeh 6:66–71, t'u-p'u 16:369–19:414. Cf. Sheng 1990:8–10.
28. SPSC 1:2b.
29. WCNS t'u-p'u 17:395–96.
30. NS 3:7b–8a.
31. Kuhn 1988:336–45.
32. TS 2a–3b; Kuhn 1988:354–64.
33. TS 3b; WCNS t'u-p'u 16:369–74; Kuhn 1988:247–72.
34. ICC chih-ting 7:1023.
35. ICC chih-ching 7:935.
36. LWTT 6:64.
37. Kuhn 1988:1.
38. TanYC 3:12a.
39. CTCCC 12:13a.
40. On these rules, see Sheng 1990:119–21.
41. LHWC 7:2b.
42. WCNS t'u-p'u 20:427–28; LWTT 6:64.
43. NSCY 6:111–12.

44. CWKWC 18:24b; TCMHL 3:19; MLL 18:282; cf. Wu and T'ien 1986:198–200; Li Jen-p'u 1983:132–33.
45. See Ch'üan 1935.
46. Cf. Yanagida 1960.
47. Cf. Sheng 1990:71–113.
48. Sudō 1962:331–32.
49. Shiba 1968:274–76.
50. Sudō 1962:345–47.
51. ICC chih-kuei 5:1254.
52. SHY shih-huo 64:25b; Sheng 1990:142–45.
53. Chang Hsüeh-shu 1983:119–21; Li Jen-p'u 1983:129–32; Shiba 1968:278–85.
54. WuHC 20:5a; KSC 51:621; ICC i 17:325.
55. NS 3:4a–b; Hsia 1987:150.
56. SHCSSC 3:34; cf. Liu and Lo 1975:387–88.
57. Chang Hsüeh-shu 1983:115–18; SHY shih-huo 64:23b, 64:25b–26a; Li Jen-p'u 1983:123–24.
58. Chang Hsüeh-shu 1983:113, 118.
59. K.-Y. Lin 1986; Lin and Liu 1984; Chao Feng 1986. For a slightly later Freer version, a copy of the same original painting but more clearly reproduced, see Suzuki 1982 1:228–29. The Freer painting shows no babies. On these paintings, see also Needham and Wang 1965:166–69; Ho et al. 1980:78–80; Lawton 1973: 54–57.
60. ICC ting 7:590.
61. ICC pu 4:1580.
62. SHY shih-huo 64:17a.
63. E.g. SS 437:12951.
64. SS 460:13485; TLC 11:2a–b; SWKWC 62:955.
65. SS 460:13479; HTL 2:6b.
66. Cf. Sheng 1990.
67. TanYC 3:12a–b.
68. ChiehHC 25:9b.
69. Ch'ienSC 5:8a.
70. HLSK 19b–20a.

8. HUSBAND-WIFE RELATIONS

1. KCTSCC ts'e 395:11a.
2. See J. Murray 1990:125.
3. T.-J. Liu 1985:26; Cartier 1973:1345; Sa 1985:298.
4. HCCS 40:6b.
5. LKC 31:360.
6. HTHS 148:16a.
7. ChiehCC 21:357.
8. SMCC 78:968–69.
9. PCWC 77:11b.
10. OYHCC 36:251–52; SSWC 15:472; FJC 20:8b–11b; WCC 76:1b–2a.

11. Cf. Owen 1986:80–98.
12. LCCC 71–75. See also Hu 1966; Ching 1976; L. Chung 1985.
13. LCCC 11.
14. CLLL 27–28; Rexroth and Chung 1979:47.
15. ICC ping 14:482.
16. SCPMHP 142:9b.
17. ICC chih-ting 5:1008. Cf. ICC ting 9:610.
18. LeCC 28:10b.
19. See Liu Yung's songs in Hightower 1981, 1982.
20. Li-li Ch'en 1976.
21. Van Gulik 1961; Beurdeley et al. [1969] 1989:7–38; Needham and Lu 1983: 184–218; Harper 1987; Wile 1992.
22. Cf. Paul 1985:3–10; Bodde 1991:270–84.
23. Honig and Hershatter 1988:181–86; Kristof 1991.
24. FJLF 9:1b–2b, 4b–5b.
25. FJLF 10:1a–b.
26. FJLF 10:11a. For later ideas on conception and heredity, see Waltner 1990:28–47.
27. FJLF 9:14b–15b.
28. WLHPCH 3a–4a, 12a.
29. YenSC 33:12b; MTC 34:9a; ICC chia 11:92.
30. E.g. LCLC pieh 1:74.
31. CF 9:679.
32. ICC pu 14:1675–76.
33. JCSP san 3:447–48.
34. ICC pu 6:1608.
35. ICC chia 17:148–49, pu 22:1753–54; KCC 4:4a–5a.
36. ICC chih-ting 8:1029–30, 6:1012; YSSF 3:49–50; Ebrey 1984b:287–88.
37. ISHP 17:831–32; Djang and Djang 1989:666.
38. MC 1:14; SCPMHP 143:5a; ISHP 5:197, 16:771–72; Djang and Djang 1989: 229, 634.
39. KHTC hsü 2:209–10; ISHP 18:919–20; Djang and Djang 1989:721.
40. SS 252:8849.
41. CMC 10:381–82.
42. M. Wolf 1972:41.

9. MOTHERHOOD

1. LFC 12:11b–12a.
2. Cf. Furth 1986, 1987, and 1988 on this literature in later periods.
3. T'ungC 69:813; WSC; FJLF.
4. SSCC 14:178–79.
5. FJLF 16:3b, 17:2b.
6. FJLF 16:4a; ICC san-hsin 4:1416.
7. FJLF 17:3a–9a.
8. ICC chia 10:83.
9. ICC ting 19:696–97; i 15:311.

10. ICC pu 18:1715-16.
11. Sawada 1968:37-42. On pollution ideas in modern Taiwan, see Ahern 1975 and Seaman 1981.
12. FJLF 18:1a-2a, 26b-35a, 19:1a-8b.
13. PTC 90:8b-10a; HPSJC 50:7b-10b; CHC 5:42b-43a.
14. SSWCL 18:193.
15. SS 248:8771-90.
16. ICC pu 10:1640.
17. WSC 8:112.
18. E.g. ICC san-hsin 4:1417.
19. FJLF 24:9a-b.
20. FJLF 16:2a.
21. SSWC 15:473; SMSSI 4:44; YSSF 3:54-55; Ebrey 1984b:297-98.
22. ChiehCC 21:356-57.
23. ChiehHC 11:8b-9a.
24. KHTC hsü B:190. Cf. SS 46:891 on his not talking.
25. SSWCL 18:192; LSL 9:7b-8b.
26. ICC san-jen 2:1479, ting 5:573-74.
27. TSCH 14; HCL yü-hua 1:945; CTYY 6:103.
28. Cf. Eichorn 1976.
29. ChuS 1:21a-22a.
30. WeiCC 10:11b-13b.
31. ICC chih-keng 10:1214, chih-chia 6:757-58.
32. YSSF 1:15; Ebrey 1984b:213.
33. E.g. CKC 23:38b-41a, 44a-b; WuHC 8:7a-8a; CYIL 117:1889; CWKWC 27: 1a-2b. See also Imahori 1955.
34. See Lee 1984.
35. ECC wen-chi 12:653-55.
36. YSSF 1:5; Ebrey 1984b:189-90.
37. ChiehCC 21:353; HLWC 12:13a; LHHS 170:13b; CWKWC 92:13a.
38. NYC 30:1b-2a.

10. WIDOWHOOD

1. HCCS 35:13a-b.
2. HCCS 40:9a-b.
3. NCCIK 18:370.
4. Cf. Holmgren 1985; Liu Li-yen 1991.
5. WLC fu-lu 405-7; SWKWC 62:951; CWKWC 92:13b.
6. TaoHC 37:12b; HTHS 149:12a; CWKWC 90:13b. See also CLC 30:436.
7. See Yüan 1988:296-307.
8. SHY hsing-fa 4:70a-b.
9. THPL 11:83-84.
10. ChiLC 68:7b-8a.
11. YSSF 1:18; Ebrey 1984b:221; CMC 6:191-92.

12. CMC 13:504.
13. CMC 8:269–70.
14. CMC 7:214.
15. CMC 7:217–23.
16. CMC 8:246, 7:211–12.
17. CMC 8:250.
18. CMC 7:229–30.
19. CMC 8:258–59.
20. CMC 8:291–92.
21. Cf. Liu Li-yen 1991.
22. LC 26:19a; cf. Legge 1885 1:439.
23. CWTTT 5:1390.
24. SC 3A:1a–3a; Waley 1937:53.
25. LNC 4:8b, 9a, 5:5b; O'Hara 1945:122, 123, 139; KCTSCC ts'e 395:9a; Swann 1932:87; Holmgren 1981, 1981–83.
26. KCTSCC ts'e 395:11a.
27. KCTSCC ts'e 395:10a.
28. E.g. CMC 7:217–18.
29. SHY li 61:4a–b.
30. SS 437:12951.
31. SHY li 61:1a–15a. See also Elvin 1984:115–18.
32. WLCC 99:631.
33. KKC 105:1486–89.
34. ICC pu 1:1554–55.
35. Cf. Elvin 1984:118–20 on Confucian miracles.
36. HCWC 27:4a–7b. For other examples, see SS 460:13485; Davis 1986:37, 40.
37. CF 8:622.
38. E.g. CF 8:665–68. For an example among his own relatives, see SMCC 79: 980–81.
39. E.g. CF 8:665–66, 671–72, 672–73, 674–75, 676–77.
40. CF 8:676–77.
41. ECC i-shu 22B:301.
42. CWKWC 26:28b–29a.
43. See Ropp 1976; Hsieh and Spence 1980; Waltner 1981; Elvin 1984; Holmgren 1985; Mann 1985, 1987; T'ien 1988; Tao 1991.
44. YSSF 1:18; Ebrey 1984b:220; CMC 9:301–2, 10:364. See also CMC 8:284.
45. ICC ting 9:613–14.
46. HTHS 153:1b.
47. HTHS 160:2b–4a.
48. HTHS 158:11a–12a, 160:2b–3a, 4a–b.
49. HTHS 153:1b.
50. HTHS 5:16b–17a, 153:2b–3b; HTT 64–65.
51. HTHS 76:3a–5a, 153:3a, 6a, 157:3a–b; Chang Ch'üan 1934–35:16. See also Ebrey 1984c.
52. Cf. Sangren 1983.

11. SECOND MARRIAGES

1. CMC 9:344.
2. SSWC 35:1009–10; CP (SC ed.) 484:19b–20b.
3. Chang Pang-wei 1989:68–72, though some of his cases are of extramarital affairs rather than remarriages; de Pee 1991:74 counts thirty-three.
4. CCCCK ping 3:22b.
5. E.g. HLPY hou 10:4b–6b.
6. SSCW 10:184; SS 314:10267, 456:13397, 349:11051; HTHS 154:10a.
7. TaoHC 37:10a, CYIL 120:1938; HPHS 20:18a; Liu Li-yen 1991:46.
8. SS 282:9555; ECC wai-shu 11:413; CYIL 140:2254; HTHS 149:11b–12a.
9. HCCS 40:9b; YSC 15:291; MTC 33:27a; CSCSC 14:36a; HTHS 156:16a; KHTC pieh A:244. For more examples, see T'ang 1986.
10. CMC 9:349–51, 353–56, 10:377–79, 12:443, fu-lu 602–3.
11. KCC 4:4a–5a; ICC i 15:311, ping 14:482, ting 7:591, ting 18:689, chih-chia 5:744.
12. Ching 1976; Rexroth and Chung 1979:92–93.
13. NCCIK 22:462–63.
14. CP (CH ed.) 56:1225–26; SS 243:8630–31.
15. SWKWC 62:951; NCCIK 22:460–61; PSWC 15:188; FHC 28:363–64.
16. Ch'ü-chou 1983:1009–11.
17. CP (SC ed.) 190:20a.
18. CP (CH ed.) 158:3836.
19. HPHS 20:18a.
20. HuaiHC 36:247–48.
21. AYC 49:2a.
22. YHCH 2:21.
23. KuHTC 34b.
24. ISHP 14:676–77; Djang and Djang 1989:534–35.
25. ICC chia 2:15–16.
26. ICC san-hsin 9:1454.
27. ICC chih-chia 4:744.
28. ECC wai-shu 11:413.
29. SSWCL 16:177–78.
30. CMC 4:124–26, 7:242–43, 8:274–75, 10:375–76; YSSF 1:17; Ebrey 1984b:217.
31. Even then, she was not getting full ownership, only rights to use the property, for judges cited a law that "any widow without children or grandchildren who on her own authority pawns or sells land or houses is subject to a beating of one hundred blows and the property is returned to its owner" (SHT 12:12b; CMC 9:304). In other words, all a childless widow could do was live off family income, preserving it for those who would receive it according to the law on broken lines after she died.
32. YSSF 1:9; Ebrey 1984b:200; ICC chia 2:15–16; SS 282:9555; CMC 10:365–66. Cf. Yanagida 1989; Birge 1992:151–63.
33. CMC 5:141; see also Huang Kan's ruling discussed at the end of Chapter 5.
34. ICC san-hsin 2:1399.
35. CMC 6:177.
36. CMC 8:273.

37. LYCS 5:8a–b; CMC 8:294; CP (SC ed.) 291:12b, 471:10a.
38. ICC chih-chia 8:772–73.
39. Chaves 1976:154–58.
40. WLHSC 10:16a; Chaves 1976:147.
41. WLHSC 24:12a–b; Chaves 1976:150–51.
42. Chaves 1976:158.
43. YSSF 1:17; Ebrey 1984b:219.
44. CTC 298. Cf. ECC i-shu 22B:303.
45. ICC chia 16:143–44.
46. CF 3:505.
47. ICC chia 2:11–12.
48. LSL 6:12b–13a.
49. CMC 5:141–42.
50. CMC 10:365–66.
51. YSSF 1:17; Ebrey 1984b:219.

12. CONCUBINES

1. Ch'en P'eng 1990:667–736.
2. Cf. Wagner 1984:80–91.
3. Cf. Sheieh 1992:134–66.
4. SHT 21:2a, 22:4b, 7a.
5. SHT 13:15a–16a.
6. SHT 26:18b–19a.
7. SHT 26:21a.
8. KCML 1b; LCLC pieh 74; HACM 3:1b–2a.
9. CTYY 16:294–95; Lo 1971:121; CYTC 23.
10. CMC 14:525–27. On government courtesans, see Ch'en Tung-yüan 1928:96–102.
11. KHTC pieh 1:244–45; CTYY 20:374–76.
12. On this market in later centuries, see Gronewold 1982; Hershatter 1991; R. Watson 1991; Sheieh 1992:82–98.
13. MLL 19:301–2.
14. CHTL 5.
15. YKML 6a–7b.
16. HLYL 4:192; SS 415:12452; CTL 1612; TIHY 13a–b.
17. CKL 7:110–11.
18. ICC pu 8:1620–21.
19. ISHP 11:510; HTHS 158:14a.
20. YSC 22:432; THPL 12:90; TSC 16:177.
21. Cf. Jaschok 1988 for modern examples.
22. LSL 4:8a–b.
23. E.g. ICC chia 13:115.
24. YSSF 3:55–56; Ebrey 1984b:299–300.
25. ICC ping 15:491, ting 11:632, pu 3:1566–67, pu 22:1754–55.
26. JCSP ssu 7:699–700.
27. CMC 7:232–33.

28. KHTC pieh B:272–74. Inflation probably accounts for her wages being higher than the prices cited by Hung Mai; see Ch'üan 1964.
29. TIHY 13a–b.
30. CHTL 5.
31. ICC pu 3:1566–67.
32. K. Chao 1986:218.
33. Assuming 20 *mu* and figures for average rents and prices of rice given in Liang 1984:146–47, 239–46.
34. E.g. SS 415:12452.
35. ICC chih-i 10:869.
36. E.g. ICC chih-hsü 10:1131.
37. ISHP 18:919; Djang and Djang 1989:721.
38. ICC chia 13:115.
39. ICC pu 22:1753–54.
40. SSC 39:7a (p. 8075).
41. ICC pu 8:1624–25, ting 11:631–32; LSL 6:6a.
42. Hsieh Tao-yün (4th cent.) and Pan Chao (ca. 48–ca. 120).
43. ChiehHC 11:7a–8a.
44. SSWC 15:473.
45. E.g. CMC 12:442–44; ICC pu 10:1641; FJC 20:11a–b.
46. MKHH 8:2b–3a.
47. E.g. HouCL 7:67; LCYH 5:25.
48. LCLC 4:20; SS 247:8749; ICC pu 8:1621–23.
49. E.g. CMC 8:251.
50. E.g. ICC chia 17:148, i 19:347, chih-ting 2:978–99, san-chi 6:1346, pu 22:1753–54.
51. SSHY 6:59a.
52. ISHP 5:186–89; YSSF 3:50; Ebrey 1984b:288; THPL 7:48.
53. HCL hou 7:551–52.
54. HTHS 161:10a–b.
55. Cf. Ebrey 1986a.
56. KHTC pieh B:272–74.
57. CYTF 77:4a–15b.
58. Ebrey 1986a:4–5.
59. NWFC 3:4b.
60. HTHS 193:11b.
61. LFC 12:12a.
62. AYC 46:11a–12b.
63. ICC pu 10:1641.
64. CF 7:643.
65. AYC 46:12a.
66. CLC 28:414–15; MTC 26:20b–23a.
67. CP (CH ed.) 211:5121, 213:5173–74, 217:5272–73; LHAPC 1:4; TTSL 98:4b–5a.
68. CP (CH ed.) 212:5143.
69. SS 456:13405. See also WLCC 31:174; SWKWC 3:31; SSWC 22:643–44.
70. CP (CH ed.) 212:5143–44.
71. SHT 14:3a; ICC ping 15:491.
72. ICC san-chi 6:1346–47.

73. SS 412:12381–82.
74. YSC 22:432–33.
75. CMC 7:230–32.
76. E.g. CMC 7:211–12.
77. CMC 7:238–39.
78. CMC 7:232–33, 8:268.
79. TCC 8:22b; KHTC pieh A:249–52.

13. CONTINUING THE FAMILY THROUGH WOMEN

1. KYC 19:10a.
2. MLL 20:304; HLPY hou 8:8b–11a; PTC 82:4b, 11a–b, 14a–b, 83:3b–4b.
3. E.g. ICC ping 13:474, ping 16:504, san-jen 4:1496, san-jen 6:1513, san-jen 10: 1544, pu 5:1588–89, pu 16:1702.
4. ICC san-jen 4:1496.
5. ICC san-jen 10:1544.
6. SS 293:9802.
7. SSWCL 9:94; NCCIK 21:442.
8. CP (CH ed.) 31:705; SHY hsing-fa 2:4a; YYFTC 17a–b; SS 437:12954.
9. Von Glahn 1987:162–63.
10. KSCC 4:11a–13b.
11. SHSWC 10:183–84.
12. YYC 5:73–77, 16:243.
13. SHSWC 46:812.
14. YSSF 1:20; Ebrey 1984b:224; CWKWC 30:17a–b; Chan 1986:150–52.
15. CMC 9:316; CYC 14:148.
16. SHT 12:13b–14b.
17. See Ebrey 1992a.
18. CMC 6:177.
19. Cf. SS 293:9802.
20. CMC 8:277–78.
21. CMC 7:236–37.
22. CMC 7:215.
23. CMC 7:216.
24. CMC 7:217.
25. CMC 7:215–17.
26. CMC 7:205–6.
27. Cf. Ebrey 1986b.
28. See Waltner 1990:94–97 for Ming examples.
29. SHT 12:8b; CMC 8:245, 246–47, translated in Ebrey 1984a:234.
30. HSC 72:17b; CMC 7:225–26; MCLH 25:3a; WKCC 1:13.
31. YYC 5:80.
32. CMC 7:201. Cf. CMC 8:269–70, where a judge upheld adoption of a boy from the wife's family when agnatic relatives tried to get their own sons established thirty years later.
33. E.g. CMC 7:225.
34. CMC 7:217–22.

35. WKCC 1:12.
36. CMC 7:205.
37. Cf. Ebrey 1984a.

14. ADULTERY, INCEST, AND DIVORCE

1. SHT 26:18b, 21a.
2. CLP 2:58.
3. E.g. ICC chih-ting 9:1037–38, ting 19:694–95, pu 5:1590, chih-kuei 4:1252. See also de Pee 1991:60–65.
4. CMC 12:448–49.
5. CMC 12:446–47.
6. SHT 26:19a–20a.
7. SHT 1:6b.
8. LCLC 4:20.
9. SC 2C:14b–16a; Legge 1893 4:70.
10. CMC 10:388.
11. CMC 10:387–88.
12. CMC 10:388–89.
13. CMC 9:343.
14. James T. C. Liu 1967:65–67, 80–81; CP (CH ed.) 209:5078–79.
15. ICC chih-chia 5:746–47.
16. LFWCC Wei-nan wen-chi 49:305; B. Watson 1973:26–27.
17. E.g. CMC 9:345–46, 353, 13:499.
18. Niida 1942:696–97, transcribing Pelliot 3220. See also Niida 1962:586–97.
19. Cf. CMC 9:352; Ch'en P'eng 1990:539–40.
20. Cf. Tai 1978.
21. ICC ping 14:484–85.
22. CMC 10:380–81.
23. CF 5:575, 7:656–57, 3:525–26.
24. Cf. HHS 29:101
25. ECC i-shu 18:243.
26. ICC chih-ting 9:1036.
27. ICC san-pu 1806. For other examples, see de Pee 1991:69–73.
28. CF 7:657.
29. ICC chih-ting 1:974.
30. ICC san-jen 2:1482–83.
31. CP (CH ed.) 31:705.
32. CMC 9:345; SHT 14:7a–8a; SYTC 10.
33. WCC 36:19a; ICC ting 9:610, san-jen 7:1519.
34. Rexroth and Chung 1979:92–93.
35. CP (SC ed.) 294:9a–b; CMC 10:379, 382–83. For other examples of the woman's side initiating divorce, see Chang Pang-wei 1989:78–79.
36. CMC 10:379–80, 12:449–50.
37. CMC 4:107.
38. Cf. Lerner 1986:100–122.

SOURCES CITED

CHINESE PRIMARY SOURCES

AYC *An-yang chi* 安陽集, 50 ch., by Han Ch'i 韓琦 (1008–75). Ssu-k'u ch'üan-shu ed.

CCCC *Hsin-pien shih-wen lei-yao ch'i-cha ch'ing-ch'ien* 新編事文類要啟箚青錢, 51 ch. (Yüan). Tokyo: Koten kenkyūkai facsimile reprint of 1324 ed., 1963.

CCCCK *Hsin-pien t'ung-yung ch'i-cha chieh-chiang kang* 新編通用啟箚載江綱, 68 ch., ed. Hsiung Hui-chung 熊晦仲 (Sung). Sung ed. of Seikadō Library.

CCPP *Ching-ch'uan pai-pien* 荊川稗編, 120 ch., ed. T'ang Shun-chih 唐順之 (1507–60). Ssu-k'u ch'üan-shu ed.

CCTS *Chih-ch'ing tsa-shuo* 摭青雜説, 1 ch., anon. In *Shuo-fu* 説郛, 100 ch., ed. T'ao Tsung-i 陶宗儀 (fl. 1360–68), ch. 37. Shanghai: Commercial Press, 1927.

CF *Chia-fan* 家範, 10 ch., by Ssu-ma Kuang 司馬光 (1019–86). Chung-kuo tzu-hsüeh ming-chu chi-ch'eng ed.

CHC *Ch'ing-ho chi* 清河集, 7 ch.+1, by Yüan Ming-shan 元明善 (1269–1322). In *Ou-hsiang ling-shih* 藕香零拾, ed. Miao Ch'üan-sun 繆荃孫 (1844–1919). Taipei: Kuang-wen shu-chü reprint of late-19th-cent. ed., 1968.

CHCCHC *Chu-hsi chüan-chai shih-i kao hsü-chi* 竹溪鬳齋十一藁續集, 30 ch., by Lin Hsi-i 林希逸. Ssu-k'u ch'üan-shu ed.

Ch'engCC *Ch'eng-chai chi* 誠齋集, 133 ch., by Yang Wan-li 楊萬里 (1127–1206). Ssu-pu ts'ung-k'an ed.

ChiaoCC *Chiao-ch'i chi* 腳氣集, 2 ch., by Ch'e Jo-shui 車若水 (13th cent.). Pai-pu ts'ung-shu chi-ch'eng ed.

ChiehCC *Chieh-chai chi* 絜齋集, 24 ch., by Yüan Hsieh 袁燮 (1144–1224). Ts'ung-shu chi-ch'eng ed.

ChiehHC *Chieh-hsiao chi* 節孝集, 32 ch., by Hsü Chi 徐積 (1028–1103). Ssu-k'u ch'üan-shu ed.

Ch'ienSC *Ch'ien-shan chi* 潛山集, 12 ch., by Wen-hsiang 文珦 (1210–after 1276). Ssu-k'u ch'üan-shu ed.

Ch'ienTC *Ch'ien-t'ang chi* 錢塘集, 12 ch., by Wei Hsiang 韋驤 (1033–1105). In *Wu-lin wang-che i-chu* 武林往哲遺著. Taipei, 1971.

ChiLC *Chi-le chi* 雞肋集, 70 ch., by Ch'ao Pu-chih 晁補之 (1053–1110). Ssu-pu ts'ung-k'an ed.

ChinS *Chin shu* 晉書, 130 ch., by Fang Hsüan-ling 房玄齡 (578–648) et al. Peking: Chung-hua shu-chü, 1974.

ChouL *Chou li* 周禮, 42 ch. In *Shih-san ching chu-shu* 十三經注疏. Taipei: I-wen yin-shu-kuan reprint of 1821 ed., 1981.

CHTC *Ch'ing-hsiang tsa-chi* 青箱雜記, 1 ch., by Wu Ch'u-hou 吳處厚. In *Chiu hsiao-shuo* 舊小説 ting 2. Kuo-hsüeh chi-pen ts'ung-shu ed.

CHTL *Chiang-hsing tsa-lu* 江行雜錄, by Liao Ying-chung 廖瑩中 (Sung). Ts'ung-shu chi-ch'eng ed.

ChuHC *Chu-hu chi* 燭湖集, 20 ch.+2, by Sun Ying-shih 孫應時 (1154–1206). Ssu-k'u ch'üan-shu ed.

ChuS *Chu-shih* 麈史, 3 ch., by Wang Te-ch'en 王得臣 (c.s. 1059). Pi-chi hsiao-shuo ta-kuan, ser. 6 ed.

CHWHK *Chin-hsiu wan-hua-ku* 錦繡萬花谷, anon., preface 1185. Taipei: Hsin-hsing shu-chü, 1969.

CHWL *Cheng-ho wu-li hsin-i* 政和五禮新儀, 201 ch.+17, ed. Cheng Chü-chung 鄭居中 (1059–1123) et al. Ssu-k'u ch'üan-shu ed.

CI *Chou-i* 周易, 9 ch. In *Shih-san ching chu-shu* 十三經注疏. Taipei: I-wen yin-shu-kuan reprint of 1821 eds., 1981.

CKC *Chien-k'ang chih* 建康志, 50 ch., by Chou Ying-ho 周應合 (1213–80). Sung-Yüan ti-fang chih ts'ung-shu ed. Taipei: Kuo-t'ai wen-hua shih-yeh, 1980 reprint.

CKL *Cho-keng lu* 輟耕錄, 30 ch., by T'ao Tsung-i 陶宗儀 (fl. 1300–68). Ts'ung-shu chi-ch'eng ed.

CL *Chia-li* 家禮, 1 ch., by Chu Hsi 朱熹 (1130–1200). In *Chu Tzu ch'eng-shu* 朱子成書, 1341 ed. (Reproduced in Ebrey 1991a.)

CLC *Ch'en Liang chi* 陳亮集, 30 ch., by Ch'en Liang 陳亮 (1143–94). Peking: Chung-hua shu-shü, 1974.

CLP *Chi-le pien* 雞肋編, 3 ch., by Chuang Ch'o 莊綽 (ca. 1090–ca. 1150). Ts'ung-shu chi-ch'eng ed.

CMC *Ming-kung shu-p'an ch'ing-ming chi* 名公書判清明集, 14 ch., anon. Peking: Chung-hua shu-chü, 1987.

CP (CH ed.) *Hsü tzu-chih t'ung-chien ch'ang-pien* 續資治通鑑長編, 520 ch., by Li T'ao 李燾 (1115–84). Peking: Chung-hua shu-chü, 1985.

CP (SC ed.) *Hsü tzu-chih t'ung-chien ch'ang-pien* 續資治通鑑長編, 600 ch., by Li T'ao 李燾 (1115–84). Taipei: Shih-chieh shu-chü, 1961.

CPTC *Ch'ing-po tsa-chih* 清波雜志, 12 ch., by Chou Hui 周煇 (1127–after 1198). Ts'ung-shu chi-ch'eng ed.

CPTSHS *Ching-pen t'ung-su hsiao-shuo* 京本通俗小説, anon. Shanghai: Chung-kuo ku-tien wen-hsüeh ch'u-pan-she, 1954 ed.

CSC *Chung-su chi* 忠肅集, 20 ch., by Liu Chih 劉摯 (1014–81). Ts'ung-shu chi-ch'eng ed.

CSCSC *Chiang-su chin-shih chih* 江蘇金石志, 24 ch., anon. Shih-k'o shih-liao hsin-pien ed. Taipei: Hsin-wen-feng, 1977.

CSKI *Ch'ing-so kao-i* 青瑣高議, 10 ch.+8, by Liu Fu 劉斧 (1040–after 1113). Shanghai: Shang-hai ku-chi ch'u-pan-she, Sung-Yüan pi-chi ts'ung-shu, 1983.

CSL *Chin-shih lu* 金石錄, 60 ch., by Chao Ming-ch'eng 趙明誠 (1081–1129). Shih-k'o shih-liao hsin-pien ed. Taipei: Hsin-wen-feng, 1977.

CSLPKS *Ch'ün-shu lei-pien ku-shih* 群書類編故事, 24 ch., ed. Wang Ying 王鎣 (Yüan). Taipei: Commercial Press reprint of Wan-wei pieh-ts'ang ed.

CTC *Chang Tsai chi* 張載集, by Chang Tsai 張載 (1020–77). Peking: Chung-hua shu-chü, 1978.

CTCCC *Chia-ting Chen-chiang chih* 嘉定鎮江志, 22 ch., by Lu Hsien 盧憲 (early 13th cent.). Sung-Yüan ti-fang chih ts'ung-shu ed. Taipei: Kuo-t'ai wen-hua shih-yeh, 1980 reprint.

CTL *Ch'ing-tsun lu* 清尊錄, 1 ch., by Lien Hsüan 廉宣 (Sung). Pi-chi hsiao-shuo ta-kuan, ser. 5 ed.

CTW *Ch'üan T'ang Wen* 全唐文, 1,000 ch., ed. Tung Kao 董誥 (1740–1818) et al. Tainan, Taiwan: Ching-wei shu-chü reprint of 1814 ed., 1965.

CTYL *Chu Tzu yü-lei* 朱子語類, 140 ch. (1270), by Chu Hsi 朱熹 (1130–1200). Peking: Chung-hua shu-chü, 1986.

CTYY *Ch'i-tung yeh-yü*, 齊東野語, 20 ch., by Chou Mi 周密 (1232–1308). Peking: Chung-hua shu-chü, T'ang-Sung shih-liao pi-chi ts'ung-k'an, 1983.

CWC *Ching-wen chi* 景文集, 62 ch., by Sung Ch'i 宋祁 (998–1061). Ts'ung-shu chi-ch'eng ed.

CWCW *Chung-wu chi-wen* 中吳紀聞, 6 ch., by Kung Ming-chih 龔明之 (1091–1182). Shanghai: Shang-hai ku-chi ch'u-pan-she, 1986.

CWKWC *Chu Wen-kung wen-chi* 朱文公文集, 100 ch., by Chu Hsi 朱熹 (1130–1200). Ssu-pu ts'ung-k'an ed.

CWTTT *Chung-wen ta tz'u-tien* 中文大辭典, 10 vols., ed. Chang Ch'i-yün 張其昀 et al. Rev. ed. Taipei: Chung-hua hsüeh-shu yüan, 1973.

CYC *Chia-yu chi* 嘉祐集, 15 ch., by Su Hsün 蘇洵 (1009–66). Kuo-hsüeh chi-pen ts'ung-shu ed.

CYCY *Chan-yüan ching-yü* 湛淵靜語, 2 ch., by Po T'ing 白珽 (1248–1328). Ts'ung-shu chi-ch'eng ed.

CYIL *Chien-yen i-lai hsi-nien yao lu* 建炎以來繫年要錄, 200 ch., by Li Hsin-ch'uan 李心傳 (1166–1243). Ts'ung-shu chi-ch'eng ed.

CYTC *Ch'ing-yüan tang-chin* 慶元黨禁, 1 ch., anon. Ts'ung-shu chi-ch'eng ed.

CYTF *Ch'ing-yüan t'iao-fa shih-lei* 慶元條法事類, 80 ch., by Hsieh Shen-fu 謝深甫 (12th cent.). Taipei: Hsin-wen-feng reprint of Seikadō Sung ms. copy, 1976.

ECC *Erh Ch'eng chi* 二程集, 25 ch., by Ch'eng Hao 程顥 (1032–85) and Ch'eng I 程頤 (1033–1107). Peking: Chung-hua shu-chü, 1981.

EY *Erh-ya* 爾雅, 10 ch. In *Shih-san ching chu-shu* 十三經注疏. Taipei: I-wen yin-shu-kuan reprint of 1821 ed., 1981.

FCHC *Fan Chung-hsüan chi* 范忠宣集, 18 ch.+5, by Fan Ch'un-jen 范純仁 (1027–1101). Ssu-k'u ch'üan-shu ed.

FHC *Fou-hsi chi* 浮溪集, 32 ch., by Wang Tsao 汪藻 (1079–1154). Ts'ung-shu chi-ch'eng ed.

FHHWC *Fan Hsiang-hsi hsien-sheng wen-chi* 范香溪先生文集, 22 ch., by Fan Chün 范浚 (1102–50). Ssu-pu ts'ung-k'an ed.

FJC *Fei-jan chi* 斐然集, 30 ch., by Hu Yin 胡寅 (1098–1156). Ssu-k'u ch'üan-shu ed.

FJLF *Fu-jen ta-ch'üan liang-fang* 婦人大全良方, 24 ch.+3, by Ch'en Tzu-ming 陳自明 (fl. 1237). Ssu-k'u ch'üan-shu ed.

FTSC *Fan T'ai-shih chi* 范太史集, 55 ch., by Fan Tsu-yü 范祖禹 (1041–98). Ssu-k'u ch'üan-shu ed.

FWCKC *Fan Wen-cheng kung chi* 范文正公集, 20 ch., by Fan Chung-yen 范仲淹 (989–1052). Ssu-pu ts'ung-k'an ed.

HACM *Hua-an chüeh-miao tz'u-hsüan* 花庵絕妙詞選, 10 ch., by Huang Sheng 黃昇 (d. after 1245). In *Chi-ku-ko tz'u-yüan ying-hua* 汲古閣詞苑英華, ed. Mao Chin 毛晉 (1598–1659). Chi-ku-ko ed.

HCC *Hsiu-chung chin* 袖中錦, 1 ch., by T'ai-p'ing lao-jen 太平老人 (pen-name, 12th cent.). Pai-pu ts'ung-shu chi-ch'eng ed.

HCCS *Hung-ch'ing chü-shih wen-chi* 鴻慶居士文集, 42 ch., by Sun Ti 孫覿 (1081–1169). In *Ch'ang-chou hsien-che i-shu* 常州先哲遺書, ed. Sheng Hsüan-huai 盛宣懷 (1849–1916). Taipei, facsimile reprint of 1895 ed., 1971.

HCL *Hui-chu lu* 揮麈錄, 4 ch., by Wang Ming-ch'ing 王明清 (1127–after 1214). Ts'ung-shu chi-ch'eng ed.

HCWC *Hsün-chai wen-chi* 巽齋文集, 27 ch., by Ou-yang Shou-tao 歐陽守道 (1209–after 1267). Ssu-k'u ch'üan-shu ed.

HH *Hsiao-hsüeh chi-chieh* 小學集解, 6 ch., by Chu Hsi 朱熹 (1130–1200), *chi-chieh* by Chang Po-hsing 張伯行 (1651–1725). Ts'ung-shu chi-ch'eng ed.

HHS *Hou Han shu* 後漢書, 120 ch., by Fan Yeh 范曄 (398–445). Peking: Chung-hua shu-chü, 1971.

HHWC *Hsi-hsi wen-chi* 西溪文集, 10 ch., by Shen Kou 沈遘 (1025–67). In *Shen-shih san hsien-sheng wen-chi* 沈氏三先生文集, 61 ch. Ssu-pu ts'ung-k'an ed.

HIC *Hsüeh-i chi* 學易集, 8 ch., by Liu Ch'i 劉跂 (d. 1117). Ts'ung-shu chi-ch'eng ed.

HJCYT *Hao-jan chai ya-t'an* 浩然齋雅談, 3 ch., by Chou Mi 周密 (1232–1308). Ssu-k'u ch'üan-shu ed.

HLPY *Hsin-pien hun-li pei-yung yüeh-lao hsin-shu* 新編婚禮備用月老新書, 24 ch., anon. National Central Library microfilm of Sung ed.

HLSK *Hsi-lu shih-kao* 西麓詩藁, 1 ch., by Ch'en Yün-p'ing 陳允平 (13th cent.). In *Liang-Sung ming-hsien hsiao-chi* 兩宋名賢小集, 380 ch., ed. Ch'en Ssu 陳思 (Sung) and Ch'en Shih-lung 陳世隆 (Yüan), ch. 315. Ssu-k'u ch'üan-shu ed.

HLWC *Hsiang-ling wen-chi* 襄陵文集, 12 ch., by Hsü Han 許翰. Ssu-k'u ch'üan-shu ed.

HLYL *Ho-lin yü-lu* 鶴林玉露, 16 ch., by Lo Ta-ching 羅大經 (d. after 1248). Peking: Chung-hua shu-chü, 1983.

HMCS *Hsin-pien shih-wen lei-chü han-mo ch'üan-shu* 新編事文類聚翰墨全書, by Liu Ying-li 劉應李 (d. 1311). 1307 ed.

HNHS *Ho-nan hsien-sheng wen-chi* 河南先生文集, 27 ch., by Yin Chu 尹洙 (1001–46). Ssu-pu ts'ung-k'an ed.

HouCL *Hou-ch'ing lu* 侯鯖錄, 8 ch., by Chao Ling-chih 趙令時 (ca. 1051–1134). Ts'ung-shu chi-ch'eng ed.

HPC *Hsüeh-p'o chi* 雪坡集, 50 ch., by Yao Mien 姚勉 (1216–62). Ssu-k'u ch'üan-shu ed.

HPHS *Heng-p'u hsien-sheng wen-chi* 橫浦先生文集, 20 ch., by Chang Chiu-ch'eng 張九成 (1092–1159). Facsimile reprint of Ming ed., 1925.

HPSJC *Hsüeh-p'o she-jen chi* 雪坡舍人集, 50 ch.+1, by Yao Mien 姚勉 (1216–62). In *Yü-chang ts'ung-shu* 豫章叢書, ed. Hu Ssu-ching 胡思敬. Nan-ch'ang, 1915–18 ed.

HSC *Ho-shan chi* 鶴山集, 109 ch., by Wei Liao-weng 魏了翁 (1178–1237). Ssu-k'u ch'üan-shu ed.

HsienTC *Hsien-t'ien chi* 先天集, 10 ch., by Hsü Yüeh-ch'ing 許月卿 (1216–85). Ssu-pu ts'ung-k'an ed.

HsiTC *Hsi-t'ai chi* 西台集, 20 ch., by Pi Chung-yu 畢仲游 (1045–1119). Ts'ung-shu chi-ch'eng ed.

HTC *Heng-t'ang chi* 橫塘集, 20 ch., by Hsü Ching-heng 許景衡 (1072–1128). Ssu-k'u ch'üan-shu ed.

HTHS *Hou-ts'un hsien-sheng ta-ch'üan-chi* 後村先生大全集, 196 ch., by Liu K'o-chuang 劉克莊 (1187–1269). Ssu-pu ts'ung-k'an ed.

HTL *Hou-te lu* 厚德錄, 4 ch., by Li Yüan-kang 李元綱 (fl. ca. 1170). Pi-chi hsiao-shuo ta-kuan ed.

HTT *Hou-ts'un tz'u chien-chu* 後村詞箋注, by Liu K'o-chuang 劉克莊 (1187–1269), *chien-chu* by Ch'ien Chung-lien 錢仲聯. Shanghai: Shang-hai ku-chi ch'u-pan-she, 1980.

HuaiHC *Huai-hai chi* 淮海集, 40 ch., by Ch'in Kuan 秦觀 (1049–1100). Ssu-pu ts'ung-k'an ed.

ICC *I-chien chih* 夷堅志, 207 ch., by Hung Mai 洪邁 (1123–1202). Peking: Chung-hua shu-chü, 1981.

IL *I-li* 儀禮, 50 ch. In *Shih-san ching chu-shu* 十三經注疏. Taipei: I-wen yin-shu-kuan reprint of 1821 ed., 1981.

ISHP *Sung-jen i-shih hui-pien* 宋人軼事彙編, 20 ch., ed. Ting Ch'uan-ching 丁傳靖 (1870–1930). Taipei: Commercial Press, 1935.

JCSP *Jung-chai sui-pi* 容齋隨筆, 74 ch., by Hung Mai 洪邁 (1123–1202). Shanghai: Shang-hai ku-chi ch'u-pan-she, 1978.

KCC *K'uei-ch'e chih* 睽車志, 6 ch., by Kuo T'uan 郭彖 (fl. 1165). Pai-pu ts'ung-shu chi-ch'eng ed.

KCML *Kao-chai man-lu* 高齋漫錄, 1 ch., by Tseng Ts'ao 曾慥 (1131–ca. 1163). Pai-pu ts'ung-shu chi-ch'eng ed.

KCTSCC *Ku-chin t'u-shu chi-ch'eng (Ch'in-ting)* 古今圖書集成, 欽定, 10,000 ch. (1725), ed. Ch'en Meng-lei 陳夢雷 (1651–ca. 1723) et al.

KEC *Kuei-erh chi* 貴耳集, 3 ch., by Chang Tuan-i 張端義 (1179–1250). Ts'ung-shu chi-ch'eng ed.

KFWC *Kao-feng wen-chi* 高峰文集, 12 ch., by Liao Kang 廖剛 (Sung). Ssu-k'u ch'üan-shu ed.

KHTC *Kuei-hsin tsa-chih* 癸辛雜識, by Chou Mi 周密 (1232–1308). Peking: Chung-hua shu-chü, 1988.

KKC *Kung-k'uei chi* 攻媿集, 112 ch., by Lou Yüeh 樓鑰 (1137–1213). Ts'ung-shu chi-ch'eng ed.

KSC *Kung-shih chi* 公是集, 54 ch., by Liu Ch'ang 劉敞 (1019–68). Ts'ung-shu chi-ch'eng ed.

KSCC *K'un-shan chün chih* 崑山郡志, 6 ch., by Yang Hui 楊譓 (Yüan). Sung-Yüan ti-fang chih ts'ung-shu ed. Taipei: Kuo-t'ai wen-hua shih-yeh, 1980 reprint.

KuanYC *Kuan-yüan chi* 灌園集, 20 ch., by Lü Nan-kung 呂南公 (Sung). Ssu-k'u ch'üan-shu ed.

KueiSC *Kuei-shan chi* 龜山集, 42 ch., by Yang Shih 楊時 (1053–1135). Ssu-k'u ch'üan-shu ed.

KuHTC *Ku-Hang tsa-chi* 古杭雜記, 1 ch., by Li Yu 李有. In *Shuo-fu* 説郛, 100 ch., ed. T'ao Tsung-i 陶宗儀 (fl. 1360–68), ch. 4. Shanghai: Commercial Press, 1927.

KYC *Kung-yang chuan* 公羊傳, 28 ch. In *Shih-san ching chu-shu* 十三經注疏. Taipei: I-wen yin-shu-kuan reprint of 1821 ed., 1981.

LC *Li-chi* 禮記, 63 ch. In *Shih-san ching chu-shu* 十三經注疏. Taipei: I-wen yin-shu-kuan reprint of 1821 ed., 1981.

LCC *Le-ch'üan chi* 樂全集, 40 ch.+1, by Chang Fang-p'ing 張方平 (1007–91). Ssu-k'u ch'üan-shu ed.

LCCC *Li Ch'ing-chao chi* 李清照集, by Li Ch'ing-chao 李清照 (1084–ca. 1160). Peking: Chung-hua shu-chü, 1962.

LCCTL *Li Ch'ing-chao tzu-liao hui-pien* 李清照資料彙編, ed. Ch'u Pin-chieh 褚斌杰 et al. Peking: Chung-hua shu-chü, 1984.

LCLC *Lung-ch'uan lüeh-chih* 龍川略志, 10 ch., by Su Ch'e 蘇轍 (1039–1112). Peking: Chung-hua shu-chü, T'ang-Sung shih-liao pi-chi ts'ung-k'an, 1982.

LCT *Lung-chou tz'u* 龍洲詞, 2 ch., by Liu Kuo 劉過 (1154–1206). Ssu-k'u ch'üan-shu ed.

LCYH *Leng-chai yeh-hua* 冷齋夜話, 10 ch., by (monk) Hui-hung 慧洪 (1071–1128). Ts'ung-shu chi-ch'eng ed.

LeCC *Le-ching chi* 樂靜集, 30 ch., by Li Chao-ch'i 李昭玘. Ssu-k'u ch'üan-shu ed.

LFC *Lang-feng chi* 閬風集, 12 ch., by Shu Yüeh-hsiang 舒岳祥 (1217–1301). Ssu-k'u ch'üan-shu ed.

LFWCC *Lu Fang-weng ch'üan-chi* 陸放翁全集, 186 ch., by Lu Yu 陸游 (1125–1210). Hong Kong: Kuang-chih shu-chü punctuated ed., n.d.

LHAPC *Lao-hsüeh-an pi-chi* 老學庵筆記, 10 ch., by Lu Yu 陸游 (1125–1210). Ts'ung-shu chi-ch'eng ed.

LHC *Le-hsüan chi* 樂軒集, 8 ch., by Ch'en Tsao 陳藻 (13th cent.). Ssu-k'u ch'üan-shu ed.

LHHS *Liang-hsi hsien-sheng wen-chi* 梁谿先生文集, 180 ch.+6, by Li Kang 李綱 (1083–1140). Taipei: Han-hua reprint of Tao-kuang ed., 1970.

LHWC *Lu-hsi wen-chi* 盧溪文集, 50 ch.+2, by Wang T'ing-kuei 王庭珪 (1079–1171). Ssu-k'u ch'üan-shu ed.

LKC *Li Kou chi* 李覯集, by Li Kou 李覯 (1009–59). Taipei: Han-ching, 1983 ed.

LNC *Lieh-nü chuan* 列女傳, 7 ch., by Liu Hsiang 劉向 (ca. 77 B.C.–ca. 6 B.C.). Ssu-pu pei-yao ed.

LSL *Le-shan lu* 樂善錄, 10 ch., by Li Ch'ang-ling 李昌齡 (fl. 1233). Taipei: Ssu-pu shan-pen ts'ung-k'an reprint of Sung ed., 1971.

LWTT *Ling-wai tai-ta* 嶺外代答, 10 ch., by Chou Ch'ü-fei 周去非 (d. after 1178). Ts'ung-shu chi-ch'eng ed.

LYCS *Lo-yang chin-shen chiu-wen chi* 洛陽搢紳舊聞記, 5 ch., by Chang Ch'i-hsien 張齊賢 (943–1014). Pai-pu ts'ung-shu chi-ch'eng ed.

MC *Mo chi* 默記, 3 ch., by Wang Chih 王銍 (d. ca. 1154). Peking: Chung-hua shu-chü, T'ang-Sung shih-liao pi-chi ts'ung-k'an, 1981.

MCC *Mien-chai chi* 勉齋集, 40 ch., by Huang Kan 黃榦 (1152–1221). Ssu-k'u ch'üan-shu ed.

MCLH *Min-chung li-hsüeh yüan-yüan k'ao* 閩中理學淵源考, 92 ch., by Li Ch'ing-fu 李清馥 (fl. 1749). Ssu-k'u ch'üan-shu ed.

MCML *Mo-chuang man-lu* 墨莊漫錄, 10 ch., by Chang Pang-chi 張邦基 (12th cent.). Ts'ung-shu chi-ch'eng ed.

MengCC *Meng-chai chi* 蒙齋集, 20 ch., by Yüan Fu 袁甫 (c.s. 1214). Ts'ung-shu chi-ch'eng ed.

MKHH *Mo-k'o hui-hsi* 墨客揮犀, 10 ch., by P'eng Ch'eng 彭乘 (fl. 1050–80). Pai-pu ts'ung-shu chi-ch'eng ed.

MLL *Meng-liang lu* 夢粱錄, 20 ch. (1274), by Wu Tzu-mu 吳自牧 (ca. 1256–after 1334). In *Tung-ching meng-hua lu wai ssu chung* 東京夢華錄外四種. Shanghai: Chung-hua shu-chü, 1962.

MT *Meng-tzu* 孟子, 14 ch. In *Shih-san ching chu-shu* 十三經注疏. Taipei: I-wen yin-shu-kuan reprint of 1821 ed., 1981.

MTC *Man-t'ang chi* 漫塘集, 36 ch., by Liu Tsai 劉宰 (1166–1239). Ssu-k'u ch'üan-shu ed.

NanS *Nan-shih* 南史, 80 ch., by Li Yen-shou 李延壽 (7th cent.). Peking: Chung-hua shu-chü, 1975.

NCCIK *Nan-chien chia-i kao* 南澗甲乙稿, 22 ch., by Han Yüan-chi 韓元吉 (1118–87). Ts'ung-shu chi-ch'eng ed.

NS *Nung-shu* 農書, 3 ch., by Ch'en Fu 陳旉 (1076–after 1149). Pai-pu ts'ung-shu chi-ch'eng ed.

NSCY *Nung-sang chi-yao* 農桑輯要, 7 ch., anon. (Yüan). Ts'ung-shu chi-ch'eng ed.

NWFC *Nei-wai fu-chih t'ung-shih* 內外服制通釋, 7 ch., by Ch'e Kai 車垓 (d. 1276). In *Chen-pi lou ts'ung-shu* 枕碧樓叢書, comp. Shen Chia-pen 沈家本 (1840–1913). 1913 ed.

NYC *Nan-yang chi* 南陽集, 29 ch.+2, by Han Wei 韓維 (1017–98). Ssu-k'u ch'üan-shu ed.

OYHCC *Ou-yang Hsiu ch'üan-chi* 歐陽修全集, 157 ch., by Ou-yang Hsiu 歐陽修 (1007–72). Taipei: Shih-chieh shu-chü, 1961.

PCC *P'eng-ch'eng chi* 彭城集, 40 ch., by Liu Pin 劉攽 (1022–88). Ts'ung-shu chi-ch'eng ed.

PCKT *P'ing-chou k'o-t'an* 萍州可談, 3 ch., by Chu Yü 朱彧 (Sung). Ts'ung-shu chi-ch'eng ed.

PCP *Po-chai pien* 泊宅編, 10 ch.+3, by Fang Shao 方勺 (1066–after 1141). Peking: Chung-hua shu-chü, T'ang-Sung shih-liao pi-chi ts'ung-k'an, 1983.

PCSCS *Pa-ch'iung shih chin-shih pu-cheng* 八瓊室金石補正, 130 ch., by Lu Tseng-hsiang 陸增祥 (1816–82). Shih-k'o shih-liao hsin-pien ed. Taipei: Hsin-wen-feng, 1977.

PCWC *P'an-chou wen-chi* 盤洲文集, 80 ch.+1, by Hung Kua 洪适 (1117–84). Ssu-k'u ch'üan-shu ed.

PHSC *Po Hsiang-shan chi* 白香山集, 71 ch., by Po Chü-i 白居易 (772–846). Kuo-hsüeh chi-pen ts'ung-shu ed.

PLC *P'i-ling chi* 毘陵集, 16 ch., by Chang Shou 張守 (c.s. 1102). Ts'ung-shu chi-ch'eng ed.

PSC *Pei-shan chi* 北山集, 40 ch., by Ch'eng Chü 程俱 (1078–1144). Ssu-k'u ch'üan-shu ed.

PSWC *Pei-shan wen-chi* 北山文集, 30 ch., by Cheng Kang-chung 鄭剛中 (1088–1154). Ts'ung-shu chi-ch'eng ed.

PTC *Pen-t'ang chi* 本堂集, 94 ch., by Ch'en Chu 陳著 (1214–97). Ssu-k'u ch'üan-shu ed.

PTL *Pin-t'ui lu* 賓退錄, 10 ch., by Chao Yü-shih 趙與時 (13th cent.). Shanghai: Shang-hai ku-chi ch'u-pan-she, Sung-Yüan pi-chi ts'ung-shu, 1983.

SC *Shih-ching* 詩經, 20 ch. In *Shih-san ching chu-shu* 十三經注疏. Taipei: I-wen yin-shu-kuan reprint of 1821 ed., 1981.

SCCC *Shih-ching chi-chuan* 詩經集傳, 8 ch., by Chu Hsi 朱熹 (1130–1200). In *Ssu-shu wu-ching* 四書五經, with commentaries by Sung and Yüan authors. Peking: Chung-kuo shu-tien, 1985.

SCPMHP *San-ch'ao pei-meng hui-pien* 三朝北盟會編, 250 ch., by Hsü Meng-hsin 徐夢莘 (1126–1207). Shanghai: Shang-hai ku-chi ch'u-pan-she reprint of 1908 ed., 1987.

SHCSSC *Shih-hu chü-shih shih-chi* 石湖居士詩集, 34 ch., by Fan Ch'eng-ta 范成大 (1126–93). Kuo-hsüeh chi-pen ts'ung-shu ed.

ShihC *Shih-chi* 史記, 130 ch., by Ssu-ma Ch'ien 司馬遷 (145?–86? B.C.). Peking: Chung-hua shu-chü, 1969.

SHSWC *Sung hsüeh-shih wen-chi* 宋學士文集, 75 ch., by Sung Lien 宋濂 (1310–81). Kuo-hsüeh chi-pen ts'ung-shu ed.

SHT *Sung hsing-t'ung* 宋刑統, 30 ch., by Tou I 竇儀 (914–66) et al. Taipei: Wen-hai reprint of 1918 ed., 1964.

SHY *Sung hui-yao chi-kao* 宋會要輯稿, 460 ch., ed. Hsü Sung 徐松 (1781–1848) et al. Peking: Chung-hua shu-chü, 1957.

SKTP *Sun-kung t'an-p'u* 孫公談圃, 3 ch., by Sun Sheng 孫升 (c.s. 1065). Pai-pu ts'ung-shu chi-ch'eng ed.

SLKC (*Hsin-pien tsuan t'u tseng-lei ch'ün-shu lei-yao*) *shih-lin kuang-chi* (新編纂圖增類群書類要) 事林廣記, 50 ch., by Ch'en Yüan-ching 陳元靚 (ca. 1200–1266). Unpublished photocopy of Naikaku bunko Yüan ed.

SLPY (*Ku-chin ho-pi*) *shih-lei pei-yao* (古今合璧) 事類備要, 366 ch., by Hsieh Wei-hsin 謝維新 (Sung). Taipei: Hsin-hsing reprint of 1556 San-ch'ü ed., 1969.

SLSMCT *Sung liu-shih ming-chia tz'u* 宋六十名家詞, ed. Mao Chin 毛晉 (1598–1659). Kuo-hsüeh chi-pen ts'ung-shu ed.

SLYY *Shih-lin yen-yü* 石林燕語, 10 ch., by Yeh Meng-te 葉夢得 (1077–1148). Peking: Chung-hua shu-chü, T'ang-Sung shih-liao pi-chi ts'ung-k'an, 1984.

SMCC *Ssu-ma Wen-cheng kung ch'uan-chia chi* 司馬文正公傳家集, 80 ch. (1741), by Ssu-ma Kuang 司馬光 (1019–86). Kuo-hsüeh chi-pen ts'ung-shu ed.

SMCYHL *Sung ming-ch'en yen-hsing lu* 宋名臣言行錄, 75 ch., ed. Hung Ying 洪瑩. 1842 ed.

SMSSI *Ssu-ma shih shu-i* 司馬氏書儀, 10 ch., by Ssu-ma Kuang 司馬光 (1019–86). Ts'ung-shu chi-ch'eng ed.

SouSC *Sou-shen chi* 搜神記, 20 ch., by Kan Pao 干寶 (4th cent.). Peking: Chung-hua shu-chü, 1979.

SPSC *Shih-ping shih-chi* 石屏詩集, 10 ch., by Tai Fu-ku 戴復古 (1169–after 1246). Ssu-pu ts'ung-k'an hsü-pien ed.

SS *Sung shih* 宋史, 496 ch., ed. T'o T'o 脱脱 (1313–55) et al. Peking: Chung-hua shu-chü, 1977.

SSC *San-shan chih* 三山志, 42 ch., by Liang K'o-chia 梁克家 (1128–87). Sung-Yüan ti-fang chih ts'ung-shu ed. Taipei: Kuo-t'ai wen-hua shih-yeh, 1980 reprint.

SSCC *Su Shun-ch'in chi* 蘇舜欽集, 16 ch.+2, by Su Shun-ch'in 蘇舜欽 (1008–48). Shanghai: Shang-hai ku-chi ch'u-pan-she, 1981 ed.

SSCW *Su-shui chi-wen* 涑水記聞, 16 ch., by Ssu-ma Kuang 司馬光 (1019–86). Peking: Chung-hua shu-chü, T'ang-Sung shih-liao pi-chi ts'ung-k'an, 1989.

SSHY *Shu shih hui-yao* 書史會要, 9 ch.+1, by Tao' Tsung-i 陶宗儀 (fl. 1360–68). Ssu-k'u ch'üan-shu ed.

SSWC *Su Shih wen-chi* 蘇軾文集, 73 ch., by Su Shih 蘇軾 (1036–1101). Peking: Chung-hua shu-chü, 1986.

SSWCL *Shao-shih wen-chien lu* 邵氏聞見錄, 20 ch., by Shao Po-wen 邵伯溫 (1056–1134). Peking: Chung-hua shu-chü, T'ang-Sung shih-liao pi-chi ts'ung-k'an, 1983.

SSYI *Su-shih yen-i* 蘇氏演義, 2 ch., by Su O 蘇鶚 (c.s. 886). Ts'ung-shu chi-ch'eng ed.

STJC *Shui-tung jih-chi* 水東日記, 40 ch., by Yeh Sheng 葉盛 (1420–74). Pai-pu ts'ung shu chi-ch'eng ed.

SuiS *Sui-shu* 隋書, 85 ch., by Wei Cheng 魏徵 (580–643) and Ling-hu Te-fen 令狐德棻 (ca. 640). Peking: Chung-hua shu-chü, 1973.

SungSWC *Sung-shan wen-chi* 嵩山文集, 20 ch., by Ch'ao Yüeh-chih 晁説之 (1059–1129). Ssu-pu ts'ung-k'an ed.

SWC *Sung wen-chien* 宋文鑑, 150 ch., by Lü Tsu-ch'ien 呂祖謙 (1137–81). Kuo-hsüeh chi-pen ts'ung-shu ed.

SWCTC *Shuo-wen chieh-tzu chu* 説文解字注, 32 ch., by Hsü Shen 許慎 (30–124), *chu* by Tuan Yü-ts'ai 段玉裁 (1735–1815). Kuo-hsüeh chi-pen ts'ung-shu ed.

SWCY *Shih-wu chi-yüan* 事物紀原, 10 ch., by Kao Ch'eng 高承 (11th cent.). Ts'ung-shu chi-ch'eng ed.

SWKWC *Su Wei-kung wen-chi* 蘇魏公文集, 72 ch., by Su Sung 蘇頌 (1020–1101). Peking: Chung-hua shu-chü, 1988.

SYKS *Shu-yen ku-shih* 書言故事, 12 ch., by Hu Chi-tsung 胡繼宗 (Sung). 1589 ed.

SYTC *Shih-yu t'an-chi* 師友談記, 1 ch., by Li Chien 李廌 (1059–1109). Ts'ung-shu chi-ch'eng ed.

TanYC *Tan-yüan chi* 丹淵集, 40 ch., by Wen T'ung 文同 (1018–79). Ssu-pu ts'ung-k'an ed.

TaoHC *Tao-hsiang chi* 道鄉集, 40 ch., by Tsou Hao 鄒浩 (1060–1111). In *Sung ming-chia chi hui-k'an* 宋名家集彙刊. Taipei: Han-hua reprint of 1833 ed., 1970.

TC *Tso-chuan* 左傳, 58 ch. In *Shih-san ching chu-shu* 十三經注疏. Taipei: I-wen yin-shu-kuan reprint of 1821 ed., 1981.

TCC *T'ung chiang chi* 桐江集, 8 ch., by Fang Hui 方回 (1227–1306). Wan-wei pieh-ts'ang ed. Shanghai: Commercial Press, 1935.

TCCS *Tu-ch'eng chi-sheng* 都城紀勝, 1 ch. (1235), anon. In *Tung-ching meng-hua lu wai ssu chung* 東京夢華錄外四種. Shanghai: Chung-hua shu-chü, 1962.

TCMHL *Tung-ching meng-hua lu* 東京夢華錄, 10 ch. (1147), attrib. to Meng Yüan-lao 孟元老 (fl. 1126–47). In *Tung-ching meng-hua lu wai ssu chung* 外四種. Shanghai: Chung-hua shu-chü, 1962.

THC *T'iao-hsi chi* 苕溪集, 55 ch., by Liu I-chih 劉一止 (1079–1160). Ssu-k'u ch'üan-shu ed.

THL *T'ou-hsia lu* 投轄錄, 1 ch., by Wang Ming-ch'ing 王明清 (1127–after 1214). In *Sung-Yüan jen shuo pu-shu* 宋元人説部書, anon. Shanghai: Commercial Press, 1919–20.

THPL *Tung-hsüan pi-lu* 東軒筆錄, 15 ch., by Wei T'ai 魏泰 (ca. 1050–1110). Ts'ung-shu chi-ch'eng ed.

THY *T'ang hui-yao* 唐會要, 100 ch., by Wang P'u 王溥 (922–82). Taipei: Shih-chieh shu-chü, 1968.

TIHY *Ts'ang i hua-yü* 藏一話腴, 1 ch., by Ch'en Yü 陳郁 (d. 1275). In *Shuo-fu* 説郛, 100 ch., ed. T'ao Tsung-i 陶宗儀 (fl. 1360–68), ch. 60. Shanghai: Commercial Press, 1927.

TiehSC *Tieh-shan chi* 疊山集, 15 ch.+1, by Hsieh Fang-te 謝枋得 (1226–89). Ssu-pu ts'ung-k'an hsü-pien ed.

TKC *Tseng Kung chi* 曾鞏集, 52 ch., by Tseng Kung 曾鞏 (1019–83). Peking: Chung-hua shu-chü, 1984.

TLC *Tung-lai chi* 東萊集, 15 ch.+25, by Lü Tsu-ch'ien 呂祖謙 (1137–81). Ssu-k'u ch'üan-shu ed.

TML *Ta Ming ling* 大明令, 1 ch. In *Huang-Ming chih-shu* 皇明制書. Tokyo: Koten kenkyūkai facsimile reprint of Ming ed., 1966.

TMLHP *T'ang-Ming lü ho-pien* 唐明律合編, by Hsüeh Yün-sheng 薛允升. Shanghai: Commercial Press, 1937.

TPKC *T'ai-p'ing kuang-chi* 太平廣記, by Li Fang 李昉 (925–96) et al. Peking: Chung-hua shu-chü, 1961.

TS *Ts'an-shu* 蠶書, 1 ch., by Ch'in Kuan 秦觀 (1049–1100). Pai-pu ts'ung-shu chi-ch'eng ed.

TSC *T'ao-shan chi* 陶山集, 16 ch., by Lu Tien 陸佃 (1042–1102). Ts'ung-shu chi-ch'eng ed.

TSCH *Tao-shan ch'ing-hua* 道山清話, 1 ch., anon. Ts'ung-shu chi-ch'eng ed.

TSLC *Tu Shao-ling chi hsiang-chu* 杜少陵集詳註, by Tu Fu 杜甫 (712–70), ed. Ch'iu Chao-ao 仇兆鰲. Hong Kong: T'ai-p'ing, 1966.

TTSL *Tung-tu shih-lüeh* 東都事略, 130 ch., by Wang Ch'eng 王偁 (12th cent.). Taipei: Wen-hai, Sung-shih tzu-liao ts'ui-pien ed., 1967.

TTTP *Ts'ao Ts'ao, Ts'ao P'i, Ts'ao Chih shih hsüan* 曹操曹丕曹植詩選, ed. Yü Kuan-ying 余冠英. Hong Kong: Ta-kuang ch'u-pan-she, 1972.

T'ungC *T'ung-chih* 通志, 200 ch., by Cheng Ch'iao 鄭樵 (1104–62). Kuo-hsüeh chi-pen ts'ung-shu reprint ed. Taipei: Hsin-hsing shu-chü reprint of Shih-t'ung ed., 1962.

TWTL *Tsui-weng t'an-lu* 醉翁談錄, 20 ch., by Lo Yeh 羅燁 (13th cent.). Shanghai: Ku-tien wen-hsüeh ch'u-pan-she, 1957.

TYC *Tan-yang chi* 丹陽集, 24 ch., by Ko Sheng-chung 葛勝仲 (1072–1141). Ssu-k'u ch'üan-shu ed.

TYTC *Ta Yüan t'ung-chih t'iao-ko* 大元通制條格, 30 ch. Taipei: Hua-wen reprint of Ming ms ed., 1980.

WCC *Wen-chung chi* 文忠集, 200 ch.+6, by Chou Pi-ta 周必大 (1126–1204). Ssu-k'u ch'üan-shu ed.

WCL *Wu-ch'uan lu* 吳船錄, 2 ch., by Fan Ch'eng-ta 范成大 (1126–1293). Pai-pu ts'ung-shu chi-ch'eng ed.

WCNS *Wang Chen Nung-shu* 王禎農書, 20 ch., by Wang Chen 王禎 (fl. 1333), ed. Wang Yü-hu 王毓瑚. Peking: Nung-yeh ch'u-pan-she, 1981.

WeiCC *Wei-chai chi* 韋齋集, 12 ch.+2, by Chu Sung 朱松 (1097–1143). Ssu-k'u ch'üan-shu ed.

WH *Wen hsüan* 文選, 60 ch., by Hsiao T'ung 蕭統 (501–31). Hong Kong: Commercial Press punctuated ed., 1965.

WHC *Wu-hsi chi* 武溪集, 20 ch., by Yü Ching 余靖 (1000–1064). Ssu-k'u ch'üan-shu ed.

WHTK *Wen-hsien t'ung-k'ao* 文獻通考, 348 ch., by Ma Tuan-lin 馬端臨 (ca. 1250–1325). Shanghai: Commercial Press, Shih-t'ung ed., 1936.

WKCC (*Wu Ch'ao-tsung hsien-sheng*) *Wen-kuo chai chi* (吳朝宗先生)聞過齋集, 4 ch., by Wu Hai 吳海 (14th cent.). Ts'ung-shu chi-ch'eng ed.

WLC *Wang Ling chi* 王令集, 20 ch., by Wang Ling 王令 (1032–59), ed. Shen Wen-cho 沈文倬. Shanghai: Shang-hai ku-chi ch'u-pan-she, 1980.

WLCC *Wang Lin-ch'uan chi* 王臨川集, 100 ch., by Wang An-shih 王安石 (1021–86). Taipei: Shih-chieh shu-chü, 1966.

WLHPCH *Wan-liu hsi-pien chiu-hua* 萬柳溪邊舊話, 1 ch., by Yu Ch'i 尤玘 (13th cent.). Pi-chi hsiao-shuo ta-kuan, ser. 6 ed.

WLHSC *Wan-ling hsien-sheng chi* 宛陵先生集, 60 ch., by Mei Yao-ch'en 梅堯臣 (1002–60). Ssu-pu ts'ung-k'an ed.

WSC *Wei-sheng chia pao-ch'an-k'o pei-yao* 衛生家寶產科備要, 8 ch., by Chu Tuan-chang 朱端章 (12th cent.). Ts'ung-shu chi-ch'eng ed.

WuHC *Wu-hsing chih* 吳興志, 20 ch., by T'an Yüeh 談鑰 (ca. 1150–1220). Sung-Yüan ti-fang chih ts'ung-shu ed. Taipei: Kuo-t'ai wen-hua shih-yeh, 1980 reprint.

YenSC *Yen-shan chi* 演山集, 60 ch.+1, by Huang Shang 黃裳. Ssu-k'u ch'üan-shu ed.

YHCH *Yü-hu ch'ing-hua* 玉壺清話, 10 ch., by Wen-ying 文瑩 (11th cent.). Peking: Chung-hua shu-chü, T'ang-Sung shih-liao pi-chi ts'ung-k'an, 1984.

YKML *Yang-ku man-lu* 暘谷漫錄, 1 ch., by Hung Hsün 洪巽 (Sung). In *Shuo-fu* 説郛, 100 ch., ed. T'ao Tsung-i 陶宗儀 (fl. 1360–68), ch. 73. Shanghai: Commercial Press, 1927.

YLMC *Yün-lu man-ch'ao* 雲麓漫鈔, 15 ch., by Chao Yen-wei 趙彥衛 (d. after 1206). Ts'ung-shu chi-ch'eng ed.

YSC *Yeh Shih chi* 葉適集, by Yeh Shih 葉適 (1150–1223). Peking: Chung-hua shu-chü, 1961.

YSSF *Yüan-shih shih fan* 袁氏世範, 3 ch., by Yüan Ts'ai 袁采 (fl. 1140–95). Ts'ung-shu chi-ch'eng ed.

YTC *Ta-Yüan sheng-cheng kuo-ch'ao tien-chang* 大元聖政國朝典章, 60 ch. (1307), anon. Facsimile reproduction of Yüan ed.

YYC *Yen-yüan chi* 剡源集, 30 ch., by Tai Piao-yüan 戴表元 (1244–1310). Ts'ung-shu chi-ch'eng ed.

YYFTC *Yüeh-yang feng-t'u chi* 岳陽風土記, by Fan Chih-ming 范致明 (c.s. 1100). In *Shuo-fu i-pai erh-shih han* 説郛一百二十号, ed. T'ao Tsung-i 陶宗儀 (fl. 1360–68), han 62. Shanghai: Shang-hai ku-chi ch'u-pan-she, 1988 reprint.

YYTT *Yu-yang tsa-tsu* 酉陽雜俎, 20 ch.+10, by Tuan Ch'eng-shih 段成式 (d. 863). Taipei: Han-ching, 1983.

SECONDARY WORKS AND TRANSLATIONS

Ahern, Emily M. (*See also* Martin, Emily.) 1974. "Affines and the Rituals of Kinship." In *Religion and Ritual in Chinese Society,* ed. Arthur P. Wolf. Stanford: Stanford University Press.

———. 1975. "The Power and Pollution of Chinese Women." In *Women in Chinese Society,* ed. Margery Wolf and Roxane Witke. Stanford: Stanford University Press.

Ames, Roger T. 1981. "Taoism and the Androgynous Ideal." In *Women in China,* ed. Richard W. Guisso and Stanley Johannesen. Youngstown, N.Y.: Philo Press.

Anagnost, Ann. 1989. "Transformations of Gender in Modern China." In *Gender and Anthropology: Critical Reviews for Research and Teaching,* ed. Sandra Morgen. Washington, D.C.: American Anthropological Association.

Aoyama Sadao 青山定雄. 1965. "Sōdai ni okeru Kahoku kanryō no kon'in kankei" 宋代における華北官僚の婚姻關係. *Chūō daigaku hachijūnen kinei ronbun shū*, 362–88.

Barmé, Geremie, and Linda Jaivin. 1992. *New Ghosts, Old Dreams: Chinese Rebel Voices*. New York: Times Books.

Barnes, Nancy Schuster. 1987. "Buddhism." In *Women in World Religions*, ed. Arvind Sharma. Albany: State University of New York Press.

Barnhart, Richard M. 1983. *Along the Border of Heaven: Sung and Yuan Paintings from the C. C. Wang Family Collection*. New York: Metropolitan Museum of Art.

Beurdeley, Michel, Kristofer Schipper, Chang Fu-jui, and Jacques Pimpaneau. [1969] 1989. *Chinese Erotic Art*. Secaucus, N.J.: Chartwell Books. Originally published as *The Clouds and the Rain: The Art of Love in China*. Fribourg, Switz.: Office du Livre.

Bickford, Maggie. 1985. *Bones of Jade, Soul of Ice: The Flowering Plum in Chinese Art*. New Haven: Yale University Art Gallery.

Birge, Bettine. 1989. "Chu Hsi and Women's Education." In *Neo-Confucian Education: The Formative Stage*, ed. Wm. Theodore de Bary and John W. Chaffee. Berkeley and Los Angeles: University of California Press.

———. 1992. "Women and Property in Sung Dynasty China (960–1279): Neo-Confucianism and Social Change in Chien-chou, Fukien." Ph.D. diss., Columbia University.

Birrell, Anne M. 1985. "The Dusty Mirror: Courtly Portraits of Woman in Southern Dynasties Love Poetry." In *Expressions of Self in Chinese Literature*, ed. Robert E. Hegel and Richard C. Hessney. New York: Columbia University Press.

Black, Allison H. 1986. "Gender and Cosmology in Chinese Correlative Thinking." In *Gender and Religion: On the Complexity of Symbols*, ed. Caroline Walker Bynum, Stevan Harrell, and Paula Richman. Boston: Beacon Press.

Bodde, Derk. 1991. *Chinese Thought, Society, and Science: The Intellectual and Social Background of Science and Technology in Pre-modern China*. Honolulu: University of Hawaii Press.

Bol, Peter K. 1992. *This Culture of Ours: Intellectual Transitions in T'ang and Sung China*. Stanford: Stanford University Press.

Bossler, Beverly Jo. 1991. "Powerful Relations and Relations of Power: Family and Society in Sung China, 960–1279." Ph.D. diss., University of California, Berkeley.

Brownmiller, Susan. 1984. *Femininity*. New York: Ballantine.

Burns, Ian Robert. 1973. "Private Law in Traditional China (Sung Dynasty)." Ph.D. diss., Oxford University.

Cahill, James. 1960. *Chinese Painting*. Geneva: Skira.

———. 1980. *An Index of Early Chinese Painters and Paintings: T'ang, Sung, and Yüan*. Berkeley and Los Angeles: University of California Press.

———. 1988. *The Alternative Histories of Chinese Painting*. The Franklin D. Murphy Lectures IX. Lawrence: Spencer Art Museum, University of Kansas.

Cahill, Suzanne. 1986. "Performers and Female Taoist Adepts: Hsi Wang Mu as Patron Deity of Women in T'ang China." *Journal of the American Oriental Society* 106:155–68.

———. 1990. "Practice Makes Perfect: Paths to Transcendence for Women in Medieval China." *Taoist Resources* 2.2:23–42.

Carlitz, Katherine. 1991. "The Social Uses of Female Virtue in Late Ming Editions of Lienü Zhuan." *Late Imperial China* 12(2):117–48.

Cartier, Michel. 1973. "Nouvelles données sur la démographie chinoise à l'époque des Ming (1368–1644)." *Annales: économies sociétés civilisations* 28.6:1341–59.

Chaffee, John W. 1985. *The Thorny Gates of Learning in Sung China: A Social History of Examinations.* Cambridge: Cambridge University Press.

———. 1991. "The Marriage of Clanswomen in the Sung Imperial Clan." In *Marriage and Inequality in Chinese Society,* ed. Rubie S. Watson and Patricia Buckley Ebrey. Berkeley and Los Angeles: University of California Press.

Chan, Wing-tsit, trans. 1986. *Neo-Confucian Terms Explained (the "Pei-hsi tzu-i") by Ch'en Ch'un, 1159–1223.* New York: Columbia University Press.

———. 1989. *Chu Hsi: New Studies.* Honolulu: University of Hawaii Press.

Chang Ch'üan 張荃. 1934–35. "Hou-ts'un hsien-sheng nien-p'u" 後村先生年譜. *Chih-chiang hsüeh-pao* 1.3:1–26.

Chang, Chun-shu, and Joan Smythe. 1981. *South China in the Twelfth Century: A Translation of Lu Yu's Travel Diaries, July 3–December 6, 1170.* Hong Kong: Chinese University Press.

Chang Fu-jui. 1964. "Les thèmes dans le *Yi-Kien Tche.*" *Cina* 8:51–55.

———. 1968. "Le *Yi kien tche* et la société des Song." *Journal asiatique* 256:55–91.

Chang, H.C. 1973. *Chinese Literature: Popular Fiction and Drama.* Edinburgh: Edinburgh University Press.

Chang Hsiu-jung 張修蓉. 1976. *T'ang-tai wen-hsüeh so piao-hsien chih hun-su yen-chiu* 唐代文學所表現之婚俗研究. M.A. essay, National Cheng-chih University.

Chang Hsüeh-shu 張學舒. 1983. "Liang-Sung min-chien ssu-chih-yeh ti fa-chan" 兩宋民間絲織業的發展. *Chung-kuo-shih yen-chiu* 1983.1:110–25.

Chang, Kang-i Sun. 1991. *The Late-Ming Poet Ch'en Tzu-lung: Crises of Love and Loyalism.* New Haven: Yale University Press.

Chang Pang-wei 張邦煒. 1986. "Sung-tai pi-ch'in pi-chi chih-tu shu-p'ing" 宋代避親避籍制度述評. *Ssu-ch'uan Shih-ta hsüeh-pao* 1986.1:16–23.

———. 1989. *Hun-yin yü she-hui (Sung-tai)* 婚姻與社會(宋代). Ch'eng-tu: Ssu-ch'uan Jen-min ch'u-pan-she.

Chao Ch'ao 趙超. 1987. "Yu mu-chih k'an T'ang-tai ti hun-yin chuang-k'uang" 由墓誌看唐代的婚姻狀況. *Chung-hua wen-shih lun-ts'ung* 1987.1:193–208.

Chao Feng 趙丰. 1986. "'Ts'an-chih t'u' ti pan-pen chi so-chien Nan-Sung ts'an-chih chi-shu"《蠶織圖》的版本及所見南宋蠶織技術. *Nung-yeh k'ao-ku* 1986.1:345–59.

Chao, Kang. 1977. *The Development of Cotton Textile Production in China.* Cambridge: Harvard University, East Asian Research Center.

———. 1986. *Man and Land in Chinese History: An Economic Analysis.* Stanford: Stanford University Press.

Chao Shou-yen 趙守儼. 1963. "T'ang-tai hun-yin li-su k'ao-lüeh" 唐代婚姻禮俗考略. *Wen-shih* 1963.3:185–95.

Chaves, Jonathan. 1976. *Mei Yao-ch'en and the Development of Early Sung Poetry.* New York: Columbia University Press.

Ch'en Ku-yüan 陳顧遠. [1936] 1978. *Chung-kuo hun-yin shih* 中國婚姻史. Reprint. Taipei: Commercial Press.

Ch'en, Li-li. 1976. *Master Tung's Western Chamber Romance ("Tung Hsi-hsiang chu-kung-tiao"): A Chinese Chantefable.* Cambridge: Cambridge University Press.

Ch'en P'eng 陳鵬. 1990. *Chung-kuo hun-yin shih-kao* 中國婚姻史稿. Peking: Chung-hua shu-chü.

Ch'en Tung-yüan 陳東原. [1928] 1980. *Chung-kuo fu-nü sheng-huo shih* 中國婦女生活史. Reprint. Taipei: Commercial Press.

Cheng Chen-to 鄭振鐸, Cheng Heng 鄭珩, and Hsü Pang-ta 徐邦達, eds. 1959. *Sung-jen hua-ts'e* 宋人畫冊. Peking: Chung-kuo ku-tien i-shu ch'u-pan-she.

Chia Shen 賈申. 1925. *Chung-hua fu-nü ch'an-tsu k'ao* 中華婦女纏足考. Peking: Tz'u-hsiang.

Chiang-hsi sheng wen-wu k'ao-ku yen-chiu so 江西省文物考古研究所 and Te-an hsien po-wu kuan 德安縣博物館. 1990. "Chiang-hsi Te-an Nan-Sung Chou-shih mu ch'ing-li chien-pao" 江西德安南宋周氏墓清理簡報. *Wen-wu* 1990.9:1–13.

Ching, Julia. 1976. "Li Ch'ing-chao." In *Sung Biographies,* ed. Herbert Franke. Wiesbaden: Franz Steiner Verlag.

Chu Jui-hsi 朱瑞熙. 1986. *Sung-tai she-hui yen-chiu* 宋代社會研究. Taipei: Hung-wen.

———. 1988. "Sung-tai ti hun-yin li-i" 宋代的婚姻禮儀. *Wen-shih chih-shih* 1988.12: 46–50.

Chu, Ron-Guey. 1989. "Chu Hsi and Public Instruction." In *Neo-Confucian Education: The Formative Stage,* ed. Wm. Theodore de Bary and John W. Chaffee. Berkelcy and Los Angeles: University of California Press.

Ch'ü, T'ung-tsu. 1965. *Law and Society in Traditional China.* Paris: Mouton.

Ch'ü-chou shih wen-kuan hui 衢州市文管會. 1983. "Che-chiang Ch'ü-chou shih Nan-Sung mu ch'u-t'u ch'i-wu" 浙江衢州市南宋墓出土器物. *K'ao-ku* 1983.11:1004–11, 1018.

Ch'üan Han-sheng 全漢昇. 1935. "Sung-tai nü-tzu chih-yeh yü sheng-chi" 宋代女子職業與生計. *Shih-huo* 1.9:5–10.

———. 1964. "Sung-mo ti t'ung-huo p'eng-chang chi ch'i tui-yü wu-chia ti ying-hsiang" 宋末的通貨膨脹及其對於物價的影響. In *Sung-shih yen-chiu chi* 宋史研究集, vol. 2. Taipei: Chung-hua ts'ung-shu pien-shen wei-yüan-hui.

Chung, Ling. 1985. "Li Qingzhao: The Moulding of Her Spirit and Personality." In *Women and Literature in China,* ed. Anna Gerstlacher, Ruth Keen, Wolfgang Kubin, Margit Miosga, and Jenny Schon. Bochum: Studienverlag Brockmeyer.

Chung, Priscilla Ching. 1981. *Palace Women in the Northern Sung, 960–1126.* Monographies du T'oung Pao, 12. Leiden: E.J. Brill.

Chung-kuo mei-shu ch'üan-chi pien-chi wei-yüan-hui 中國美術全集編輯委員會. 1984. *Chung-kuo mei-shu ch'üan-chi* 中國美術全集. Shanghai: Shang-hai Jen-min mei-shu.

Clark, Hugh R. 1991. *Community, Trade, and Networks: Southern Fujian Province from the Third to the Thirteenth Century.* Cambridge: Cambridge University Press.

Coale, Ansley J. 1985. "Fertility in Rural China: A Reconfirmation of the Barclay Assessment." In *Family and Population in East Asian History,* ed. Susan B. Hanley and Arthur P. Wolf. Stanford: Stanford University Press.

Cohen, Myron L. 1976. *House United, House Divided: The Chinese Family in Taiwan.* New York: Columbia University Press.

Comaroff, J. L. 1980. "Introduction." In *The Meaning of Marriage Payments,* ed. J. L. Comaroff. New York: Academic Press.

Croll, Elisabeth Joan. 1978. *Feminism and Socialism in China*. Boston: Routledge & Kegan Paul.

Davis, Richard L. 1986. *Court and Family in Sung China, 960–1279: Bureaucratic Success and Kinship Fortunes for the Shih of Ming-chou*. Durham, N.C.: Duke University Press.

de Bary, Wm. Theodore. 1953. "A Reappraisal of Neo-Confucianism." In *Studies in Chinese Thought*, ed. Arthur F. Wright. Chicago: University of Chicago Press.

de Bary, Wm. Theodore, and John W. Chaffee, eds. 1989. *Neo-Confucian Education: The Formative Stage*. Berkeley and Los Angeles: University of California Press.

de Pee, Christian. 1991. "Women in the *Yi jian zhi:* A Socio-historical Study Based on Fiction." M.A. thesis, University of Leiden.

Djang, Djang, and Jane C. Djang. 1989. *A Compilation of Anecdotes of Sung Personalities*. New York: St. John's University Press.

Doolittle, Justus. 1865. *Social Life of the Chinese, with Some Account of Their Religious, Governmental, Educational, and Business Customs and Opinions, with Special but Not Exclusive Reference to Fuhchau*. New York: Harper & Brothers.

Dudbridge, Glen. 1978. *The Legend of Miao-shan*. London: Ithaca Press.

Dull, Jack. 1978. "Marriage and Divorce in Han China: A Glimpse at 'Pre-Confucian' Society." In *Chinese Family Law and Social Change in Historical and Comparative Perspective*, ed. David C. Buxbaum. Seattle: University of Washington Press.

Dworkin, Andrea. 1974. *Woman-Hating*. New York: E.P. Dutton.

Ebrey, Patricia Buckley. 1978. *The Aristocratic Families of Early Imperial China: A Case Study of the Po-ling Ts'ui Family*. Cambridge: Cambridge University Press.

————, ed. 1981a. *Chinese Civilization and Society: A Sourcebook*. New York: Free Press.

————. 1981b. "Women in the Kinship System of the Southern Song Upper Class." *Historical Reflections* 8:113–28.

————. 1984a. "Conceptions of the Family in the Sung Dynasty." *Journal of Asian Studies* 43.2:219–45.

————. 1984b. *Family and Property in Sung China: Yüan Ts'ai's Precepts for Social Life*. Princeton: Princeton University Press.

————. 1984c. "The Women in Liu Kezhuang's Family." *Modern China* 10.4:415–40.

————. 1986a. "Concubines in Sung China." *Journal of Family History* 11:1–24.

————. 1986b. "The Early Stages in the Development of Descent Group Organization." In *Kinship Organization in Late Imperial China, 1000–1940*, ed. Patricia Buckley Ebrey and James L. Watson. Berkeley and Los Angeles: University of California Press.

————. 1988. "The Dynamics of Elite Domination in Sung China." *Harvard Journal of Asiatic Studies* 48:493–519.

————. 1990. "Women, Marriage, and the Family in Chinese History." In *The Heritage of China*, ed. Paul Ropp. Berkeley and Los Angeles: University of California Press.

————, trans. 1991a. *Chu Hsi's "Family Rituals": A Twelfth-Century Chinese Manual for the Performance of Cappings, Weddings, Funerals, and Ancestral Rites*. Princeton: Princeton University Press.

————. 1991b. *Confucianism and Family Rituals in Imperial China: A Social History of Writing About Rites*. Princeton: Princeton University Press.

————. 1991c. "Introduction." In *Marriage and Inequality in Chinese Society*, ed. Rubie S. Watson and Patricia Buckley Ebrey. Berkeley and Los Angeles: University of California Press.

———. 1991d. "Shifts in Marriage Finance from the Sixth to the Thirteenth Centuries." In *Marriage and Inequality in Chinese Society,* ed. Rubie S. Watson and Patricia Buckley Ebrey. Berkeley and Los Angeles: University of California Press.

———. 1992a. "Property Law and Uxorilocal Marriage in the Sung Period." In *Family Process and Political Process in Modern Chinese History.* Taipei: Institute of Modern History, Academia Sinica.

———. 1992b. "Women, Money, and Class: Ssu-ma Kuang and Neo-Confucian Views on Women." In *Papers on Society and Culture of Early Modern China,* Taipei: Institute of History and Philology, Academia Sinica.

———. Forthcoming. "Marriage Among the Song Elite." In *Chinese Historical Micro-demography,* ed. Stevan Harrell. Berkeley and Los Angeles: University of California Press.

Edgren, Sören. 1989. *Southern Song Printing at Hangzhou.* Stockholm: Museum of Far Eastern Antiquities.

Eichhorn, Werner. 1976. "Some Notes on Population Control During the Sung Dynasty." In *Études d'histoire et de littérature chinoises offertes au Professeur Jaroslav Prusek.* Paris: Bibliothèque de l'Institut des Hautes Études Chinoises.

Elvin, Mark. 1973. *The Pattern of the Chinese Past.* Stanford: Stanford University Press.

———. 1984. "Female Virtue and the State in China." *Past and Present* 104:111–52.

Erler, Mary, and Maryanne Kowaleski. 1988. *Women and Power in the Middle Ages.* Athens: University of Georgia Press.

Fang Chien-hsin 方建新. 1985. "Sung-tai hun-yin li-su k'ao-shu" 宋代婚姻禮俗考述. *Wen-shih* 24:157–78.

———. 1986. "Sung-tai hun-yin lun-ts'ai" 宋代婚姻論財. *Li-shih yen-chiu* 1986.3:178–90.

Ferguson, Margaret W., Maureen Quilligan, and Nancy J. Vickers, eds. 1986. *Rewriting the Renaissance: The Discourses of Sexual Difference in Early Modern Europe.* Chicago: University of Chicago Press.

Finegan, Michael Harold. 1976. "Urbanism in Sung China: Selected Topics in the Society and Economy of Chinese Cities in a Premodern Period." Ph.D. diss., University of Chicago.

Fong, Wen. 1973. *Sung and Yuan Paintings.* New York: Metropolitan Museum of Art.

Frankel, Hans H. 1976. *The Flowering Plum and the Palace Lady: Interpretations of Chinese Poetry.* New Haven: Yale University Press.

Freedman, Maurice. 1958. *Lineage Organization in Southeastern China.* London: Athlone Press.

———. 1979. *The Study of Chinese Society: Essays.* Stanford: Stanford University Press.

Friedl, Ernestine. 1967. "The Position of Women: Appearance and Reality." *Anthropological Quarterly* 40:97–108.

Fu-chien sheng po-wu kuan 福建省博物館, ed. 1982. *Fu-chou Nan-Sung Huang Sheng mu* 福州南宋黃昇墓. Peking: Wen-wu ch'u-pan-she.

Furth, Charlotte. 1986. "Blood, Body, and Gender: Medical Images of the Female Condition in China." *Chinese Science* 7:53–65.

———. 1987. "Concepts of Pregnancy, Childbirth, and Infancy in Ch'ing Dynasty China." *Journal of Asian Studies* 46:7–35.

———. 1988. "Androgynous Males and Deficient Females: Biology and Gender Boundaries in 16th- and 17th-Century China." *Late Imperial China* 9:1–31.

Fusek, Lois. 1982. *Among the Flowers: The "Hua-chien chi."* New York: Columbia University Press.

Gamble, Sidney D. 1954. *Ting Hsien: A North China Rural Community.* New York: International Secretariat, Institute of Pacific Relations.

Gates, Hill. 1989. "The Commoditization of Chinese Women." *Signs* 14.4:799–832.

Gernet, Jacques. *Daily Life in China on the Eve of the Mongol Invasion, 1250–1276.* Trans. H. M. Wright. Stanford: Stanford University Press, 1970.

Giles, Herbert A. 1963. *San Tzu Ching.* 2d ed. rev. New York: Ungar.

Gold, Penny Schine. 1985. *The Lady and the Virgin: Image, Attitude, and Experience in Twelfth-Century France.* Chicago: University of Chicago Press.

Goody, Jack. 1973. "Bridewealth and Dowry in Africa and Eurasia." In Jack Goody and S. J. Tambiah, *Bridewealth and Dowry.* Cambridge: Cambridge University Press.

———. 1976a. "Introduction." In *Family and Inheritance: Rural Society in Western Europe, 1200–1800,* ed. Jack Goody, Joan Thirsk, and E.P. Thompson. Cambridge: Cambridge University Press.

———. 1976b. *Production and Reproduction: A Comparative Study of the Domestic Domain.* Cambridge: Cambridge University Press.

———. 1990. *The Oriental, the Ancient, and the Primitive.* Cambridge: Cambridge University Press.

Gronewold, Sue. 1982. *Beautiful Merchandise: Prostitution in China, 1860–1936.* New York: Institute for Research in History and the Hasworth Press.

Guisso, R. W. L. 1978. *Wu Tse-t'ien and the Politics of Legitimation in T'ang China.* Bellingham: Western Washington University, Program in East Asian Studies Occasional Papers.

———. 1981. "Thunder over the Lake: The Five Classics and the Perception of Woman in Early China." In *Women in China,* ed. Richard W. Guisso and Stanley Johannesen. Youngstown, N.Y.: Philo Press.

Hajnal, J. 1965. "European Marriage Patterns in Perspective." In *Population in History,* ed. D. V. Glass and D. E. C. Eversley. Chicago: Aldine.

Handlin, Joanna F. 1975. "Lü K'un's New Audience: The Influence of Women's Literacy on Sixteenth-Century Thought." In *Women in Chinese Society,* ed. Margery Wolf and Roxane Witke. Stanford: Stanford University Press.

Hansen, Valerie. 1990. *Changing Gods in Medieval China, 1127–1276.* Princeton: Princeton University Press.

Harper, Donald. 1987. "The Sexual Arts of Ancient China as Described in a Manuscript of the Second Century B.C." *Harvard Journal of Asiatic Studies* 47:539–93.

Harrell, Stevan, and Sara A. Dickey. 1985. "Dowry Systems in Complex Societies." *Ethnology* 24.2:105–20.

Hartwell, Robert M. 1982. "Demographic, Political, and Social Transformation of China, 750–1550." *Harvard Journal of Asiatic Studies* 42:365–442.

Hershatter, Gail. 1991. "Prostitution and the Market in Women in Early Twentieth-Century Shanghai." In *Marriage and Inequality in Chinese Society,* ed. Rubie S. Watson and Patricia Buckley Ebrey. Berkeley and Los Angeles: University of California Press.

Hightower, James R. 1981. "The Songwriter Liu Yung: Part I." *Harvard Journal of Asiatic Studies* 41. 2:323–76.

———. 1982. "The Songwriter Liu Yung: Part II." *Harvard Journal of Asiatic Studies* 42.1:1–66.

Ho, Wai-kam, Sherman E. Lee, Laurence Sickman, and Marc F. Wilson. 1980. *Eight Dynasties of Chinese Painting: The Collections of Nelson Gallery – Atkins Museum, Kansas City, and the Cleveland Museum of Art.* Bloomington: Indiana University Press.

Holmgren, Jennifer. 1981. "Widow Chastity in the Northern Dynasties: The Lieh-nü Biographies in the *Wei-shu.*" *Papers on Far Eastern History* 23:165–86.

———. 1981–83. "Women and Political Power in the Traditional T'o-pa Elite: A Preliminary Study of the Biographies of Empresses in the *Wei-shu.*" *Monumenta Serica* 35:33–74.

———. 1983. "The Harem in Northern Wei Politics—398–498 A.D." *Journal of the Economic and Social History of the Orient* 26:71–90.

———. 1985. "The Economic Foundations of Virtue: Widow-Remarriage in Early and Modern China." *Australian Journal of Chinese Affairs* 13:1–27.

———. 1986. "Observations on Marriage and Inheritance Practices in Early Mongol and Yüan Society, with Particular Reference to the Levirate." *Journal of Asian History* 20:127–92.

———. 1991. "Imperial Marriage in the Native Chinese and Non-Han State, Han to Ming." In *Marriage and Inequality in Chinese Society,* ed. Rubie S. Watson and Patricia Buckley Ebrey. Berkeley and Los Angeles: University of California Press.

Honig, Emily, and Gail Hershatter. 1988. *Personal Voices: Chinese Women in the 1980's.* Stanford: Stanford University Press.

Hsia Nai 夏鼐. 1987. *Sung-tai ching-chi shih* 宋代經濟史. 2 vols. Shanghai: Shang-hai Jen-min ch'u-pan-she.

Hsieh, Andrew C. K., and Jonathan S. Spence. 1980. "Suicide and the Family in Pre-Modern Chinese Society." In *Normal and Abnormal Behavior in Chinese Culture,* ed. A. Kleinman and T.-Y. Lin. Dordrecht, Holland: Reidel.

Hsü, Dau-lin. 1970–71. "The Myth of the 'Five Human Relations' of Confucius." *Monumenta Serica* 29:27–37.

Hsü Hung 徐泓. 1989. "Ming-tai ti hun-yin chih-tu" 明代的婚姻制度. *Ta-lu tsa-chih* 78.1:26–37 (pt. 1), 78.2:68–82 (pt. 2).

Hu P'in-ch'ing. 1966. *Li Ch'ing-chao.* New York: Twayne.

Hu Wen-k'ai 胡文楷. 1985. *Li-tai fu-nü chu-tso k'ao* 歷代婦女著作考. Rev. ed. Shanghai: Commercial Press.

Huang, Hong-quan. 1988. *Anthology of Song-Dynasty Ci-Poetry.* Peking: People's Liberation Army Publishing House.

Huc, M. 1855. *The Chinese Empire.* 2 vols. London: Longman, Brown, Green, & Longmans.

Hughes, Diane Owen. 1978. "From Brideprice to Dowry in Mediterranean Europe." *Journal of Family History* 3.3:262–96.

Hymes, Robert P. 1986a. "Marriage, Descent Groups, and the Localist Strategy in Sung and Yüan Fu-chou." In *Kinship Organization in Late Imperial China, 1000–1940,* ed. Patricia Buckley Ebrey and James L. Watson. Berkeley and Los Angeles: University of California Press.

———. 1986b. *Statesmen and Gentlemen: The Elite of Fu-chou, Chiang-hsi, in Northern and Southern Sung.* Cambridge: Cambridge University Press.

Ihara Hiroshi 伊原弘. 1971. "Sōdai Minshu ni okeru kanko no kon'in kankei" 宋代明州における官戶の婚姻關係. *Chūō daigaku daigakuin kenkyū nenpō* 1:157–68.

Imahori Seiji 今堀誠二. 1955. "Sōdai ni okeru eiji hogo jigyō ni tsuite" 宋代における嬰兒保護事業について. *Hiroshima daigaku bungakubu kiyo* 8:127–51.

Jaschok, Maria. 1988. *Concubines and Bondservants: A Social History.* London: Zed Books.

Jay, Jennifer. 1990. "Vignettes of Chinese Women in T'ang Xi'an (618–906): Individualism in Wu Zetian, Yang Guifei, Yu Xuanji, and Li Wa." *Chinese Culture* 31.1:77–89.

Johnson, David G. 1977. "The Last Years of a Great Clan: The Li Family of Chao Chün in Late T'ang and Early Sung." *Harvard Journal of Asiatic Studies* 37:5–102.

Johnson, Kay Ann. 1983. *Women, the Family, and Peasant Revolution in China.* Chicago: University of Chicago Press.

Judd, Ellen R. 1990. "'Men are More Able': Rural Chinese Women's Conceptions of Gender and Agency." *Pacific Affairs* 63.1:40–61.

Kao, Karl S. Y., ed. 1985. *Classical Chinese Tales of the Supernatural and the Fantastic: Selections from the Third to the Tenth Century.* Bloomington: Indiana University Press.

Kao Shih-yü 高世瑜. 1988. *T'ang-tai nü-shih* 唐代女史. Sian: San-ch'in ch'u-pan-she.

Kassoff, Ira E. 1984. *The Thought of Chang Tsai, 1020–1077.* Cambridge: Cambridge University Press.

Kelleher, M. Theresa. 1987. "Confucianism." in *Women in World Religions,* ed. Arvind Sharma. Albany: State University of New York Press.

———. 1989. "Back to Basics: Chu Hsi's *Elementary Learning (Hsiao-hsüeh).*" In *Neo-Confucian Education: The Formative Stage,* ed. Wm. Theodore de Bary and John W. Chaffee. Berkeley and Los Angeles: University of California Press.

Klapisch-Zuber, Christiane. 1985. *Women, Family, and Ritual in Renaissance Italy.* Trans. Lydia G. Cochrane. Chicago: University of Chicago Press.

Ko, Dorothy. 1992. "Pursuing Talent and Virtue: Education and Gentry Women's Culture in Seventeenth- and Eighteenth-Century China." *Late Imperial China* 13.1:9–39.

Kondo, Dorinne K. 1990. *Crafting Selves: Power, Gender, and Discourses of Identity in a Japanese Workplace.* Chicago: University of Chicago Press.

Kracke, E. A. 1954–55. "Sung Society: Change Within Tradition." *Far Eastern Quarterly* 14.4:479–88.

———. 1975. "Sung K'ai-feng: Pragmatic Metropolis and Formalistic Capital." In *Crisis and Prosperity in Sung China,* ed. John Winthrop Haeger. Tucson: University of Arizona Press, 1975.

Kristof, Nicholas D. 1991. "A Peek Through the Keyhole at a New China." *New York Times,* July 19, 1991, 1.

Ku-kung po-wu yüan ts'ang-hua chi pien-chi wei-yüan-hui 故宮博物院藏畫集編輯委員會. 1978. *Chung-kuo li-tai hui-hua, 1* 中國歷代繪畫, 1. Peking: Jen-min ch'u-pan-she.

———. 1981. *Chung-kuo li-tai hui-hua, 2* 中國歷代繪畫, 2. Peking: Jen-min ch'u-pan-she.

Kuhn, Dieter. 1988. *Textile Technology: Spinning and Reeling.* Pt. 9 of Science and Civilisation in China, vol. 5: *Chemistry and Chemical Technology.* Cambridge: Cambridge University Press.

Kuo-li Ku-kung po-wu yüan 國立故宮博物院. 1970. *Ku-kung ming-hua hsüan-ts'ui* 故宮名畫選萃. Taipei: Ku-kung.

Lawton, Thomas. 1973. *Chinese Figure Painting*. Washington, D.C.: Freer Gallery of Art.

Lee, Bernice J. 1981. "Female Infanticide in China." In *Women in China*, ed. Richard W. Guisso and Stanley Johannesen. Youngstown, N.Y.: Philo Press.

Lee, Thomas H. C. 1984. "The Discovery of Childhood: Children's Education in Sung China (960–1279)." In *"Kultur": Begriff und Wort in China und Japan*, ed. Sigrid Paul. Berlin: Dietrich Reimer Verlag.

Legge, James, trans. 1885. *Li Chi, Book of Rites*. 2 vols. Oxford: Oxford University Press.

———. 1893. *The Chinese Classics*. 5 vols. Oxford: Oxford University Press.

Lerner, Gerda. 1986. *The Creation of Patriarchy*. New York: Oxford University Press.

Levering, Miriam L. 1982. "The Dragon Girl and the Abbess of Mo-shan: Gender and Status in the Ch'an Buddhist Tradition." *Journal of the International Association of Buddhist Studies* 5.1:19–35.

———. 1987. "Ta-hui and Lay Buddhists: Ch'an Sermons on Death." In *Buddhist and Taoist Practice in Medieval Chinese Society*, Buddhist and Taoist Studies II, ed. David W. Chappell. Honolulu: University of Hawaii Press.

Levy, Howard Seymour. 1958. *Harem Favorites of an Illustrious Celestial* (漢宮專寵). Taichung: Ching-tai.

———. 1962. "T'ang Courtesans, Ladies, and Concubines." *Orient/West* 8:49–64.

———. 1966. *Chinese Footbinding: The History of a Curious Erotic Custom*. New York: Bell.

Li Ao 李敖. 1980. "Sung-tai ti li-hun—Fu-ch'i t'ung-t'i chu-i hsia ti Sung-tai hun-yin ti wu-hsiao ch'e-hsiao chieh-hsiao chi ch'i hsiao-li yü shou-hsü" 宋代的離婚—夫妻同體主義下的宋代婚姻的無效撤消解消及其效力與手續. *Li Ao ch'üan-chi* 李敖全集, vol. 1. Taipei: Ssu-chi.

Li, Dun J. 1971. *The Ageless Chinese: A History*. New York: Charles Scribner's Sons.

Li Jen-p'u 李仁溥. 1983. *Chung-kuo ku-tai fang-chih shih-kao* 中國古代紡織史稿. Ch'ang-sha: Yüeh-lu.

Li Jung-mei 李榮楣. 1936. "Chung-kuo fu-nü ch'an-tsu shih-t'an" 中國婦女纏足史譚. In *Ts'ai-fei lu hsü-pien* 采菲錄續編, ed. Yao Ling-hsi 姚靈犀. Tientsin: Shih-tai kung-ssu.

Li Yu-ning 李又寧 and Chang Yü-fa 張玉法, eds. 1975. *Chin-tai Chung-kuo nü-ch'üan yün-tung shih-liao, 1842–1911* 近代中國女權運動史料, 1842–1911. Taipei: Chuan-chi wen-hsüeh she.

Liang Keng-yao 梁庚堯. 1984. *Nan-Sung ti nung-ts'un ching-chi* 南宋的農村經濟. Taipei: Lien-ching.

Lin Kuei-ying 林桂英. 1986. "Wo-kuo tsui-tsao chi-lu ts'an-chih sheng-ch'an chi-shu ho i lao-tung fu-nü wei chu ti hua-chüan" 我國最早記錄蠶織生產技術和以勞動婦女為主的畫卷. *Nung-yeh k'ao-ku* 1986.1:341–44, 395.

Lin Kuei-ying and Liu Feng-t'ung 劉鋒彤. 1984. "Sung 'Ts'an-chih-t'u' chüan ch'u-t'an" 宋《蠶織圖》卷初探. *Wen-wu* 1984.10:31–33, 39.

Lin Yutang. 1939. *My Country and My People*. London: Heinemann.

Linck, Gudula. 1989. "Aus der fruchtbaren Erde wie einsame Schatten: zum Wandel der Wahrnehmung von Weiblichkeit bei der chinesischen Oberschicht der Sung-Zeit." In *Lebenswelt und Weltanschauung der chinesischen Oberschicht im frühneuzeitlichen China*, ed. Helwig Schmidt-Glinzer. Stuttgart: Franz Steiner Verlag.

Liu Hsien 劉咸 and Ch'en Wei-k'un 陳渭坤. 1987. "Chung-kuo chih-mien shih k'ao-lüeh" 中國植棉史考略. *Chung-kuo nung-shih* 1987.1:35–44.

Liu, James T. C. 1967. *Ou-yang Hsiu: An Eleventh-Century Neo-Confucianist.* Stanford: Stanford University Press.

Liu Jun-ho 劉潤和. 1967. "Sung-tai hun-yin ti chi-mien kuan" 宋代婚姻的幾面觀. *Chung-wen hsüeh-hui nien-k'an* 66–67:95–120.

Liu, Kwang-Ching. 1990. "Socioethics as Orthodoxy: A Perspective." In *Orthodoxy in Late Imperial China,* ed. Kwang-Ching Liu. Berkeley and Los Angeles: University of California Press.

Liu Li-yen 柳立言. 1991. "Ch'ien-t'an Sung-tai fu-nü ti shou-chieh yü tsai-chia" 淺談宋代婦女的守節與再嫁. *Hsin shih-hsüeh* 2.4:37–76.

Liu Tseng-kuei 劉增貴. 1981. *T'ang-tai hun-yin yüeh-lun* 唐代婚姻約論. Vol. 4 of *Chung-kuo shih-hsüeh lun-wen hsüan-chi* 中國史學論文選集, ed. Wang Shou-nan 王壽南 et al. Taipei: Yu-shih.

Liu, Ts'ui-jung. 1985. "The Demography of Two Chinese Clans in Hsiao-shan, Chekiang, 1650–1850." In *Family and Population in East Asian History,* ed. Susan B. Hanley and Arthur P. Wolf. Stanford: Stanford University Press.

Liu, Wu-chi, and Irving Yucheng Lo, eds. 1975. *Sunflower Splendor: Three Thousand Years of Chinese Poetry.* Garden City, N.Y.: Anchor Books.

Lo, Irving Yucheng. 1971. *Hsin Ch'i-chi.* New York: Twayne.

Lü Ch'eng-chih 呂誠之. 1935. *Chung-kuo hun-yin chih-tu hsiao-shih* 中國婚姻制度小史. Rev. ed. Shanghai: Lung-hu shu-tien.

Ma Chih-su 馬之驌. 1981. *Chung-kuo ti hun-su* 中國的婚俗. Taipei: Ching-shih shu-chü.

McCreery, John L. 1976. "Women's Property Rights and Dowry in China and South Asia." *Ethnology* 15:163–74.

McDermott, Joseph P. 1990. "The Chinese Domestic Bursar." *Ajia bunka kenkyū* 2:284–67 (15–32).

Macfarlane, Alan. 1986. *Marriage and Love in England: Modes of Reproduction, 1300–1840.* Oxford: Basil Blackwell.

Mandelbaum, David G. 1988. *Women's Seclusion and Men's Honor: Sex Roles in North India, Bangladesh, and Pakistan.* Tucson: University of Arizona Press.

Mann, Susan. 1985. "Historical Change in Female Biography from Song to Qing Times: The Case of Early Qing Jiangnan (Jiangsu and Anhui Provinces)." *Transactions of the International Conference of Orientalists in Japan* 30:65–77.

———. 1987. "Women in the Kinship, Class, and Community Structures of Qing Dynasty China." *Journal of Asian Studies* 46:37–56.

———. 1991. "Grooming a Daughter for Marriage: Brides and Wives in the Mid-Ch'ing Period." In *Marriage and Inequality in Chinese Society,* ed. Rubie S. Watson and Patricia Buckley Ebrey. Berkeley and Los Angeles: University of California Press.

———. 1992. "'Fuxue' (Women's Learning) by Zhang Xuecheng (1738–1801): China's First History of Women's Culture." *Late Imperial China* 13.1:40–62.

Mao Tse-tung. 1975. *Selected Works of Mao Tse-tung.* 4 vols. Peking: Foreign Languages Press.

Martin, Emily. (*See also* Ahern, Emily.) 1988. "Gender and Ideological Differences in Representations of Life and Death." In *Death Ritual in Late Imperial and Modern China,* ed. James L. Watson and Evelyn S. Rawski. Berkeley and Los Angeles: University of California Press.

Martin-Liao, Tianchi. 1985. "Traditional Handbooks of Women's Education." In *Women and Literature in China,* ed. Anna Gerstlacher, Ruth Keen, Wolfgang Kubin, Margit Miosga, and Jenny Schon. Bochum: Studienverlag Brockmeyer.

Mauss, Marcel. 1967. *The Gift: Forms and Functions of Exchange in Archaic Societies.* Trans. Ian Cunnison. New York: W. W. Norton.

Meijer, M. J. 1981. "The Price of a P'ai-lou." *T'oung Pao* 67.3–5:288–304.

Murray, Julia K. 1990. "Didactic Art for Women: The *Ladies' Classic of Filial Piety.*" In *Flowering in the Shadows: Women in the History of Chinese and Japanese Painting,* ed. Marsha Weidner. Honolulu: University of Hawaii Press.

Naka Michiyo 南珂通世. 1898. "Shina fujin tensoku no kigen" 支那婦人纏足の起原. *Shigaku zasshi* 9.6:496–520.

Needham, Joseph, and Lu Gwei-djen. 1983. *Spagyrical Discovery and Invention: Physiological Alchemy.* Pt. 5 of Science and Civilisation in China, vol. 5: *Chemistry and Chemical Technology.* Cambridge: Cambridge University Press.

Needham, Joseph, and Wang Ling. 1965. *Mechanical Engineering.* Pt. 2 of Science and Civilisation in China, vol. 4: *Physics and Physical Technology.* Cambridge: Cambridge University Press.

Neill, Mary Gardner. 1982. *The Communion of Scholars: Chinese Art at Yale.* New York: China Institute in America.

Ng, Vivien W. 1987. "Ideology and Sexuality: Rape Laws in Qing China." *Journal of Asian Studies* 46.1:57–70.

Niida Noboru 仁井田陞. 1942. *Shina mibunhōshi* 支那身分法史. Tokyo: Zayūhō kankōkai.

———. 1962. *Chūgoku hōseishi kenkyū* 中國法制史研究. Vol. 3: *Dorei nōdō hō, kazoku sonraku hō* 奴隸農奴法, 家族村落法. Tokyo: Tōkyō daigaku Tōyō bunka kenkyūjō.

———. [1937] 1967. *Tōsō hōritsu bunsho no kenkyū* 唐宋法律文書の研究. Reprint. Tokyo: Daian.

Niu Chih-p'ing 牛志平. 1985. "Ts'ung li-hun yü tsai-chia k'an T'ang-tai fu-nü ti chen-chieh kuan" 從離婚與再嫁看唐代婦女的貞節觀. *Shan-hsi shih-ta hsüeh-pao (che-hsüeh, she-hui k'o-hsüeh)* 1985.4:108–13.

———. 1987. "T'ang-tai tu-fu shu-lun" 唐代妒婦述論. *Jen-wen tsa-chih* 1987.3:92–97.

Ocko, Jonathan K. 1990. "Hierarchy and Harmony: Family Conflict as Seen in Ch'ing Legal Cases." In *Orthodoxy in Late Imperial China,* ed. Kwang-Ching Liu. Berkeley and Los Angeles: University of California Press.

———. 1991. "Women, Property, and the Law in the PRC." In *Marriage and Inequality in Chinese Society,* ed. Rubie S. Watson and Patricia Buckley Ebrey. Berkeley and Los Angeles: University of California Press.

O'Hara, Albert Richard. 1945. *The Position of Women in Early China According to the "Lieh nü chuan," "The Biographies of Eminent Chinese Women."* Washington, D.C.: Catholic University. (Reprinted Taipei: Mei-ya shu-chü, 1971.)

Ortner, Sherry B., and Harriet Whitehead, eds. 1981. *Sexual Meanings: The Cultural Construction of Gender and Sexuality.* Cambridge: Cambridge University Press.

Owen, Stephen. 1986. *Remembrances: The Experience of the Past in Classical Chinese Literature.* Cambridge, Mass.: Harvard University Press.

Paar, Francis W., ed. 1963. *Ch'ien Tzu Wen: The Thousand Character Classic.* New York: Ungar.

Pao, Chia-lin 鮑家麟. (*See also* Tao, Chia-lin Pao.) 1987. "Yin-yang hsüeh-shuo yü fu-nü ti-wei" 陰陽學說與婦女地位. *Han-hsüeh yen-chiu* 5.2:501–12.

Pasternak, Burton. 1985. "On the Causes and Demographic Consequences of Uxorilocal Marriage in China." In *Family and Population in East Asian History,* ed. Susan B. Hanley and Arthur P. Wolf. Stanford: Stanford University Press.

Paul, Diana Y. 1985. *Women in Buddhism: Images of the Feminine in the Mahāyāna Tradition.* 2d ed. Berkeley and Los Angeles: University of California Press.

P'eng Li-yün 彭利芸. 1988. *Sung-tai hun-su yen-chiu* 宋代婚俗研究. Taipei: Hsin-wen-feng.

Rawski, Evelyn. 1991. "Ch'ing Imperial Marriage and Problems of Rulership." In *Marriage and Inequality in Chinese Society,* ed. Rubie S. Watson and Patricia Buckley Ebrey. Berkeley and Los Angeles: University of California Press.

Reed, Barbara E. 1987. "Taoism." In *Women in World Religions,* ed. Arvind Sharma. Albany: State University of New York Press.

Rexroth, Kenneth, and Ling Chung, trans. and eds. 1979. *Li Ch'ing-chao: Complete Poems.* New York: New Directions.

Robertson, Maureen. 1992. "Voicing the Feminine: Constructions of the Female Subject in the Lyric Poetry of Medieval and Late Imperial China." *Late Imperial China* 13.1:63–110.

Ropp, Paul S. 1976. "Seeds of Change: Reflections on the Condition of Women in Early and Mid Ch'ing." *Signs* 2.1:5–23.

Rorex, Robert A., and Wen Fong. 1974. *Eighteen Songs of a Nomad Flute: The Story of Lady Wen-chi, a Fourteenth Century Handscroll in the Metropolitan Museum of Art.* New York: Metropolitan Museum of Art.

Rose, Mary Beth, ed. 1986. *Women in the Middle Ages and the Renaissance: Literary and Historical Perspectives.* Syracuse: Syracuse University Press.

Rossabi, Morris. 1989. "Kuan Tao-sheng: Woman Artist in Yüan China." *Bulletin of Sung-Yüan Studies* 21:67–84.

Rowe, William T. 1992. "Women and the Family in Mid-Ch'ing Social Thought: The Case of Ch'en Hung-mou." In *Family Process and Political Process in Modern Chinese History.* Taipei: Institute of Modern History, Academia Sinica.

Sa, Sophie. 1985. "Marriage Among the Taiwanese of Pre-1945 Taipei." In *Family and Population in East Asian History,* ed. Susan B. Hanley and Arthur P. Wolf. Stanford: Stanford University Press.

Sanday, Peggy Reeves, and Ruth Gallagher Goodenough, eds. 1990. *Beyond the Second Sex: New Directions in the Anthropology of Gender.* Philadelphia: University of Pennsylvania Press.

Sangren, P. Steven. 1983. "Female Gender in Chinese Religious Symbols: Kuan Yin, Ma Tsu, and the 'Eternal Mother.'" *Signs* 9.1:4–25.

Sawada Mizuho 澤田瑞穂. 1986. *Jigokuhen: Chūgoku no meikaisetsu* 地獄變: 中國の冥界說. Ajia no shūkyō bunka 3. Kyoto: Hozokan.

Schafer, Edward H. 1984. "Notes on T'ang Geisha." In *Schafer Sinological Papers* 2, 4, 6, and 7.

Scott, Joan W. 1986. "Gender: A Useful Category of Historical Analysis." *American Historical Review* 91:1053–75.

Seaman, Gary. 1981. "The Politics of Karmic Retribution." In *The Anthropology of Taiwanese Society,* ed. Emily Martin Ahern and Hill Gates. Stanford: Stanford University Press.

Sharma, Ursula. 1980. *Women, Work, and Property in North-West India*. London: Tavistock.

Sheieh, Bau-hwa. 1992. "Concubines in Chinese Society from the Fourteenth to the Seventeenth Centuries." Ph.D. diss., University of Illinois, Urbana-Champaign.

Sheng, Angela Yu-yun. 1990. "Textile Use, Technology, and Change in Rural Textile Production in Song China (960–1279)." Ph. D. diss., University of Pennsylvania.

Shiba Yoshinobu 斯波義信. 1968. *Sōdai shōgyōshi kenkyū* 宋代商業史研究. Tokyo: Kazama shobo.

————. 1970. *Commerce and Society in Sung China*. Trans. Mark Elvin. Ann Arbor: University of Michigan, Center for Chinese Studies.

Shiga Shūzō 滋賀秀三. 1967. *Chūgoku kazoku hō no genri* 中國家族法の原理. Tokyo: Sōbunsha.

————. 1978. "Family Property and the Law of Inheritance in Traditional China." In *Chinese Family Law and Social Change in Historical and Comparative Perspective*, ed. David Buxbaum. Seattle: University of Washington Press.

Shih Chih-lien 石志廉. 1979. "Pei-Sung fu-nü hua-hsiang chuan" 北宋婦女畫像磚. *Wen-wu* 1979.3:87 and pl. 7.

Smith, Arthur H. [1899]. 1970. *Village Life in China*. Reprint. New York: Little, Brown.

Speiser, Werner, Roger Goepper, and Jean Fribourg. 1964. *Arts de la Chine*. Fribourg, Switz.: Office du Livre.

Stacey, Judith. 1983. *Patriarchy and Socialist Revolution in China*. Berkeley and Los Angeles: University of California Press.

Steele, John, trans. 1917. *The I-li, or Book of Etiquette and Ceremonial*. 2 vols. London: Probsthain.

Su Pai 宿白. 1957. *Pai-sha Sung-mu* 白沙宋墓. Peking: Wen-wu ch'u-pan-she.

Sudō Yoshiyuki 周藤吉之. 1962. *Sōdai keizaishi kenkyū* 宋代經濟史研究. Tokyo: Tōkyō daigaku shuppankai.

Sung, Marina H. 1981. "The Chinese Lieh-nü Tradition." In *Women in China*, ed. Richard W. Guisso and Stanley Johannesen. Youngstown, N.Y.: Philo Press.

Suzuki, Kei. 1982. *Comprehensive Illustrated Catalog of Chinese Paintings*. Tokyo: University of Toyko Press.

Swann, Nancy Lee. 1932. *Pan Chao: Foremost Woman Scholar of China*. New York: Century.

Tai, Yen-hui. 1978. "Divorce in Traditional Chinese Law." In *Chinese Family Law and Social Change in Historical and Comparative Perspective*, ed. David Buxbaum. Seattle: University of Washington Press.

Tan Ch'iao-erh 丹喬二. 1978. "Sōdai konōmin kazoku to josei: jidai to josei" 宋代小農民家族と女姓: 時代と女姓. *Nihon daigaku bungaku kenkyūjo kiyo* 20:101–17.

T'ang Tai-chien 唐代劍. 1986. "Sung-tai ti fu-nü tsai-chia" 宋代的婦女再嫁. *Nan-ch'ung shih-yüan hsüeh-pao* 1986.3:80–84.

Tao, Chia-lin Pao. (*See also* Pao, Chia-lin.) 1991. "Chaste Widows and Institutions to Support Them in Late-Ch'ing China." *Asia Major*, 3d ser., 4.1:101–19.

Tao, Jing-shen. 1976. *The Jurchen in Twelfth-Century China: A Study of Sinicization*. Seattle: University of Washington Press.

T'ao Hsi-sheng 陶希聖. [1935] 1966. *Hun-yin yü chia-tsu* 婚姻與家族. Taipei: Jen-jen wen-k'u ed.

Telford, Ted A. 1992. "Covariates of Men's Age at First Marriage: The Historical Demography of Chinese Lineages." *Population Studies* 46:19–35.

Thatcher, Melvin. 1991. "Marriage of the Ruling Elite in the Spring and Autumn Period." In *Marriage and Inequality in Chinese Society*, ed. Rubie S. Watson and Patricia Buckley Ebrey. Berkeley and Los Angeles: University of California Press.

T'ien Ju-k'ang. 1988. *Male Anxiety and Female Chastity: A Comparative Study of Chinese Ethical Values in Ming-Ch'ing Times*. Leiden: E. J. Brill.

Tilly, Louise A. 1987. "Women's History and Family History: Fruitful Collaboration or Missed Connection?" In *Family History at the Crossroads*, ed. Tamara Hareven and Andrejs Plakans. Princeton: Princeton University Press.

Tseng Tsao-chuang 曾棗莊. 1986. "San-Su yin-ch'in k'ao" 三蘇姻親考. *Chung-hua wen-shih lun-ts'ung* 1986. 2:237–49.

Twitchett, Denis. 1960. "Documents on Clan Administration, I: The Rules of Administration of the Charitable Estate of the Fan Clan." *Asia Major*, n.s., 8:1–35.

———. 1983. *Printing and Publishing in Medieval China*. New York: Beil.

Umehara Kaoru 梅原郁. 1985. *Sōdai kanryō seido kenkyū* 宋代官僚制度研究. Kyoto: Dōhōsha.

———, trans. 1986. *Meikō shohan seimeishū* 名公書判清明集. Kyoto: Dōhōsha.

Van Gulik, R. H. 1961. *Sexual Life in Ancient China*. Leiden: E. J. Brill.

von Glahn, Richard. 1987. *The Country of Streams and Grottoes: Expansion, Settlement, and the Civilizing of the Sichuan Frontier in Song Times*. Cambridge, Mass: Council on East Asian Studies, Harvard University.

Wagner, Marsha L. 1984. *The Lotus Boat: The Origins of Chinese Tz'u Poetry in T'ang Popular Culture*. New York: Columbia University Press.

Waley, Arthur. 1937. *The Book of Songs*. London: Allen & Unwin.

———. 1941. *Translations from the Chinese*. New York: Alfred A. Knopf.

———. 1960. *Ballads and Stories from Tun-huang: An Anthology*. New York: Macmillan.

Waltner, Ann. 1981. "Widows and Remarriage in Ming and Early Qing China." In *Women in China*, ed. Richard W. Guisso and Stanley Johannesen. Youngstown, N.Y.: Philo Press.

———. 1987. "Visionary and Bureaucrat in Late Ming: T'an-yang-tzu and Wang Shih-chen." *Late Imperial China* 8:105–27.

———. 1990. *Getting an Heir: Adoption and the Construction of Kinship in Late Imperial China*. Honolulu: University of Hawaii Press.

Walton, Linda. 1984. "Kinship, Marriage, and Status in Song China: A Study of the Lou Lineage of Ningbo, c. 1050–1250." *Journal of Asian History* 18.1:35–77.

Watson, Burton, trans. 1965. *Su Tung-p'o: Selections from a Sung Dynasty Poet*. New York: Columbia University Press.

———. 1973. *The Old Man Who Does as He Pleases: Selections from the Poetry and Prose of Lu Yu*. New York: Columbia University Press.

———. 1984. *The Columbia Book of Chinese Poetry: From Early Times to the Thirteenth Century*. New York: Columbia University Press.

Watson, Rubie S. 1981. "Class Differences and Affinal Relations in South China." *Man* 16:593–615.

———. 1984. "Women's Property in Republican China: Rights and Practice." *Republican China* 10.1a:1–12.

———. 1991a. "Afterword: Marriage and Gender Inequality." In *Marriage and Inequality in Chinese Society,* ed. Rubie S. Watson and Patricia Buckley Ebrey. Berkeley and Los Angeles: University of California Press.

———. 1991b. "Wives, Concubines, and Maids: Servitude and Kinship in the Hong Kong Region, 1900–1914." In *Marriage and Inequality in Chinese Society,* ed. Rubie S. Watson and Patricia Buckley Ebrey. Berkeley and Los Angeles: University of California Press.

Weidner, Marsha. 1988. "Women in the History of Chinese Painting." In *Views from Jade Terrace: Chinese Women Artists, 1330–1912,* ed. Marsha Weidner, Ellen Johnston Laing, Irving Yucheng Lo, Christina Chu, and James Robinson. Indianapolis: Indianapolis Museum of Art.

———, ed. 1989. *Flowering in the Shadows: Women in the History of Chinese and Japanese Paintings.* Honolulu: University of Hawaii Press.

Weidner, Marsha, Ellen Johnston Laing, Irving Yucheng Lo, Christina Chu, and James Robinson. 1988. *Views from Jade Terrace: Chinese Women Artists, 1330–1912.* Indianapolis: Indianapolis Museum of Art.

Weiner, Annette B., and Jane Schneider. 1989. *Cloth and Human Experience.* Washington, D.C.: Smithsonian Institution Press.

Weller, Robert P. 1984. "Social Contradiction and Symbolic Resolution: Practical and Idealized Affines in Taiwan." *Ethnology* 23:249–60.

Widmer, Ellen. 1989. "The Epistolary World of Female Talent in Seventeenth-Century China." *Late Imperial China* 10.2:1–43.

———. 1992. "Poems Saved from Burning: Xiaoqing's Literary Legacy and the Place of the Woman Writer in Late Imperial China." *Late Imperial China* 13.1:111–55.

Wile, Douglas. 1992. *Art of the Bedchamber: The Chinese Sexual Yoga Classics, Including Women's Solo Meditation Texts.* Albany: State University of New York Press.

Wilhelm, Richard, trans. 1967. *The I Ching or Book of Changes.* Princeton: Princeton University Press.

Wolf, Arthur. 1985. "Fertility in Prerevolutionary China." In *Family and Population in East Asian History,* ed. Susan B. Hanley and Arthur P. Wolf. Stanford: Stanford University Press.

Wolf, Arthur, and Chieh-shan Huang. 1980. *Marriage and Adoption in China, 1845–1945.* Stanford: Stanford University Press.

Wolf, Arthur, and Susan Hanley. 1985. "Introduction." In *Family and Population in East Asian History,* ed. Susan B. Hanley and Arthur P. Wolf. Stanford: Stanford University Press.

Wolf, Margery. 1972. *Women and the Family in Rural Taiwan.* Stanford: Stanford University Press.

———. 1985. *Revolution Postponed: Women in Contemporary China.* Stanford: Stanford University Press.

Wong, Sun-ming. 1979. "Confucian Ideal and Reality: Transformation of the Institution of Marriage in T'ang China (A.D. 618–907)." Ph.D. diss., University of Washington.

Workman, Michael E. 1976. "The Bedchamber *Topos* in the T'zu Songs of Three Medieval Chinese Poets: Wen T'ing-yün, Wei Chuang, and Li Yü." In *Critical Essays on Chinese Literature,* ed. William H. Nienhauser, Jr. Hong Kong: Chinese University Press.

Wu Pao-ch'i 吳寶琪. 1989. "Shih-hsi Sung-tai yü-hun-sang su ti ch'eng-yin" 試析宋代育婚喪俗的成因. *Pei-ching shih-fan ta-hsüeh hsüeh-pao* 1989.5:92–98.

Wu Shu-sheng 吳淑生 and T'ien Tzu-ping 田自秉. 1986. *Chung-kuo jan-chih shih* 中國染織史. Shanghai: Shang-hai jen-min ch'u-pan-she.

Yanagida Setsuko 柳田節子. 1960. "Sōdai no yōsan nōka keiei—Ka'nan o chūshin to shite" 宋代の養蠶農家經營―江南を中心として. In *Wada hakushi koki kinen Tōyōshi ronsō* 和田博士古稀記念東洋史論叢. Tokyo: Kodansha.

———. 1989. "Nanshōki kasan bunkatsu ni okeru joshōbun ni tsuite" 南宋期家產分割における女承分について. In *Ryū Shiken [Liu Tzu-chien] hakushi shōju kinen Sōshi kenkyū ronshū*, 劉子健博士頌壽紀念宋史研究論集, ed. Kinugawa Tsuyoshi 衣川強. Tokyo: Dōhōsha.

Yang, Lien-sheng. 1957. "The Concept of 'Pao' as a Basis for Social Relations in China." In *Chinese Thought and Institutions,* ed. John K. Fairbank. Chicago: University of Chicago Press.

Yang, Martin C. 1945. *A Chinese Village: Taitou, Shantung Province.* New York: Columbia University Press.

Yang Shu-ta 楊樹達. [1933] 1976. *Han-tai hun-sang li-su k'ao* 漢代婚喪禮俗考. Reprint. Taipei: Hua-shih ch'u-pan-she.

Yang, Xian-yi, and Gladys Yang, trans. 1981. *The Courtesan's Jewel Box: Chinese Stories of the Xth-XVIIth Centuries.* Peking: Foreign Languages Press.

Yao, Esther S. Lee. 1983. *Chinese Women: Past and Present.* Mesquite, Tex.: Ide House.

Yao Ling-hsi 姚靈犀. 1936. *Ts'ai-fei lu hsü-pien* 采菲錄續編. Tientsin: Shih-tai kung-ssu.

Yü, Chün-fang. 1990. "Images of Kuan-yin in Chinese Folk Literature." *Han-hsüeh yen-chiu* 8.1:221–85.

Yüan Li 袁俐. 1988. "Sung-tai nü-hsing ts'ai-ch'an-ch'üan shu-lun" 宋代女性財產權述論. In *Sung-shih yen-chiu chi-k'an* 宋史研究集刊, vol. 2, ed. Hang-chou ta-hsüeh li-shih hsi Sung-shih yen-chiu shih 杭州大學歷史系宋史研究室. Hang-chou: Che-chiang sheng she-lien t'an-so tsa-chih.

Zurndorfer, Harriet T. 1992. "The 'Constant World' of Wang Chao-Yüan: Women, Education, and Orthodoxy in 18th-Century China—A Preliminary Investigation." In *Family Process and Political Process in Modern Chinese History,* Taipei: Institute of Modern History, Academia Sinica.

INDEX

abortion, 181

Admonitions for Girls, 120, 184

adoption: and patrilineal descent, 111, 235, 246–48; of unwanted children, 183; and widowhood, 191–93, 194

adultery: by monks, 250, 251; penalties for, 49, 250–51; and remarriage, 212; and women's sexuality, 162

advice books, 10

affinal relationships, 63, 83, 84, 103, 247–48

age: of courtesans, 30; of marital partners, 154–55, 213, 216; at marriage, 74–77; and remarriage, 205, 213; and sexual segregation, 24, 26; of widows, 189

Analects, 121, 123, 124, 158, 170, 185, 197

Analects for Girls, 24, 195

ancestor worship: introduction of bride to ancestors, 92–93; and localized kinship, 4; Neo-Confucian revitalization of, 4; and orphans, 76; and patriarchy, 7, 262

androgyny, 36, 37

architecture, separation of public and private space in, 21

authority. *See* male dominance

betrothal: breaking of, 88; of children, 63–64; confirmation of, 58; and exchange of gifts, 55, 56, 83–88; legal status of, 47–48, 60; parental authority in, 48; rituals of, 83–84

bias, in historical sources, 17–19

bigamy, 47, 49

Biographies of Great Women, 119, 123, 170, 195, 207

blood, 28

Bloody Bowl Sutra, 175

bodhisattvas, as androgynous, 37

Book of Agriculture (Ch'en Fu), 139

Book of Agriculture (Wang Chen), 136, 139

Book of Changes, 27, 28, 86

Book of Documents, 121

Book of Poetry, 53, 56, 197, 252

Book of Rites: and age at marriage, 75; and dowries, 104; and education of women, 123; marriage defined in, 45, 51, 55; and matchmaking, 74; and remarriage, 195; sexual segregation dictated in, 23–24, 25, 28

Book of Sericulture, 140

Book of Songs, 25, 121, 195

brideprice, 85. *See also* betrothal, exchange of gifts

brides. See wedding ceremony

Buddhism: and education of women, 121, 122; women's interest in, 124–28, 170–71

celibacy, 78, 163, 164–65, 202

Chan Ch'ing, 236

Chang, Miss (1012–1063), 119

Chang, Miss (1023–1082), 157

Chang, Miss (1074–1122), 125

Chang, Miss (1146–1195), 108

Chang, Miss (concubine), 229

Chang, Miss (dowried property owner), 100, 194

Chang, Miss (eleventh century), 198

Compositor: Central Typographers
Text: 10/12 Baskerville
Display: Baskerville